GILBERT MURRAY REASSESSED

Bust of Gilbert Murray, by Oscar Nemon, who emigrated from his native Croatia to Britain in 1939 and settled in Oxford; his house and studio were near the Murrays' home on Boars Hill, on land bought from Robert Graves. Nemon, who was taught English by Max Beerbohm, became a naturalized British citizen in 1948, his application supported by Murray. The bust was probably made in 1942; Nemon had previously made a bust of Freud, and went on to portray Winston Churchill. By permission of the Estate of Oscar Nemon.

Gilbert Murray Reassessed

Hellenism, Theatre, and International Politics

Edited by
CHRISTOPHER STRAY

OXFORD
UNIVERSITY PRESS

OXFORD
UNIVERSITY PRESS

Great Clarendon Street, Oxford OX2 6DP

Oxford University Press is a department of the University of Oxford.
It furthers the University's objective of excellence in research, scholarship,
and education by publishing worldwide in

Oxford New York

Auckland Cape Town Dar es Salaam Hong Kong Karachi
Kuala Lumpur Madrid Melbourne Mexico City Nairobi
New Delhi Shanghai Taipei Toronto

With offices in

Argentina Austria Brazil Chile Czech Republic France Greece
Guatemala Hungary Italy Japan Poland Portugal Singapore
South Korea Switzerland Thailand Turkey Ukraine Vietnam

Oxford is a registered trade mark of Oxford University Press
in the UK and in certain other countries

Published in the United States
by Oxford University Press Inc., New York

First published 2007

British Library Cataloguing in Publication Data
Data available

Library of Congress Cataloging in Publication Data
Data available

Typeset by SPI Publisher Services, Pondicherry, India
Printed in Great Britain
on acid-free paper by
Biddles Ltd, King's Lynn, Norfolk

ISBN 978-0 19-920879-1

3 5 7 9 10 8 6 4 2

To the memory of those who died in the terrorist attack on London on 7 July 2005

Preface

Most of the contributions in this book derive from papers given at a conference on Gilbert Murray which was held at the Institute of Classical Studies, University of London, between 6 and 8 July 2005. My thanks are due to all those who spoke at the meeting, and to the staff of the Institute: Tim Cornell, Mike Edwards, and Kim Ayodeji. Murray's grandchildren, Alexander Murray and Ann Paludan, cast a spell over the conference: their perceptive accounts of their grandfather, their contributions to discussion, and their charm made it a special occasion. I am also indebted to Alexander Murray for permission to quote from Gilbert Murray's papers: MSS Gilbert Murray, Bodleian Library, Oxford. References in the form 'GM 123.456' are to box and folio numbers in this collection. I am also grateful to Hilary O'Shea and Jenny Wagstaffe at Oxford University Press; to Bill Bruneau, who went well beyond the call of a contributor's duty; to Francis West, for his generosity in providing information to other contributors; to Richard Ashdowne and Chris Collard, for checking Greek text; and to Cliff Davies, Paul Naiditch, and Graham Whitaker, for help with references for Chapter 8.

Christopher Stray
7 July 2006

Contents

Contributors

William Bruneau Emeritus Professor of the History of Education, University of British Columbia

Martin Ceadel Professor of Politics, University of Oxford, and Fellow of New College

Christopher Collard Emeritus Professor of Classics, University of Wales Swansea

Malcolm Davies Fellow of St John's College, Oxford, and University Lecturer in Classics

Mark Griffith Professor of Classics and Theater, University of California, Berkeley

N. J. Lowe Senior Lecturer in Classics, Royal Holloway, University of London

Fiona Macintosh Senior Research Fellow, Archive of Performances of Greek and Roman Drama, University of Oxford

Barbara F. McManus Professor of Classics Emerita, College of New Rochelle

Mick Morris Arts Tutor, the Open University in Scotland

James Morwood Dean of Wadham College, Oxford

Alexander Murray Emeritus Fellow, University College, Oxford

Ann Paludan Independent researcher on Chinese sculpture

Robert Parker Wykeham Professor of Ancient History, University of Oxford, and Fellow of New College

Julia Stapleton Senior Lecturer in Politics, University of Durham

Christopher Stray Honorary Research Fellow in the Department of Classics, Ancient History and Egyptology, University of Wales Swansea

Francis West Emeritus Professor of History and Government, formerly Pro-Vice Chancellor (Research) Deakin University, Victoria, Australia, and Overseas Fellow, Churchill College, Cambridge

Peter Wilson Senior Lecturer in International Relations, London School of Economics and Political Science

Russell Wodell Writer and editor based in Vancouver

Introduction

Christopher Stray

Writing to a friend in 1951 about a proposal to commemorate the centenary of Jane Harrison's birth, Gilbert Murray commented, 'It is a frightfully difficult thing to know what is worth remembering or preserving for posterity in the mass of anybody's remains, and probably the judgment of fifty years hence will be quite different from that of the present.'[1] The present volume is published 'fifty years hence': half a century after Murray's death in 1957. His comment referred to the preservation of personal papers, but the point applies equally to the intangibles of oral memory and reputation. Just how should we assess Murray's life, his achievements and his legacy? The question helped to shape my article on Murray for the new *Oxford Dictionary of National Biography.* In the university where Murray had held the Regius Chair of Greek from 1908 to 1936, there were conflicting opinions on how best to record his life and work. Some felt the article contributed to the (old) *Dictionary of National Biography* by his pupil Isobel Henderson (M. I. Henderson 1971) should be retained out of pietas, supplemented where necessary; others thought it essential to make a fresh start. A reading of Henderson's article, in the light of what I knew of Murray's career, convinced me that a new account was needed.[2] The preparation of the article on Murray further persuaded me both of the importance of its subject,

[1] Murray to J. A. K. Thomson, 8 March 1951: GM 175.56.

[2] Henderson's eloquent and committed memoir retains an independent value as a historical document; it can be consulted in the *DNB*, and online via the *ODNB* website.

and of the near-impossibility of dealing adequately with the full range of his activities: Greek scholar, historian of literature and of religion, political activist and polemicist, internationalist, translator, man of the theatre, editor, psychic researcher; a public figure for several decades, and a friend and mentor to many—a range at which the subtitle of this volume can only hint. This conclusion led eventually to a conference on Murray held at the Institute of Classical Studies, University of London, between 6 and 8 July 2005, from which most of the papers in the present volume derive. On 7 July, as Murray's views on the morality of the international order were being discussed, a bus was blown up a few hundred yards away during the terrorist attack on London of that day. The attack not only prevented some participants from reaching the conference, but also brought home, to those who were able to attend, the human reality of the issues to which Murray devoted so much of his life. This volume is dedicated to the memory of those who lost their lives in London on that day.

Writing of Murray three years after his death, Arnold Toynbee drew attention to his father-in law's many-sidedness, suggesting that only Murray himself could have given an 'adequate and comprehensive account' of it. The justification Toynbee offers for this is much more intriguing than the obvious one, that the achievement to be recorded was Murray's own: 'He could have done it because, for him, there was unity in all he thought and felt and did'. Quoting Murray's statement that he had constantly thought about 'peace and Hellenism', Toynbee went on to explain that 'His work for peace was an expression of his life-long liberalism... He identified both the Hellenic genius and the modern Western genius with the liberal spirit, and so identified them with each other. This was the master idea that gave unity to all his pursuits...' (Toynbee 1960, 212). There is a great deal of truth in this, though it cannot explain everything in Murray's life.

The author of *The Study of History* had the gift of seeing the grand pattern in the scattered particulars, but also a tendency to impose Procrustean patterns on them. A similar problem confronts anyone who writes about Murray's achievement and his position in history. Can his life and work be accorded some kind of enduring value, or may we situate them only in the moment of their existence? The tension between these strategies is perhaps not to be resolved, but rather to be remembered. We ought also to remember that the same tension was central to Murray's engagement with Hellenism. He began his career as a scholar just as a longstanding tradition which saw Greece as a source of eternal value was challenged by a historicizing vision. In that new perspective, Greek art and literature were to be (re)located firmly in their time, place, and social context. Murray's fusing of Hellenism with liberalism enabled him to transcend this dichotomy by seeing Hellenism as a process. Frank Turner aptly labelled Murray's version of it 'evolutionary humanistic Hellenism' (F. M. Turner 1981, 61; cf. Stray 1998, 222–5).

This new progressive absolute was itself historically located in the world of late nineteenth-century Oxford. Like his friends Richard Livingstone and Alfred Zimmern, Murray absorbed a vision of Hellenism as the basis of a reforming and educative mission. These young men had read Greats (Literae Humaniores) at the zenith of its popularity (Walsh 2000), when an intense immersion in ancient Greek philosophy and history led some undergraduates to a commitment to change the world, or at least to become enlightened administrators of the British Empire (Symonds 1986, Vasunia 2005).

Murray was assiduous in preserving his papers. In referring to 'the mass of anybody's remains', he may well have been thinking how substantial his own papers were. (They now fill several hundred boxes in the Bodleian Library.[3]) The fate of personal papers is of interest in its own right: not just their survival or destruction, but the way they are organized and used. Murray's papers were sorted (and in some cases, apparently, weeded) by his pupil and literary executor Isobel Henderson and his former secretary Jean Smith, and given to the Bodleian Library in 1958; they were then catalogued by Margaret Clapinson. The memorial volume published just after Murray's death (Toynbee and Smith) contains intriguing and irritating unsourced statements, based either on oral knowledge or on papers now difficult to identify. For example, Henderson wrote that Richard Jebb, Murray's predecessor in the Glasgow Greek chair, when consulted by one

[3] Bodleian Library, Oxford, MSS Gilbert Murray (referred to in text as GM with box and folio numbers following).

of the electors about a successor, referred to Murray as 'the most accomplished Greek scholar of the day' (M. I. Henderson 1960, 128). She was followed by Murray's two biographers (F. J. West 1984, 59; D. Wilson 1987, 34); like her, they give no source, and it is fair to assume that her account *was* their source. It remains unclear what her own source was.[4] The history of Murray's biographies has been a complicated one. Francis West was commissioned to write a biography in 1970 by Murray's executor Arnold Toynbee, who had read West's biography of Murray's brother Hubert (F. J. West 1968). When appointments to senior university posts prevented West from meeting the agreed deadline, the commission was transferred to Duncan Wilson. Wilson, however, died before finishing his book, which was completed by his widow. Meanwhile West had returned to the task, and in the event his biography appeared before Wilson's (F. J. West 1984, D. Wilson 1987).[5]

MURRAY IN THE MAKING

In 1912, the history of Greek religion had, in Murray's view, four stages; in 1925 he detected five (Murray 1912b, 1925a). Murray's life, we might say, also had five stages. First came his early life in Australia, ending when he was brought to England aged 11 in 1877; then his

[4] Nothing relevant has been identified in Murray's papers, nor in Jebb's; in his testimonial for Murray, Benjamin Jowett described him as 'the most distinguished undergraduate of his time' (D. Wilson 1987, 34). The elector in question may have been Edward Caird, the Principal of Glasgow University; we know that Jebb sent him comments on the candidates.

[5] Murray's friend Jane Harrison, who died in 1928, had burnt her papers before leaving England for France in 1922; her letters to Murray, preserved in his papers, constitute a major source for her biography. The story of the attempts to commemorate Harrison on the basis of her papers after her death in 1928 is a long and convoluted one (Beard 2000, 129–60). Her pupil Jessie Stewart's memoir appeared more than thirty years after Harrison's death (Stewart 1959), and only recently have two full-scale biographies appeared (Peacock 1988, Robinson 2002). Peacock's was driven by a Freudian agenda to which its subtitle *The Mask and the Self* alludes: though not without merit, it was seriously weakened both by its constricting agenda and by its author's lack of understanding of the English context (Stray 1991). Robinson's research was much more thorough, and her telling of Harrison's story is, at least for now, definitive.

education at Merchant Taylors' School and Oxford, where he graduated in 1888. The third stage consisted of his time as professor of Greek at Glasgow, from which he resigned in 1899, followed by an interlude of convalescence and writing; the fourth began with his return to Oxford in 1905, and was dominated by his career as Regius Professor of Greek from 1908 to 1936. The fifth and final stage represents his long and active retirement, until his death in 1957. This scheme is comfortably based on conventional turning points such as graduation, appointments, and retirement, but it fails to do justice to a many-stranded life like Murray's. It makes no sense at all, for example, of his long commitment to the League of Nations and to the Home University Library, which in both cases straddled the fourth and fifth stages listed above. Nor does it help us to see how Murray pursued both technical scholarship (for instance, the editing of texts) and the communication of a vision of Hellenism to a general public.[6] More fundamentally, it is an obstacle to the understanding of a man who evolved from youth to age in a straight line, whose fundamental views and attitudes were established fairly early on, and who then held firmly to them (though his liberalism, unsurprisingly, veered late in life toward conservatism). This Murray is a serene and somewhat detached person, able to deal with the young with affection, but always to a degree aloof. J. A. K. Thomson wrote in concluding his obituary, 'while he was one of the friendliest, he was one of the remotest of men'.[7] He is able to deal with emergencies, with changes in circumstance, and with difficult issues, at speed and with confidence.

This is the Murray of the present volume (with the obvious exception of West's chapter on his early years). It is all the more revealing, then, to find a young and relatively clumsy Murray struggling to negotiate a relationship with the man he had succeeded as professor of Greek at Glasgow, Richard Claverhouse Jebb. This

[6] Hence Griffith's decision, in his chapter in this volume, to speak both of 'phases' of Murray's career and of 'modes' of work.

[7] Thomson 1957, 254; cf. Toynbee 1960, 217. Martin Ceadel, in this volume, perceptively suggests that Murray's serenity provoked adolescent revolt by his children. Alexander Murray commented on my reference (Stray 2004a) to 'rows' between Murray and his wife that in their generation people did not have 'rows': conflict was repressed.

moment in his life merits brief exploration, especially as Murray's side of the correspondence was not available to his biographers.[8] The relationship between the young Oxford whippersnapper and the established Cambridge scholar (a man always sensitive to criticism and in need of praise) can be followed in their correspondence between 1889, when Murray was elected to the Glasgow chair, and Jebb's death in 1905.

Jebb had suggested three Cambridge-trained scholars in their forties or fifties as candidates to succeed him at Glasgow, and it must have come as a shock to find that a 23-year-old Oxford man had been appointed.[9] He cannot have been amused, either, by finding that in his inaugural lecture Murray had failed to make any mention of his predecessor in the Greek chair.[10] In their correspondence we can see a Murray who had not acquired the serene confidence of his maturity. In 1893 he sent Jebb a copy of a proposal for a new series of classical texts with minimal critical comment attached (GM 3.84, with some reactions at GM 3.90–173). Writing as he was to a man whose edition of Sophocles had been appearing since 1883 to great acclaim, he felt obliged to declare that

> I am afraid that I seem to speak disparagingly of Commentaries—the last thing I could wish to do, as my chief ambition is to write a good commentary some day. The kind of book I had in mind was Tyrrell's Bacchae—and similar books in Macmillan's small red series. (Murray to Jebb, 9 Dec. 1893)

This was a diplomatic choice of example, since Murray probably knew that R. Y. Tyrrell of Trinity College Dublin was one of Jebb's closest friends and allies. The plan was not the only one proposed by Murray in this period but soon abandoned. His several attempts to secure a commitment to it from Jebb went as far as offering him

[8] Jebb's letters are preserved in MSS Gilbert Murray, Bodleian Library, Oxford; Murray's in Jebb's papers, in a family archive. I hope to publish them in a forthcoming edited selection of Jebb's correspondence.

[9] His letter is lost, but they seem to have been James Gow, William Ridgeway, and John Sandys. The last-named was runner-up. It is curious that in Terence Rattigan's play *The Browning Version*, the worn-out classics master Crocker-Harris is replaced by a bright young Oxford scholar, loaded with prizes for classical composition, called Gilbert—though admittedly this is his surname rather than his forename.

[10] The lecture was published as *The Place of Greek in Education* (Murray 1889).

editorship of the whole series, but they were unsuccessful, and the series itself never appeared.[11] The rather extreme offer, and the nervous distancing from his own printed circular, both suggest a lack of confidence. In the following year, Murray complimented Jebb on the 'depth of insight and the linguistic tact' shown in the translation in his edition of the *Oedipus Coloneus* (Jebb 1886: Murray to Jebb, 30 Mar. 1894). The older man's flattered reply encouraged Murray to write, on 14 April, that 'I am so exceedingly glad that my remarks about the Oedipus translation should have given you any satisfaction. I am half afraid that it was impertinent of me to say as much as I did.' Again, Murray's nervousness is on the surface.

When Murray's first academic book, the short *History of Ancient Greek Literature*, appeared in 1897, he sent Jebb a copy, and hearing nothing from him, wrote to assure him that any copy he had received had indeed come from the author, not just from the publisher, adding: 'I merely write now lest you should think I had been guilty of the discourtesy—and indeed the ingratitude—of not sending you a copy of my first book written in your old chair' (Murray to Jebb, 14 June 1897). Jebb did not reply till 30 September (GM 5.26–7), and his measured prose must have made plain his lack of sympathy with Murray's book:

I suppose we belong, in some sense, to rather different schools. The brilliant & daring Wilamowitz (in whom, as I gather, you place unreserved confidence), appears to me rather too fond of hypotheses which he propounds as ascertained facts, and rather too haughtily negligent of all opinions except his own, to be always a safe guide. On the other hand, your attitude towards English scholars and their work is not exactly that which I should have adopted in such a case. You treat them, as it seems to me, somewhat cavalierly. With rare and somewhat arbitrary exceptions, they are, indeed, not mentioned at all: e.g., why not refer to the standard English edition of the *Πολιτεία* by Sandys—Cantab though he is?[12] Then I imagine that you have more sympathy than I have with the style of the New Journalism.[13] But

11 Murray appears to have been ignorant of the contemporary flurry of activity in Oxford which led in 1896 to the commissioning of the first volumes in the Oxford Classical Texts series.

12 Aristotle's *Constitution of Athens*. Sandys had published an edition of this newly discovered work: Sandys 1893.

13 The popular style of the new mass-audience newspapers of the 1880s, exemplified by W. T. Stead. The phrase had been coined by Matthew Arnold (Arnold 1887, 638).

it is one of the charms of the classics that they afford room for endless variety of treatment.

The remark about Sandys, a friend and colleague of Jebb's whom Murray had defeated for the Glasgow chair, suggests that the choice of a young man from Oxford still rankled. But there will have been other grounds for dissatisfaction on Jebb's part. In his preface Murray had written that 'To read and re-read the scanty remains now left to us of the Literature of Ancient Greece, is a pleasant and not a laborious task; nor is that task greatly increased by the inclusion of the Scholia, or ancient commentaries'.[14] In the margin of his copy, it has been claimed, Jebb's friend, rival and successor Henry Jackson wrote 'Insolent puppy'.[15] Murray certainly stored large amounts of Greek literature in his memory. In 1953, a talented undergraduate who had just, like Murray himself nearly seventy years before, won the Gaisford prize for Greek verse, contacted the great man and was invited to Yatscombe. Over tea with the Murrays he boldly quoted a sentence of Demosthenes, at which Murray commented, 'Ah yes: but you have not got it quite right', and recited the whole paragraph without hesitation.[16]

Jebb had another reason to be galled by Murray's inscouciance: he had himself planned to write a history of Greek literature in three volumes, but the project had foundered after he became a hard-working and conscientious MP for his university in 1891. While at Glasgow he had taken full advantage of the six months' free time it afforded each year. Now his successor had the same advantage.

The chapters in this volume include investigations of Murray's relationships with three friends: the classicist and poet A. E. Housman, the philosopher Bertrand Russell, and Murray's protégé the classicist J. A. K. Thomson.[17] The first two cases involve striking contrasts in

[14] Murray 1897, p. vii. The mention of the scholia is interesting in the light of Murray's earlier plan to include them in his Glasgow series of classical texts.

[15] Smith 1960, 133, presumably the source for Bowra 1966, 220. Jackson was elected to the Greek chair at Cambridge after Jebb's death in 1905. Smith refers to 'the margin of a copy still extant', but the copy has not been traced.

[16] The brash undergraduate was Colin Leach, who kindly allows the story to be told here.

[17] Friendships of different kinds, admittedly. That with Housman was 'cautious' (D. Wilson 1987, 115): see Davies's chapter in this volume.

emotional and intellectual style. Adding the Murray–Jebb relationship to this list highlights the possibility that in other circumstances, Murray might himself have become a protégé.[18] In at least two cases, those of Francis Storr at Merchant Taylors' School and Thomas Snow at St John's College, his erstwhile teachers became his enthusiastic supporters—Snow, in fact, offered to go to Glasgow as Murray's assistant. In Jebb's case, however, not only was there no pre-existing relationship, but Murray offended Jebb initially, and then irritated him with his literary style and his liking for Euripides, whom Jebb could not stand. As his pupil (and Murray's friend) Arthur Verrall put it, Jebb 'could not speak of Euripides without pain in his voice, and seldom, without necessity, spoke at all. He had no strong desire, I think, to comprehend such a person' (Verrall 1907, 467). Jebb subscribed to the Arnoldian Hellenism for which Sophocles was the great literary exemplar of classical value. Murray, like Verrall, preferred the human pathos of Euripides.[19]

'Fifty years hence', tastes changed. Writing to Murray in 1921, almost half a century after Jebb's Sophocles editions had begun to appear, J. A. K. Thomson remarked that 'you and I know that those Introductions of Jebb's are irredeemably commonplace', and Murray agreed: 'About taste and style in literature, and how little they seem to be generated by pure scholarship ... Certainly Jebb had only a good commonplace style, and ditto judgement' (Thomson to Murray, 27 Sept. 1921, Murray to Thomson, 4 Dec. 1921: GM 172.24, 27; for the context, see McManus's chapter in this volume). Fifty years after Murray's death, a perceptive and fair-minded critic can remark that 'Murray's views on Greek literature and culture were mainly conventional and derivative' (Griffith, this volume, p. 58). Murray's own verdict on Jebb was very much of its time in its linking of literary style and judgement. (It was of course delivered before the rise of the rebarbative technicalities of professionalized scholarship, let alone the arcane vocabulary of postmodernist theory.) This was a time when classical culture still held a residual place of honour in English

18 The topos is a familiar one in biography: for a discussion of its application to the relationship between Murray and the German classical scholar Wilamowitz-Moellendorff, see Calder and Kopff 1977.

19 See the contributions of Davies and Griffith in this volume.

high culture, and when its study was a matter of the aesthetics and rhetoric of contemporary social position, as much as, or perhaps more than, the investigation of historical evidence. Curiously, something of that earlier mode of assessment has reappeared. Griffith goes on to say that Murray was 'authoritative and . . . perfectly representative of some important critical positions in the Great Britain of his day' (ibid.) This points to a history of scholarship in which being remembered by later scholars is not the only criterion of evaluation. It has accurately been observed of Murray that 'In spite of his great fame when alive, he might never have written so far as most scholars are concerned today' (Fowler 1991, 79). It might be added that this is a judgement on contemporary scholars as much as on the past scholars—like Murray—whom they forget. Or perhaps it is a judgement on their teachers: for how many students are now sent to read Murray, to form their own opinion of him? Here Griffith's reassessment of Murray as a supremely talented interpreter of ancient Greece for his own time comes into its own. Murray skilfully articulated the cultural themes he identified as Hellenic, and deployed them in his own society. In his own words, 'The Scholar's special duty is to turn the written signs in which old poetry or philosophy is now enshrined back into living thought or feeling. He must so understand as to relive'.[20] It is remarkable that he deployed his chosen themes on such a wide front: theatre, scholarship, and politics. One has to go back to the nineteenth century, and most obviously to Gladstone, to find this kind of deep personal engagement linking classical culture and contemporary politics (Bebbington 2004, 142–215).

Gladstone and Murray were both Oxford men, pulled in from the provinces and remade in the crucible of Oxford classics. But Murray's arrival in Oxford in the 1880s, half a century later than Gladstone's, came during the zenith of Greats: that remarkable phenomenon of the late nineteenth century, referred to above, when young men were inspired by the blend of history and philosophy on the Greats course to take their idealism into an imperfect world in order to make it a better one. Most famously, a carefully constructed conveyor belt led from Jowett's Balliol to the home and imperial civil service: the men who read of the Guardians in Plato's *Republic* went on to become

[20] Murray 1918c, 82; cf. Dodds 1960, 15–16.

Guardians themselves. Murray's experience of Oxford was a major source of the blend of Hellenism and Liberalism which was central to his later thought and action. It is hardly surprising that this blended vision was shaped by conventional attitudes and social position.

It is similarly unsurprising that Murray identified with particular classical authors. As Mark Griffith suggests, in Murray's book devoted to him Aristophanes is presented as a 'gentlemanly, well-read comic playwright' who hated war. The identification can be made even more precisely, in fact, since Murray himself was a comic playwright. There survives in his family a short farce set at a meeting of the League of Nations, entitled 'Saved again, or, the Assembly as it might be. A serious drama'. The cast includes not only several national delegates to the League, but also the cloakroom attendant in the Assembly building. This unpretentious little piece vividly conveys the confusion engendered by large numbers of people talking past each other at speed. National stereotypes are on display, but the gentle poking of fun is aimed at the British as well as other nations.[21]

Murray was both a member of the British social elite, notably through his marriage to Lady Mary Howard, and a liberal gadfly of the establishment. The simplistic distinction between 'integrated' and 'alienated' intellectuals promulgated in the 1950s by writers like Edward Shils is thus of little help in understanding his position.[22] His elite social connections and his links to those in high political office were reinforced by his location in Oxford, the British academic site most closely tied in to the metropolitan world of government. This entanglement between the academic and political worlds was paralleled in the fusion of Hellenism and Liberalism in Murray's life. Until his retirement from the Greek chair at Oxford in 1936, he was at once a leading scholar, promoter, and popularizer of ancient Greece, and a leading figure in national life and international politics.

21 My thanks to Ann Paludan for providing me with a copy of Murray's script (pp. 16, undated), which I understand has been performed by his descendants during family gatherings.

22 See Shils 1955. For a good discussion of Shils's views, see Collini 2006, 145–50. Murray is mentioned only in passing in Collini's book. This does not pretend to comprehensive coverage, or indeed 'coverage' at all (ibid., 7), but it may also be that Murray is simply not Collini's *kind* of intellectual.

At times, indeed, the strain told, as when in 1923 his Vice-Chancellor suggested that his political activities were making it impossible for him to carry out his academic duties.[23]

MANY-SIDED MURRAY

This brings us back to the sheer range of Murray's activities. The essays in this volume cannot hope to cover them all, but taken together they offer a more comprehensive picture of Murray than has hitherto been available. His grandchildren Ann Paludan and Alexander Murray vividly evoke their childhood, when the Murrays' home at Yatscombe on the edge of Oxford was a familiar place, distinctive in its sights, its smells, but above all for the grandparents who gave it life as a centre of experience and of advice. Francis West, the author of biographies of both Murray and his brother Hubert (F. J. West 1968, 1984), takes us back to Gilbert Murray's own childhood, letting new light into dark corners, and showing us not only what we did not know before, but what Murray forgot or misremembered. The next four chapters discuss aspects of Murray's work as a classicist. Mark Griffith situates his writing on Greek literature and philosophy in the culture of his own time; he argues that Murray is best seen as a man who articulated contemporary concerns with supreme skill in a period of transition. Robert Parker discusses Murray's writing on Greek religion between 1907 and 1915, showing how he found in it an imaginative ideal which reflected his own mixture of rationalism and aspirational agnosticism. Christopher Collard and James Morwood consider different aspects of Murray's engagement with Greek texts. Collard's is a pioneering examination of Murray's textual editing, an area of his work which is conventionally dismissed, and hence ignored. Without challenging the consensus that this was not Murray's strong point, he provides a much more nuanced account than has previously been available. Morwood discusses Murray's work as a translator of Greek tragedy, examining the

[23] D. Wilson 1987, 301–2. Murray denied the charge, but gave up half his salary for the appointment of a Reader in Greek.

linguistic and dramatic aspects of his versions, and emphasizing the scale of his achievement in bringing tragedy to an enormous audience. Fiona Macintosh reviews Murray's involvement with the theatre, situating his translations firmly in the performance traditions of early twentieth-century England but also in a wider context, ranging from the activities of the Salvation Army (seen by Shaw and others as a modern parallel to the maenadic revels of the *Bacchae*) to the influence of Nietzsche. She ends by exploring the influence of Murray's translations on the reworking of Greek tragic plots by the Nigerian writer Wole Soyinka.

The next three chapters deal with Murray's friendships with two contemporaries (A. E. Housman and Bertrand Russell) and a junior (J. A. K. Thomson). Malcolm Davies and William Bruneau explore his relationship with men who were in many ways very different from him, but who like him combined academic distinction with a wider public reputation. Housman was like Murray a professional classical scholar who engaged with a wider public through poetry; but was unlike him both in his austere textual criticism and in his often savage reviewing of other scholars. Similarly Russell, who moved in social and intellectual circles which overlapped Murray's, and like him was a liberal in politics, had a very different mindset. In both cases, the maintenance of the relationship involved a continuing tension between distinct emotional patterns and world-views. Barbara McManus brings back to the light an almost forgotten classical scholar whom Murray adopted as his protégé, recommended for academic posts, regularly holidayed with and made his literary executor. The obscurity into which J. A. K. Thomson has fallen as a scholar may be justified,[24] but his relationship with Murray, previously unexplored, is of great interest to any student of Murray's life. And as with Murray's textual criticism, the history of failure and obscurity has its own importance.

William Bruneau's chapter on Murray and Russell introduces us to Murray's involvement in politics; the next three chapters continue this theme. Martin Ceadel and Peter Wilson consider his activity and his thinking in international relations. Ceadel traces the building up

[24] A minor indication: in his foreword to Smith and Toynbee 1960, Arnold Toynbee misspelled his name as Thompson (Smith and Toynbee 1960, 8).

of what was always an aristocratic Liberalism, one which included a disdain for 'small dark races'. He shows how Murray the apologist for British policy in World War I slowly transmuted into Murray the internationalist in the late 1910s and 1920s, and how his liberalism turned to conservatism in his later years: in Ceadel's words, 'his Hellenism turned sour'. Wilson uses the disciplinary tradition of International Relations to draw up a balance sheet of achievement and failure; his conclusion is on balance negative, Murray being classed as one of the 'idealists' whose thinking was superseded by the 'realist' thinking of E. H. Carr and others. Yet some of Murray's views can be classed as 'realist', and in any case, as Wilson concludes, 'it is always salutary to revisit civilized books and civilized minds'. Julia Stapleton assesses Murray as a liberal intellectual, looking at his involvement with his fellow-Liberal Alfred Zimmern and with the Home University Library, for which he worked from its foundation in 1910 almost to his death in 1957. She traces the development of both men's ideas on internationalism and social reform from the heady days of the 1910s through the disillusionments of later decades, when the late-Victorian matrix of Hellenism and Liberalism became too narrow a basis for theorizing and reform. Murray the public educator is further explored in Mick Morris's pioneering study of his long involvement with the neglected medium of radio.[25] Murray's broadcasts ranged from classical drama to current affairs to memories of his youth; from translations to lectures to the Brains Trust, a programme which cemented his status as a public intellectual. Morris's account is supplemented by comprehensive listings of Murray's broadcasts, and of the subsequent publications in the *Radio Times* and *Listener*. His translations were broadcast on the Light and Home Services, and in the late 1940s the new Third Programme added selections in the original Greek.[26] The selection of his letters to *The Times* made by William Bruneau and Russell Wodell gives us a chance to sample the mixture of rigorous argument, sly humour, and adroit rhetoric which Murray employed as a public

[25] The discussion in Collini 2006, 434–50 is a welcome exception to this neglect.

[26] It is worth remembering that Michael Ventris saw the Third Programme as a suitable forum for announcing his successful decipherment of Linear B: Carpenter 1996, 114–15.

figure in another medium. Their selection is made from nearly 300 letters published between 1908 and 1956, and illustrates not only his mastery of the genre but his views on a variety of topics, both serious and trivial. Finally we come to Murray himself as medium, in N. J. Lowe's discussion of his involvement in experiments in telepathy. Lowe's previous exploration of the involvement in psychical research of Murray's friends the Verralls (Lowe 2005) makes him ideally equipped to investigate the remarkable story of Murray's own career in this field. Murray was, Lowe argues, England's leading telepath; and his account of Murray's experiments in this field underlines with especial force the width of Murray's interests and achievements.

In 1960, Murray's pupil and successor E. R. Dodds wrote: 'Whether he is to be ranked with the greatest scholars depends on one's conception of scholarship; but that he was a truly great man no one who knew him could doubt' (Dodds 1960, 19). Murray was, to put it another way, a phenomenon; and one we are used to recognizing in our reading of nineteenth-century history and literature. Gladstone, J. S. Mill, Grote, Macaulay: all combined intellectual distinction with fame in public affairs, all drew on their knowledge of the ancient world in attempting to influence their contemporaries. It is as a later member of this small group of gifted and versatile men, perhaps, that Murray should be reassessed, fifty years after his death.

1

Remembering our Grandfather I

Ann Paludan

My grandparents' house, Yatscombe, on Boars Hill, was a sunny house. In my memory the large, airy rooms were always sunlit and from this you can see that I was happy there. My father, their son Basil, died when I was eight and my parents had split up when we were very young, so my sister and I probably spent more time there than we would otherwise have done. As far back as I can remember, we spent our Easter holidays there and later, when I was at Oxford, I bicycled up each Sunday for the day, coming down in the evening with an armful of flowers for my room at St Hugh's. My memories are therefore mainly from the early 1930s until 1949 when I married and started a life abroad.

I cannot see one grandparent without the other and for me, they were always at Yatscombe, with its garden sweeping down to the azaleas and bamboos which Grandfather loved so much. In the spring the woods below were filled with bluebells and there was a notice on the gate that all were welcome to come in and see them. There was a wooden, revolving summer house on the hill where Grandfather sometimes worked in the summer, pushing it round to face the sun.

By the time I knew them, the storms of earlier years had passed and they were both loving and dependent on each other. In the evenings Grandmother brought Grandfather his slippers (in my innocence I though that this must be the recipe for a happy marriage). Looking back, I can see that they must have appeared to many as ill-matched but this was wrong. They were, perhaps, like yin/yang, the union of two opposites forming an harmonious whole. Grandfather was of course easier to appreciate: he was full of charm and very funny. Grandmother was woefully lacking in humour but made up for it with love. Her tolerance was shown when we wanted to play tennis on a Sunday morning and she said: 'I don't mind at all but I don't think you should do anything which might upset others'.

One day in 1940, Grandfather came in to lunch laughing to tell how he had heard two of the little evacuees billeted next door describe how they had seen a little old woman hitchhiking that morning on a lorry. And one had said to the other 'Do you know who that was? It was Lady Mary Murray.' Grandmother saw nothing funny and merely said, 'Well, Gilbert, I had to get down into Oxford and Edgington had no more petrol.'

For a child, it was the continuity, the knowledge that each time you went there, things would be the same, that was so satisfying. When you opened the front door, there would be the smell of polished linoleum in the hall, and Grandmother running and calling to Edgington, the gardener cum driver, to come and help with the luggage. Meals were always at the same time and the pattern of the days unchanged. Unlike at home, children ate with the grown-ups and my Nanny remembers with wonder hearing Grandmother switch from one language to another when talking to the many visitors who came. On Sundays there was a sort of open house; dons and undergraduates were welcome to come to lunch (I suppose they must have received an encouragement or invitation of sorts) but they were expected to be interesting. Perhaps the sharpest remark I ever heard Grandfather say was to a young undergraduate who came two weeks in a row and was very boring, 'Please do not think it necessary to bicycle all the way up here next Sunday, Mr X'.

The background to these years was what was happening on the Continent and events there were reflected in the refugees: first from Nazi Germany, then from Austria and Czechoslovakia. For years afterwards, whenever I heard some one talking English with a German accent, it took me back to Yatscombe. My grandparents had built a small house, just inside the garden, in memory of my aunt Agnes, who died in 1922, and this was lent to families who had been forced to flee and needed time to find a new life in exile. In that atmosphere, it seemed quite normal when my grandmother one day explained that the Czech professor staying with us had been forced to leave his family behind and was waiting daily for news of their escape and that I should therefore do my best to distract him. I was nine at the time; she did not feel it necessary to suggest what I should do, and I remember getting him to go for walks in the bluebell woods and teach me some Czech.

But life was not all serious. We had funny games of croquet on what Maurice Bowra later described as the Murrays' '18-hole tennis court'. There were games after tea—spillikens, consequences, and a version of Happy Families based on the counties and towns of England. Sometimes Grandfather could be persuaded to show how he could put his chin on the floor with a full bottle of squash on his head, or take us over to the Preservation—an open hillside on the other side of the road—and teach us to throw a boomerang and tell how the aborigines in Australia counted—something to do with walla, wallawalla and then walla walla-one boy, and how important it was for a young Aborigine man to keep all his fingers. No girl would marry a man without the full complement because when a man worked in the sawmills he was insured and each finger, if cut off, would bring a good-sized lump of money.

The love of seeing children happy never left him. When I took my eldest son to stay in 1954, he thought that Mark was too serious and the next morning at breakfast there were little woolly mice on the sugar and marmalade pots and his famous wind-up mouse roared across the table to hit Mark's plate. Grandmother wrote a postcard to all her grandchildren every Sunday morning; Grandfather wrote more rarely, but when he did, it would often be a letter filled with pictures cut out from magazines to make a funny story.

The house was filled with books. Grandfather's study was of course lined with them but they were also in the hall, in the drawing room, and all round a little room called the den; upstairs there were bookcases on the landing and then in all the bedrooms. (When she was about ten, their eldest daughter, Rosalind, who later became a Roman Catholic and married Arnold Toynbee, came into Sunday lunch a bit late. She apologized but said, 'I've just discovered a most exciting book. It's called the "Holly Bibel" and is all about a man's head on a plate'.) There were pictures, mostly by my great-grandfather, but no talk about art and no music. Grandmother was musical but Grandfather was tone deaf. He told me how much he regretted this but wondered if his inability to hear tonal music had not concentrated or heightened his love for the sound and rhythm of words. He is one of the few people whom I can hear when I read his works.

The life of the house centred on two rooms: both in the middle of the house facing south. On the ground floor there was the dining room—a hub of activity from where Grandmother ran the house and family. In a way, it was rather a modern room—not at all a room just for eating in; the only telephone was on the wall as you came in; then a long bookcase ran along the right hand wall to the wide bow windows at the end. In the corner of the window was Grandmother's desk on which was her little black and red tin money box from which she would take 13*s.* 8*d.* to repay us for our return ticket from London. On the left side of the room was the fireplace, with photographs of young friends who had been killed in the Great War on the mantlepiece above; to the left, another bookcase with pictures of their three deceased children.

Directly above this room was Grandfather's study. This was sacrosanct. No one except Grandmother was allowed to disturb him. He worked there all morning, and then again after his afternoon walk. I remember only one occasion when we were allowed to break in. My sister and I had spoken of 'the next war' and Grandmother was so horrified that she took us straight up to Grandfather so that he could explain to us that there should never be another war—that that was what the League of Nations was all about. I remember well her strong reaction, but not what he said.

Grandfather was a brilliant teacher. In the autumn of 1943, I had my appendix out just before school started and in those days you had to rest for six weeks. Grandfather said he would help with my Latin and gave me an ode of Horace to learn. Next day I went to recite it and stumbled half way through. Very gently he said: 'Ann, I asked you to learn it. You had better come back tomorrow.' I may have absorbed some of this since in later years, when I had to teach one of my younger children because once again they were changing countries and schools, I heard them agree that I was much more strict than any teachers they had had.

It was on the afternoon walks that he really talked. He used to ask one person to accompany him and off we set, through the woods, he with his secateurs to keep the paths clear, and of course, later, with a stick. These walks were a treasured joy. You knew that it was a slight privilege to be asked but at the same time, it was perfectly natural—conversation flowed—sometimes about subjects I was studying (modern history and later international relations)—sometimes about what he had thought and done. He had that rare gift of being genuinely interested in what you said.

He talked about his childhood, how Yarralumla was always filled with books, sent in large consignments from Britain, and how this attracted visitors from far around; he told with pride how in the earlier days when a convict misbehaved, his punishment would be to accompany his father on his long and fast walks round the land. Later, in the Boer War, it was about being pelted with rotten eggs for his unpopular anti-war views. And then came the days at Glasgow University. Well into his eighties he still had nightmares that he was back in the large lecture hall faced with a hundred or so students, almost all older than him; and how he had to stand at the door to collect the money they paid to attend.

When young he had gone to the House of Commons and heard Gladstone speak. Gladstone was small and old and started in a quiet, elderly voice. Then he gradually worked himself up into a crescendo, arms raised and eyes flashing, often lasting an hour or so, during which it seemed as if the whole world was concentrating on what he was saying; then slowly his voice fell and by the end, there was just this little old man again.

Several times he talked about the pre-1914 belief that European nations had become so civilized that there could never be war again. Here, he admitted that he had been short-sighted, blinded by his own faith in the power of reason to influence man. Shortly before the war broke out in August 1914, he was walking through St James's Park and met Sir Edward Grey; to Grandfather's remark that surely war was unthinkable, Grey answered that it was certain and that it was coming. Whenever he referred to this moment, you could still feel the deep shock and impression that this had made.

There were funny anecdotes: at the Committee for Intellectual Co-operation they had successfully introduced the practice whereby different countries accepted each other's postal rates on the grounds that post each way would probably be about equal; then this was thrown into disarray by Christian missionaries bombarding the Arab countries with their pamphlets.

He told me that his interest in psychic matters stemmed from the long sea journey when his mother took him and his brother to England after his father's death. A woman on board claimed to be clairvoyant and when Grandfather gave her a small object which had belonged to his father, she told him things about his father which there was no way she could have known, and which were not even generally known in the family. His interest in psychical phenomena was genuine—as we all know he had an unusual rapport with his eldest daughter, Rosalind, and they could thought read each other—but he explained that he resigned from his position as president of the society because he feared that association with the subject might harm his more important work. If he were regarded as a quack, people would not listen to what he said about the League of Nations.

Through the mid- and late-1930s it seems to me that his prime interest was very much concentrated on international affairs. He later regretted not having accepted a peerage (he had refused Asquith on the grounds that he felt his elder brother Hubert, Governor of Papua New Guinea, deserved an honour more that he did), because he felt that a title would have given his views more weight. In his later years, he laughed that it was the Brains Trust which brought him fame and how he often found himself in the Oxford to London train listening to stories told about himself, including famous Spoonerisms ('the half-warmed fish', for example) which he had heard when young about earlier professors.

Running through all this, whether on walks or in the house, was the strong, unspoken feeling that you must work for what is right and you must be firm. Both my grandparents were very proud of the memorial which they instigated at New College, Oxford, in memory of German undergraduates of the college who had died in the First World War.

Shortly before he died, I was back in England on leave and he told me he was going up to London for a meeting of the Anglo-Hellenic League. He was very tired 'but it is when things are going badly that you must make the greatest effort'. From the same period, 1954, there is another story which I cannot remember in full. It seems that at one moment, late in life, Plato was wearing or doing something religious, contrary to his beliefs, and when a friend asked him about this, answered 'I know, but it keeps the women happy'. I often thought of this in connection with the events surrounding my grandfather's last days.

It took a long while before I realized that he was well known outside the family and I would like to end with a story my late sister's son, Rupert Birch, told me a few weeks ago. He is a wine-grower and was travelling round the world to sell his wine. In South Korea he was particularly well looked after, and when thanked for this, his host explained that he had met Rupert's parents in London as a young man fleeing from North Korea during the war. When he heard that my sister was a granddaughter of Gilbert Murray, he told her that when he had studied Classics in North Korea before the war they had used Gilbert Murray's translations. It is hard to think of a more isolated country than North Korea. I think Grandfather would have smiled.

Remembering our Grandfather II

Alexander Murray

To write for publication on 'memories of my grandfather'—whoever one is and whoever one's grandfather—is to face two small obstacles; small, because I hope they can be overcome in this case, but still obstacles. The first has to do with memory. To Ann and me and my two brothers—we four are the only grandchildren left of ten—the thought of our grandfather conjures up a world. It is full of people, vanishing beyond the horizon: Dr Nasmyth, the family doctor and a neighbour on Boars Hill (the green paradise that looks down on Oxford's towers), Mr and Mrs Gurney, next-door neighbours at Yatscombe, Kathleen Haines, the housekeeper, the embodiment of loving loyalty, Edgington, the gardener, and a succession of secretaries creamed year after year from the Somerville classicists, all destined for great things on their own account later; and countless more. It is also a world of things: the peculiar click of the brass door-handles at Yatscombe, the floppy rubber table mats with birds painted on, the green lino along the upstairs corridors, the smell of lavender all along the front of the house, the crunch of the gravel, and so ad infinitum. It was a world in the strict etymological sense, *ver-öld*, 'an age of men'. For our word 'world' comes in fact from the only approximation early Germanic languages had to denote an abstract period of time, *öld*, and it was not abstract at all: *öld* is related to the Latin *alo*, I nourish—it connotes a generation, full of people, and things, and associations.

It is this world that I have to remember. And for the younger among my readers let me say that, through changes that have happened imperceptibly over the sixty or seventy years since, it will seem quite a different world from that of 2007, and hard to recapture. Much of the globe was still coloured red. People travelled abroad by ship, and in Britain by steam-train (the Oxford-to-London version of which took most of two hours). There were housekeepers and gardeners, called by their surnames. Manners were stricter: the condoms and rapes that feature in our daily news bulletins would never have been so much as mentioned in polite company, in news bulletins or anywhere else. As a boy of fourteen or so I was in one respect ahead of my time, and was once sent out of the room by my grandmother for (as I thought) spilling soup. 'Leave the room!' 'Why, Grandmother?' I pleaded. 'You said "damn"'. And I had, without thinking, and meekly departed. So it was in some ways a different world from this one now. Like all worlds it was infinite. To take one or two 'memories' out of it is to pick flowers from an endless landscape. The posy I offer can consist of no more than one or two representative emblems.

The second little obstacle has to do with writing about these memories. The experiences that matter to us are just that, experiences. They remain as that in our memories. The moment we try and describe them we deconsecrate them. The flowers are not just emblems, but dying emblems, from the moment they are picked, and on the way to becoming verbal formulae or images, subject to the vicissitudes of all other material, present-day things. In the 'worst-case scenario' we may find, like the 49-year-old W. B. Yeats (who perhaps had himself to thank), that 'all my sacred things are but a post the passing dogs defile'.

I hasten to say that I am far from thinking there might be any 'passing dog' here. Indeed this volume plays a wonderful tribute to our grandfather. I am confident that its 'reassessment' will leave someone we grandchildren can recognize, and which he, too, if he had lived to 140—how lonely that would be (I once had a dream that it had happened, and he was sitting alone at Yatscombe, wrapped in a blanket)—that he, too, would have recognized as fair and comprehensible. In that happy confidence, I shall overcome these reservations and find some fresh memories, not those already in the biographies.

Here, to start with, is a small one absolutely fresh, because I have not told it to anyone before. It must have been 'imprinted' on my memory, as the psychologists say, by the attached emotion. I was about seven, had to be rebuked for one of my bouts of misbehaviour, and the job fell to Grandfather. He 'stood me up' against the bookcase in the big Yatscombe dining room (all rooms had huge bookcases), and said 'You used to be such a *nice* little boy, but now you have become quite horrid'. I shouted 'I don't *care*!' Tears must have come into it. Of course I did care. Although I have told this story just to give a fresh flower, it does incidentally show that my gentle, vegetarian, League of Nations grandfather could be a disciplinarian when he had to be, and perhaps more so with age and experience. My father, Stephen, Grandfather's youngest son, enjoyed teasing us four boys with minor verbal impieties at our grandparents' expense, and used to say (with the disdain of a man who thought children needed whacking), that when *he*, my father, was delinquent (which appears to have been often) he would be sent to the professor's study, where his father would admonish him by quoting an example from Greek history.

Grandfathers have less admonishing to do than fathers, anyway; and the vast majority of my memories of Grandfather were of the friendship—that is what it was—we grandchildren had with him. In any public context the friendship was combined with awe. Once, when he was addressing a huge meeting in Central Hall, Westminster—on world peace or something like that—he said at the end: 'I now have a mysterious message to add. I believe there are members of the clan Murray in the audience. Will they meet me in the front vestibule after this lecture?' He meant my elder brother Gilbert and me, then about 13 and 11. I blushed purple, though no one around me can have known who was meant. He met us, and took us afterwards to lunch at the National Liberal Club. Two other examples of this awe in the context of the world at large rather than within the family come to mind from a few years after that one. I was a fresher at New College, Oxford, and, as freshers will, had become secretary of the College 'History Society', responsible for getting speakers. One tea-time at Yatscombe I mentioned this responsibility. Grandfather thought, and suggested Salvador de Madariaga, then probably the most famous of Spanish liberals. The very idea of having such an international colossus descend on our little society set me trembling, but Grandfather had his hand already on the telephone before the incongruity struck him, too, and he dropped the idea. Awe in the young can be unwittingly cruel. I was a student musician. In the last year of his life, my grandfather once proposed coming down to Oxford to hear a performance by my orchestra. I am sorry, now, that I discouraged it, and it never happened. It would have been an outing, perhaps with modest grandparental pride attached. (As to music, Grandfather was always alleged to be tone-deaf. My father—there was a touch of Aubrey in all his stories—alleged that his father had once listened briefly to a Beethoven quartet on the radio and turned it off, saying 'Really, I cannot understand why Americans like dancing to this sort of thing!')

Now I have begun plucking these little live flowers I must stop, because they never will. Perhaps two more may be allowed, since again they *are* memories, fresh flowers, and take us all back some fifty-six years. In our mid teens my brother Gilbert and I got a craze for long-distance cycling. I, on my own, was to visit Yatscombe at the end of summer term from our school in Hampshire. That meant cycling sixty miles (easier on roads then than now). The marathon was almost over, the long garden wall of Yatscombe was on my right and evening was falling. There, to my surprise, was Grandfather, standing on the pavement by the main road in front of me. A few minutes before the thought had struck him: 'I wonder where he is?', and he had walked down the drive to see. Utterly irrational, of course; when I do this sort of thing it never works. Thought-reading aficionados may see it as a case of serendipity. I don't tell it for that, but simply because it is one of countless little instances of the grandfatherly care he showed for all of us. Another of these instances concerns one of my school reports. I had had some bad ones, then, to everyone's relief, came a good one. My parents sent it to Grandfather, who wrote to me. The letter must be somewhere but I quote a bit from memory. He said *he* had once had a good report like that, and went on: 'I put it in a place hard of access, so that if I felt I was falling away, I could go and find it, to see what I had once been and could continue being'. After he died I found the document he must have been referring to, on top of a high bookshelf in his Yatscombe study. It consisted of the undistributed copies of the printed booklet of testimonials he was given, aged 23, for the chair in Glasgow. (I need hardly say, my good school report was in nothing like the same league.)

Ann has told of the walks, and explained that walk also meant talk. Our grandfather was a founder-member of the Oxford Preservation Trust, lived opposite its biggest purchase, the so-called 'Prez' on Boars Hill, and rarely missed a walk there or roundabout. Talk included his telling us stories of childhood, often repeated by popular demand. Two Murray relations—or was it neighbours?—in Australia, mother and daughter, had mushrooms for breakfast. Suddenly one said to the other, 'How funny your face looks.' The other: 'So does yours.' Both started laughing, and were soon laughing so uncontrollably that when the cook came in she thought something must be amiss, and checked on the mushrooms. They turned out to be the 'sardonic' kind that make you die in convulsions; so she produced an emetic, and all was well. And a hundred more like that. We wanted to hear them again and again. 'Tell us how you got lost in the bush.' 'But I told you that the day before yesterday.' But we insisted, and out it came, our grandfather as a boy in Australia, lost during a long day of unscheduled wandering on the edge of the bush, hearing at evening the howling of the yellow dog dingos, and, at last, at dusk, meeting on a bridge with a mounted ranger, who took the little boy home. (That story *does* come in the biographies and apparently does not fit with the dates of the Murrays' departure from Yarralumla. Too bad. He must have been staying with friends or relations. I would sooner spend the rest of my life in chains than doubt a word of anything our grandfather told us as true. He was perfectly capable of playing deliberate tricks, for fun, but that is another matter.) Here is another story. Some other boys (of whom I seem to remember he was one) were playing 'follow my leader' on the sea coast, all in their swimming trunks. The leader climbed a diving board and dived into a pool, and as he went down saw a shark below. He shrieked a warning to the others. But the boy behind him was already on the diving board, and simply took the shriek as part of the game until it was too late; and so did the others. The shark was frightened by the noise and swam away. Or two more from his days in Glasgow. Glasgow professors had to collect their wages in the form of a sovereign, to be collected from each student at the first lecture, put in a bag, and taken to the bank. This practice was sufficiently well known in criminal circles that professors were advised to take a stout knobkerrie with them en route for the bank. Another Glasgow custom was for a lecture class to display boredom or disapproval by banging feet or making a noise. To a debutant professor this was naturally a source of apprehension. Grandfather was once travelling in a railway sleeping-car from London to Glasgow for the beginning of term. He was in the upper of two bunks. In the small hours he was woken by the man below, a clergyman, who was saying 'I am *so* sorry. I *do* apologize. I am *so* sorry. My wife also finds it tiresome. I *do* apologize.' Grandfather asked him what on earth he thought he had to apologize for. 'My snoring,' said the clergyman. It turned out that grandfather had been dreaming of the Glasgow class he was soon to address. In his dream they were making a noise, and Grandfather, though still essentially asleep, had said *en haute voix*, 'I am afraid I must insist on silence!'

Some walks might involve a visit to neighbours en route, on Boars Hill, and there would be more talk. Once we called on C. A. Macartney, the expert on Hungary. It must have been just before my grandfather's 90th birthday. 'How are you keeping, Professor Murray?' asked Macartney. 'I have only one ailment.' 'I believe you are celebrating it this week.' A raw undergraduate is naturally impressed by that kind of ellipsis. Wise men can say everything with few words. But among walk-talk stories I must add one more about Ann, because she has not told it. Our grandmother was an indefatigable organizer and liked to know how we planned to spend our days. After one Sunday lunch she was reviewing our projects, and when she got to Ann (who was an undergraduate at St Hugh's and the plan had already been arranged: there was an essay to write), our grandmother said, 'Ann is to walk on the Preservation with her grandfather and discuss liberty'.

That brings in Grandmother (and incidentally that inveterate institution, Sunday lunch; another world, of which I will confine myself now to saying—because it has become an inherited characteristic in some branches of the family—that Sunday lunch guests would nearly always include one or more foreigners, so that our grandmother's initial introductions customarily included something like 'I would like you to meet Dr Rademacher/Sinowitz/ (etc)'. This was truest of course in the war years, when Yatscombe was a noted welcoming post for refugees, especially academic; but it went on being true afterwards). But a bit more on our grandmother. I am glad Ann has mentioned her, because to miss her out is to get everything wrong. The two of them were in 'symbiosis'. By the time people like me became conscious, in the late 1930s, they had been through so much, most painfully of all the early deaths of three of their five children. The bond endured even when our grandmother lost her memory some five years before she died, and all that was left of her strong social presence was a beautifully benign smile. I should say, all that *seemed* to be left, and can put in a story to illustrate the 'seem'. The date must have been early 1955. I was at Yatscombe for tea, which was laid on the big oak table in the dining room. Our grandmother was brought down to her time-honoured position at the head, with the tea-things on a tray in front of her, though I guess Kathleen must have helped her pour. Conversation was mainly between grandfather and grandson, to whose mental age the professor easily adjusted his own. At one point he demonstrated a recently discovered wonder: if you rolled a circular napkin ring across the oak table it would not roll off, but go slow, halt before the edge, and roll back towards you. The professor's demonstration was only half-way through before Grandmother, who had taken no part whatever in proceedings otherwise, said 'Gilbert!', in reproof at the informality of his table manners. Even then, aged 90 and with no memory left, she remained herself deep down.

These are all little things, no doubt; but some archaeologists build much of their history on the basis of minutiae, so I hope these are not useless. Occasionally the great world impinged on us. When Grandfather broadcast, we dutifully listened. I was once taken as the smallest member of a Yatscombe contingent to sit in the front row of a performance, at Somerville, of Aristophanes' *Frogs*. In my undergraduate days, in what must have been 1956, the great world became very present when I learned that Sir Antony Eden's private secretary had been in Yatscombe that day, sent by the Prime Minister to ask Grandfather's advice on what to do about the Suez crisis.

Among my domestic memories, some relate to my grandfather's last years, because they coincided with my own early time as an Oxford undergraduate. I was quite often up at Yatscombe, and got to know well those who looked after Grandfather, especially Kathleen

Haines, and also, when Kathleen had her breaks, Adèle Rankl (the *relicta* of the Viennese conductor Karl Rankl: they had been given Yatscombe Cottage to live in, then Karl had vanished to London with another wife). For those who have daily to coax their imagination back over many centuries, let me insert a memory which may help project it over one. Adèle Rankl had invited Grandfather over to dine at Yatscombe Cottage with, as fellow-guests, Egon and Emmi Wellesz (he the composer and musicologist). When we moved to armchairs after the dinner Grandfather drifted into sleep, while the others slipped into their native German, of which I had learned just enough to follow their conversation without joining in. They were talking about pre-First-World-War Vienna, *Die Welt von Gestern.* For half an hour I was there; and, all but a hundred years later, here I am, as sole survivor, telling *you.*

Kathleen and Adèle often told me of things Grandfather had said. Once, when it was Adèle's turn to help him to bed, he muttered 'It's so hard to be good'. Another time, Adèle surreptitiously borrowed a note with Grandfather's writing on it and showed it to someone she knew who was said to read character from handwriting. On seeing Gilbert Murray's handwriting the expert said, 'The person who wrote this had a character very like Jesus Christ'. Delighted, Adèle confessed to Grandfather what she had done. He said, 'I am not like Jesus Christ. I don't lose my temper.' He was not Bernard Shaw's friend for nothing.

Right to the end, in all he said and did, there was nothing at all out of character: not a trace of those devils of bitterness or delusion that sometimes torture the very old, only a fully conscious, fully sensitive, exposure to life itself, and exposure most painful of all on the early morning when Kathleen came through to the small bedroom where he slept, and was up, in his dressing-gown, sitting in his chair, to tell him that Lady Mary had just died.

My grandfather's jocular reference to Jesus Christ raises the matter of our grandfather's alleged interest in Roman Catholicism in the year after our grandmother died. Happily I do not have to tell that story, since its outline—as far as history can relate, which is never far in such matters—has now been told in print, in the April 1991 issue of the periodical *New Blackfriars.* The author of that article was Father Crozier, the Roman Catholic priest with whom our grandfather had contact in that last year. I will only add that, although Father Crozier's conversations with Grandfather were naturally private, nothing I heard from Kathleen, Adèle, or Dr Nasmyth clashed with what he says in that article, and the very little they said on the subject rather goes along with it. Nor, when I was introduced to Father Crozier and talked with him in 1980, did there seem to me any reason to mistrust his account.

About ten years ago I went to see Yatscombe, which had shortly before become empty. (The American college which had bought it had gone, and the house was for sale.) I went round, looking in through the windows. There was of course no furniture; one clumsy alteration had spoiled one end of the sitting-room; it was all somewhat derelict. But it was Yatscombe all right: dining-room (where I had been rebuked, aged seven), veranda, drawing-room, hall, den (once my father's nursery), everything. It all came back. Then, suddenly, I saw it was not Yatscombe at all. Not at all. It was a different house. Ours had gone for ever, with the *ver-öld* which it had once held, a *ver-öld* now surviving, as far as this planet is concerned, only in four memories, all of them edging their way to dissolution with every tick of the clock.

2

A Broken Mirror: Gilbert Murray's Reflections of an Australian Childhood

Francis West

'The memories of a small child are like a broken mirror: bright spots and blanks and ocasional misarrangements' (Murray 1960, 23): the opening sentence of Gilbert Murray's *Unfinished Autobiography*, which began as a memoir of his father, Sir Terence (Aubrey) Murray, Australian pastoralist and politician, and his brother, Sir (John) Hubert (Plunkett) Murray, Australian colonial governor of Papua. The autobiography was unfinished, Arnold Toynbee, his son-in-law explained, because when Murray came to the chapters in which he himself was the central figure, he disliked carrying on, for he felt that autobiography was egotistical (Murray 1960, 7). He began to write about his father in April 1949, his memory having recently been reawakened by looking over some packets of old letters, three volumes of notes and newspaper cuttings making a sort of commonplace book, and a journal for the year 1841 (Murray to Lady Mary Murray, 11 Apr. 1949: GM 474.129-30).[1] Apart from Murray's own memories of his Australian childhood, these few documents were 'eked out again by memories not of things I saw but of things I was told, mostly no doubt a little shaped and simplified in accepted family tradition. Unfortunately my two elder brothers, Aubrey and Hubert, are no longer here to correct and amplify my record. It is all fragmentary. It is probably often inexact' (Murray 1960, 23).

[1] GM = Bodleian Library, Oxford, MSS Gilbert Murray; numbers refer to boxes and folios.

BRIGHT SPOTS IN THE MIRROR

Murray intended to give some picture of an 'almost forgotten period' and a 'remarkable and unrecorded life', but he accepted that in old age—he was 83 when he began to write—memory had lapses, played tricks. A noted raconteur, he had told and retold stories from his Australian childhood to family and friends throughout his long life, stories that inescapably became polished over time; Lady Mary once objected: 'Gilbert, you know that's not true', and he replied, with his charming smile, 'I may have improved it in my mind'.[2] Polished and re-polished stories may become false memories, not only Murray's but also those of his parents and siblings who told him of things he had not seen for himself. His father's story, for example, that 'King' Cakobau of Fiji told him that he had been a cannibal, but white men spoiled their flesh by eating too much salt (Murray 1960, 49): this cannot be true, for Cakobau came to Sydney only once, two years after Murray's father, who never visited Fiji, had died. Certainly intending to be accurate, Murray recognized that his autobiography might nevertheless often be inexact.

His autobiography, like most others, contains errors of fact. He was actually seven years old, not nine, when his father died (Murray 1960, 7). His boarding school in the Australian bush was not near Nattai in the Blue Mountains (ibid., 53), but over the Dividing Range south-west of Sydney at Moss Vale and at nearby Mittagong, scarcely the Australian bush by the mid-1870s. Two former convicts, 'Old Tom' and 'Old Jimmy', were not living in cottages on his father's fine 'Yarrowlumla' station, now Canberra, the federal capital of Australia, in what Murray called 'my time' there (ibid., 33), for his father had lost that property in 1858, eight years before his youngest son was born. Murray's much older half-sisters Leila and Evelyn, who had been born and brought up there, certainly told him stories about 'Yarrowlumla', as also about his father's other great station near Lake George, 'Winderadene',[3] where they lived as a family after moving

[2] F. J. West 1984, 1, *e relatione* Margery Murray, wife of Hubert's son Patrick, Murray's nephew, who heard it while staying at Boars Hill.

[3] These are Murray's spellings of the names. 'Yarrowlumla' is more commonly written 'Yarralumla', and 'Winderadene' as 'Winderradeen' (Anna Maria's spelling in a letter to her nephew and godson Aubrey, 8 Mar. 1880).

from Yarrowlumla in 1856, where their mother Minnie died in 1858, shortly after giving birth to Aubrey (G. Wilson 1968, 161, 206, 253, 255), and where their father married Agnes, Murray's mother, in 1860; but Winderadene too was lost in September 1865, four months before Murray's birth (F. J. West 1968, 19). He may not have seen the written family name of his father's first wife that he misspells Gibbs, not Gibbes, but he must have seen his half-sister's name written as Evelyn, not Eveline, and certainly one of his own registered names which he misspelled as Forster instead of Foster (Murray 1960, 26). Carelessness, perhaps?

These are trivial errors of commission. The omissions from his autobiography are more serious. Murray portrays in his father both constant support for progressive causes and hostility to authoritarian, sectarian religion that were his own characteristics, his father being 'the greatest person in the world', 'the ultimate arbiter on all doubtful questions' (ibid., 31). In looking back at his Australian childhood to explain how a ragged little boy from the Australian bush came to be a great man in his British present—a distinctively Whig approach to the past by light of the present (F. J. West 1973, 17–18)—Murray made his father central. But did he re-make him in his own image? Omissions, whether from forgetfulness or choice or lack of knowledge, certainly lead to some lack of perspective in the portrait of his father, whose early death, he supposed a modern psychologist would say, unconsciously caused him to look for a guiding father-figure in later life (Murray 1960, 89). Since Murray had little, if any, knowledge of psychoanalytical theories of infant development as the determinant of adult personality, his use of a psychological term is what Lionel Trilling called 'the slang of our culture' (Trilling 1955, 12).

Murray depicts his father as tall, strong, majestic, a great pastoral landowner through his own hard work as a young man in the harsh, lonely, often dangerous conditions of the Australian bush, who entered politics at the insistence of others as an honest man passionate for the public good. When he had finished his classical schooling in Dublin, his father, Gilbert Murray's grandfather, sent for him to come out to Sydney where he was serving as Paymaster to the British forces in the penal colony of New South Wales, after fighting at Waterloo (Murray 1960, 36). Once in New South Wales, at the remarkably young age of 20 or 21 Murray's father was made a 'Frontier Magistrate', and given a grant of land near Lake George with some 'ticket-of-leave' convicts as servants (ibid., 37). Originally he had the two fine stations 'Yarrowlumla' and 'Winderadene', and generously gave away a third (ibid., 34). Almost a feudal proprietor or oriental kadi, keeping open house with free lodging for old servants, passing travellers, and distressed Irish gentlemen, he was invited by a deputation to represent them in parliament (ibid., 33, 38). Unwilling to canvass votes for himself—a troop of Irishmen went round electioneering for him while he stayed at home—he was continuously re-elected despite being extremely independent, in particular differing from fellow Irish Catholics over his opposition to denominational education (ibid., 40–1). His causes were those of liberal and humane practice: religious liberty, abolition of capital punishment, prevention of cruelty to animals, improved working conditions for servants, concern for Australian aborigines who came to him for advice and help (ibid., 44, 48).

BLANKS IN THE REFLECTION OF HIS FATHER

As Murray suspected, this picture of his father has been misarranged, shaped, and simplified in accepted family tradition. He knew nothing at first hand of his father's life as a great landowner. What he knew was second-hand from his mother and his siblings, but they actually knew little at first-hand themselves. His mother met his father only in 1860 and lived intermittently for only five years at Winderadene. His half-sisters Leila and Evelyn knew more, for they were born and brought up at Yarrowlumla between 1844 and 1857, and his half-brother Aubrey, born at Winderadene in 1857 and often there until 1865, knew something. His full brother Hubert, born in Sydney in 1861, knew little of his father's earlier life. Murray never met nor corresponded with his two relations who knew very much more than anyone else: his father's elder sister Anna Maria, who came with him to New South Wales in 1827, and her son William, who lived with her near Yarrowlumla after 1840. His father's few papers offered Murray little to correct family oral tradition.

Not surprisingly, therefore, Murray's account needs amplification and correction. His grandfather did not fight at Waterloo—his army paymaster's commission, obtained through the influence of Mrs Fitzherbert with the Prince Regent, restricted him 'from any military command or duties with arms'[4]—but served in Wellington's army in Portugal from 1811 to December 1814.[5] He was not recommissioned until five months after Waterloo as paymaster to the 48th (Northampton) Regiment of Foot, posted in New South Wales from 1817 to 1825. He did not send for Terence Aubrey to Sydney while serving there; returning to London, he retired on half-pay in 1826. Selling his commission to raise capital, he brought Terence Aubrey and Anna Maria to Sydney in 1827, for his service entitled him to a free grant of 2,560 acres of land; his elder son James joined them in 1830 after medical studies in Edinburgh (G. Wilson 1968, 20–2). Terence Aubrey was not appointed a frontier magistrate at a remarkably young age, and then given a grant of land. His 1,280 acres, adjoining his father's larger grant at Collector, near Lake George, in 1829, were compensation to his father for administrative errors that had forced him to give up his first two selections, and were granted only on condition that Captain Murray provided him with £1,000 of capital. Murray's father became a magistrate in 1833 after his father had presented him to the new governor, Lieutenant-General Sir Richard Bourke, a fellow veteran of the Peninsular War from Limerick, where the Murrays had been resettled after the Boyne. Bourke needed more magistrates because he faced an outbreak of bushranging in the Lake George district (ibid., 68).

[4] H. Murray 1970, 165. Hubert told Rosalind Toynbee that he and Aubrey often wondered how their grandfather and two of his brothers, although Catholics, got commissions in the British army and navy. His explanation was that they all married Fitzgerald sisters, and the Fitzgerald family were friends of Mrs Fitzherbert who married George IV. Gilbert did not know or did not choose to give this explanation: he thought the law was loosely administered in the case of paymasters. In fact there was still a royal dispensing power, but his grandfather's commission, as he told the governor of New South Wales in 1820, 'positively restricted' him from any military command or duties with arms: G. Wilson 1968, 11. Wilson was unclear when he bore the title captain, but in 1798 the Prime Minister, William Pitt the Younger, introduced army commissions for paymasters, selected by regimental colonels but reporting directly to the War Office, who could be ranked as captains: Hinchcliffe 1983, 20.

[5] The Murray Family Papers in the National Library of Australia contain a copy of a Horseguards certificate of this service.

These factual errors do not seriously distort Murray's image of his father as a young man in the Australian bush, clearing, fencing, stocking his land, gaining a reputation as a fearless horseman and fine shot in pursuit of bushrangers. But a blank in the broken mirror of childhood memory does. His grandfather is a missing person. It was Captain Murray, not Murray's father, who established the family as Australian landed gentry, adding to the original grants by purchase and entailing everything on Terence Aubrey and his heirs at his death in 1835 (ibid., 74). James, the elder son, is another missing person. After his medical service, he bought 'Woden', a station six miles from Yarrowlumla, which he left to Terence Aubrey at his death in 1857. Anna Maria, whom Murray never mentions, inherited her husband's 'St Omer' station in 1834, but kept house for her brother James at Woden. These missing persons alter the perspective of Murray's picture of his father.

After Terence Aubrey inherited in 1835, he built a handsome, twelve-roomed stone house, with kitchen and stable ranges, at Winderadene, and a family vault in which he laid his father's and later his brother's bodies (ibid., 74, 79–80). He had lived at a third station, 'Ajamatong', six miles from Winderadene, land his father had bought in his son's name in 1833, but he did not give this away; he still owned it in the 1850s (ibid., 232–3). Yarrowlumla, a stone hunting lodge with land and pack of hounds, thirty-five miles south of Lake George, he bought in 1837 (ibid., 80–1), then having 20,000 acres of freehold land, running 13,000 sheep; by 1850 he had fifty-four thousand acres of freehold with 20,000 sheep. He had also 'squatted' on six out-stations and 'hundreds of thousands of acres' beyond the official boundary of settlement.[6] Murray either did not know, or did not choose to say, that this expansion depended on borrowed money. Thomas Walker, whom his father took hunting at Ajamatong, put up

[6] *Sydney Morning Herald* (24 June 1847). The term 'squatter' changed its meaning over a short period of time: Roberts 1964, 186–7. At first a term of abuse for ex-convicts or vagrants who occupied land close to freehold settlers and stole their stock, after 1836 it meant a settler who occupied land beyond the official boundary of settlement under a squatting licence of £10 p.a., and after 1839 one who had right of possession, but not freehold, in land on which he squatted. Michael Roe regarded Murray as one of a group of conservative settlers who were gentry, as distinct from squatters: Roe 1965, 41, 47–8, 54, 57, 68, 73–4.

money to enable him to buy Yarrowlumla from Francis Mowatt, to whom Terence Aubrey remained in debt for part of its price, as well as to two Trust Companies.[7] When severe economic depression struck in the early 1840s, creditors threatened ruin. He managed to rearrange, but not to pay off, his debts, surviving immediate threat of insolvency but not the later loss of his land. Murray attributed this to natural disasters, although he must have heard from his half-sisters that a major part of the loss came from lack of foresight.

In 1843 his father married Mary ('Minnie'), second daughter of Lieutenant-Colonel John George Nathaniel Gibbes, Collector of Customs in New South Wales and rumoured to be an illegitimate son of Frederick, Duke of York, second son of George III.[8] Minnie was ten years younger than Terence Aubrey, who hoped to put his lands beyond his creditors' reach by settling them on his wife, except for Winderadene and 2,000 acres around the house to meet the property qualification for election to parliament. After bearing him six children, three of whom died shortly after birth, in the isolated conditions of the bush, Minnie herself died early in 1858, two months after giving birth to Aubrey. Under her will, the property her husband had transferred passed to her Gibbes family, who treated it, Terence Aubrey complained to George Foster Wise (after whom Murray was named at birth), 'as if it had been a wedding portion from Colonel Gibbes to his daughter... that old hag Mrs Gibbes who rules everything at Yarrowlumla... will do all she can to prevent... any arrangement that will meet my ends' (G. Wilson 1968, 286; see Ryan 1976).

It is hard to believe that Murray did not hear this story from his half-sisters. When he was 6, Leila, close to the mother she had nursed and deeply attached to country life, called on the Gibbes at Yarrowlumla in 1872; they refused to receive her. Murray's father told Evelyn how very much he felt this insult.[9] It is even harder to believe that

[7] Murray to Mowle, 11 Sept. 1843. Mowle Papers, Mitchell Library, Sydney.

[8] See Pike 1966. Hubert Murray told a garbled version of this rumour to Murray's daughter Rosalind in 1934, in which Gibbes became the son of George IV and Mrs Fitzherbert; he described this as 'a strong family tradition, though it was not known to me until recently': H. Murray, 1970, 165.

[9] Murray to Evelyn, 3 Sept. 1872. Murray Family Papers, National Library of Australia.

Aubrey and Hubert did not tell Murray of their adventure in September 1865 when, alone at Winderadene as bailiffs swept through the house to remove all its contents—knives and forks, chairs and tables, beds and blankets—they had been driven by mail coach to Sydney in tempest, thunder, lightning, and rain.[10] It was public knowledge that their father owed £25,000, an enormous sum at the time; only his friends, rallying round to raise enough for him to avoid bankruptcy, enabled him to continue in parliament.

Understandably, Murray did not depict his father as lacking in judgement and foresight—his generation believed the dead were entitled to discretion[11]—but instead said, recalling a story of his mother's (Murray 1960, 34–5), that he was careless in money matters, and explained his ruin by natural disasters, agents' mismanagement, and over-generosity to the needy. Loss of his remaining land in 1865 was triggered by the loss of 20,000 sheep to disease in 1860–1,[12] but the underlying cause was his alienation of most of his land on marriage while still owing debts contracted through ambition to achieve a great landed position and a place in the world. Murray must have known Aubrey's view of their father as a 'reckless, improvident old Irish gentleman' (G. Wilson 1968, 282). Hubert told him in 1889 that Aubrey was thinking of having a shot at recovering the entailed Lake George property; his aunt Anna Maria told Aubrey that the Gibbeses had wrongfully disposed of it (F. J. West 1970, 8). Murray's mother told him of meeting that fine old lady: 'you would be more in sympathy with her than anyone I have met. She is not ashamed of high motives'.[13] He could not have known her son

[10] Murray to Anna Maria 20 Feb. 1869. Bunn Papers, Mitchell Library, Sydney. Anna Maria married Captain George Bunn in 1828; he died in 1834. She inherited a life interest in his station 'St Omer' (called after the French town where her mother died in 1814 en route to visit Captain Murray, then serving in Portugal), near Braidwood, thirty-five miles south-east of Lake George.

[11] Murray to Lady Mary Murray, 3 Dec. 1892: GM 449.108. On his only return visit to Australia, Murray was told by Stewart Mowle that, as he had half-suspected 'my father drank to excess'. He also learned that his half-brother Aubrey had been 'a desperate drunkard'. He certainly knew that Hubert was expelled from Brighton College for striking a master after drinking in a pub during Sports Day. He was discreet about all of this in his autobiography.

[12] Murray to Anna Maria, 7 Sept. 1865. Bunn Papers, Mitchell Library, Sydney.

[13] Agnes Murray to Gilbert and Mary Murray, 10 Apr. 1890: GM 483.250.

William's opinion of his uncles James and Terence Aubrey: 'like all Irish gentry they felt all trade or work was degrading'.[14]

MISARRANGEMENTS IN THE REFLECTION

If Murray knew nothing at first hand of his father's improvident life as a great landowner whose lordly swagger attracted the local nickname of 'the Duke', although he knew an old Irish gentleman later called him 'the Emperor' (Murray 1960, 34) he knew no more of his father's earlier political career. Brought up in a succession of smaller and smaller rented houses in Sydney, Murray 'dimly remembered' denunciations of politicians who were 'schemers' (ibid., 32), his father being an honest man in politics although sometimes inconsistent. President of the Society for the Abolition of Capital Punishment, he was taunted in parliament over what should be done with the Fenian who attempted to assassinate the Duke of Edinburgh, Queen Victoria's son, in 1868; he angrily replied: 'Hanged as high as Haman' (ibid., 42). But Murray never detected in his father social or political ambition for great position in the world. He believed his father had had to be invited to stand for parliament, although he actually put himself forward in January 1843 as a long-term settler who would 'unlock the elements of prosperity and greatness lying dormant in the land' (*Sydney Morning Herald*, 24 Jan. 1843). He left his bride of three weeks in order to join his young protégé and agent, Stewart Mowle, in canvassing votes, promising him that 'If I rise in the world, you shall rise with me'.[15] In parliament, his consistent cause was opposition to the high selling price of Crown land that he believed blocked settlement by desirable colonists: English country gentlemen with their families and connections, the clergyman, the physician, tradesmen, and labourers (*Sydney Morning Herald*, 6 Dec. 1843). He condemned the 'new breed' of squatters who operated through monopolistic squatting companies with speculative capital to occupy land under licence—and often without it—so shutting out

[14] William's manuscript autobiography. Bunn Papers, Mitchell Library, Sydney.

[15] T. A. Murray to Mowle, 2 and 24 June, 1843. Mowle Papers, Mitchell Library, Sydney.

retired officers who in any case could not afford the high price (ibid., 29 May 1847, 6 Aug. 1853). Not a liberal cause but that of a squirearchy, a gentry as distinct from a rude, lawless squattocracy.

Or, indeed, of a nobility. In 1852, although he thought to retire from public life, Murray's father was pressed to stand again—the occasion Murray misidentifies as his first reluctant entry into politics. He joined a committee that recommended a new Constitution with a nominated upper house whose members should receive patents of nobility and hereditary titles. At a packed public meeting in the Royal Victoria Theatre in Sydney, a young Irish radical lawyer, Daniel Deniehy, caricatured on stage 'these harlequin aristocrats', this 'bunyip aristocracy'. Imitating Terence Aubrey's haughty swagger, he cried: 'Observe the colonial starred' Murray, 'with more crosses and orders—not perhaps orders of merit—than a state of mandarinhood'. The proposal perished, but a nominated Legislative Council was established. Murray ran again for the lower House of Assembly, telling voters he favoured a partly elected upper chamber. Henry Parkes, a leading radical, publicly described Murray's political career as 'chequered by the effects of a temper more or less unbending, and a judgement often precipitate and perverse', although he detected 'an inclination to liberalism' (G. Wilson 1968, 224). Daniel Deniehy, hearing Murray's support for a partly elected upper house, called him the only representative of the old territorial aristocracy to come out from those with whom he had been connected by long years of sympathy to join the ranks of the reformers when he saw the squattocracy attempting to use responsible government in order to perpetuate its domination (ibid., 256–7). But Murray in fact wanted a conservative house in order to restrain the excessive democracy of a lower into which an inferior type of man was being brought by the absence of any property qualification;[16] liberal suffrage introduced an ultrademocratic tendency by letting in men of deficient education (*Sydney Morning Herald*, 13 May and 13 Nov. 1858). He opposed the liberal or progressive causes of a wholly elected upper house, universal adult male suffrage, and the secret ballot. Fellow members of the lower house saw him as aristocratically arrogant in appearance and manner

[16] T. A. Murray to James Macarthur, 11 June 1858. Macarthur Papers, Mitchell Library, Sydney.

with, said the radical Scottish clergyman, John Dunmore Lang, 'magniloquent delivery of unimportant matters' (ibid., 24 Sept. 1859).

Gilbert Murray was plainly unaware of the realities of mid-nineteenth-century New South Wales politics. There were no political parties as in Britain; parliamentary politics were more like eighteenth-century factions, combining to form relatively short-lived ministries (Loveday and Martin 1969, 1–5, 24–6). He was unaware of his father's earlier ambition to see a responsible gentry shaping the colony, and does not mention his acceptance of office as Secretary for Lands and Public Works when the moderate liberal faction of 'Slippery Charlie' Cowper formed a government in 1856. Murray wanted a Lands Bill to control squatting monopolies and encourage smaller settlers (*Sydney Morning Herald*, 27 Nov. 1857). He never got it through parliament, resigning office when criticized for neglecting his duties by absence from the debate to be with his dying wife at Winderadene. He at first declined to stand in 1859 because, he told a fellow pastoralist, there was nothing in public life to attract men of character into a lower house that had 'a tide of ignorance and indifferent honesty... swelling through it'.[17] But stand again he did, in the hope of passing a Lands Bill. He sat with the opposition to the liberal Cowper who, defeated on a financial vote, resigned, advising the governor to send for Murray who had ambitions to become premier (G. Wilson 1968, 262).

Having no faction of his own, he failed to attract those he considered fit to hold office, reluctantly returning his commission. Henry Parkes, declining to serve, asked Murray if he thought he would make a good premier (Martin 1980, 170); he replied that he could devote himself to his duties but could never stoop to conciliate support. Ineffective in factional politics, on the unexpected retirement of the Speaker in 1860 Murray sought this honourable but politically neutral post, supported by Parkes who publicly said there were one or two other gentlemen he would have preferred. Duly elected, Murray complained to him that the Duke of Newcastle had refused him the knighthood his predecessors had received.[18] After

[17] T. A. Murray to James Macarthur, 27 Apr. 1859. Macarthur Papers, Mitchell Library, Sydney.

[18] T. A. Murray to Parkes, 18 Sept. 1861. Parkes Papers, Mitchell Library, Sydney.

a constitutional crisis over the upper house rejection of two bills in 1862, Murray accepted nomination as President of the Legislative Council (Loveday and Martin 1969, 32–3). This was the politically neutral office his father occupied throughout Murray's early childhood; his earlier chief cause in factional politics—to maintain and strengthen a landed gentry, as distinct from squatters, speculative companies, land dealers and traders—was unknown to the child, who naturally assumed his father had always been the liberal man he knew.

If politics happened outside Murray's family circle, religion was another matter. His religious attitudes were a direct family experience. Murray knew his father to be tolerant, opposed to sectarian religion: he had married his first wife in her Anglican parish church, and married Murray's Protestant mother at Winderadene, first in a Catholic ceremony, then in an Anglican one. Murray's half-siblings were probably baptized as Catholics, although their father expected no regular religious observance beyond family prayers at breakfast.[19] Murray's full brother Hubert was baptized as an Anglican, but there is no record of Gilbert's infant baptism; both were baptized as Catholics in 1869. Neither their father nor their mother attended the ceremony in St John's College at Sydney University, a Catholic foundation their father had strongly opposed, being called, Murray heard, one of 'the unattached' by the Catholic bishop (Murray 1960, 44). His half-sister Evelyn stood sponsor.[20] He probably heard of his father's heated reply to John Hubert Plunkett, an Irish Catholic former Attorney-General after whom Hubert had been named. In a debate on Henry Parkes' Public Schools Bill in December 1866, Plunkett argued that schoolmasters must inculcate the principles of religion. Murray interjected: it was not intended to have other than

[19] Gwendoline Wilson (G. Wilson 1968, 161, 285) says the children were all baptized as Anglicans, but Anna Maria addressed Aubrey as her godson. As a devout Catholic, she could not have become his godmother had he not been a Catholic himself; as Evelyn must have been to stand as sponsor at the Catholic baptisms of her half-brothers in 1869.

[20] Register of Baptisms, St Joseph's, Newtown, Sydney. The entry was inserted at the request of Dr Forrest, Rector of St John's College, who baptized Gilbert and Hubert, Evelyn being recorded as sole sponsor for the former, Hugh Murray Guinn for the latter. Fr Godfrey Ainsworth of the Franciscan Friary, Waverley, to Francis West, 23 Mar. 1990. Francis West Papers, National Library of Australia.

Christian masters, but they must be men of practical, not dogmatic Christianity. Plunkett retorted that Murray's religion was so different from his own and that of every other member. Murray indignantly responded: he had 'as good a right to make a religion for himself as Martin Luther had' (*Sydney Morning Herald*, 7 Dec. 1866).

As the dominant figure in his family, his father's politics and religion, in Murray's account, caused all his children to be passionately on the side of the oppressed; they were Home Rulers, keen on the protection of animals, children, foreigners, heretics, and unpopular minorities. All of them were 'greatly interested in religion and all sceptical' (Murray 1960, 26). Murray attributes this to 'birth and upbringing' in his father's household. By 'birth' he meant not genetic inheritance but descent from Irish ancestors who had fought and suffered for their convictions, as recorded in a 1758 entry in the family bible,[21] and his father was proud of descent from an early king of Connaught.[22] But it was to 'upbringing', rather than birth, that Murray attributes his own and his siblings' personalities, attitudes, and values: liberal and progressive in political and social causes, sceptical in religion, and hostile to sectarian dogma: 'When, after long separations two of us happened to meet, we nearly always found ourselves in agreement about current controversies' (Murray 1960, 25). But just as Sir Terence, as he became in 1869, was neither the liberal nor progressive in factional politics that Murray supposed him to be, he was not a religious sceptic either. It would be surprising if Murray had not seen in his father's papers the codicil added to his

21 Murray 1960, 41–2. The family bible has disappeared. Murray's quotation of the 1758 entry by Patrick Murray, great-grandson of Denis who had been too young to fight at the Boyne, differs slightly from a typed copy in the Murray Family Papers in the National Library of Australia which records the death of his great-grandfather, six of his brothers, and the greater part of his corps which was chiefly composed of relatives but adds 'and tenantry', as might be expected if the Murrays held extensive lands in Antrim and Derry. Neither Gilbert nor Hubert asked an obvious question: if the Murrays were Catholic, how did they come to hold so much land in what was the Protestant settlement of Ulster by James I of England and VI of Scotland, as Hubert implied to Rosalind, Murray's elder daughter, wife to Arnold Toynbee, in 1934. H. Murray 1970, 166.

22 F. J. West 1984, 1, quoting Murray (*e relatione* Margery Murray, staying with Murray and Lady Mary at Boars Hill): 'if the 22nd king, why not the 21st?; there must have been some funny business there'. G. Wilson 1968, 2 and n. 2, names the king as Dubhionracht. Hubert gives the line of descent from Heremon, first Milesian king of all Ireland: H. Murray 1970, 165–6.

will in 1871,[23] nor heard from his mother that she was entrusted with the religious education of all the children, free of any interference by relatives or the Roman Catholic Church. His father highly respected the Roman Catholic Church, having been brought up in it and never adopting any other, but very partially accepted its doctrines and disciplines (ibid., 40–2: the codicil is inserted by the editors as a footnote, not quoted by Murray). Although he had his sons baptized as Catholics, he never contemplated giving them a denominational or sectarian education: his object was to impress the broad principles of Christianity on their minds. Murray wrote at the beginning of his autobiography that he and his siblings as children were all sceptical of religion, but later in his account he said that it was during his three years in the Head Form at Merchant Taylors' that he began to think seriously about religion (ibid., 83). A decade earlier, he had written that his hostility to traditional religion began as a moral rebellion in early childhood against the miracle of the Gadarene swine: it was monstrously cruel to drive unoffending pigs over a precipice. Such cruelty was what wicked, bullying boys at school would do (Murray 1940b, 7). But Murray encountered such boyish wickedness only at boarding school after his father's death; he records no horror at Sir Terence casually shooting a black cockatoo with his rifle (Murray 1960, 33), and does not mention an entry in the 1841 diary in his possession: climbing Mt Coree, his father saw some lyre-birds 'singing most beautifully'; on the way down, he had a couple of shots at them.[24] Murray also quotes without comment a letter his father wrote to Stewart Mowle, asking him to boil down one or two thousand sheep for tallow (Murray 1960, 34), a process described in cuttings in his father's commonplace book: sheep were driven live into a huge boiling vat.[25]

If physical revulsion at cruelty to animals and hostility to religion were not exactly his father's attitudes, what of his mother's influence?

[23] Ibid, 40–1, n. 1. The codicil is inserted by the editors as a footnote, not quoted by Murray.

[24] Diary 8 Mar., 1841. Murray Family Papers, National Library of Australia.

[25] Roberts 1964, 203–5. The process was invented by a neighbour of Murray's, Henry ('Black Harry') O'Brien of Yass, who nominated Murray at the 1843 election. The price of wool in the 1840s depression meant that a live sheep was worth less than the tallow produced by boiling it down.

She was his sole parent in Australian childhood in the four years after 1873, and during his English schooldays until 1884; he was her 'especial care and comfort during my sixteen years of struggling widowhood'.[26] Nevertheless she is a minor figure in the autobiography.[27] A cherished family story told of her defence of Winderadene against bush rangers, offering beer to 'blacks' whom she mis-heard to ask for sherry, not cherries (Murray 1960, 47, 51). She decided that Murray should go to boarding school; he talked with her 'over and over again' for he was miserable at leaving home. She gave him half-a-sovereign in case he wished to run away (ibid., 53), and come back to the home she had made for her family in the boarding school for young ladies she had opened in Sydney. In Murray's brief references to her, she was a spirited woman, a cousin of W. S. Gilbert, descended from 'generations of schoolteachers'.[28] She spoke French and German, and was remembered as a decisive, modernizing influence by pupils both at her Sydney school and the one she opened in South Kensington after she brought Gilbert to England in 1877. Her attitudes and decision made him an expatriate, for she believed New South Wales to be a cultural desert, 'the home of the philistines': 'never think of this country for your career—break your heart and waste your talents' (F. J. West 1980). Murray's lack of acknowledgement of her role and influence in his upbringing, by contrast with his father's, is the more remarkable because he describes Hubert as 'rudderless' without her guidance (Murray 1960, 76).

[26] G. Wilson 1968, 310, quoting Agnes to Lady Mary, 27 Nov. 1889. D. Wilson 1987, 4 and n. 12, wrongly cites this as a letter to Lady Carlisle.

[27] D. Wilson 1987, 3–4, notes that Murray writes very little of his mother, that few letters survive, and speculates (p. 32) that she may have resented his close relationship with his mother-in-law, Rosalind, Countess of Carlisle, who insisted on his wedding to her eldest daughter, Mary, while his mother was away in Australia for Hubert's wedding (p. 37).

[28] Gilbert Murray, 'Myself When Young', *The Listener* (18 Aug. 1949), 272–3, says that on his mother's side he was descended from generations of schoolmasters, but his other references are few: Murray 1960, 24–5, 47, 53,71–2, 74–5, 77 contain all his brief account. On his death, a number of his mother's London pupils wrote to his youngest son, Stephen, who gave the letters to Arnold Toynbee; the phrases 'a modernist in her day', 'more influence over us than anyone else', 'a social conscience much more highly developed than was common' independently echo those quoted from her Sydney pupils in E. M. Irvine, *Certain Worthy Women*, p. 295 and *The Town and Country Journal* (4 Nov. 1908), quoted in G. Wilson 1968, 304–5.

A Freudian explanation of all this will not do: there is no evidence of the Oedipus complex nor of sibling rivalry.[29] Nurture, the formative factor Murray assumed, does not explain the differences between his half-siblings and himself and his full-brother, nor between Hubert and himself who shared common nurture, similar education, both taking 'Firsts' in Lit. Hum. at Oxford, Hubert becoming a man of action, Gilbert a man of letters. Nature, genetic inheritance from a different mother in the case of his half-siblings, a shared one with Hubert, is something he never explores. Birth order theory explains in Darwinian terms that each successive child creates a different niche that determines later personality. Murray, like his father a last-born, on this theory was 'born to rebel'. Pity, which both his father and he had, is 'a rebel passion' (Murray 1960, 25). But both enjoyed the prominence they actively sought and gained as Establishment figures.

[29] F. J. West 1983, 2006. Sulloway 1996, 71–8 sets out the development and nature of birth order theory.

Appendix
An Abbreviated Murray Genealogy*

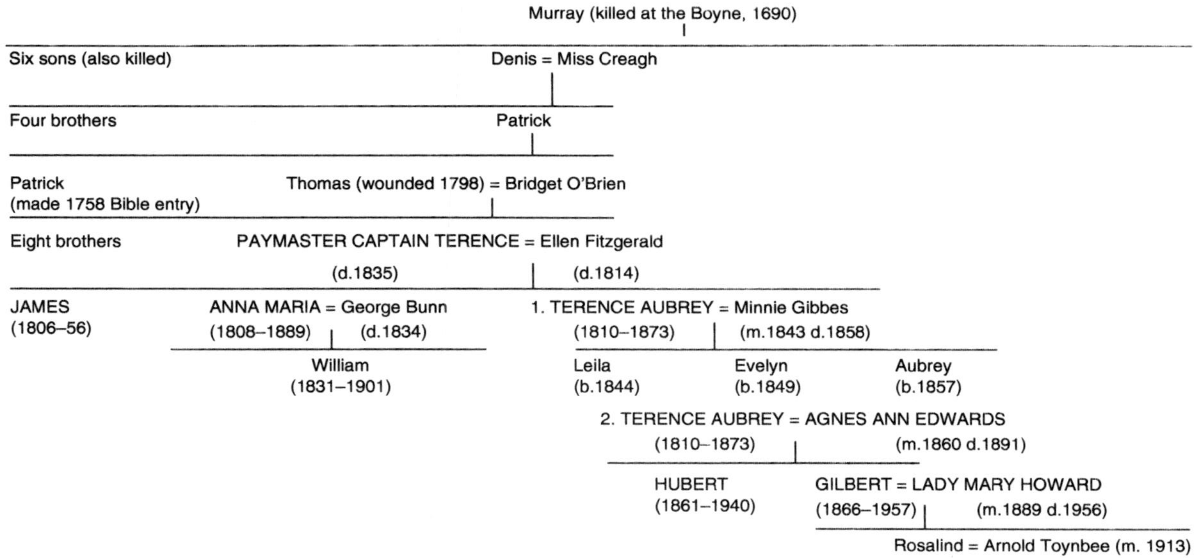

*Names in capitals are those commonly referred to in the text.

3

Gilbert Murray on Greek Literature: The Great/Greek Man's Burden

Mark Griffith

INTRODUCTION: GILBERT MURRAY AS HELLENIST

There were two main phases, or two modes, to Gilbert Murray's career as a Greek scholar. The first ('mode A') was that of an upwardly-mobile professional classicist of the conventional kind, self-consciously engaged in close philological analysis and on-going debate with rival scholars. The second ('mode B') aimed instead at a wider audience, including many non-classicists, and largely eschewed the apparatus of professional scholarship. These two modes did overlap chronologically to some

The talk from which this chapter is derived was entitled 'Murray and Greek Tragedy'. But I have broadened the scope a little to consider also some of Murray's scholarship on other aspects of ancient Greek literature, since this volume is intended to 'reassess' (among other things) Murray's importance, influence, and originality as a scholar of Greek culture in general, and there are certain aspects of his work on tragedy that can usefully be illuminated through consideration of his views on other authors and genres. So while this chapter will have indeed much more to say about Murray's views on Greek tragedy than on any other single aspect of Greek literature or culture, I will also make brief mention of his published views of Homer and Hesiod, of the Presocratics, of Herodotus and Thucydides, and of 'Orphic' literature and ideas. I should also perhaps make clear from the outset that, as a Cambridge-trained British classicist, I myself underwent some of the same educational experiences as Murray (emphasis on language skills, composition, and philology), yet remain an outsider inasmuch as I come from Cambridge (not Oxford), and am not a Ritualist. My thanks to Christopher Collard, Leslie Kurke, and Christopher Stray for helpful comments, corrections, and suggestions; also to Chris Stray for delivering the oral version of this paper at the conference in July 2005, when I was unable to attend in person.

degree—which is why 'mode' might be a better term than 'phase'. But on the whole, 'mode A' was confined to the earlier years of his career, so I shall henceforth usually refer to these as two 'phases' of Murray's illustrious career.[1] During the first phase, Murray was necessarily occupied with establishing his scholarly credentials. Like any promising young classicist in nineteenth- and early twentieth-century Britain, he had first (as an Oxbridge student) to demonstrate his skill at playing the game of linguistic refinement and flair, and then pay his national and international philological dues as a textual critic and/or author of a major critical edition. In Murray's case, this phase involved, first of all, winning prizes (mainly in composition) at Oxford and thereby proving himself an accurate, finely tuned, and sympathetic connoisseur of Greek (and incidentally Latin). Such linguistic expertise established him as a good man: grammatically sound, philologically well-groomed, and therefore authorized to express opinions about Greek literature—not vulnerable to the kinds of accusations that might be levelled at a James Frazer or Jane Harrison, whose philological training was more open to question. And his three-volume Oxford Classical Text of Euripides (Murray 1902a, 1904, 1909a) relatively quickly completed the demonstration of his scholarly credentials.

The oft-told story of Murray's first contact with Wilamowitz is revealing on this score. When he plucked up the courage to write to his learned German colleague, whose recently published *Einleitung* to his edition of Euripides' *Herakles* (Wilamowitz-Moellendorff 1889) had so completely eclipsed any British Hellenist's efforts to control the apparatus of textual history and criticism, Murray—only

[1] So, for example, 'Murray's most substantial work on Euripides was done before the First World War' (Easterling 1997, 113). The Aeschylus OCT editions (Murray 1937; 2nd edn., Murray 1955) might seem to be an exception, since these, on the face of it, should be counted as philological work done in 'mode A', yet performed during the later stages of Murray's career (phase two). But it has often been observed that the scholarship of these (especially of the first edition) did not favourably impress the community of experts for its rigour and accuracy; and most of the (considerable) improvements to the second edition were believed by many to be due to other (younger) members of the Oxford group that met regularly to work with him on that project in the 1950s—including Paul Maas, Denys Page, and Hugh Lloyd-Jones. (See further Collard in this volume; also D. Wilson 1987, 321, and n. 4 below.) It is notable that Eduard Fraenkel, in the otherwise generous and inclusive Preface to his *Agamemnon* edition (Fraenkel 1950), makes no mention of any assistance from Murray.

half-jokingly—chose (in 1894) to write his letter in classical Greek 'to show' (as he himself explained, and as Wilamowitz later recalled it) 'that [he] was not a merely frivolous person troubling him for the sake of his autograph or the like' (M. I. Henderson 1960, 129; see further D. Wilson 1987, 55). In his friendly letter of response, Wilamowitz apparently intimated that they would get more serious scholarship accomplished if they corresponded thenceforth in the vernacular—which they thenceforth did, happily and productively, though it is clear that the flow of information and critical opinion was very one-sided. Murray had little to teach Wilamowitz, though Wilamowitz liked his energy and desire to breathe life into the old Classics; but on the other side, Murray's Euripides edition was greatly indebted to Wilamowitz, as Murray himself freely acknowledged. Indeed, the differences between their respective activities and achievements as editors of the tragedians is very telling. Murray seems to have made no secret (in private) of his feeling that he was in somewhat over his head with the manuscripts of Euripides and their relationships to one another; and he did not succeed in making much progress on that front—his edition is useful more for its general good sense and eclectic use of the work of others than for any scientific principles of stemmatology, rigorous collection of data, or systematic textual criticism.[2] Wilamowitz, by contrast, though he too complains (in Latin, in the Preface to his *editio maior* of Aeschylus) that he 'takes no pleasure in swallowing the dust of libraries in collating MSS', did in fact swallow much and collate several (admittedly, at high speed), and thereby made important advances in establishing the manuscript tradition of his author.[3] And of course, for Wilamowitz this was but

[2] See especially Diggle 1984, pp. ix–x, and further Easterling 1997 and Collard (in this volume). As Diggle remarks,

'He employed for the most part a sober judgement, and accepted from his predecessors what seemed to be useful, while adding from time to time something of his own. But he selected his record of the manuscript readings almost entirely from various other sources, and one might have wished for a much fuller reporting of them.' (translation mine, from Diggle's Latin)

Diggle also points out that Murray made good use in this edition of the learned and acute critical input of both Arthur Verrall and A. E. Housman.

[3] 'ego a. 1885 in *Agamemnone* superstitionem, cui innutritus eram, nondum abieceram, etsi de triade iam dubitabam. ... deinde 1890 in scholiis Aeschyleis demonstravi ... sed taedium perquirendorum codicum declinabam, non solum

one of numerous heavy-duty editorial and philological undertakings that he worked through in the course of his immensely productive career—whereas for Murray the Euripides edition was virtually the only venture of its kind that he undertook,[4] and more, one may suspect, as a proof that he was capable of such work than because he thought the results would really make a significant difference to anything.

In addition to embarking on this solid and sustained piece of textual editing, Murray in the first phase of his career published a general *History of Ancient Greek Literature* (Murray 1897: reissued 1902, and repeatedly thereafter), which was an offshoot of his lectures and teaching at Glasgow, and seems to have been designed also to provide further confirmation of its author's range, soundness, and general expertise as a conventional Classicist. (I will discuss this *History* briefly in what follows.) He also completed a well-researched book on Homer, *The Rise of the Greek Epic* (Murray 1907b), which went into several editions and reprints (the most substantial revision occurring in 1924). This is a judicious and balanced investigation of the various 'Homeric Questions'; and it is a book which reads remarkably well today, with a broadly unitarian reading of the poems combined with an intelligent—though inevitably quite speculative—account of the highly conventional yet flexible rhapsodic tradition that produced them. Especially in the revised (post-1924) editions, it provides a sane and in many respects convincing account of the mixture of old and new, traditional and supplementary, local and panhellenic, historical and mythical, that the epics present in

quia bibliothecarum pulvere vesci minime amo, sed etiam quia alios talia multo melius ac facilius expedire probe scio. ... at vero, cum ante aliquot annos Aeschyli compluria publice interpretabar, puduit desidiae grammaticorum adeo, ut quidquid otii minime largi suppeditebat, recensendae triadi impenderem. ... atque ut erraverim—numquam edidissem Aeschylum, nisi ita errassem.' (Wilamowitz-Moellendorff 1914, pp. ix–x)

[4] See D. Wilson 1987, 321, and Collard's chapter in this volume, for the limitations of Murray's Aeschylus OCT, for which he clearly did much less work of his own on the MSS and scholia than he did for Euripides. For a particularly harsh and derisory assessment of the 1955 second edition ('edition-by-committee'), contrasting its slapdash *apparatus criticus* and lack of first-hand acquaintance with the MSS unfavourably with the previous editions of Wilamowitz and Paul Mazon, see Dawe 1964, 5–10.

their surviving form. It also offers an attractive reading of the two poems (along with thoughtful assessment of the Cyclic poems too)—with special emphasis on the final meeting between Achilles and Priam and the compassion that pervades the closing scenes of the *Iliad.* Murray's command of recent work in the field is impressive. References to other scholars are many, and respectful. This was a serious and significant contribution, and might be said to be the one real example of Murray combining both 'modes' (A and B) within the same book.[5]

The combination of these solid and demonstrably learned ventures, even despite the hiatus of his ill health and resignation from Glasgow, landed Murray, first, his return to Oxford as Fellow of New College (1905) and subsequently the Regius Chair of Greek (1908). Thus the second phase of his career was opened up for him. Once established as Regius Professor of Greek at Oxford (i.e. occupying the most prestigious professional position in the English-speaking world of Classics), he could thenceforth choose exactly what kind of work and writing he preferred, and what kind of a scholar he wanted to be. He had paid his dues, and now he could operate in the scholarly mode that he found most congenial to his goals and interests. This meant, it turned out, being an inspiring teacher, a patron of and collaborator with junior faculty, a facilitator and impresario of international Greek studies, and above all, the spreader of the word (at least, in English) and especially of the *spirit* of the ancient Greeks to a larger public: What do the Greeks and their culture mean? Why do they matter to us? What is so special about them? How can we make, or keep, them 'ours' (or, How can we come to see ourselves in them)? What do we have to find in the Greeks to justify who we are now and what we want to stand for (even struggle for) in the political and cultural world?

To many of Murray's contemporary professional classicists (as to many of my own teachers in the 1960s), such questions did not seem appropriate or answerable. Today, fifty or more years later, of course,

[5] It must have largely been the extraordinarily exclusionary attitude of the Parry–Lord oralists, once they had established their ascendancy in Britain and the USA, that drove this book completely from the field. It is, in my opinion, still worth reading—more so e.g. than most of the discussions of Homer published in English during my youth (1960s–1970s). See too Parker's contribution to this volume.

there are few classicists who are not required to confront them constantly, and at least intermittently to offer answers. But also it has become more evident to most of us that the process of 'finding ourselves' in the ancient Greeks, and claiming them as the ancestors—and/or as justification—for some contemporary status quo or political programme, has always in fact been a (more or less covert) reason for studying the Greeks and Romans. Murray was perhaps merely ahead of his time in acknowledging this so blatantly and so cheerfully.

So how did Murray operate in this second phase, as a prominent and established Hellenist? Not as a 'professional' classicist, to put it bluntly (as a good number of subsequent biographers and critics have done). He did not publish in the professional journals, nor (after the Euripides OCT) did he like to work on critical editions, textual problems, or scholarly commentaries. Shelley Arlen in her bibliography of the *Cambridge Ritualists* (Arlen 1990) lists *c.*1,300 publications of one kind or another by Murray (Arlen 1990, 80–297). Of these, many are letters, pamphlets, occasional addresses, etc.; quite a few are Introductions or by-products to his translations. Virtually none are scholarly articles of a conventional kind, submitted to and published in a classical journal. Nor did he often write critical reviews of the work of others. This has led to his being characterized by many as an 'amateur' and a mere 'popularizer'—neither of which labels he would himself necessarily have rejected.[6]

Yet his *influence* as a critic, appreciator, and interpreter of Greek literature was enormous, and in certain key respects his writings made as significant an impact as those of any of his more conven-

[6] D. Wilson 1987, 200–3, Easterling 1997, with further references. Christopher Collard informs me (*per litteras*) that among Murray's *Nachlass* is a small collection of textual notes on the Menander fragments in the Cairo codex, mainly on the *Epitrepontes*. This work, which Murray never completed, was probably done soon after 1907, when the codex was first published. Another venture that Murray once entertained, but regrettably never seriously attempted, was a commentary, perhaps on a Euripides play: see his letter to to R. C. Jebb of 9 Dec. 1893, quoted by Stray in the Introduction to this volume. It seems likely indeed that such a commentary, combining succinct philological and grammatical explanation with literary and dramatic interpretation, without gratuitous display of sheer learning for the sake of it, would have suited Murray's talents well—much better than a critical edition (OCT). But he appears never to have followed up on this idea.

tionally 'professional' contemporaries in the field of purely literary studies. This influence and impact came through five main types of activity:

(i) As a translator of drama (see Macintosh's chapter);
(ii) As a popular essayist, theatre-practitioner, broadcaster;
(iii) In the lecture hall and classroom, where his exceptionally beautiful voice and charming delivery greatly enhanced his unquestionable erudition. So his lectures and courses for undergraduates were very successful, first at Glasgow, then at Oxford, and in addition—a dimension rarely achieved by professional classicists—his public lectures were also a hit at Harvard and other places where he was invited;
(iv) He was also an effective supporter of and collaborator with other scholars, especially those less well established than himself (see McManus' chapter in this volume);
(v) He published readable and not-too-specialized books on Greek literature, especially drama.

It is these books that I will discuss in the rest of this chapter.

MURRAY AND GREEK LITERATURE

Apart from the Oxford Classical Texts of Euripides and Aeschylus, Murray was the author altogether of six[7] books on Greek literature—plus his famous contribution to Jane Harrison's *Themis* (1912), which found its way also, in mildly adapted forms, into his books on Euripides and Aeschylus (and elsewhere too).[8] The six books are the following: *A History of Ancient Greek Literature* (Murray 1897, 1902; and later reprints; subsequently reissued in 1956 as *The Literature of Ancient Greece*); *The Rise of the Greek Epic* (Murray 1907b,

[7] Perhaps we should say really 'five', since *The Classical Tradition in Poetry* does not set out to be a conventional study of Greek literature itself, but of its reception. In what follows, I shall nonetheless refer (briefly) to *The Classical Tradition in Poetry*, since Murray there makes interesting and revealing remarks about 'tradition' that are relevant to his criticism in general.

[8] See Parker in this volume, pp. 96–102, for further discussion and references.

reissued in many editions, including a fairly major revision and update in 1924); *Euripides and his Age* (Murray 1913, 2nd edition 1946; 3rd edition 1965); *The Classical Tradition in Poetry* (Murray 1927a); *Aristophanes: A Study* (Murray 1933); and *Aeschylus: The Creator of Tragedy* (Murray 1940).

If one were to ask the average professional scholar of Greek literature and culture today, how significant are (any of) these six books, i.e. how important, how influential, and how original as a scholar and critic Murray was, few would disagree with the verdict of Robert Fowler (writing in reference primarily to Murray's *Five Stages of Greek Religion*, but also to 'the rest of his scholarship'): 'In spite of his great fame when alive, he might never have written so far as most scholars are concerned today' (Fowler 1991, 79). Nor would I disagree with this verdict. In the field of Greek literary studies, Murray's contributions, in the long run, do indeed appear negligible, and his publications are rarely cited in the bibliographies to the latest contributions in the fields in which he wrote. The reasons are obvious enough: Murray's views on Greek literature and culture were mainly conventional and derivative; his 'research' (in terms of discovery of previously unknown evidence or shedding of unexpected new light on old problems) was, at least after the Homer book, relatively limited and superficial. Compared with Jane Harrison or Francis Cornford (to name perhaps the two best-known and most respected of his contemporaries and peers), his permanent legacy of important new scholarly ideas is small indeed. And as compared too with some of his successors of the next Oxbridge generations, the same is certainly true: W. S. Barrett, J. D. Beazley, A. M. Dale, J. D. Denniston, E. R. Dodds, H. D. F. Kitto, E. Lobel, D. L. Page, G. Thomson, R. P. Winnington-Ingram, and many more who could be mentioned (to say nothing of such distinguished German expatriates as E. Fraenkel and R. Pfeiffer), all of whose editions, commentaries, articles, and monographs continue to be cited and consulted, whereas almost none of Murray's are at all.

Nonetheless, it could truly be said that Murray's impact and influence as a scholar of Greek literature were extraordinarily important and distinctive—and quite interesting for us to analyse today. This is because in certain respects his work was so authoritative and so perfectly representative of some important critical positions in the Great Britain of his day; and also because the medium and manner of his communication, especially in the case of his Euripides book, were so attractive to an important segment of the scholarly and artistic community—i.e. impressionable undergraduates, practising artists, and well-read, politically influential readers from all kinds of other fields. That is to say, Murray was not only a supremely elegant, persuasive, and reader-friendly spokesperson for Victorian–Edwardian liberal–aristocratic values, and for a view of the world in which enlightened clusters of 'great men' (like Pericles and his circle: Anaxagoras, Aeschylus, Herodotus, etc.) might be seen as leading their nation towards a less superstitious and more compassionate future, but also a serious and engaged literary critic who saw the conflicts and inconsistencies that mark (especially) the texts of Euripides and Thucydides (even of Homer, too) as indicators of cultural stress and challenge from which we can all learn and benefit. And while Murray's ideas about the Greeks were not particularly original or distinctive in their main outlines, the ways in which he adopted and adapted the bold new ideas of others (most notably, Jane Harrison, and James Frazer; and, less directly and consciously, Friedrich Nietzsche), and the manner in which he presented these ideas to a general cultured public, were extraordinarily appropriate to a particular mentality and socio-political order.

Murray has been disparaged by some in the later twentieth century as merely an old-fashioned 'Gladstonian Liberal' (e.g. by Calder 1991, Fowler 1991; see the usefully corrective remarks of Easterling 1997). But I would suggest that his explicit endorsement of such 'Victorian' and 'Edwardian' values (during the period *c.*1900–40), and his direct analogizing of this liberal–progressive morality and social reformism—combined as it was with a cheerful commitment to world domination—to the period of Periclean Athens, was an enterprise of some sophistication and socio-political canniness. It was indeed a distinctive reading of the Greeks, and of what their literature can be made to mean—and by 'literature', Murray really meant the literary productions of a few of their greatest men; for unlike some of his predecessors and contemporaries, he did not buy deeply into the racist notion of a superior 'spirit' or 'character', shared by all Greeks or all Indo-Europeans. Murray was often quite scornful of 'stagnant rustic life' and the 'stupid taboos... [of] a thoroughly backward peasant in a Greek village', e.g. those from the demes of rural Attica that Aeschylus and even Euripides had to deal with, like the superstitious zealots in the audiences of medieval mystery plays.[9] And even though Fowler states, for example, that Murray's views have faded into oblivion because of 'the complete obsolescence of the Victorian world-view, or, more precisely, the world-view of a Gladstonian Liberal, which directly inspired all of Murray's work' (Fowler 1991), I would suggest instead that this world-view—and Murray's reading of Hellenism—has in fact continued to exercise a strong attraction for many segments of the educational and political establishments, even today.

So let us turn now to the books by which Murray is best known, along with his most famous contribution to Greek (and world) literary/dramatic studies, his theory of 'the Ritual Origins of Tragedy'—which in fact is reprised in each of the books on drama and operates to some degree as their backbone or guiding thread. Before we focus specifically on Murray's contributions to the criticism of Greek Tragedy, we should pause at least briefly to take stock of the *History of Ancient Greek Literature* (Murray 1897), since this most straightforwardly brings out the main lines of Murray's cultural mission. As has been observed by others, this book for the most part provides an unsurprising and unobjectionable survey of that

[9] In *The Classical Tradition in Poetry* Murray remarks, in describing the mind-set of 'traditional' societies that lack the benefit of a classical education,

> 'The mass of them acted without any thought at all, and followed the manners of speech and thought and behaviour which happened to be prevalent at that date... Tradition really held sway over all of them. But there was a difference in the attitude of different people toward the tradition. All were bound by it. But to most men, at any rate those of the lower type, it was an unconscious bondage. They spoke and ate and smoked and spat in the ways to which their fathers had been accustomed, because it had never occurred to them to do otherwise.... They mostly resented innovations, at any event when they involved effort. To the man in evening dress, on the other hand, the tradition represented an ideal ...' (Murray 1927a, 5)

In his Euripides book (Murray 1913, 112–17), he presents a picture of the Athenian masses who had been 'only lightly touched on the surface by the wisdom of the sophists ... and the spell of Pericles ...' and who quickly reverted to 'the silliest and cruelest of agricultural magic' and their 'old unregenerate mass of sentiment,' as they eagerly 'followed the lead [of] Cleon' with his violent and cruel policies—a picture that clearly accepts without demur Thucydides' strongly aristocratic views. Murray even uses the class-tinged term 'effrontery' of the misguided (and specifically Athenian) lower-class desire to justify their new self-assertion (p. 116).

large and already well-trodden field, devoting quite a bit of its space to summarizing the main works and the immediate context of their composition. One can note, however, as an incidental bonus, how well-informed and up-to-date Murray continued to be even in his later years, despite his 'non-professional' manner. Thus the new Preface for the third edition of 1956, as well as outlining several areas in which the author says his views have altered since the original publication of the first two editions of the work (1897, 1902), contains quite an engaging report on the various papyrus discoveries made between 1900 and 1955—i.e. mostly the Oxford-based Oxyrhynchus publications of Grenfell and Hunt, Lobel, and others, which brought more of Bacchylides, Menander, Alcaeus, and others back into the world (including several fragments of satyr plays, which Murray suggests further confirm the ritual theory of drama). All this serves as a nice reminder of how centrally placed Murray was, and how interested he continued to be in keeping abreast of the latest finds and theories in the world of Classics.

From our perspective, just over a century later, a few interesting peculiarities stand out in the *History.* Hesiod is assessed by Murray at a remarkably low value. Although his account of the likely composition of the *Works and Days* and *Theogony* over time in a poetic tradition of rhapsodes, rather than as the product of a single poet, is sensible and balanced, Murray's characterization of these poems (and the *Shield*) as completely devoid of continuity or unity (they 'might as well be called a dozen [poems as three]'), as 'lacking in earnest religious spirit' (apart from the Hecate hymn), and as 'a hopelessly inadequate attempt... to give a connected account of the gods... more than old, it is primeval'), betray his striking lack of sympathy for the ethical and aetiological aims of that particular tradition. The contrast between his low opinion of this rough peasant production (as he sees it), all bogged down in superstition and 'primeval'—even 'cannibalistic'—material, and his admiration for the refined sophistication of the noble Homeric epics, could not be stronger.

All the more remarkable is the long section that follows on 'Orphism', in which Murray lays the groundwork for what he imagines to have been the truest Greek religious experience, that of the mystery religions. (For Homer's gods, he claims, are merely 'elements of romance', while Hesiod's are just 'facts to be catalogued'—an extraordinary misrepresentation of the Hesiodic explorations of *dikê* and *hubris*, the myths of Prometheus, Pandora, and the Ages, and the succession to power of Zeus!) But the (alleged) 'wave of religious emotion' that fuelled Orphism and the worship of Bacchus from the sixth century BCE right through into late antiquity, largely invisible in the surviving literature, yet most truly characteristic of the 'joy' and passion felt by the best of the Hellenes and occasionally revealed in their artistic productions—most notably their dramas—all of this is detailed by Murray with reference both to the Sanskrit Vedas and to popular cults that are known only from (as he puts it) 'the discoveries of anthropologists'. Murray goes on to explain: 'The Mysteries are not mentioned by Homer. That does not mean that they are late: it means that they are either too sacred or else too popular' (Murray 1897, 63). It is easy to see why experts in the field, such as Ridgeway, Farnell, Pickard-Cambridge, and Linforth, were unhappy with the methodology of the 'Ritualists', even as one can respect Murray's eagerness to identify a genuine current of religious feeling somewhere in archaic Greek literature (see further Parker's chapter in this volume).

Within the rest of the *History of Ancient Greek Literature*, Murray devotes his warmest attention to Aeschylus and Euripides—with a very lukewarm account of Sophocles, whom he characterizes as too 'pious' and conventional-minded, too tightly bound by the primitive old heroic stories, suffering from a 'lack of speculative freedom' and 'a certain bluntness of moral imagination', and 'limited' in his intellectual focus: thus incapable of 'thinking through' the problems presented by the old sagas or of working out new and challenging solutions to them (Murray 1897, 239–40; cf. Easterling 1997, 119–21). I shall focus in more detail on Murray's Aeschylus and Euripides in the second half of this chapter. But we should not omit reference to his Herodotus and Thucydides, both of whom as authors clearly resonate strongly with Murray himself for their personalities, their careers (as he reconstructs them), and—especially—their respective sociopolitical contexts and personal dilemmas.

Herodotus came from far away... to Athens, where he made influential, aristocratic and literary friends and became an integral part of the intellectual scene. The life-story sounds familiar. Murray himself likewise came far, from Australia, and mingled with the cream of the English aristocracy. Like Herodotus, too, Murray was unreservedly admiring of Greek political achievements, especially those of Athens: democracy, the defeat of foreign tyranny: 'His [sc. Herodotus'] theme was the deliverance of Greece, and the rise of the Athenian Empire, and he died before that Empire began to totter'; 'Persia was tamed; *the seas under one law*; freedom and order won'—"Equal laws, equal speech, democracy." '; 'He [Herodotus] lived in a great city where every citizen could read and write [sic], where everybody was *deinos* and *philokalos*. ... etc.').[10] This does indeed sound very like 1890s England—before the Great War, before the currents of independence were perceived to be running too strongly or too extensively within the Empire, with *Britannia* (still) *ruling the waves*, and poets, artists, and novelists flourishing, museums and universities collecting the wonders of the world for everyone to marvel at.

Proceeding to Thucydides, Murray sketches the historian's career, emphasizing the violent implosion of Athenian democratic ideals that followed the death of Pericles and the exile of Thucydides himself. In this description, Murray's own horror of the 'herd', and his disgust at the vindictiveness and bigotry of the unenlightened, the fragility of civilized values even in a place like Athens, are palpable. In particular, his account of Thucydides' shock and disillusionment at returning home to Athens after the war to renew his interactions with a new generation of fellow-citizens, and the difficulties he faced in completing his account of the defeat of Athens and the betrayal by those citizens of that former decency and 'love of beauty'—an account that is necessarily largely fictional, or at least hypothetical—suggests a very close and personal identification between Murray himself and this great representative of the Hellenic enlightenment.[11] Indeed, apart from Euripides, there seems to be no Greek author who appeals more directly to Murray (who takes all his Greek authors very personally) than Thucydides—though the Presocratic thinker

[10] Murray 1897, 178. More recent, and less idealistic, estimates as to the proportion of the Athenian population that could effectively read and write range from *c.*50% down to *c.*20% (e.g. Harris 1989, 20–4).

[11] 'It must be borne in mind that Thucydides returned to Athens in 403 like a ghost from the tomb, a remnant of the old circle of Pericles. He moved among men who were strangers to him. His spirit was one which had practically died out of Athens nearly a generation before . . . His life is over now, without distinction, his Athens ruined beyond recognition, the old mistress of his love dead and buried.' (Murray 1897, 200–1)

Anaxagoras also seems to strike a particularly powerful chord of sympathy in him: another free-thinking immigrant (like Herodotus and Murray himself), arriving in Athens from Clazomenae and joining in with Pericles and the other enlightened elites on their brave (yet futile? or at least, frustrated) political–cultural mission.

The rest of the *History* is quite straightforward and predictable. The Hellenistic period is over quickly; Imperial Greek literature occupies very few pages indeed, though Plutarch and Lucian are briefly praised. From our perspective, there is nothing wrong with it, but not much that stands out either.

The solid merits of the Homer book—in all its many reprintings and updatings—have been mentioned already above. It was apparently Murray's work on this book that prompted him to develop his influential and successful ideas about the successive 'stages' of Greek religion (discussed by Robert Parker elsewhere in this volume). And meanwhile, of course, Murray's translations of Greek drama had already made a large and ever-increasing impact both on the world of English-speaking theatre performance and on a relatively broad readership of non-Classicists as well. Thus his ideas about Greek drama were disseminated in many forms: the translations themselves, the introductions to those published translations; lectures, pamphlets, and theatre programme-notes for the many productions that used his translations; and, at the apex, the actual books he published on Euripides, Aristophanes, and Aeschylus, to which I now turn.[12]

MURRAY ON GREEK DRAMA

Murray's most influential book is probably the slim volume on *Euripides and his Age* (Murray 1913).[13] Originally published in 1913 as Volume 73 of the Home University Library of Modern Knowledge, it was reprinted many times in that format. It was slightly revised and reset in 1946 (shrinking thereby to a mere 170 pages); and finally reissued

[12] See above n. 9 and below, pp. 67–8, for a brief discussion of *The Classical Tradition in Poetry* (Murray 1927a).

[13] On this, and for detailed discussion of Murray's interpretations of Euripides in general, see above all Easterling 1997.

in a third edition, with an appreciative preface by H. D. F. Kitto, in 1965.[14] The case is stated clearly at the outset:

> Most of the volumes of this series are occupied with large subjects and subjects commonly recognized as important to great masses of people at the present day. In devoting the present volume to the study of a single writer, remote from us in time and civilization and scarcely known by more than name to many readers of this Library, I am moved by the belief that, quite apart from his disputed greatness as a poet and thinker, apart from his amazing and perhaps unparalleled success as a practical playwright, Euripides is a figure of high significance in the history of humanity and of special interest to our own generation.

We may note here the phrase, 'Euripides is a figure of significance'. As we remarked already, it is characteristic of Murray that he presents the authors of all his favorite literary and philosophical texts (Aeschylus, Anaxagoras, Herodotus, Thucydides—and less so, Sophocles, Plato, and Aristophanes) above all as *individuals* who faced personal challenges and conflicts, especially in negotiating their (literary) way between the foolish and backward popular masses, on the one side, and the intellectual pioneers and social critics of a tiny intellectual elite, on the other. His favorite authors are the ones who find ways to reflect honestly and vividly the resultant collisions, and to present an avenue for compassionate understanding and (ideally) resolution of society's most cruel and disruptive tendencies. (Murray never wrote a book on Sophocles—and, as I noted above, in his *History of Ancient Greek Literature* he complains of Sophocles' conventional piety and his unwillingness to offend the masses or modify the storylines of the crude old heroic sagas that he had inherited.)[15]

[14] Characteristically, for Murray in his later phase of scholarly activity, even in the 1946 revision he did not see fit to add any references, in the final section of 'Bibliography', to anything written since the first edition of 1913. 'Mode B' apparently did not require such concessions to the niceties of professional scholarly discourse.

[15] This antipathy extends to Murray's assessment of Sophocles' style as well:

> '*Elektra*, brilliant as it is, [is] . . . typically uncharming. The explanation may partly lie in some natural taste for severity and dislike of sentiment in Sophocles; it seems certainly also to be connected with his archaism. His language is archaistic through and through; and it seems as if his conceptions were. . . . Sophocles is thus subject to a certain conventional idealism. He lacks the elemental fire of Aeschylus, the speculative courage and subtle sympathy of Euripides.' (Murray 1897 [3rd edn, 1917], 237–40)

See further Easterling 1997, 119–21.

As the opening chapter of the Euripides book proceeds, Murray also outlines his view of the ways in which individuals, including authors, are formed by their 'Age':

Every man who possesses real vitality [sic] can be seen as the resultant of two forces. He is first the child of a particular age, society, convention; of what we may in one word call a tradition. He is secondly, in one degree or another, a rebel against that tradition. And the best traditions make the best rebels.... A tradition is generally at its best, not when it is universally accepted, but when it is being attacked and broken.... And in a sense, the greatest triumph that any tradition can accomplish is to rear noble and worthy rebels.

And he goes on to explain that, just as 'the great age of Athens... trained an extraordinary band of critical or rebellious children', so too in Britain, in 1913, 'We are in reaction now against another great age... the Victorian Age' (Murray 1913, 14–15).

That is how Murray proceeds to read and interpret Euripides (as earlier he had interpreted Thucydides in his *History of Ancient Greek Literature*); and implicitly he sees himself as the ideal 'child' of Victorian England, shaped by its values and traditions, and in a reasonable and limited way, he sees himself also as a rebel against some of that Age's more repressive and reactionary tendencies.[16] Yet clearly he is conscious that he is also defending Victorian values, and resisting the more radical challenges of a whole new Age that threatens to dawn and to sweep away that whole traditional world. (He points to Plato as just such a threat to the Athenian world of Pericles; presumably Marx, Freud, or Nietzsche would be the modern equivalents—though he almost never seems to mention any of them, and his own work shows no overt signs of responding to Marx or

[16] After all, Murray supported the proposal to abolish compulsory Greek for admission to Oxford; and he was amiably though cautiously supportive of women's rights, etc.—i.e. definitely a 'progressive' overall, if a mildly liberal rather than radical one.

'The Victorian Age had, amid enormous differences, a certain similarity with the Periclean... And in most of the current criticism on things Victorian... one seems to feel the Victorian spirit itself speaking. It arraigns Victorian things by a Victorian standard; blames them not because they have moved in a particular direction, but because they have not moved far enough.... Euripides, like ourselves, comes in an age of criticism following upon an age of movement and action.... He accepts the Athenian ideals of free thought, free speech, democracy, 'virtue', and patriotism. He arraigns his country because she is false to them.' (Murray 1913, 16–17)

Freud and their challenges to 'humanism' at all. Nietzsche is another story, of course: see Easterling 1997, 126.)[17] What Murray recommends, then, is to be a 'noble and worthy rebel', rather than a reactionary or irresponsible one. And so he seeks to claim from the Age of Athens those elements that can be recaptured as models for preserving the best of 'the achievements' of the Victorian Age. The further question lurks in the background too, I think: Athens lost her empire, but maintained her cultural supremacy. What about Victorian England? Will this empire rebel too? (or be taken from us, by rival powers?). Will the angry victims of our oppression (like Medea, as he puts it later in the book: see below) be so maddened by the mistreatment meted out to them by unenlightened and uncompassionate members of our own society, that they will rebel in ways that cannot be contained or constructively channelled? And what of the cultural legacy that we have created? Will that be preserved? Will that make us better? Who will defend that 'tradition'?

Throughout his work, in fact, Murray is almost obsessed by the notion, and the value, of 'tradition', and of 'conventional forms' of behaviour and expression. Ceremony, ritual, decorum—these are not mere forms, but embodiments of cultural value and of a living and precious spirit—what Murray calls 'a tradition of thought and conduct and social atmosphere' that must be preserved and renewed, and perhaps refined, from generation to generation. This is the subject, in fact, of another whole book by Murray, *The Classical Tradition in Poetry* (Murray 1927a), developed from the Norton Lectures that he delivered at Harvard. There is not space enough here to discuss this book in detail, and it would in any case carry us into realms far removed from Greek tragedy; nor did this volume, for all its charm and erudition, have as great an impact or represent quite such a distinctive blend of progressive and conservative values as the two books on the tragedians do. But a couple of striking features nonetheless deserve to be mentioned. The first is the distinction that Murray draws between (primitive), unthinking tradition, an 'unconscious bondage' of the uneducated (see n. 9 above), on the one hand, and 'tradition [as] an ideal' on the other. Thus, whereas the ignorant

[17] But Parker (n. 23) in this volume observes that there is no sign that Murray was fully aware of the influence of Nietzsche's work on his own theory of the ritual origins of tragedy. His off-hand remarks about Nietzsche seem generally to have been rather dismissive.

masses 'ha[ve] no deep basis of conviction to prevent them from following the line of least resistance', better-educated traditionalists may 'cho[o]se carefully the tradition that [they] wish to follow.' (The value of a classical education, and an understanding of classical principles of form and subject, is the real point, though Murray illustrates it by the example of wearing of a dinner-jacket in the bush.) In addition, he insists that poetry is 'a thing that unites rather than separates.... It is a common worship wherein all servants of the Muses labour, a common service wherein each can help another, and wherein a "thing of beauty" lives on and is a "joy for ever", on one condition only, that it is still studied and loved and understood.' (Murray 1927a, 5, 260–1.) And in his highly engaging second chapter, entitled 'Molpe', he also anticipates many of the positions of recent studies of Greek poetic–musical performance and the 'song-culture' of archaic Greece.

In his *Euripides* book, the readings of particular plays that Murray provides are—as Kitto pointed out in his Preface to the third, posthumous edition (1965)—often quite original, pointed, and illuminating (see too especially Easterling 1997, 115–18, 121–4). Though brief, and selective in the issues and passages that he addresses, Murray often highlights social and moral problems within the texts—and Euripides' strong emotional and intellectual engagement with these problems—in helpful ways that effectively, yet unobtrusively, demolish the extreme convolutions or complaints that earlier scholars had made. His analyses often expose the limitations and implausibilities not just of the eccentric Verrall (a good friend of Murray's, though also a critic whose work on the dramatists he was constantly seeking more or less directly to oppose and neutralize), but also of a whole host of disapproving critics who had seen Euripides as being too 'clever', too 'rationalistic', too 'sophistic' or 'impious', or simply as 'undramatic'. Murray also includes excellent—though brief—general remarks about several important features of Euripides' dramatic technique, such as structural conventions, messenger speeches, and the language and 'music' of the choruses.

The book contains especially sensitive observations about the divine epiphanies of e.g. *Electra*, *Hippolytus*, and even the *Bacchae*.[18] Likewise, over and over, Murray points to scenes (and to choral odes)

[18] One attentive reader who appears to have been strongly influenced by Murray's readings of divine activity in Euripides was the Californian poet and dramatist Robinson

in which human compassion and wonder, noble self-sacrifice, and inspiring perseverance are affirmed—even in the midst of the most disturbing disruptions of social order and decency—and he argues (quite unfashionably for his time) that Euripides in fact prefers to provide what Murray terms an 'antique peaceful close' to his plays.[19] Above all, he sees Euripides struggling against the 'stupidity of public criticism' and the bigotry of 'superstitious Greeks', and attempting through the poetry and dramatic confrontations of his plays to bring his multifaceted Athenian audience to a more enlightened understanding—and feeling—for the possibilities of human, social existence. At the same time, Murray insists that Euripides, at bottom (or at the end—i.e. above all in the *Bacchae*), for all his powerful intellectual powers and enlightened moral convictions, was primarily a poet and a dramatist:

> Euripides was both a reasoner and a poet. The two sides of his nature sometimes clashed and sometimes blended. But ever since the *Heracles* he had known which service he really lived for; and in his last work it is the poet who speaks, and reveals, so far as such a thing can be revealed, the secret religion of poetry. (Murray 1913, 195)

This was on the whole a much more 'positive' and less embittered or sarcastic Euripides that Murray proposes—and his book (along with Murray's own translations, of course) certainly contributed significantly to the rehabilitation of Euripides as a serious and effective playwright that took place during the twentieth century.[20]

I have little to say about Murray's *Aristophanes: A Study* (Murray 1933). It was a pleasant, even useful, book in its time, but, as Murray himself acknowledged (in the very first words of the Preface), 'There

Jeffers, most notably in the closing scene of *The Tower beyond Tragedy* (1926). This lyric drama drew primarily from the *Oresteia*; but the final scene was clearly inspired by the appearance and language of the Dioscuri in Euripides' *Electra*: see Griffith 2003.

19 'Of course, the epiphany [*deus ex machina*] does not give what our jaded senses secretly demand, a strong "curtain". It gives the antique peaceful close.... The concrete men and women whom we have seen before us, striving and suffering, dissolve into the beautiful mist of legend.... and... we are awakened to the concrete theatre and the audience and the life about us not with a shock, but gradually, like one lying with his eyes half shut and thinking about a dream that has just gone.' (Murray 1913, 224)

20 In addition to Easterling 1997, see also Michelini 1987, for an assessment of Murray's place within 20th-cent. Euripidean studies in general.

is little or no research in this book.' It quite neatly fits the standard pattern of his work on Greek literature, both in its emphasis on the ritual origins and persistent character of Old Comedy (with Murray providing frequent reassurances to his more prudish readers that *ta phallika* were and are a vital element in nature, and hence also in human society), and in its validation of one man's distinctive and progressive vision, as contrasted with the cruel and crude misunderstandings of his fellow-citizens. Aristophanes emerges from Murray's study as a man 'who had something to say':

> He came, it would seem, from a highly cultivated home with a great knowledge of literature . . . He had further . . . been brought up in a somewhat old-fashioned gentlemanly style, which laid stress on good manners, respect for the aged, and conventional piety. He found in Athens, the fevered and ambitious Athens of the time, young men of his own age who were very different in their outlooks. Their morals were much less strait-laced. Their general lack of reverence disgusted him. They struck him as dreadfully ignorant of Homer and good literature. (Murray 1933, 19)

This gentlemanly, well-read comic playwright also hated war. The resemblance to Murray himself is thus unmistakable. At the outset, indeed, we are informed that they share the same precious, yet elusive, sense of humor, '*to geloion*, "laughter" or "humour", in which Ancient Greece and modern England sometimes seem to stand alone against the rest of the world, much as they do in their idealization of "sportsmanship"' (Murray 1933, p. ix). Aristophanes thus takes his place, along with Euripides and Thucydides, as another progressive yet embattled Athenian author, in this case one whose gentleness, political seriousness of purpose, and blend of ritualistic verve with exquisite literary taste, all combine to provide a model of English *joie de vivre* at its best.

Murray's last book, *Aeschylus: Creator of Tragedy* (Murray 1940a), is another rather slim volume, like *Euripides and his Age*; and it quickly established itself as a comparable point of reference in the field. Published, like the Aristophanes volume, by the Clarendon Press of Oxford, rather than the Home University Library, as the Euripides book originally had been, it takes up only a little over 200 pages of large print, and once again is purposely 'unscholarly' in style, and uncluttered with footnotes or Greek. (Indeed Murray makes a point of reassuring his reader in the Preface that he will not make his book 'needlessly long'.) The book begins with an account of the 'Invention of Tragedy', which is readable and not overly fanciful. Then Murray proposes three main areas in which Aeschylus may be regarded as having made especially vital contributions to the drama: the impressiveness (*semnotês*) and inventiveness of his verbal expression; his stage technique; and his ideas. Then the theory of the ritual origins of tragedy is rehearsed, with the nice added twist of a suggested connection between the *eniautos daimôn* and the 'third saviour' mentioned by the Chorus in *Agamemnon.* The surviving plays, and some of the fragmentary ones too, are then described, though not in much depth. The most extended discussion, naturally, is given to the *Oresteia,* and here Murray focuses most intently on the religious pattern (the ideas) that he sees unfolding (in accordance with his notion of the 'stages of Greek religion'), above all the idea that the ending of the trilogy affirms a progression from the earlier cruel and vindictive gods, to 'a world power that Aeschylus calls Zeus, who learns and grows', a 'God who can forgive' (Murray 1940a, 110, 199–206). The decisive factor in the acquittal of Orestes, according to Murray's reading, is thus 'pity'—and the whole reading ends up in fact seeming intensely Christian, even though Murray was of course criticized by some for his more or less agnostic views.[21]

Murray's progressivist reading of Aeschylus, and his emphasis on ideas, on 'pity, compassion' and the playwright's desire to suggest that human suffering in the end does, or may, have some justification or mitigation in sight—maybe even a divine purpose behind it—had also informed Murray's reading of Euripides at every turn, as we saw; and they are tied closely to his most celebrated 'theory', that of the ritual origins of tragedy. That theory is presented in both the books, and for most general readers it was there that they actually encountered

[21] 'In the *Agamemnon*..., Pity [the capitalization is Murray's] acts not as a personal emotion but [as] a sort of world force.... Unlike all who were before him, [Zeus] can think and learn and forgive' (Murray 1940, 196, 200). As a student in Cambridge during the 1960s, I came to realize that it was this progressive and quasi-Christianizing mode of reading that most infuriated those Oxford and Cambridge scholars who liked to deride the lightweight quality of Murray's scholarship. By contrast, the Aeschylus of D. L. Page, P. H. J. Lloyd-Jones, and R. D. Dawe was as harshly archaic, demonic–superstitious (non-rationalistic, pre-Christian), and as reactionary in his religious, moral, and political views as could be imagined. See now Parker, in this volume.

it directly, since few actually laid their hands on, and persevered through, Jane Harrison's long and difficult—and highly original—*Themis* (J. E. Harrison 1912), where the theory was first presented, in the form of an 'Excursus on the Ritual Forms Preserved in Greek Tragedy' (Murray 1912a). In any case, it is with this theory, and its place in the history of criticism and twentieth-century culture, that I will conclude this chapter.

Despite the low opinion of Murray's work held (as I mentioned above) by most Greek scholars these days, his influence on the understanding and interpretation of Greek drama, especially in Britain and the USA, has in fact been enormous. Directly, this influence came primarily from that much-cited 'Excursus', as well as the shorter versions of it that were provided in the introductions and notes to his various Euripides translations, and in the opening chapters of the Euripides and Aeschylus books. But indirectly, too, the presence of Murray's name, and the institutional authority that he brought to the 'camp' of the so-called Ritualists, played a crucial role in extending the influence of that theory in ever-widening circles. It was Murray who most handily and engagingly articulated an interpretive formula that was both simple (some have even called it 'simplistic'—e.g. D. Wilson 1987, 155) and yet full enough of technical-yet-familiar terms (Agôn, Pathos, Lamentation, Recognition, Epiphany, etc.) to sound erudite and (in the Greek context) authentic, and this combination of user-friendly factors provided the foundation for several of the most successful and long-lasting literary-critical systems and 'theories of drama' of the last century. Through the works especially of Theodore Gaster, Francis Fergusson, and Northrop Frye (and doubtless many more could be mentioned), Murray's ideas about the 'ritual origins' and essential mythic pattern of Greek tragedy (its framework? or spiritual core?) have continued to loom large, even to dominate the critical scene (especially the university scene, in departments of Drama, Comparative Literature, and English—less so, perhaps, in departments of Classics) for much of the twentieth century. Along with Nietzsche's formulation of 'Dionysian' and 'Apollinian' (which has been equally derided by classicists as inaccurate, misleading, and ahistorical), the 'Ritual Theory of Drama' still attracts adherents and is taken seriously, if not as an account of origins, then as a 'mytheme' or 'structural pattern' of real heuristic value.

Now it is probably true (as several critics have pointed out) that relatively little in these ideas is truly of Murray's own invention: since the key elements, and overall structure and sequence, were already provided by Jane Harrison and James Frazer (and some, of course, are merely adapted from Aristotle's *Poetics*).[22] But the elegant synthesis of these elements that Murray worked out, together with the confident and non-argumentative manner in which he presented the theory as if it were the orthodox view of most experts in the field, proved to be immensely persuasive. I doubt that without Murray's authority the 'ritual theory' would in fact have spread nearly so widely nor been swallowed nearly so whole as eventually turned out to be the case. And whereas Duncan Wilson[23] chose to state quite emphatically that it was 'unfortunate ... for his reputation as a scholar [that] he gave his whole-hearted backing not only to the [*eniautos-daimôn* theory] but also to the thesis that Greek tragedy had its origins in the annual rituals connected with this year-spirit', I would argue precisely the opposite: this 'backing' by Murray, even if it was poorly grounded in evidence and slippery in argumentation, was in many respects the most stimulating, creative, and important act of critical interpretation that he ever achieved. Admittedly, the theory is almost certainly wrong in most of its main positive assertions; and one may concede that by some standards such shortcomings *are* indeed 'unfortunate' for a scholarly reputation. But the interpretive power and heuristic potential of Murray's theory have been immense; and it has provoked several subsequent refinements by others that have proven to be of enduring validity and value. This was not at all 'unfortunate', in the long run. Indeed, over the last twenty years or so the critical fashion has shifted again ... and Wilson's (or Lloyd-Jones') negative assessment might not be so

22 Aristotle's opening statements that the basic impulse to compose and enjoy poetry comes from an innate appreciation of 'rhythm and harmony', and that the sources of tragedy and comedy came (respectively) from 'those leading-off the dithyramb' (or 'the satyric') and 'those conducting the phallic <ceremonies>', were obviously not far from the minds either of Nietzsche (in his *Birth of Tragedy from the Spirit of Music*) or of Murray.

23 D. Wilson 1987, 154 (heavily under the influence—as usual, it appears—of Hugh Lloyd-Jones in matters of Greekness and the history of classical scholarship).

simplistically uttered nowadays. As was reasserted from several quarters in the 1991 Conference in Urbana, Illinois, on 'The Cambridge Ritualists Reconsidered' (Calder 1991), ritual is definitely back in vogue in the Classics, and one might consider such distinctive and serious classicists as Walter Burkert, Jack Winkler, and Richard Seaford (to say nothing of cultural critics, anthropologists, and pioneers of performance studies such as Rene Girard, Victor Turner, or Richard Schechner) to be heavily indebted to Murray—in their different ways.[24]

In any case, whether 'unfortunately' or not, Murray's neat formulation of the theory of the 'ritual forms' filled a critical need for Edwardian British 'higher culture'. For at a moment when the socioeconomic–political movements (of e.g. Marxism and Socialism) and the psychological–linguistic–anthropological theories (of e.g. Freud, De Saussure, Jakobson, and Durkheim) were mounting major challenges to the secular liberal-humanism of the English upper-class establishment, and when Modernist styles and techniques were likewise challenging the Western Classics-based educational–artistic status quo, Murray's 'simplistic' theory succeeded brilliantly in combining several new and old—and often quite disparate—strands of criticism of drama and culture into a single, relatively simple pattern, and in neutralizing or modifying many of those critical approaches that were most threatening to the humanistic enterprise in general and most disruptive to its particular reading of 'the Greek spirit'. If Murray welcomed 'rebels' of a noble kind, while feeling acutely uncomfortable about the 'ugly, stupid herd' and those more dangerous and extreme rebels who might go too far and completely destroy the 'Athenian' (or Victorian) achievement, then it was of vital importance that the 'noble rebels' themselves marshal an effective strategy of self-defence, by articulating the most eloquent and compelling account possible of their own 'tradition'. The theory

[24] For example, Girard 1977, V. W. Turner 1969, 1982, Schechner 1977, 1993. In the previous generation, the key figures were Francis Fergusson, Theodore Gaster, and Northrop Frye, along with their numerous disciples; see e.g. Ackerman 1991b, 145–52, 184–94. On the other hand, it must be conceded that Murray, prude and old-fashioned gentleman that he was at heart, showed himself quite unable to grasp the implications for performance studies and gender studies that such theories of ritual so obviously presented: it remained for others to pick up where he left off (or backed away).

that Murray helped to develop and articulate therefore needed to satisfy the claims of the 'herd' (the proletarian revolution?) and of the Modernists (the hyper-intellectual rebels?) alike, by showing how and why the best elements of the 'original' energies of creativity and generation had been refined and perfected, artistically and morally, into art-forms that were being preserved and reincorporated in that very 'Victorian Age' to which Murray and his fellow-spirits themselves belonged.

The theory was thus 'populist', in its appeal to 'everyman', the land, and the seasons, and a simple uncomplicated, universally shared past. It was also 'primitivist', and thus appealing to those (Romantics; even some Modernists) who sought in art a return to purer and less industrialized or politically tainted truths. It provided a perfect compromise between religious believers and non-believers, between conservatives and scientific progressivists. Murray's version of the Harrison–Frazer model, I suggest, enabled him to form (or restore!) an appealingly progressive and optimistic reading of ancient Greek culture that was in many respects extremely old-fashioned, even as it seemed to buy in to several of the most innovative currents in anthropological, psychological, and cultural–historical analysis. I will leave it to others (and especially Robert Parker, in this volume) to discuss Murray's contribution to the understanding of Greek religion, in relation to the views of Robertson Smith, Emile Durkheim, Jane Harrison, James Frazer, etc. What I should like to highlight here instead is his clever blend of Aristotle, Nietzsche, and what one might call 'back-door Christianity' (or 'Christianity lite'), as a way of reclaiming Classical Greek tragedy as a force of morality, decorum, and tradition, and ultimately (it may not be too much to claim) as a justification and anticipation of specifically British imperial claims and achievements.

Nietzsche, in his *Birth of Tragedy* (Nietzsche 1872) had proposed a non-moralizing reading of Greek tragedy in which the Dionysian spirit of 'musical' energy (collective, physical, passionate, undirected, simultaneously destructive and creative) was harnessed by a controlling Apollinian aesthetic of order, balance, meaning—so that the sufferings of an Oedipus or a Hamlet were made 'beautiful' rather than nauseating and desperate. (See further Silk and Stern 1981, Henrichs 1984, J. I. Porter 2000.) The source of the Apollinian impulse was the artist, the musician, the playwright (or the Nietzschean philosopher himself). Attempts by weak, cowardly critics to find 'poetic justice' in the sufferings of these Greek heroes and heroines must be resisted, because they amount to a betrayal of the 'spirit' of Hellenism. The strong critic has the courage—and the aesthetic discrimination—to recognize the beauty and clarity of Classical Greek representations of loss, pain, violence, cruelty, death, and the natural order that makes them necessary; and the Greek genius (according to Nietzsche) lies in combining this clear-eyed, almost scientific, recognition with a gusto for the musical, collective, choreographical, rhythmic elements of theatrical performance. Theatre was thus an experience (a *praxis*, a *pathos*) as well as an act of contemplation (*theôria*).[25]

In formulating this iconoclastic theory of tragedy, Nietzsche was of course reacting against a number of well-established critical currents that liked to see the Greeks as rationalistic purveyors of timeless moral truths, as also against Hegel's more recently formulated dialectic model of ethical progress resulting from the conflict of opposed sociopolitical interests or forces. Nietzsche himself was not particularly interested (at least, not by the time he came to publish the *Birth of Tragedy*) in the issue (hotly debated in the mid–late nineteenth century), of when and how the Olympian gods were adopted (or imported) by the Greeks, and whether or not an older system of divinities had in fact preceded them—and if so, what those earlier divinities were like (chthonian? female? Titanic? vegetative and non-anthropomorphic? etc.). But Nietzsche's figure of the 'Dionysian', as opposed to—and in some sense as predecessor to—the Apollinian, and thus as an elemental, essential force of Nature and pre-conscious (non-rational) feeling, was clearly presented as a challenge to existing theological norms concerning the source and status of 'higher' religion.

Jane Harrison's studies of Greek ritual, topography, and iconography, as well as her reading in the anthropology and sociology of religion, were coming from a very different direction from Nietzsche

[25] For Robinson Jeffers' parallel process of recognition and incorporation of Greek (especially Aristotelian) and Nietzschean aesthetics into a post-Romantic poetics of his own, especially with regard to tragedy—partly under the influence of Murray's readings of Euripides—see Griffith 2003.

(or Freud, for that matter); but they brought her very much into Nietzsche's intellectual orbit. Her take on the power of ritual action and the primacy ('originality') of non-Olympian, non-anthropomorphic, non-Homericized divinities, overlapped quite a bit with Nietzsche's notion of the 'Dionysian', as did her suggestion that there was an immediacy of feeling, a physical-spiritual engagement and excitement, and a degree of personal fulfillment available through these sub-literary processes of 'worship' that was stronger and more authentic (in religious terms)—and also less elitist, less tidily and repressively controlled by hierarchies of gender and politics—than the Olympian religion as we encounter it in the Homeric poems or the major public monuments of the Greek *polis*.

Readings of Greek tragedy conducted under the aegis of Nietzsche or Harrison (not that either was much interested in literary or dramatic criticism, as such) might tend to zero-in on the moral chaos, the musical exuberance, the sacrificial violence and the human multiplicity of the plays: and indeed, Harrison did write an intriguing and important article on the Erinyes (J. E. Harrison 1899; also J. E. Harrison 1908b), while implicitly Nietzsche's whole book is a reading of Euripides' *Bacchae*, and it includes heavily 'pessimistic' and nihilistic remarks about *Oedipus Tyrannus*. (See Silk and Stern 1981, J. I. Porter 2000.) But what Murray achieved, it might be said, was a reclamation of Greek tragedy (and Hellenism in general) for the hierarchy of, if not law, then at least moral order, enlightened rule (whether human or divine), and the benevolent exercise of reason, against which these iconoclasts had directed their energies. (We may think of his Zeus in the *Oresteia*, growing and learning and pitying the human sufferers, as he emerges as 'third saviour' in the demonic cycle.) Thus, even as Jane Harrison welcomed and collaborated with Murray, appreciating his exquisite command of the Greek language, his wide range of literary reading, and his open mind, it is notable that the quality she commented on as having influenced her the most was his kindness and goodwill: 'You are . . . so hypermoralised and superspiritualised that you force me to think of righteousness, temperance, and judgment to come'.[26] This is the back-door Christianity ('secular humanism' in modern parlance?) that I mentioned above:

[26] Harrison to Murray, in a letter, quoted by D. Wilson 1987, 119.

the re-importation into Jane Harrison's Hellenism of a sense of (Anglican) decency, propriety, forgiveness, compromise, and kindness that Nietzsche's account threatened to eradicate.

Murray's 'ritual theory' entails a move (evolution) from ritual–authentic 'origins' that accomplishes two main (perhaps unconscious) objectives: on the one hand, the theory preserves 'tradition' (= conventional forms, including choruses, music and dance, etc),[27] even as it also eliminates those 'primitive' and crude, unrefined tendencies that Murray himself so disliked and feared—the behaviour and emotions of 'the herd', the 'ugly, stupid peasant', etc., as well as the repressive superstitions and rules of clerics and savages.

Murray in fact quite frequently lets slip in his translations and criticism[28] that—like most British or Australian men and women of his class of that period—he did not admire the lower classes, nor most foreigners except Europeans or Americans, and least of all religious fanatics, even as he also realized full well that if exploited and mistreated too badly all of those people might be goaded into angry and hideous reaction (i.e. a 'madness' of the kind displayed so powerfully by Euripides' mistreated women and foreigners, his Medea and Hecuba and Bacchants). As Murray writes:

> Medea's . . . is the madness produced by love rejected and justice denied, by the sense of helpless, intolerable wrong. A lesser poet might easily have made Medea a sympathetic character, and have pretended that long oppression makes angels of the oppressed. . . . But Euripides, tragic to the heart and no dealer in pleasant make-believe, saw things otherwise: 'when these oppressed

27 This emphasis on 'music' and 'lyric' (cf. Morwood's discussion in his chapter in this volume) is a theme that he emphasized strongly both in his Euripides book and in his lectures and book on *The Classical Tradition in Poetry*—though Murray himself, according to D. Wilson 1987, was quite unmusical, as well as being prudish, teetotal, and uptight—far from 'Dionysian'.

28 Murray refers to the sons of Aegyptus in the *Suppliant Women* as 'the Egyptian horde' (Murray 1940, 49–50), and quotes Wilamowitz's notorious phrase, 'a mob of black and yellow devils', without further comment (Murray 1940a, 52). Murray shared the widespread scholarly view of this period (up to the publication in the 1950s of an Oxyrhynchus papyrus that showed that this play must in fact date from the 460s BCE, only a few years before the *Oresteia*), that this was 'in my judgement far the earliest' surviving Greek tragedy (Murray 1940a, 48). His description of the masses of performers involved ('at least 153 persons . . . and it is just possible that the[se] figures should be doubled': Murray 1940a, 50) seems to reflect a typical colonialist anxiety about 'hordes of savages' and the dangers of anarchy, lust, and musical extravagance stemming from Africa.

women strike back', he seems to say, 'when these despised and enslaved barbarians can endure no longer, it will not be justice that comes but the revenge of madmen'.[29]

CONCLUSION

In a limited and equivocal way, Murray admired Rudyard Kipling, and expressed approval—though qualified—of the notion that an Englishman (or an Athenian) has a special responsibility to live up to the demands of 'a very great nation with a high and peculiar task (or destiny) before it'.[30] In his scholarly writings, as in his stage productions and lectures, we may see Murray as shouldering his own special 'Great Man's Burden' of responsibility for conveying the legacy of enlightenment and moral progress (as pioneered in Athens, and recreated in Victorian England), in a responsible and artistically vibrant way, to his modern charges—i.e. to the young, the teachable, the open-minded—not necessarily the Greek-reading or professionally expert—but all those who can be absorbed into the continuing

[29] Murray certainly disapproved of terrorism, and was not on the whole a supporter of revolutionary violence. But he understood that intolerable oppression and repeated provocation will eventually produce a backlash. I have found only one reference of Murray's (kindly tracked down by William Bruneau) concerning the most disturbing anti-British guerrilla/liberation campaign of the 1950s, that of the Mau Mau in Kenya (Russell Archives 710.053427):

14 November, 1952

Dear Bertie,

I wonder if this Presidential Address of mine would at all interest you? The historical part is interesting, and possibly some of the speculative part.

I dreamed last night that I had a solution of the Mau Mau difficulty by transferring the various Mau Mau parties to a large hall in which Whigs and Tories used to fraternise. I asked you for the details and you said that there were Whigs and Tories there, but they were really all scientific O.Ms. which the Government kept in a dark room ready to make in-ven-tions when wanted, and you doubted whether the Mau Mau would do.

Yours ever, G.M.

It is characteristic of Murray that this reference intertwines dreaming and fantasy (poetry?) with politics, with a strong (defusing) component of humour.

[30] Quoted in D. Wilson 1987, 76–7. Murray and Kipling met as teenagers, an encounter that Murray recalled in a letter subsequently published by Christopher Collard (Collard 1993): 'I... find him absurdly attractive... I also find... that he is really not essentially a poet or artist but a narrow-minded moralist' (ibid., 63). For Murray's continuing ambivalence toward Kipling, see D. Wilson 1987, 96, 338, 342.

tradition for which, and about which, Murray spoke and wrote so politely, so melodiously, and so unpretentiously. And with his formulation of the 'Ritual Theory' of Greek drama, in particular, he succeeded in developing an especially versatile and attractive myth, or metaphor, according to which the most primeval and universal human impulses could be imagined as having been channelled and refined into a moral and artistic tradition capable of being continually adjusted, re-perfected, and reproduced. These adjustments and refinements could only be achieved, of course, by exceptionally gifted individuals (Aeschylus and Euripides, Anaxagoras and Thucydides, Shakespeare and Ibsen—or perhaps Wilamowitz and Murray himself); but if such individuals could continue to be found, and educated, there might be no limit to the length of time for which things could continue to be maintained in their proper alignment, in the arts, in the schools, and among the nations of the world. The sun should never set on the *eniautos daimôn*—or if it should ever set, it will surely rise again tomorrow.

4

Gilbert Murray and Greek Religion

Robert Parker

Speakers and writers often begin with an assertion of the importance of their topic: I shall enlist Murray himself to make such an assertion vicariously on my behalf. Reviewing two volumes of L. R. Farnell's *The Cults of the Greek States* in the *Albany Review* for 1907, Murray begins:

> It seems a bold statement, yet on reflection we are prepared to maintain it, that one of the greatest practical advances made by the human race in the last fifteen or twenty years has been in our improved understanding of ancient and especially of Greek religion. We are not forgetting Japan, or wireless telegraphy, or radium, or the Hague conference, or even flying machines. To understand the meaning of Religion, if mankind could ever attain it, would be a greater end than is suggested by any of these.[1]

Arlen 1990 (with the web supplement at www.uflib.ufl.edu/cm/history/Cambridge-Ritualists) is a valuable bibliography (for a small omission see Murray 1936). I am most grateful to Chris Stray for the invitation to participate and for subsequent editorial advice; also to participants in the conference for their comments on the day. I have learned much from the thesis in progress of Michael Konaris (Balliol College, Oxford) on the study of Greek religion in the late 19th and early 20th cents.

[1] Murray 1907a. I have not traced a second, more technical review which he there alludes to. Farnell replied in a personal letter (14 Nov. 1907: Bodleian Library, Oxford, MSS Gilbert Murray (hereafter GM) 12. 209–10) that he was more interested in the primitive and mystical than Murray allowed: 'I am really devoured with love of origins, and I am most interested in early Orphism'. But only 'lack of anthropological and religious perspective' could sanction the idea that the idea of personalized gods arose late in Greece. Murray reviewed Farnell's *Higher Aspects of Greek Religion* in *The Nation* (vol. X, 9 Mar. 1912, 954) and declared it a good book full of good points despite or perhaps because of Farnell's rejection of the 'desire to analyse the

The belief that they were living through a pioneering, a heroic, age in the study of Greek religion is found in other writers of the period,[2] though no one else is bold enough to give the thought such a world-historical twist. When he wrote those words, Murray was himself just entering upon the period in which he participated actively in this, as he saw it, epochal movement in the history of human consciousness. His first extensive engagement with Greek Religion was in *The Rise of the Greek Epic*, published in that same year of 1907. His most famous single theory, the derivation of tragedy from laments for Dionysus seen as an *eniautos daimôn* or year-spirit, was worked out in 1910 or thereabouts and presented in a contribution to Jane Harrison's *Themis* of 1912. *Four Stages of Greek Religion* was, as its subtitle states, 'based on a Course of Lectures delivered in April 1912 at Columbia University'. It was reissued as *Five Stages of Greek Religion* with an extra chapter in 1925, but much of the material for the extra chapter had already been covered in lectures on the Stoic philosophy given in 1915 (Murray 1915f, reprinted in Murray 1950a, 19–85). So most of Murray's most important writing about Greek religion was done in

Olympians into their elements' ('he wishes to hear nothing of matrilinear societies, nothing of totems or initiations'). In a letter of 6 Dec. 1922 to J. A. K. Thomson (GM 172.46–7) Murray writes: 'I have been reading Farnell's Hero Cults and am astonished at the way a learned man can go on writing quite reasonably well on a subject without shedding any scintilla of light on a subject anywhere'. In a letter of 1955 he contrasted the living influence of Harrison's work with Farnell's 'five learned volumes' which 'now seem to belong to the Dark Ages' (Stewart 1959, xi). For the unfavourable reviews exchanged by Farnell and Jane Harrison see Robinson 2002, 169–70, 193–6, 231. Harrison's unpublished letters to Murray preserved in Newnham are said to be full of criticisms of Farnell (F. M. Turner 1981, 130 n. 89); in one in Oxford she jokes that the gift of Murray's *Rise of the Greek Epic* has made her feel 'so happy and holy that I no longer desire to bang Mr Farnell's head' (11 Nov. 1907: GM 143.12). When A. S. Farquharson in 1927 urged Murray to put Harrison up for an honorary doctorate in Oxford, Murray replied that previous soundings had revealed 'a solid body of prejudice' against her (letters of 10 and 14 Mar. 1927: GM 52.144–6).

[2] Campbell 1898, p. v (rather muted); Farnell 1920, 7; above all a famous passage of Jane Harrison, *Reminiscences of a Student's Life* (J. E. Harrison 1925, 82–4). For the same thought in Murray himself see the preface to the first edn. of *Rise of the Greek Epic* (Murray 1907b, p. v) or to *Four Stages of Greek Religion* (Murray 1912b). In the *Albany Review* article, Murray lists the scholars whose work has revolutionized the field as 'Dr. Tylor and the anthropologists, Frazer and Miss Harrison, Rohde, Marquardt (sic: for Mannhardt?), Lang, Jevons, Ridgeway, A. B. Cook, Reinach, Foucart, Usener, Dieterich—to mention only the first names that occur'. Scholars cited in *Four Stages* are listed by Fowler 1991, 85 n. 15.

the short period from 1907 to 1915, and it is on this period that I shall concentrate. (Of later contributions which I pass by, the most discussed has probably been the theory of the 'perfectibility of Zeus' presented in *Aeschylus: The Creator of Tragedy*.)[3] Whatever one thinks about his theory of the origin of tragedy, the influence of *Four* (and then *Five*) *Stages of Greek Religion* in creating general interest in the subject is beyond dispute. In 1920 L. R. Farnell published an *Outline-History of Greek Religion* which omitted *Four Stages* from its bibliography and was, I suspect, designed to replace it.[4] But it failed of its intent if so; for many years *Four/Five Stages*, regularly reprinted, was the almost inevitable first book for anyone interested in the subject in the English-speaking world to turn to. I can offer no statistics, but it may well have been more widely read than any other English book ever written on the subject.

In the *Albany Review* article, Murray credits the scientific study of religion with two beneficial qualities: it protects the student from superstition, and it allows an escape from the mentality which requires one, faced by a particular religion, either simply to accept or simply to reject its claims. Murray's own attitude to religion was characterized by his son-in-law Arnold Toynbee as a mixture, sometimes uneasy, of 'polemical rationalism' and 'tolerant agnosticism reaching out toward something beyond itself' (Murray 1960, 217). As illustration of the 'polemical rationalism' we can adduce, from many possibilities, the fact that one edition of *Five Stages* was published by the Rationalist Press Association,[5] or indeed Murray's commendation of Arnold Toynbee to Bertrand Russell as 'a quite satisfactory free-thinker with no nonsense about the absolute' (letter of 29 July 1913 (GM 165.137), cited in D. Wilson 1987, 211). But he

[3] Murray 1940a. But this was not originated by Murray: see Lloyd-Jones 1956, 55 (= Lloyd-Jones 1990, 238–9).

[4] Farnell 1920. *Four Stages* was the first book noticed by Farnell in *The Year's Work in Classical Studies* for 1913, in a section which began 'The last year has not witnessed the production, in England at least, of any works of primary importance in the sphere of Greek religion and mythology' (Farnell 1913b, 129). He found the third and fourth chapters much better than the first two. Such was also the verdict of J. T. Sheppard, *Classical Review* 27 (1913), 197–8, and of Murray's pupil W. R. Halliday in a letter (28 Feb. 1913: GM 21.202–3) which anticipated his review of *Five Stages* in the *Classical Review* (Halliday 1925), where much in the first two chapters is declared 'fantastic'.

[5] No. 52 in its The Thinker's Library series (London 1935). It is from this edition that I quote.

could not but be attracted by the moral earnestness of many religious teachers, including even St Paul, who, most unusually for a classical scholar, he once declared to be 'next to Greek poets almost my favourite author'.[6] He also held that there is an incomprehensible element in human experience which religious thought addresses and which dogmatic materialism denies to its cost. 'The Uncharted surrounds us on every side and we must needs have some relation to it' (Murray 1925a, 171; cf. 7–9, 195–6). Late in life, he mentioned approvingly to Bertrand Russell 'Conan Doyle's story of the little French atheist who refused to trample on the Cross when some Sudanese fanatics tried to make him'.[7]

Good religion is a tentative quest and a probing, therefore. But a tentative quest and a probing is liable to be conducted at a rather high metaphysical level, and it was chiefly at this level that he could engage sympathetically with ancient religion; his greatest enthusiasm was for Stoicism, a fully developed philosophical system. Sympathy with ritual is harder to discover in him, and for this enthusiastic reader of Frazer's *Golden Bough* almost all ritual was probably irredeemably primitive and superstitious. The religion of so-called primitive peoples is not, far from it, inevitably fanatical and dogmatic. Faced with Evans-Pritchard's questioning, his Nuer informants told him that they did not know what Kwoth, Spirit, was like; they

[6] *Christian Commonwealth*, 26 Nov. 1913 (cited by D. Wilson 1987, 444 n. 42). Cf. Fowler 1991, 82: 'Murray was happy enough on many occasions to use "Christian" and "Hellenic" as equivalent terms.' The whole tendency of his occasional writings on early Christianity was to emphasize continuity with Greek thought rather than rupture; see e.g. the section 'The Creeds, Christian and Pagan: the Area of Agreement' in his chapter 'Religion and Philosophy' in *The History of Christianity in the Light of Modern Knowledge* (London and Glasgow 1929), 42–82. In his introduction to A. Loisy, tr. L. P. Jacks, *The Birth of the Christian Religion* (London 1948), he can even write (p. 6) 'The idea of a son of God born to save the world is essentially a Greek idea' (he is referring to the year spirit); cf. 'Religion and Philosophy', 70. 'The strong measure of suppressed Calvinism that lay behind Murray's lifelong agnosticism may plainly be perceived in his treatment of Aeschylus': Lloyd-Jones 1982, 203.

[7] Letter of 26 July 1954, quoted by Toynbee in Murray 1960, 218. See too the passages cited by Fowler, 1991, 82; and on Murray's religious development D. Wilson 1987, 5–6, 21–2, 99, 160, 185, 398. The fullest statements of his position are 'What is Permanent in Positivism' (the Comte Memorial Lecture for 1939, reprinted in Murray 1950a, 153–89) and the preface to Murray 1940b (partly quoted in D. Wilson 1987, 398). The controversy concerning the unpleasant but unimportant possibility that he was received into the Catholic church when near death is well discussed by F. J. West 1984, 245–51.

were merely simple people, and how could simple people know about such matters? If the European was so clever, perhaps he could tell them the answer (Evans-Pritchard 1956, 215–16). But such was not the image of the primitive ritualist available to Murray in the works of anthropology that he read in his prime.[8]

Murray's first book, *A History of Ancient Greek Literature* published in 1897,[9] antedates the period of his main engagement with Greek religion. But many *en passant* remarks illustrate the assumptions from which he started. The preface contains one of the great themes of the period: it contrasts the bloodless and idealized Greek of classicizing tradition, in art above all, with 'the Greek of the anthropologist, the foster-brother of Kaffirs and hairy Ainos'. Of the two images Murray states his preference for the second—'he is at least human and simple and emotional'—but adds 'his fault, of course, is that he is not the man we want, but only the raw material out of which that man was formed: a Hellene without the beauty, without the spiritual life, without the Hellenism'. 'Only the raw material out of which that man was formed': Murray here indicates his allegiance to what Frank Turner calls 'evolutionary humanistic hellenism'.

[8] In the preface to *Four Stages* Murray writes: 'it was the writings of my friend Mr. Andrew Lang that first awoke me, in my undergraduate days, to the importance of anthropology and primitive religion to a Greek scholar'; a quite extensive correspondence between the two survives. In 1891 Murray wrote (as a stranger) to Frazer, with what seems to have been a suggestion in Frazerian spirit about the 'oak' and 'winter fire' of Pind. *Pyth.* 4. 264–6; Frazer is politely sceptical (15 Aug. 1891: GM 2. 212–17). The essential validity of Frazer's work is always taken for granted by Murray (despite mild scepticism in Murray 1907a, 205): see e.g. *The Classical Tradition in Poetry*: 'We all know, since the work of Sir James Frazer, how the whole religion of the Mediterranean world centred on what we call agriculture' (Murray 1927a, 37). Malinowski sent Murray a copy of *The Sexual Life of Savages in North-Western Melanesia* (Malinowski 1929); Murray seems politely to have deprecated an explicitness inappropriate in a work addressed to a lay audience, to which Malinowski responded, 'As a fellow humanist, wouldn't you agree that sex plays an enormous part in serious interests, social ties, artistic inspiration?' (15 Sept. 1929: GM 56. 49)—alas, no reply survives. The two men also corresponded over business, for instance in relation to Murray's quondam secretary, the ethnographer Audrey Richards. But I know no evidence for serious engagement on the part of Murray with Malinowskian/post-Malinowskian ethnography.

[9] Murray 1897. New prefaces were added in 1898 and 1907. Much later, Murray apparently began a full-scale revision which was never completed (though it seems to have got further than is allowed by D. Wilson 1987, 311–12): a letter to J. A. K. Thomson of 22 Sept. 1926 (GM 172.168) speaks of the revision as 'half-finished', and one of 16 Aug. 1927 (GM 172.201–2) mentions rewriting the chapter on Pindar.

Turner has identified a tradition of Victorian comment on Greek mythology whereby the achievement of the greatest Greek writers was to transcend the tradition from which they emerged, to criticize and purify the mass of myths which they inherited.[10] The attractions of this 'getting better' approach for any Victorian hellenist, whether Christian or free-thinker, are obvious: the goal may not have been reached, but the Greeks were moving decisively in the right direction. Murray's identification of the proto-Greek as a 'foster-brother of Kaffirs and hairy Ainos' is novel and characteristically vivid, but the broad approach is very traditional. Indeed Lewis Campbell, a distinguished Sophoclean and Platonic scholar born in 1830, said much the same in his *Religion in Greek Literature* published in the following year.[11]

The body of Murray's text is written in the same spirit. The Greeks are praised for their 'spiritual vividness and religious freedom' on page 1.[12] Xenophanes, who attacked the Homeric conception of deity, is commended for 'saying boldly the things that every one was secretly feeling' (74). In the crisis of the Persian invasion of 480, the refusal of the Greeks to be swayed by the pessimistic advice of Apollo of Delphi is characterized as 'the rising of the greater part of

[10] F. M. Turner 1981, 101–3; this tradition was inaugurated according to Turner by Grote, and provided a kind of charter for progressive purification of the 'myths' of contemporary Christianity. For later statements in the same vein see ibid., 129.

[11] Campbell 1898. The title is misleading, as the book includes chapters on e.g. 'Antecedents and Survivals', 'Period of Transition—Hero-worship', 'Athenian Worships', 'The Mysteries'. Campbell states that in order to 'gather out of every civilisation what it contains of good' we must consider not 'crude beginnings' but 'originality and bloom' (ibid., 5, cf. 14). Campbell's book arose from an endowed lecturership in Natural Theology (the Gifford), as did so much writing on ancient religion in this period: E. Caird, *The Evolution of Religion* (Glasgow 1893) (Gifford); idem, *The Evolution of Theology in the Greek Philosophers* (Glasgow, 1904) (Gifford); J. Adam, ed. A. M. Adam, *The Religious Teachers of Greece*, Edinburgh 1908 (Gifford); Farnell, *The Evolution of Religion* (London 1905) and *Higher Aspects* (cf. n. 1) (both Hibbert); idem, *Greek Hero Cults and Ideas of Immortality* (Oxford 1921) and *The Attributes of God* (Oxford 1925) (both Gifford); idem *Greece and Babylon. A Comparative Sketch of Mesopotamian, Anatolian and Hellenic Religion* (Edinburgh 1911) (the first Wilde lectures). Murray was to have given Gifford lectures in the winter of 1908/9 but withdrew in consequence of election to the Oxford chair, to Jane Harrison's distress (Robinson 2002, 214–15).

[12] Cf. Campbell 1898, 12: 'Greece was from first to last the home of spiritual freedom'.

Greece above its religion' (139). On the scandalous matter of phallic rites Murray enters various pleas in mitigation, of which one is a reminder that 'where religion gives sanctity to a bad custom it palsies the powers of the saner intellect' (212). Stesimbrotus of Thasos is a deplorable figure, a spreader of vicious lies and libels, but he has one redeeming feature: 'he did not, as is commonly supposed, combine his rascality with sanctimoniousness. His book on The Mysteries must have been an attack' (166). The best attitude to be adopted to this religion was, it seems, one of criticism, and fortunately most Greek poets were indeed critical. One should not mistake Aeschylus, for all his piety, for a conventional polytheist: in religious thought he is in fact 'the precursor of Euripides' (224). Indeed, Murray boldly claims, 'the only orthodox Greek writer preserved to us is Pindar' (225); Sophocles receives a rather unconvincing exemption from the imputation of thoroughgoing orthodoxy, on the ground that he has caught something of the temper of a rationalist age (ibid.).[13] Pindar is well known for his rewritings of traditional myths, and had often been praised on those grounds by writers who adopted the 'getting better' approach to Greek religion mentioned earlier (see F. M. Turner 1981, 101–2 (J. A. Symonds and R. W. Mackay)). But for Murray 'getting better' is in this case not good enough: 'he expounded the rehabilitation of traditional religion, which radiated from Delphi', and this meant that he was still in thrall to priestcraft. His attitude both to the Persian invasion of 480 and to genuinely progressive thought was deplorable, and revealed him as 'the unreasoning servant of sacerdotal tradition and racial prejudice' (110–11).

At a different point in the book, Murray forgets the errant Pindar and declares that 'the literature as preserved is entirely secular' (62). Authentically religious writing existed in good quantity, but is almost entirely lost. Murray goes on to talk a little about what he takes to be the genuinely popular and emotionally appealing elements in Greek religion: the Eleusinian Mysteries, the worship of Dionysus, and

[13] The discussion in the chapter on Sophocles (232–49) makes him much more conventional. But I cannot resist quoting a delightful attempt to modernize Sophocles a little by comparing *OT* and the late Ibsen: 'one of the strongest scenes is made by the husband and wife deliberately and painfully confessing to one another certain dark passages of their lives, which they had hitherto kept concealed' (241: Lewis Campbell in a letter of 21 May 21 1897 [GM 4.204] declared himself unconvinced).

Orphism—Orphism, the vehicle of which was books, allows a link back to the theme of lost religious literature (62–8). 'The mystical and "enthusiastic" explanation of the world was never without its apostles in Greece', he emphasizes, but promptly puts it in its place by adding, 'the main current of speculation, as directed by Athens, set steadily contrariwise, in the line of getting bit by bit at the meaning of things through hard thinking' (68). As he was to write to his mother-in-law a few years later, 'Greece has a proud and permanent message to mankind, a message quite untouched by "supernaturalism" and revealed religion; it is human, rational and progressive, and affects not Art only but the whole of life' (letter of 31 Jan. 1900 (GM 476. 191–4), quoted in D. Wilson 1987, 78).

In 1896, the year before Murray's *History of Ancient Greek Literature*, there had appeared the first two large volumes of Farnell's *Cults of the Greek States*, the first work of detailed and comprehensive scholarship on Greek religion ever published in English. Frazer's six-volume commentary on Pausanias, launched on the world as a whole in 1898, was a contribution of similar ambition. In the same year, as we have noted, Lewis Campbell published *Religion in Greek Literature*, a substantial work of much broader scope than the second part of its title would suggest. It seems to have had little influence, but as a synthesis could count as something of a pioneer work in English scholarship. By contrast, no distinctive work of the so-called Cambridge ritualists had yet appeared, except in so far as Frazer himself is to be counted a member of that group.[14] The ritualists were not the origin of the upsurge of interest in Greek religion in this country, but a product of it. The first great book by one of them, Jane Harrison's *Prolegomena to the Study of Greek Religion*, was published in 1903; Murray, a close friend and regular correspondent of Jane Harrison since 1900 (Robinson 2002, 127–30), lived with the work in its period of gestation, and contributed to it a technical appendix on the text of the Orphic Gold Leaves. *Prolegomena* is famous for, to speak crudely, dethroning the Olympians and portraying the primitive religion of Greece as a religion of fear and propitiation addressed to the dead, to

[14] It is true that two key themes of *Prolegomena* (myth deriving from ritual; superficiality of the Olympians) are already present in J. E. Harrison, with M. de G. Verrall, *Mythology and Monuments of Ancient Athens* (London 1890), e.g. pp. xxxiii–iv (F. M. Turner 1981, 123), but that work seems not to have been largely influential.

Keres and other chthonians, to mother goddesses, to animal gods and to ill-defined special gods who were (*Themis* later revealed) a projection of the emotion generated in a particular rite. In his Memorial Address on Jane Harrison, Murray described the *Prolegomena* as 'what I can only call a work of genius' and 'a book which, in the current phase, made an epoch', and he quite often cites it in *The Rise of the Greek Epic*, of 1907.[15] But the influence of the *Prolegomena* on that work perhaps lies less in particular discussions than in a certain pervasive tendency of the argument.

The Rise of the Greek Epic defies ready summary. It jumps abruptly between very diverse topics (some of them probably mediated to Murray through Harrison); ideas hurtle from all sides, many vivid historical analogies are presented, but the chronology is rather vague, and for lack of evidence the argument is often obliged to assume 'how it must have been' form. The best way to catch its tendency is perhaps through the binary oppositions that Murray introduces at various points. One is between a settled 'tribal' religion and the religion of migrants: for migrants, ties to home, to cults of the earth, to graves and tribal gods are broken, and the walled place of refuge, the city, becomes the central focus of loyalty (61–92). Greek religion is a religion crucially shaped, deracinated, by the experience of migration. Another is that between the Homeric poems as we have them and the tradition or the milieu from which they derive. This is the famous thesis of the expurgation from the Homeric poems of barbarous practices such as homosexuality, human sacrifice, the dispatch of scapegoats, the worship of god-kings, bloody rites of purification (120–45). But this opposition between Homer and his tradition or milieu transforms itself into one between the 'Northern and the aboriginal elements in the Homeric poems'. Pre-hellenic inhabitants of the Aegean were conquered by invaders from the north, the proto-Achaeans or proto-Hellenes, and the purification of the tradition by the Homeric poets represented the triumph of the northern ideal (144–5). A further antithesis, partially identifiable with the one just discussed, is that between the Homeric gods, resolutely anthropomorphic and non-local, and the actual objects of religious devotion and enthusiasm in Greece. 'The real worship of

[15] See the index; and for the phrases quoted, Murray 1928, 11–12.

Greece in the fourth century almost never attached itself to those luminous Olympian forms [a very Harrisonian note, this]. There were many ecstasies of enthusiasm and outbreaks of superstition in Greece, but they all depend on deities of quite a different sort' (265). A final antithesis is that between Ionia and Attica. The Homeric gods have passed, in sceptical Ionia, through anthropomophism into buffoonery; transported to Attica, they recover some religious seriousness and depth (267–81).

The element common to all these antitheses is a contrast between an intense, superstitious form of religion and one calmer and more rational, much 'cleaner and colder' (144) than its opposite. The point of this contrast in turn is to exalt this calmer and more rational religion as a distinctive and magnificent achievement of Hellenism, a stronghold of decency heroically established, and defended against constant attack, in a savage land. (Only in Ionian frivolity did rationalism overreach itself and require some moral bracing from Athens.) The introductory chapter, revealingly entitled 'Greece and the Progress of Man', had presented yet another antithesis which is in fact the template for all the others, one between 'Hellenism' and 'Paganism': though the Greek has often been mistaken for the ideal type of Pagan man, 'in the main, as all classical literature shows, the Greek and the Pagan are direct opposites'. Yet Paganism preceded, and surrounded, Hellenism, whose ever-threatened achievement it was to resist the temptations to barbarism all around it (9–10). As Murray explains in his contemporary piece in *Albany Review*, 'In religion as in other matters, the essential characteristic of Greece is that, while in itself the direct antithesis of savagery, and a very incarnation of the spirit of progress, it yet stands close to savagery at every point. The battle which Greece waged for human enlightenment was a battle hand to hand, against enemies whose feet stood upon its own hearthstone' (Murray 1907a, 201).

In a sense we are back, it is clear, with the old 'getting better' tradition mentioned above. But the portrayal of the swamp of primitive bestiality out of which Greek religion emerged has gained enormously in detail and vividness. Jane Harrison in *Prolegomena* had thrown down a challenge to received notions about the civilized and enlightened character of Greek religion. Farnell, affronted, argued that Harrison was historically mistaken on crucial issues: the attempt to reach back to a pre-Olympian era in Greek religion was a vain one, since the various strands separated out by Harrison did not represent chronological stages; they were different levels of belief and action that co-existed at any given time. Murray, by contrast, accepted Harrison's findings with enthusiasm, and put them to use in his progressivist account of the Hellenic achievement in religion: not all the instances of 'barbarism overcome' that he deploys here and elsewhere derive from Harrison, but many do, and nothing that she presented resisted assimilation within the various capacious and flexible schemata and antitheses which he deployed to set off Hellenic from barbarian or pagan or pre-hellenic. The combination of intellectual energy and stylistic charm in *Prolegomena* was bound to attract Murray strongly. But he had no need to resist that attraction: the book presented him not with a threat but an opportunity. It was just a matter of tweaking Harrison's position a little to fit within his progressivist assumptions.[16]

The engagement with Jane Harrison continues in *Four Stages in Greek Religion*, of 1912. The preface announces that the study of Greek religion, long a deserted territory, is now a battle-ground. Murray announces that, 'if ever the present differences resolved themselves into a simple fight with shillelaghs between the scholars and the anthropologists, I should without doubt wield my reluctant weapon on the side of the scholars', but goes on to insist that anthropology has identified real phenomena below the surface of the texts. This is a reprise of the antithesis (classicism v. hairy Ainos) drawn in the preface to *A History of Ancient Greek Literature*, but the embodiment of 'anthropology' is now Harrison, whose work is

16 Contrast the simple rejection of speculation about origins by another progressivist, admittedly writing prior to the *Prolegomena*: putative origins 'have no bearing on what an ordinary Athenian felt or believed' (Campbell 1898, 15). Jane Harrison's own position was ambiguous (cf. Ackerman 1991a, 11 n. 22): despite her reputation for hostility to the Olympians, she was capable on occasion of adopting very Murrayite positions, as in her short sketch *Religion of Ancient Greece*: '(in Greece) by the action of art and philosophy savage elements are eliminated, and, by this purgation from ignorance, ugliness and fear, religion became, not only powerless to harm, but potent exceedingly for good' (J. E. Harrison 1905, 13; cf. 64, the last page). In the second edition of *Themis*, she professed to have been reconciled somewhat to the Olympians by Murray's *Five Stages* (J. E. Harrison 1927, viii). Murray was faithful to Andrew Lang, who according to F. M. Turner 1981, 118, 'recognized the savage intellect in order to banish its influence from civilized life'.

immediately praised. Despite the book's title, Murray reveals early on (2) that the history of Greek religion falls in its most important outline into just three stages; of the three stages, which had formed the subjects of the three lectures on which the book was based (D. Wilson 1987, 158), the first two related to Harrison's work very directly. The first was designated 'The Raw Material' in the original lecture and 'Saturnia Regna' in the published book; what Murray offers under this heading is in essence a presentation of Jane Harrison's pre-Olympian world, as depicted not only in *Prolegomena* but also, with an enriched palette, in *Themis*, also published in 1912. But Murray distances us and the Greeks from it by labelling it as 'the primitive Euêtheia or Age of Ignorance', the stage to which the Berlin ethnographer K. S. Preuss had applied what Murray calls 'the charming word "Urdummheit", or "Primal Stupidity".' He ingeniously seeks ancient authority for his periodization by identifying the Age of Ignorance with the 'Pelasgian' proto-form of Greek religion as described by Herodotus (2.52–3), when the gods lacked names, genealogies, and clearly delineated functions. In the account of stage two ('The Olympian Conquest' in the book; 'The Attempt at Order' as a lecture) Murray defends the Olympians against Jane Harrison's 'scornful challenge to the canonical gods of Greece', as he puts it in his preface, by attempting 'to explain their historical origin and plead for their religious value'. Stage Three is 'the change that took place in Greek thought between, say, Platonists and the neo-Platonists' (p. xiii), the 'rise of asceticism, of mysticism, in a sense, of pessimism; a loss of self-confidence, of hope in this life and of faith in normal human effort', a transformation 'which is not specifically Christian: it is just as marked in the Gnostics and Mithras-worshippers as in the Gospels and the Apocalypse, in Julian and Plotinus as in Gregory and Jerome' (123). Stage Four is a coda to Stage Three, the 'Last Protest' of Julian 'against the all-conquering "atheism" of the Christians' (4); and as a coda to the coda Murray presents as an appendix a translation of 'a very curious and little known ancient text, which may be said to constitute something like an authoritative Pagan creed', the *On the Gods and the World* of Julian's friend Sallustius.

In Stage Three (and Stage Four) the concerns of Jane Harrison have been left far behind. And evidently the attempt to explain the transformation in the character of Greek thought between one philosophical school and another represented a change of direction for a study which began with the bizarre rituals addressed to dimly apprehended pre-Olympian powers. The charge that Murray wrote the first half of one book and the second half of another would not lack force; certainly, the actual religious practices of Greece after the fifth century BC are, with the exception of ruler-cult, extraordinarily neglected.[17] But the power of the book to inspire lay in its range. Nobody now attempts to present a history of Greek religion which sweeps from earliest beginnings to the age of Julian;[18] in Murray's day too the norm seems to have been to treat the period after, at latest, the fourth century in a cursory final chapter. But Murray's comprehensive vision is the vision of his greatest pupil, E. R. Dodds, and of another great historian of ancient religion, A. D. Nock, who ascribed his interest in the subject to a reading of *Four Stages of Greek Religion* shortly before leaving school (Nock to Murray, 23 Sept. 1926: GM 51.226). Murray's interest in, say, Gnosticism and the so-called Mithras liturgy and the Corpus Hermeticum and Plotinus are by no means to be taken for granted in a Professor of Greek who was also deeply engaged with Greek drama and epic. We are told that when Albrecht Dieterich held a class on Greek magical papyri in Heidelberg in 1905, he disguised it in the lecture list under the title 'selected Greek papyri' in order not to be seen to be leading his pupils so far astray from the paths of rationality and of literature (Preisendanz 1928, p. v). Stage Three takes Murray almost as far from what was generally deemed exemplary about Greek culture as had Stage One. He duly puts it, like Stage One, under the mark of imperfection: it embodied (in a famous phrase first suggested to him by his friend J. B. Bury) a 'failure of nerve' (p. xiii). And he sometimes seeks, not very convincingly, to detect in late antique religious phenomena a reversion to the mentality of the Urdummheit. But he had access to Stage Three, as not to Stage One, through actual texts, and direct

17 As O. Weinreich noted in a review of *Five Stages*, *Philologische Wochenschrift* 46 (1926), 643–4 = *Ausgewählte Schriften* II (Amsterdam 1973), 205–7.

18 But Simon Price's *Religions of the Ancient Greeks* (S. R. F. Price 1999) has unusual chronological depth. Two heroic works of the first half of the twentieth century did match Murray's scope, in much greater detail, but with a consequent loss in eusynoptic appeal: U. von Wilamowitz-Moellendorff, *Glaube der Hellenen*, 2 vols. (Berlin 1931–2) and M. P. Nilsson's *Geschichte der griechischen Religion*, 2 vols. (1st edn, Berlin, 1940 and 1950).

evidence steered his imagination in this case in much better directions. What is in general most striking is the sympathy with which he describes the 'failure of nerve'.

When he re-issued *Four Stages* in 1925 he added a new chapter and a new stage.[19] Between 'The Olympian Conquest' and 'The Failure of Nerve' is now inserted an account of 'The Great Schools' of the fourth century, the Cynics, Stoics, and Epicureans above all. In one way the book profits greatly. Murray's all but incomparable excellences as an expositor are here applied to a gripping and well-focused subject with which he had deep sympathy. But in a different way the addition underlines a weakness in a central thesis of the original book. A main aim had been 'to plead for the religious value of the Olympians' in answer to their devaluation by Jane Harrison. But it now emerges that the real peak from which the Failure of Nerve represented a decline was not 'Olympianism but the great spiritual and intellectual effort of the fourth century B.C.'. Murray's attempt to defend the Olympians had never been very powerful.[20] A late Victorian rationalist, he was not the man to mount a robust neo-pagan defence of their self-loving vitality in the spirit of Nietzsche or Walter Otto or Hugh Lloyd-Jones. The Stoic compromise between monotheism and traditional belief suited him, as the new edition with the new chapter made plain, much better. But it was the Olympians whom he had set himself to defend. And his defence fails to convince not just because even by his own account the Olympian revolution failed, representing, as he splendidly puts it, 'a superb and baffled endeavour, not a *telos* or completion but a movement and effort of life' (61). Barbarous rites lingered on; the attempt to achieve order and coherence within polytheism could only go so far, and the Greeks were not ruthless enough to break through to monotheism;[21] even the attempt to create a unifying religion of the city encountered obstacles (61–72).

[19] E. R. Dodds supplied Murray with some comments to aid the revision, which unfortunately do not survive (letter of 25 July 1924: GM 48.129). The changes were negligible, addition of the new chapter aside.

[20] I leave aside the extra difficulty created for him by his belief in the irreligiousness of the Homeric gods. As in *Rise of the Greek Epic*, he has to have them pass through Pisistratean Athens in order to recover some seriousness.

[21] Cf. Murray 1936, 627: the Greeks could never manage 'clean, wholesome denial. They scarcely ever dared to say "There is no such being as Apollo or Dionysus."'

The real weakness in Murray's defence lies not in this admission of partial failure but in the difficulty he finds in ascribing substantial virtues to the Olympians (72–8). He claims, in vague general terms, that the Olympian religion 'debarbarized the worship of the leading states of Greece' and 'generally permitted progress'; it helped to unify Greece; and it was a great thing to 'envisage the world as governed, not by Giants and Gorgons... but by beings of quiet splendour like many a classical Zeus and Hermes and Demeter'. This last claim comes perilously close to an aesthetic idealization in the manner of Winckelmann, such as Murray himself had declared to have been superseded by the discoveries of anthropology. Defenders of Greek religion have often credited Apollo of Delphi with a moralizing mission, but the rationalist in Murray prevails here, and oracles are firmly if unhistorically treated as a distasteful manifestation of the Urdummheit (37–8). His most original argument is distinctly double-edged. To the proposition that 'There is, in one sense, far more faith in some hideous miracle-working icon which sends out starving peasants to massacre Jews than in the Athena of Phidias' (74) he attempts a double response, of which one element is more stressed than the other: on the one hand (minor thesis), 'once we have rid our minds of trivial mythology, there is religion in Athena also'; but on the other hand (major thesis), the thinness, the rootlessness, the unreality of the Olympians is not a weakness but a strength, because it allows them to become a vessel for whatever their worshippers care to pour into them; in the fifth century, they are vehicles for a religion of the city (the city being at this date the real focus of fervour); later they are 'Gods of half-rejected tradition, of unconscious make-believe, of aspiration... not gods in whom any one believes as a hard fact', pointers to the 'uncharted' rather than palpable figures. Murray's own ideal of suspension of judgement about the uncharted (p. 84 above) is here seen as a necessary response to the character of the Olympians.

A novel form of apologetics, whereby the virtue of a god is that the god defies belief! Murray's mistake perhaps was to tie a thesis about the place of religion in Greek society to a defence of a particular way of imagining the gods. What Murray admired was, on the one hand, the comparatively free scope for speculation in religious matters that was available to the Greeks, the absence of stifling dogma; on the other, the fact that one was not obliged to agree with Lucretius that, among them, 'tantum religio potuit suadere malorum': brutalities committed in the name of religion were almost unknown. And who would deny that these are very real virtues in a society? But it is very unclear why dogmatism and barbarous cruelty would have been impossible in defence of the Olympians, or tolerance and mildness even where pre-Olympian mother goddesses as imagined by Jane Harrison were honoured. The Greeks did indeed regularly suspend judgement about the uncharted, and to that extent Murray is describing a central characteristic of their religion (see T. Harrison 2000, 191, and the works he cites). But it is not because Zeus had traditionally been visualized as a monarch on a throne that they recognized that ultimately they could not know his mind. What was crucial was the way in which religious life was organized, what one might call the predominance of city over priest, not the character of the pantheon. As it happens, Farnell published in the same year as *Four Stages* a short book entitled *The Higher Aspects of Greek Religion* (Farnell 1912, based on Hibbert lectures). Farnell's prose is quite free from those flashes of vivid imagination that illuminate any page, nay, almost any sentence, of Murray. But the apologia for classical Greek religion that it contains is much more soundly based.[22]

Murray's most famous theory in the field of religion was presented not in *Four Stages* but as an 'Excursus on the Ritual Forms preserved in Greek Tragedy' in Jane Harrison's *Themis* of the same year (Murray 1912a).[23] Tragedy originated in a ritual dance presenting the destiny of Dionysus, to be understood as one of those gods embodying the

[22] For some reactions to *Four Stages* see nn. 4 and 17. A. B. Cook praised it for being interested both in 'origins' and 'endings' (letter of 22 Aug. 1913: GM 22.184–5); J. B. Bury commented that religions are either ineffective or pathological, and the Olympian religion is the former, for which reason 'I like it best' (letter of 17 Jan. 1913: GM 21.140–1); Wilamowitz expressed warm approval, despite their differences in approach, especially for the defence of the Olympians and the treatment of Sallustius (letter of 2 Jan. 1913: GM 21.118–19 = Wilamowitz-Moellendorff 1991, 112–15, no. 56); L. Radermacher described it as 'der erste Versuch einer wirklichen Geschichte des religiösen Denkens' (letter listed in the catalogue of Murray papers as of 16 July 1926: GM 51.184c-d, but the 6 of 1926 is unclear and in that year Murray would surely have sent *Five Stages*, not *Four*).

[23] And, very engagingly, in lecture form as 'The Ritual of Dionysus' (Murray 1912d); see too Murray 1912c (with strong emphasis on the idea of spring renewal);

vegetation who die and are resurrected or reborn each year, what Jane Harrison rashly named (but the concept goes back to J. G. Frazer) an *eniautos daimôn* or year spirit. The ritual often takes the form of a conflict between the old year and the new, yet both years are really the same spirit, who is thus involved in a perpetual cycle of avenging his own death by killing himself.[24] Thus far the theory was, as Murray frankly acknowledges, developed by Farnell out of Usener.[25] But for Farnell this was strictly a theory about origins, and shed no light on surviving tragedies. Murray's contribution was to associate it with recurrent formal features of plays which we can still read. (The idea of deriving certain formal features of tragedy from ritual had already been advanced, as Murray again acknowledged, by Dieterich; but Dieterich adduced fewer features, and associated them with a different ritual, the Eleusinian Mysteries.[26]) Tragedy's *agôn*, for instance, was the conflict of the old year and the new; its lament, a lament for the dead year; its theophany or *deus ex machina* the old year's resurrection in glory. Such was, of course, no longer the content of the plays; other characters had long since replaced the Dionysus (or

Murray 1965, 28–32 (summarized in D. Wilson 1987, 155, who calls it 'Murray's clearest statement of his thesis'). It is quite clear that any influence Nietzsche may have had on Murray's theory was indirect: he had doubtless read and been impressed by *Die Geburt der Tragödie*—in 'German Scholarship' (Murray 1915d), 339, Nietzsche is said to have done fine, imaginative work 'before he gave up Greek and went a-whoring after false philosophies'—but a long interval intervened between that reading and the emergence of the theory, during which Murray's thoughts about the origins of tragedy were going in other directions (see the new preface of 1907 to the *History of Ancient Greek Literature*, pp. xxiv–xxv). In the second edition of *Themis*, Murray added what he regarded as a conclusive new argument from Hdt. 2 about the supposed content of the 'Mysteries of Dionsyus' (Murray 1927b, 342–3).

24 'The Year Daemon . . . waxes proud and is slain by his enemy, who becomes thereby a murderer and must in turn perish at the hands of the expected avenger, who is at the same time the Wronged One re-risen': Murray 1913, 29–30.

25 *Cults of the Greek States*, v (Oxford 1908), 230–7; he cites H. Usener, *Archiv für Religionswissenschaft* 7 (1904), 303–13 (= *Kleine Schriften von Hermann Usener*, iv, 439–47) and also 'the old Thrako-Greek mummers' play' discovered by R. M. Dawkins (Dawkins 1906). Farnell defended his theory against criticism by Ridgeway in Farnell 1913a.

26 *Archiv für Religionswissenschaft* 11 (1908), 163–96 (= *Kleine Schriften*, Leipzig and Berlin 1911, 414–39).

the doubled Dionysus—Dionysus and his adversary/alter ego Pentheus) of the original drama. But the form persisted.[27]

According to Duncan Wilson, Murray's theory 'shows the influence of Jane Harrison and Verrall at its most pernicious' (D. Wilson 1987, 155). Certainly, a very intense exchange of ideas between Murray, Harrison, and F. M. Cornford must have led up to *Themis*, a work to which both Cornford and Murray contributed sections which fit seamlessly into the pattern of the whole.[28] The discovery at Palaiokastro in Crete in the excavations of 1902–5 of a hymn to Zeus must have seemed to the group an almost miraculous confirmation of the value of the concept of the *eniautos daimôn*: it addresses him as 'mightiest youth' and summons him to come to his worshippers 'for the year' (ἐς ἐνιαυτόν). But it is wrong to suppose that Murray was, as it were, ensnared into inventing a theory which his better reason would have rejected. Already in the *History of Ancient Greek Literature* he had questioned the accepted view that Dionysus was a latecomer to the Greek pantheon: he suggested instead, in the passage in the book perhaps most likely to interest a modern professional student of Greek religion, that 'Dionysus is rather a newcomer than a foreigner: he is like the new year, the spring, the harvest, the vintage. He is each year, in every place, a stranger who comes to the land and is welcomed as a stranger; at the end of his time he is expelled, exorcised, cut to pieces or driven away' (Murray 1897, 63). And despite the trenchant criticism which his new theory of the origin of tragedy soon received,[29] there was, it seems, no other

[27] 'An outer shape dominated by tough and undying tradition, formal and conventional to the last degree; an inner life, fiery with sincerity and spiritual freedom: that is the sort of paradox which from beginning to end is presented by Greek drama; and I think probably presented by the greatest art of many ages beside.' (Murray 1912d, 45)

[28] Note too how closely Harrison's statement of her own religious position (J. E. Harrison 1912, pp. xviii–xix) resembles that of Murray as presented in *Four Stages* and elsewhere (nn. 6 and 7 above): Murray drew attention to the passage in his memorial address: Murray 1928, 16–18.

[29] The well-known critique by Murray's friend A. W. Pickard-Cambridge (Pickard-Cambridge 1927, 185–207) was already sketched out in a letter of 18 Oct. 1911 (GM 19.15—Murray had invited comments on a draft) and in a paper read at the Oxford Philological Society on 12 June 1914, as Pickard-Cambridge pointed out after the publication of his book to a somewhat wounded Murray (letter of 22 Sept. 1927: GM 53.49). Murray gave his friend's book a very mixed review in the *Classical Review* (Murray 1927b), and in a letter to J. A. K. Thomson charged Pickard-Cambridge with

scholarly position to which he held so devotedly. He restates it again and again in different places, with changed nuances to suit new contexts.[30] In his British Academy Shakespeare lecture of 1914 he extended the approach to Hamlet; he greeted the parallel explanation of the origin of Attic comedy by F. M. Cornford with acclaim, and in *The Classical Tradition in Poetry* of 1927 it almost seems that literature in all its forms derives ultimately from ritual dances for the year-spirit (Murray 1927a, 28–51); in that work, under the influence of his friends Janet Spens and Francis Cornford, he associates another ritual figure, the Scapegoat, with the origins of drama (ibid., 63–7).[31] Later he even decided that the rapes of maidens and resultant births so characteristic of Euripides and New Comedy embodied a motif of the traditional plot in disguised form: the exposed children of this plot structure were none other than the little *daimôn* of the New Year (Murray 1943c; Murray 1951; and already (in brief) in Murray 1927c, 341 n. 1). His quicksilver intelligence always enabled him to see connections and encouraged him to engage in cultural cryptography, to detect, say, behind the figure of Helen a statue carried off during a ritual at Sparta (where brides were always seized).[32] A little-noticed article of 1915 traced 'The conception of another life' back to tribal coming-of-age rites: Christian conceptions of heaven derive from pagan conceptions of a blessed afterlife, as

'a queer inability to take in new ideas or to make an effort of imaginative understanding' (3 Sept. 1927: GM 172.205). On 24 May 1926 (GM 51.129–33) Pickard-Cambridge sent Murray a detailed critique of a paper (not preserved in the correspondence: unpublished?) in which Murray sought to link $\delta\rho\hat{\alpha}\mu\alpha$ with $\delta\rho\acute{\omega}\mu\epsilon\nu\alpha$, taken to connote a mystery, and advanced his new argument from Hdt. 2 (above, n. 23).

[30] In addition to nn. 23 and 24 and the passages of *Classical Tradition* mentioned in the text, see e.g. Murray 1933, 13; Murray 1940a, 5–8, 155–9.

[31] Letters to and from Spens and J. A. K. Thomson of the period are full of such matters. Hamlet: 'Hamlet and Orestes', reprinted as ch. VIII of Murray 1927a; first in *Proceedings of the British Academy* 1914. (For a sympathetic view of Murray's comparison, though not his *eniautos daimôn* explanation, see Nuttall 1988.) Note too the appearance of the *eniautos daimôn* even in Murray's occasional remarks on Christian origins (n. 6 above).

[32] Murray 1924, 205–6; the same chapter contains similar treatment of other figures. Murray went on having new ideas in this area: the treatments of Helen, Achilles, and Agamemnon were substantially altered in the third edition and that of Odysseus was added; but the approach is already there in the treatment of Thersites, derived from Usener, in the first edition (unchanged later, like that of Diomedes).

propagated in the Eleusinian Mysteries above all; but Eleusinian 'initiation' is merely puberty initiation transposed into a new key. (Unfortunately the equivocation on 'initiation' works better in English than in Greek.) The mud of the underworld starts as the real mud in which the candidate for initiation has been plastered; the choirs of heaven have their origin in the happy songs that greet the youth whose ordeal has been completed. (Murray 1915a; reprinted in Murray 1940b, 121–50.)

Murray's theory of the origin of tragedy was not, then, a single or a temporary aberration. Yet he was fully capable of appreciating the plays as plays; and his obstinate commitment to what has generally seemed so reductive and implausible a theory is puzzling. After listing all the instances in Euripides of a concluding divine epiphany, Murray comments 'if this were free and original composition the monotony would be intolerable and incomprehensible: we can understand it only when we realize that the poet is working under the spell of a set traditional form' (Murray 1927c, 352). In the *History of Ancient Greek Literature* he had already spoken of 'inexplicable pieces of conventionalism' in the form of Attic tragedy (Murray 1897, 203). Part of the explanation may then be that the theory helped to reconcile Murray, used to a freer form of drama, to formal restrictions against which he chafed, or feared that modern readers would chafe. But he surely also felt, or at least hoped, that a ritual explanation plumbed not just the origins but also the depths of tragedy. In his Memorial Address on Jane Harrison, he suggested that *Prolegomena* was a book about Greek religion, whereas *Themis* was a book about 'the religious ventures and aspirations of the human mind everywhere'. Applying the ritual theory to Hamlet was a step in the direction of making it into a general theory of tragedy. He ends that lecture with a contrast between the surface splendour of plays like *Hamlet* or the *Agamemnon* or the *Electra*, products of the poet's conscious skill, with 'a strange unanalyzed vibration below the surface, an undercurrent of desires and fears and passions, long slumbering yet eternally familiar, which have for thousands of years lain near the root of our most intimate emotions and been wrought into the fabric of our most magical dreams' (Murray 1927a, 239–40; similar rhetoric on p. 261). At this point, one may feel, Murray's unfailing verbal fluency has taken over where something more ruggedly analytical would have been better in place. We need to be told what relation exists between the evocation of these 'desires and fears and passions' in the 'primitive folk-tale' and in the complex and brilliant plays. In chapter 3 of *The Classical Tradition in Poetry* he briefly attempts to give such an account, and to link the distinctive character of tragic pleasure with the genre's ritual origins (Murray 1927a, 55–67). But what he offers is not very clear or satisfying. He also appeals to the 'overwhelming influence wielded over the art and thought of mankind by unconscious imitation and tradition' (ibid., p. v). But it was probably above all his own ritual theory that caused him to believe in that 'overwhelming influence'. Still, it seems clear that a main attraction of the ritual theory for Murray was the way in which (so to speak) it allowed everything to connect with everything else. *Five Stages of Greek Religion* brought phenomena usually treated as disparate together in a single progressive history. The ritual theory linked Sophocles and Shakespeare too with their rude romantic forebears.

There is a different though related context in which Murray's general sympathy for the Cambridge ritualists should be set. In an article on 'German scholarship' in the *Quarterly Review* for 1915, he advanced, in contrast to German Wissenschaft, the ideal of a kind of writing which combined the virtues of scholarship with 'the impulse of an artist' (Murray 1915d). He considered it a quite recent and in the main an English development, and he presented as examples the works of Cornford, Zimmern, Livingstone, Bevan, and J. A. K. Thomson, works which 'stand as much by their sense of beauty and their imaginative suggestiveneness as by the particular conclusions which they try to prove'. Jane Harrison had also just been mentioned and clearly belongs in the group; engagement of the writer's whole being in the work is said to be another, potentially dangerous, characteristic of such writing. The issue of the *Quarterly Review* in question was entitled 'German "Kultur"' and, published in 1915, was designed to undermine the credentials of that Kultur, but Murray was not writing vulgar propaganda, and in a letter of 1921 to J. A. K. Thomson (4 Dec. 1921: GM 172.27–28) reverts to his ideal of a 'style of scholarship which consists essentially in the perception of beauty, and to some extent in the representation of it': Murray himself, Thomson, Livingstone, Zimmern, Cornford, Jane Harrison, and 'Robinson of Eton'[33] are here listed as its exponents. Cornford and Harrison did not in fact write about 'beauty', but they wrote beautifully and their works were very rich in 'imaginative suggestiveness'. They also provided what one might call (though the phrase is not Murray's) big explanations for things, broad hypotheses which brought many things together and made many things cohere; this was a kind of scholarship which, if one could only bring oneself to believe in it, could really shed floods of light on matters worthy of a serious person's attention. The appetite for big explanations may be a misguided one, but it was certainly one that Murray shared with those Cambridge ritualists to whom he was closest. Big explanations demand imagination, and imaginativeness was one of the key values of the group. Jane Harrison ends a glowing review of Murray's *Rise of the Greek Epic* with a magnificent rhetorical flourish:

> Another reader will say 'Most interesting and delightful, very suggestive and stimulating as a whole—but surely at least half the book is pure work of the imagination'.
> *It is.*
> (J. E. Harrison 1908a, cited by D. Wilson 1987, 127.)

The danger of such an idealization of imagination is doubtless the scope that it allows for the intrusion of the writer's own values, assumptions, and dreams, unobstructed by evidence. On a stern view, Murray's *Five Stages* is mostly unconscious propaganda for the values of Victorian liberalism (so Fowler 1991). Whether the 'sound scholars' such as Farnell whom Jane Harrison so heartily despised fared any better in extruding themselves from their works is matter for another enquiry.

[33] Probably a mistake for (Cyril) Robinson of Winchester. Cf. the discussion of this letter in McManus's chapter (p. 189) in this volume.

5

Gilbert Murray's Greek Editions

Christopher Collard

I INTRODUCTION

Acclaim for Murray during his lifetime as an interpreter of Greek culture and poetry for the widest possible audience, and his unparalleled success as a translator of Greek drama, especially for performance, outdid his reputation in traditional Greek scholarship. His career began with such unusual distinction at Oxford, especially in the Greek language itself, that he was elected to a fellowship at New College in 1888 and only a year later appointed to a chair at Glasgow at the age of 23.[1] Once there he quickly aspired to produce critical editions of Greek authors for students' use, while writing also his

I thank Professor Francis West most warmly for helpful correspondence about some of Murray's letters in the Oxford University Press Archive which were unavailable during my attempt to consult them there in late 2005, and for his permission to cite his personal notes upon them used for his biography of Murray (F. J. West 1984), as also upon some letters in the Gilbert Murray Papers, Bodleian Library (referred to in text and notes as GM), which I was unable to locate from the catalogue. I am grateful also to the Press Archivist, Dr Martin Maw, for permission to cite a few other documents. I particularly thank the President and Fellows of Corpus Christi College, Oxford for permission to cite from the Fraenkel Papers held in their Archive (see Section IV and nn. 52, 55, 58).

I owe special gratitude to James Diggle and the volume's editor Chris Stray for their readiness to read a draft of this paper at short notice, and to aid its improvement.

1 Both appointments had one cause: 'so deep was the impression that his personality and promise made upon his seniors' (Dodds 1960, 13 = Dodds 1957, 476); cf. Lloyd-Jones 1982, 198. Some names of Murray's supporters are given by F. J. West 1984, 59. For Murray's own account of the Glasgow appointment see Smith and Toynbee 1960, 93–4.

earliest book of general appreciation, the *History of Ancient Greek Literature* (Murray 1897). His proposed Glasgow Critical Texts (Section II below) faded away when he was invited from Oxford in the middle 1890s to edit Euripides; his edition was to become standard throughout the world for almost eighty years (Section III below). His retirement from the Regius Chair of Greek at Oxford in 1936 coincided with his Oxford edition of Aeschylus (Section IV below) which disappointed both the world and hardly less the editor himself. Both editions were for the Oxford Classical Texts.[2] It is less well known that Murray contributed textual notes to some of the early volumes of the Oxyrhynchus Papyri, and gave general help to J. U. Powell's *Collectanea Alexandrina* (Powell 1925).[3] The only other evidence I have found for Murray's critical work upon original texts consists in a few manuscript pages of suggestions and supplements *exempli gratia* to the Cairo codex of Menander first published in 1907.[4] Murray

[2] *Euripides* Vol. I, 1902; Vol. 1st edn, II, 1904; 2nd edn, 1908; 3rd edn, 1913; Vol. III, 1st edn, 1909; 2nd edn, 1913. *Aeschylus*, 1st edn 1937; 2nd edn, 1955 (reissued with corrections 1957).

[3] *Oxyrhynchus Papyri* Part VI (1908), where the editors B. P. Grenfell and A. S. Hunt acknowledge Murray's 'most valuable suggestions and criticism upon (No.) 852' (Euripides' *Hypsipyle*, pp. 19–106); Part VII (1910, ed. Hunt) upon 1011 (Callimachus' *Aetia* and *Iambi*, pp. 15–82); Part IX (1912, ed. Hunt) upon 1174 (Sophocles' *Ichneutae*, pp. 30–86) and 1175 (Eurypylus, pp. 86–123); Part XI (1915, ed. Grenfell and Hunt) upon 1358–63 (Hesiod, Alcaeus, Bacchylides, Callimachus, pp. 44–92); also Part XV (1922, ed. Hunt), an undefined contribution. Murray receives thanks in the Praefatio of Hunt's *Tragicorum Graecorum Fragmenta Papyracea Nuper Reperta* (Oxford Classical Texts, 1912); most of his contributions to these texts, some shared with other scholars, may be found at (Hunt's line-numbers) Soph. *Ichn.* apparatus, 13 text, 15 app., 262 text, 234 app., 321 text, 365 text, 390 text, 394 app.; *Euryp.* 3–6 app.; *Ach. Conv.* col. ii.1 text; Eur. *Hyps.* 3 ii app., 3 iv.2 text, 3 v.11 text, 34.12 app., 34.67 app., 34.112 app., 41.87 app., 41.96 text, 41.99–100 app., 41.105 app., 45.111 app.; *Cretes* 39 text.

Murray published the first edition of the famous Palaikastro (Cretan) 'Hymn of the Kouretes': Murray 1908–9; cf. Murray's brief exposition of the Hymn in Powell and Barber 1921, 50–3. For Powell's *Collectanea* see his Praefatio p. ix; also n. 6 below. Murray is however not acknowledged in Powell's editorial 'Preface' to his *New Chapters in the History of Greek Literature. Third Series* (Powell 1933), nor by A. W. Pickard-Cambridge in his long section in that volume upon fragmentary Greek tragedies (ibid., 68–155). It remains to be established how far, or whether at all, Murray made fresh, original alterations in the texts which he chose for the *Oxford Book of Greek Verse* (Bowra 1930).

[4] Bodleian Library, Oxford, MSS Gilbert Murray (hereafter GM) 433, a 28-page notebook; it is undated. I have collated many of Murray's suggestions, which are most frequent for *Epitrepontes*, with the apparatus of Sandbach's OCT and A. Montari's

declined an invitation to follow his Oxford edition of Euripides with one of Sophocles or, if not of him, of Herodotus or the lyric poets.[5] Lastly, there was his advice, if not overt help, to some editors of individual plays of Euripides.[6]

Epitrepontes (Vol. I, Rome, 1997). There is little for future editors of Menander (indeed Murray seems to make a few and surprising metrical blunders), but there are coincidences between Murray and early twentieth-century editors (e.g. those who question the presence of Syriscus, and an address to him, at *Epitr.* 269, or Croiset in his conjecture at 321). The only interest may be whether Murray's ideas are reflected in his much later English version of the play, *The Arbitration* (Murray 1945). Murray offered no Greek texts, only translations, when he treated the newly discovered Menander fragmentary plays in J. U. Powell, E. A. Barber, *New Chapters in the History of Greek Literature*, Second Series (Oxford, 1929), 9–34.

5 GM 397 contains the invitations: for Sophocles by Charles Cannan, on behalf of the Press, in a letter to Murray of 11 Aug. 1903; that for Herodotus was repeated by Humphrey Milford, 7 May 1904, and for Sophocles repeated informally by Cannan, 18 Jan. 1906, including the words 'Do you think you could finish off Euripides . . . and seriously tackle Sophocles?'; and more formally by Cannan, 7 Feb. 1906. 'Murray' however 'was anxious to find scholarly work other than textual criticism' (once he finished Euripides): D. Wilson 1987, 116. Eventually B. P. Grenfell suggested to the Press that A. C. Pearson should undertake Sophocles, and Cannan wrote to Murray on 16 Nov. 1917, seeking his approval; the idea may have been provoked by Pearson's earlier work in reducing some of Jebb's editions of the plays for the use of schools, and by the publication in that year of his *The Fragments of Sophocles*. A Press document by R.W. Chapman of 16 Nov. 1922 says 'Murray resigned in favour of Pearson, who completed the edition, which is now in the press'.

6 Acknowledged in the Prefaces of J. U. Powell, *Phoenissae* (London, 1911); O. R. A. Byrde, *Heracles* (Oxford, 1914); M. Platnauer, *Iphigenia in Tauris* (Oxford, 1938); J. D. Denniston, *Electra* (Oxford, 1939); A. S. Owen, *Ion* (Oxford, 1939); E. R. Dodds, *Bacchae* (Oxford, 1944[1]). D. L. Page acknowledges Murray's help in his *Actors' Interpolations in Greek Tragedy* (Page 1934: see D. Wilson 1987, 317), but not in his *Medea* (Oxford, 1938)—probably in his angry reaction when Dodds, rather than Denniston, was appointed to the Regius Chair in succession to Murray. This was at Murray's recommendation to the Prime Minister Stanley Baldwin: see R. B. Todd in Todd 2004, 1.248. Murray's letter to Stanley Baldwin, with whom alone the appointment then lay, is in GM 77. 138–40; its wording is reflected in Lloyd-Jones 1982, 289; cf. also n. 20 below. Page's angry letter to Murray of 24 June 1936 is also in GM 177; it cites Euripides, *Bellerophon* F 286.1–2, quoted by D. Wilson 1987, 328 at n. 62, 445. For the reaction of C. M. Bowra, another disappointed aspirant (whom Murray ranked third behind both Dodds and Denniston), see M. Davies 2006, 11 and n. 65. For Dodds's reaction to the appointment see Dodds 1977, 124–7.

II MURRAY'S PROPOSED GLASGOW CRITICAL TEXTS

Murray was circulating this proposal from Glasgow towards the end of 1893. Some of those he consulted at Oxford, particularly Ingram Bywater, the Regius Professor of Greek, had since the late 1880s been deliberating in conjunction with Oxford University Press what were to become the Oxford Classical Texts. It would have been strange if Murray knew nothing of these plans, stranger if, when Bywater's colleagues received his proposal, they did not at once tell him of their own—but both may well have happened, since in the summer of 1894 Murray sent his proposal as if still active to Wilamowitz in Germany. It was part of Murray's request for advice about working on Euripides.[7]

Probably the idea of the Critical Texts began while Murray was intending a lexicon to Euripides, a preliminary it appears (from Wilamowitz' answer) to a critical edition of the poet.[8] Either project would have seemed an ambitious project for a young scholar; in combination they required a good deal of thought and advice. For his Critical Texts Murray named the three tragedians to Wilamowitz; but he circulated to a number of persons printed sample pages not only of Sophocles, *Ajax* 810–49 but also of Aristophanes, *Nubes* 15–51;

[7] In fact Bywater at first encouraged Murray: see D. Wilson 1987, 56, n. 14. 'In the summer of 1894': Murray's letter (in ancient Greek) has not survived, but Wilamowitz' reply (also in Greek) has: it is GM 3. 216–22, dated 12 Oct. 1894 and containing two apologies for its slowness. This is Letter 1 in Wilamowitz-Moellendorff 1991, 9–21 (reproduced both in the original Greek and in [partial] English translation), together with full commentary. The editors, Bierl et al., record (ibid., 1, 117 n. 526) that all Murray's original letters to Wilamowitz were preserved in Berlin until 1945, when they were 'burned by thieves' for fuel during the terrible winter. For Murray's initial approach to Wilamowitz see (writing before Bierl et al.) M. I. Henderson 1960, 129; F. J. West 1984, 68–70; D. Wilson 1987, 55–6.

[8] Wilamowitz gave succinct advice upon the making of a lexicon, insisting that its basis should be a text into which should be entered all manuscript variants and conjectures seemingly of value to the lexicon: Letter 2 to Murray of 10 Mar. 1895 in Wilamowitz-Moellendorff 1991, 21–2, cited by F. J. West 1984, 70 and D. Wilson 1987, 56. One year later Murray, after he had agreed to edit Euripides for Oxford, wrote to his wife that the lexicon he contemplated 'really implies the making of a text in one's mind and it will be much simpler as well as far more satisfactory to do it thoroughly': letter of 8 June 1896, which I draw from Prof. West's personal notes.

and to Wilamowitz at least he sent also a typed sample of the first part of the lyric passage *Phoenissae* 288–354. The printed samples offer an edited Greek text, with beneath it (selected) ancient scholia and a very brief apparatus criticus; the typed sample for *Phoenissae* differs, having instead of an apparatus a brief note 'Lectiones Codicum' in the right-hand margin.[9] Wilamowitz' response states that Murray would add 'something about metre'; indeed Wilamowitz generously returned a quite detailed metrical commentary (in ancient Greek) on the whole lyric passage, together with a suggested summary metrical analysis in Latin; he also advised how much of the scholia on the passage to reproduce.[10] There is however no section on 'metre' in the samples surviving in Oxford, just as none of them includes the proposed ancient biographical matter mentioned by G. Whitaker[11] as having been sent to British scholars, of which Wilamowitz' letter reveals that he too knew, if only as a possible inclusion (Wilamowitz-Moellendorff 1991, 11–15).

Murray had discouraging responses in Britain, among them one which might have weighed more heavily than others, from his valued Oxford mentor and friend Arthur Sidgwick, who was 'not so sure (the Critical Texts) will pay: the British schoolmaster is so very adhesive to old methods'.[12] Wilamowitz' response was typical of all his letters to Murray upon issues of pure scholarship: firmly directive opinion inside a carefully reserved affability, marked nevertheless by great generosity from his own work.[13] He approved the principles of

[9] I have examined both the printed and the typed samples surviving in GM 438. Chris Stray points out that Murray probably chose *Ajax* from Sophocles' plays because Jebb had still to produce this seventh and last volume of his great edition (Cambridge, 1896).

[10] Wilamowitz-Moellendorff 1991, 17–21, not translated into English. The editors (ibid., 17 n. 52) state that 'Murray adopted none of Wilamowitz' suggestions' (that is, for the text and metrical analysis of this passage), in his eventual Oxford edition of 1909.

[11] G. Whitaker, '... brevique adnotatione critica ...: A Preliminary History of the Oxford Classical Texts' (Whitaker 2007, forthcoming). I owe sight of this remarkable article to the author's kindness.

[12] GM 168, letter of 15 Dec. 1893. For Sidgwick see my entry in Todd (2004) 3.893–4, and my much fuller treatment, with wider bibliography, 'Schoolmaster, Don, Educator: Arthur Sidgwick Moves to Corpus in 1879' (Collard 2007, forthcoming).

[13] See Wilamowitz-Moellendorff 1991, 5, 6, 29 n. 107. For Wilamowitz' true evaluation of Murray ('I take him seriously only as a poet') see ibid., 6 at n. 26 = 67 n. 284; at 36 n. 137 is reproduced Wilamowitz' opinion of Murray's proof-text of *Cyclops*, as

Murray's proposed Glasgow editions, stressing the importance of giving students the primary evidence, but foresaw extreme difficulties in editing scholia selectively in a way useful for them (Wilamowitz-Moellendorff 1991, 11–12 = (translated) 15–16). He pours his coldest water in the middle of a long exposition of the problems: 'But on the whole I would be lying if I commended the plan: the more I think about it, the more difficult it seems' (Wilamowitz-Moellendorff 1991, 11 = (translated) 15). Instead, Wilamowitz preferred a modern editor's paraphrase to a report of the ancient scholia.

Murray abandoned his proposal. Within eighteen months or so he had agreed to edit Euripides for the Oxford Classical Texts.[14]

III THE OXFORD *EURIPIDES*

The gestation and progress of this edition are well documented in (i) the (partly) surviving correspondence between the chief officers of the Press and Murray, and (ii) that from Wilamowitz to Murray; further, in (iii) Murray's copious correspondence with his wife, and (iv) an account of Murray's work on Euripides over the years 1896–1909 given by Francis West.[15] Murray discussed with both the Press and Wilamowitz his first intention to begin work upon a critical edition of Euripides through the making of a lexicon; and in negotiating with the Press he declared that he intended an edition of the fragments too.[16]

expressed to his great friend G. Kaibel in 1901: (translated) 'He produces almost only nonsense . . . a pupil of Verrall . . . he produces extraordinary stupidities in it.'

[14] The formal invitation came from Lyttelton Gell on behalf of the Press on 26 June 1896: GM 397.

[15] (i) Press Archive files bearing on the Classical Texts (unnumbered letters; many gaps in time; Murray's own letters are usually missing), together with letters, some the originals of those sent to Murray by the Press, others copies of his responses to theirs, in GM 397 (for a full account of the Classical Texts and their beginning see Whitaker 2007); (ii) Letters 1–43 in Wilamowitz-Moellendorff 1991, 9–91, of Wilamowitz to Murray between 12 Oct. 1894 and 14 Dec. 1909, and the editors' introduction and commentary; (iii) GM 451–6; (iv) F. J. West 1984, 68–70, 112–21; for other accounts and assessments cf. D. Wilson 1987, 113–16; and Easterling 1997, 114–15, with bibliography at 113 n. 1.

[16] The lexicon was quite quickly forgotten, the fragments very slowly: the last mentions of the latter I have found are by the Press's Charles Cannan, on 21 Apr. 1917

Murray's awareness that he needed advice, and his consultation of Wilamowitz, marked his good judgement, because Wilamowitz had published the two fundamental works of contemporary scholarship on Euripides, *Analecta Euripidea* (Berlin, 1875) and *Euripides, Herakles* (Wilamowitz 1889). There was no one more authoritative anywhere.[17] The complete critical edition of Euripides by Wilamowitz' Berlin predecessor A. Kirchhoff (Berlin, major edition 1855, minor edition 1867–8) had already been overtaken by that of A. Nauck (3rd edn, Leipzig, 1870)—who had died in 1892 just before Murray first wrote to Wilamowitz. When Murray was starting work, N. Wecklein was nearing completion of the edition he had begun in 1878 with R. Prinz (19 fascicles, one for each play, Leipzig, 1878–1902)—an edition which Murray evaluated a little less harshly than Wilamowitz himself.[18] Like Nauck's, Wecklein's edition was too free with its textual conjectures, and Murray determined to be more conservative.

It is the common opinion of later scholars that Murray was insufficiently prepared, energetic, or rigorous in method for the task, not by Wilamowitz' standards alone, but by those already well established in German scholarship and demonstrated in Britain for the Press by Ingram Bywater, the *auctor princeps* of the Oxford Classical Texts, in his *Aristotle, Nicomachean Ethics* (1890; it became an Oxford Text in 1899). It was all the more remarkable therefore that Wilamowitz not only gave Murray advice in their very first exchange

(GM 397), a sad judgement that they would never be published, and in an internal Press document by R. W. Chapman of 16 Nov. 1922, succinctly: 'Murray—Euripides. This means the fragments, and is unlikely to come along.'

17 Murray's much later, fullest, and most glowing appreciation of Wilamowitz (Murray 1915d, 336–7) is cited at Wilamowitz-Moellendorff 1991, 5 n. 23: for example, 'impatient, brilliant, original, magnificent, unmethodical, a man of genius as well as of enormous learning'. Interestingly, these words were published while Wilamowitz was still alive, and during World War I. After 1913 Murray maintained a very interrupted correspondence with him until 1930 (Wilamowitz-Moellendorff 1991, Letters 57–60).

18 '(Wecklein) is not likely to be revolutionary', cited in P. Lyttelton Gell's letter from the Press to Murray of 8 Dec. 1897, cf. Charles Cannan to him of 7 Apr. 1904 (both GM 397)—what, however, did 'nothing revolutionary' intend to say? Wecklein was in fact over-free with his own conjectures (see n. 41 below). Later, Murray wrote of '(Wecklein's) thoroughness, or rather that of Prinz who did the collating for him' in a letter to his wife of 1 April 1903 (cited by F. J. West 1984, 117: GM 456). The cause and history of Wilamowitz' 'contempt' for Wecklein is documented in Wilamowitz-Moellendorff 1991, 23 n. 76 and 62 n. 260; cf. also n. 41 below.

of letters in 1894, but regularly until the Euripides was complete in 1909. It may have been that he was charmed and impressed by the young and unknown British professor's courtesy in seeking his help (Murray had not as yet published anything). From the start both appeared to realize that Murray would need guidance in practically every aspect of a scholar's task; biographers and others have written of Murray's approaching Wilamowitz, and being treated by him, like a graduate student under supervision—a phenomenon almost unknown in Britain at that date, but regular in Germany. Furthermore he sent Murray matter from his own unpublished collations, and from his published and unpublished critical notes upon the plays; and he offered from the earliest time to read Murray's proofs. This last he seems to have done with great thoroughness, on the evidence of his letters (no annotated proofs survive).[19] He interrupted his own work, often at times of great personal commitment or exhaustion, to do this kindness for a fellow-scholar, whom he admired more as a poet–translator for the stage (see n. 13). Murray was aided too by the erratic Arthur Verrall (whose brilliant intellect Wilamowitz at least recognized—but also its waywardness), through discussion, correspondence, and, again as with Wilamowitz, the reading of proofs (similarly not preserved, it appears).[20] Here were helpers as different

[19] The statement by Wilson 1987, 424 n. 3 that fragmentary proofs marked by Wilamowitz survive in GM 8 is a slip: there are only letters and notes accompanying the (lost) proofs.

[20] Reasonable inferences about Verrall's manner of annotating Murray's proofs are made in Ackerman 1973, 103–4, cf. 106: Ackerman reproduces and discusses Verrall's over-ingenious defence of Ms. L at Eur. *Supp.* 939.

Some of Murray's opinions of Verrall: 'very original and teasingly seductive; general result of his revision satisfactory', in a letter to Lady Mary of 19 Aug. 1901 which I cite from Prof. Francis West's correspondence with me (GM 455); 'the most brilliant of all modern critics of Euripides' (Murray 1913, 1, cited at Wilamowitz-Moellendorff 1991, 50 n. 196); 'the dangerous delights of his work', in Murray's obituary of Verrall (*Oxford Magazine*, 24 Oct. 1912) cited by D. Wilson 1987, 116 n. 16, cf. 424 n. 16. Perhaps most revealing of all for Murray's own Greek scholarship is a sentence in his letter to Stanley Baldwin (see n. 6 above): '(J. D.) Denniston is universally... respected. In actual knowledge of Greek I doubt if he has his equal in Oxford or Cambridge. Whenever I am in doubt on a point of idiom, he is the man I consult, as I used in old days to consult Verrall.'

Even before Murray finished his Euripides, there was concern about Verrall's 'baleful influence': a phrase used by A. E. Housman in a letter to Murray of 4 Nov. 1904, cited by M. I. Henderson 1960, 143 and later published in Housman 1971, 404; cited by F. J. West 1984, 116. Housman's wording is reflected in Lloyd-Jones 1982, 201 and id.

in approach and temperament as any two could be; and Murray was bound to find it hard to reconcile their judgements, let alone his own with theirs.

Murray's identification of the principal manuscripts on which to base his edition followed that of Prinz (and his successor Wecklein) in theirs which began appearing in 1878 and itself followed that of Kirchhoff (see above); and Murray was guided to these fundamental textual witnesses by Wilamowitz. In the course of his work Murray nevertheless needed to use further manuscripts, again with Wilamowitz' rather pained but continued guidance. The entire manuscript basis of his edition was sensible and practical, within the scope and purpose of the Oxford Classical Texts, a consideration of which Wilamowitz was aware (and he was himself later to contribute the Greek Bucolic Poets to the series: 1906; 2nd edn 1910).[21]

Murray's own work did not begin promisingly. One reason why he did little or no collating before producing his first volume was urgency within the Press to have it completed and published; this, in part, lay behind his early request (February 1897) to Wilamowitz for advice and help with dependable collations, either his own or others'.[22] Another reason may have been that he was already beginning to suffer from the long illness which brought him to resign from the Glasgow chair in 1898. Isobel Henderson believed that the illness affected his early progress with the edition; in 1900 Charles Cannan

1991, 204 (the latter a reprinted review of D. Wilson 1987 which came out in 1988). Cf. also Diggle 1984, p. x n. 17, with evaluation of Verrall's conjectures; Diggle here illustrates Housman's help to Murray, and will do so more fully in Diggle 2007.

Wilamowitz' judgement of Verrall is documented in Wilamowitz-Moellendorff 1991, 50 n. 196, e.g. (translated) 'Verrall's idea... is very ingenious, it's very seductive' (a letter to Murray of 16 July 1901); cf. their p. 68 n. 284: (translated) 'Verrall, who causes much harm in England too' (a letter to G. Finsler, 30 Mar. 1908). Wilamowitz was also struck by Verrall's personal charm: ibid., 80. Similar criticism of Verrall from Germany was advanced by N. Wecklein in his review of Murray's Vol. I: Wecklein 1902, col. 932. For Verrall see N. J. Lowe in Todd 2004, 3.1001–4, and Lowe 2005.

[21] Wilamowitz' advice to Murray was chiefly in Letters 3, 4, 8 and 10 in Wilamowitz-Moellendorff 1991, between March 1897 and July 1901. He expressed his dismay at Murray's uncertain knowledge of the manuscript tradition when proposing to produce a complete edition of Euripides, rather than a text from which to compose a lexicon (Letter 4 of 16 Sept. 1897: ibid., 27). Murray's choice and range of manuscripts is judiciously assessed by K. J. Matthiessen, *Studien zur Textüberlieferung der* Hekabe *des Euripides* (Heidelberg, 1974), 30–1.

[22] Wilamowitz' reply, with information and undertakings, is dated 1 Mar. 1897: Letter 3 in Wilamowitz-Moellendorff 1991, 22–5.

at the Press became anxious not to force completion of the first volume 'if (he) ought not to work'.[23] Murray may at least have intended to collate while holidaying in Florence in 1897, and a visit to Paris for collation in 1901 (by which time the first volume was in proof) is recorded in his wife's diary; in the event, his only prolonged spell collating on the continent was in 1903, in time for results to be included in the second volume.[24] When eventually he did collate, his health had clearly recovered strongly; he found the work alternately strenuous and fascinating, but was pleased by his findings, enough to question some of Wilamowitz' results; as significantly, he regathered confidence in his Greek scholarship, and started hoping for a professorship again.[25]

[23] M. I. Henderson 1960, 134; Cannan to Murray, 9 May 1900 (GM 397). For the incompletely diagnosed nature of Murray's illness see F. J. West 1984, 47–50 and D. Wilson 1987, 64–8. Murray wrote to his friend the dramatic critic W. Archer on 9 Sept. 1897, after work on his first batch of Euripides' plays for his Vol. 1, 'my stomach has positively refused to do any more work' (cited by M. I. Henderson 1960, 134, but with no reference).

[24] The evidence for Murray's collating, and its times, is examined by R. L. Fowler in Wilamowitz-Moellendorff 1991, 28 n. 105. He inclines to believe that actual collation in 1897 is a false inference from a letter which Murray wrote to the Italian scholar G. Vitelli after his visit to Florence. Prof. Francis West has noted a letter from Murray to his wife of 15 Mar. 1897 (GM 452) in which he says '(I) might look in at Florence to collate C (the great Laurentian ms. now known as L) in difficult passages'; but it seems he did not 'look in', for in 1903 he wrote to his wife of his 'shy' demeanour in approaching the library, when intending an initial visit (see n. 28). James Diggle (i) tells me that when he examined the record in the Laurentian Library of those who had consulted ms. L, he did not find Murray's name at all, for any year; and (ii) notes that Murray did not even 'go as far as London to collate the Harleian ms. of *Rhesus*, although Wilamowitz had indicated that this was a manuscript which needed to be used (see Wilamowitz-Moellendorff 1991, 23: Letter 3). His reports of it (incomplete and inaccurate) are taken entirely from Wecklein'. M. Davies 2006, 14 compares Housman with Murray for their dependence upon others' collations, at least in the case of Housman's edition of Juvenal (Housman 1905: Praefatio, p. v), and comments that Housman was defended by another non-collator, D. R. Shackleton Bailey (M. Davies 2006, 26 n. 54).

[25] Letters to his wife from Italy, from February to April 1903, recorded variously by Prof. Francis West in his notes and correspondence with me (cf. F. J. West 1984, 86 and, for 'shy' [n. 27 above] 116); for Murray's questioning of Wilamowitz' collations see D. Wilson 1987, 115. In particular, Murray's letter of 29 Mar. has a wish that 'they would make me professor of Greek at some nice place. But of course there is no place except Oxford.' Murray returned to a Fellowship at New College in 1905; but his naming to the Regius Chair in 1908 was not straightforward (see e.g. Lloyd-Jones 1982, 202), and he himself doubted his suitability in a letter to his wife of 25 June 1908 (GM 459), cited by M. I. Henderson 1960, 148 and D. Wilson 1987, 130 n. 79.

One document at least from Murray's preliminary work survives for public access: the Sackler Library in Oxford holds, among its inheritance from his library, his copy of Volume 3 of Kirchhoff's minor edition of 1867–8; it contains *Ion* (Murray's eventual Vol. II), *Cyclops* and *Medea* (Vol. I), *Orestes, Phoenissae*, and *Rhesus* (Vol. III). Into it Murray entered various manuscript readings not in Kirchhoff's brief apparatus—mostly, it appears to me, from his major edition of 1855 (this is consistent with his own acknowledgement in his first volume (Murray 1902a, p. viii). The margins have a few conjectures, possibly occurring to Murray himself but which were not in fact original; in his edition itself they are correctly attributed on the basis of Wecklein's apparatus, e.g. *Ion* 764 (Hermann), *Medea* 781 (Burges), and 1374 (Weil). Most interestingly, Murray pasted in against *Medea* 214–26 in this book a first draft of the 'dramatic paraphrase' printed in his later apparatus (on this paraphrase see Wecklein's review [1902], cited at n. 42). The first and second volumes of Murray's smaller Kirchhoff contain no marginalia at all, however; this is hard to explain.

Murray describes the main principles underlying his economical apparatus: he disregards as many minutiae and obvious errors as possible, except where they may be material to establishing the text or purifying it of error (Vol. I, p. ix); he sets out his approach to orthography (p. x); he follows Wecklein in the attribution of conjectures, while allowing that this may result in errors (p. x). His Praefatio in Vol. II enlarges on the status of conjectures he reports: he has tried not to pass over any likely to be correct, but he warns that he may not himself support every conjecture he reports.[26] The result was

[26] Second unnumbered page. In Vol. 1 p. x, he had said generally about attributions, 'no doubt I have often been wrong, for convincing conjectures should occur to any critic, and it makes little difference which one, or even whether an anonymous scribe, first wrote them down'; these words remind me of a very much older but similar formulation by J. Markland in his edition of Statius' *Silvae* (Markland 1728, p. xiii): (translated) 'for what difference does it make, from what quarter Truth comes, provided that it does come?' In a letter to R. W. Chapman of the Press of 8 Aug. 1912 Murray wrote, 'I never took much trouble to find out who first' (I cite from Prof. Francis West's correspondence with me). Later that year, Chapman responded to Pearson's review of Murray's Euripides OCT Vol. III (Pearson 1912: see the main text at n. 48, below) with '*Pearson on Attributions* will give you some trouble... The matter of attribution leaves me cold; but truth is truth, no doubt' (16 Oct. 1912: GM 397)—a surprising remark from a classicist who contemplated an exact study of Greek particles before Denniston,

an apparatus concise in accord with the general practice of the Oxford Classical Texts, and one logically and clearly arranged. Quite often he gives help through translation or paraphrase, especially where he defends the manuscript tradition, and he regularly gives parallels for usage or meaning; he interweaves occasional appreciation of the play's movement, a habit true to his special interest in the dramatic and theatrical[27]—a very live habit, since some plays in his translation were first produced on the stage while the critical edition was in progress.[28] In this regard the well-known sentence from his Praefatio to Vol. I (p. xi) is all-important: 'Plus interpretationis eget, me iudice, Euripides quam emendationis' ('It is interpretation that Euripides needs, in my judgement, more than emendation').[29]

and judged his 'big book' on the subject (Denniston 1934) unfavourably—as did Murray in his letter to Stanley Baldwin (n. 6 above): 'though very exact and careful, (it) has not much illumination about it', a judgement with which very few grateful users would agree. Chapman later produced the critical edition of Jane Austen which became, like Murray's Euripides, standard for eighty years.

While M. Davies 2006, 14 compared Murray and Housman for their dependence upon others' collations (n. 24 above), James Diggle contrasts Murray's lack of care over attributions with Housman's scruple, and refers to Housman's *Manilius* v (Housman 1930, p. xxxii): (translated) 'some (editors) so much prefer error to knowledge that even when we patient drudges have ascertained the facts for them they continue to disseminate misinformation.' Diggle cites also D. L. Page's *Poetae Melici Graeci* (D. L. Page 1962, p. ix): (translated) 'in naming the authors of emendations I have used considerable effort' (but for his OCT of Aeschylus Page was able to rely for attributions on Dawe 1965: Page 1972, p. v). For Murray's claimed corrections and conjectures in Aeschylus, see Section IV.

27 Amusing here is a letter cited by C. Archer in his account of his father's friendship with Murray (Archer 1936, 36–7), which includes Murray's definition of an apparatus for a layman: 'An apparatus criticus is a list of Ms. variations, with occasional remarks thereon. Only men of the highest moral character, religion, and social grace can produce one satisfactorily.' The definition is cited by D. Wilson 1987, 114. Again I am reminded of Markland in his *Statius*, writing of textual scholarship and editing: (translated) 'The truth is, learning is absurd without a good character' (Markland 1728, iv).

28 Cf. the main text at n. 30 above and the n. itself. See Ackerman 1986 on T. S. Eliot's attack on Murray's translations, cf. Lloyd-Jones 1982, 204–8; and now both J. Morwood's Introduction to the reprint of Gilbert Murray's Euripides translations (Morwood 2005), and his chapter in this volume.

29 The passage was picked up by Pearson 1912: see below. It is cited at greater length by Easterling 1997, 115, who describes it as 'magnificent' and as summing up Murray's 'consistent attitude to all aspects of his work on Euripides'; earlier, by e.g. R. Kannicht, *Helena* (Heidelberg, 1969), 1.128; recently by M. Davies 2006, 27 n. 84.

While Murray worked on his edited text and apparatus, he simultaneously translated Euripides, a procedure he later followed for Aeschylus.[30] He discussed his editing regularly with the officers of the Press, and with both Wilamowitz and Verrall before and after he sent them proofs. He corresponded at times with E. Bruhn, W. G. Headlam, A. E. Housman, E. C. Marchant, J. U. Powell, and R. Y. Tyrrell, whom he thanked in his first two volumes; a little of their correspondence survives in the Gilbert Murray Papers (chiefly GM 8 and 9). The great loss of the proofs marked by Wilamowitz and Verrall, which would have illuminated Murray's methods and judgements in response very clearly, is partly offset by the survival of one very detailed letter from Wilamowitz when he returned proofs for *Alcestis* and *Medea*: it is Letter 8 (16 June 1901) in Wilamowitz-Moellendorff 1991, 35–47; the editors have carefully compared it with Murray's eventual text. Murray is revealed as variably receptive to Wilamowitz' suggestions for change, and for reducing his apparatus; but since Wilamowitz' name is so frequent in Murray's apparatus throughout the entire edition, it may be inferred that Murray chose to use a very considerable proportion of his suggestions.

In the Praefatio to Vol. I (Murray 1902a, p. x), Murray said that he had made innovations in the setting-out of the lyric verses; he continued his method in his two later volumes. It caused disquiet, and in his Vol. III (Murray 1909a, pp. v–vii), he tried to explain it fully in response to a request by Paul Maas, who was already a prominent metrical scholar.[31] Murray had evidently been aware of the disquiet, for he defended his unaltered presentation of the lyrics

[30] F. J. West 1984, 88, 224. Chris Stray reminds me of Jebb's remark that 'A translator of the Characters is forced to become also an editor', in his edition of Theophrastus (Jebb 1870, vi). Stray raises also the interesting question, whether Murray's occasional desire for echoing in his translations something of the original Greek lyric rhythms, may actually have influenced in reverse the constitution of his text in Euripides and Aeschylus. For Murray's desire see his note on his translation of Euripides' *Bacchae* (Morwood 2005, 468)); cf. Morwood in this volume on Aeschylus' *Persians* 647–81 (p. xxx). I have discussed this question with James Morwood; we see no obvious way to answer it, except through a difficult and subjective comparison of Greek and English in those plays for which he was working almost simultaneously on the text and the translation, and through a search for any hints in his correspondence which his biographers (F. J. West 1984, D. Wilson 1987) may not have picked up.

[31] This appears to have been the first contact between the two men. Later they worked closely together in Oxford upon the second edition of Murray's *Aeschylus*: see Section IV.

in the second edition of his Vol. II (1908). The issue was technical, and related to the practice initiated by editors as early as the third century BC, in Alexandria: they used 'indenting' or 'in-setting' (Greek *eisthesis*) to signal a change of metre, especially from spoken to lyric verse. By Murray's time, scholarship had begun to employ 'indenting' within lyric passages to mark close prosodic continuity between adjacent verses, particularly at the end of sequences of identical or related metres or 'periods'. Murray explained in his Vol. III that he steered a middle course, but at times inconsistently, between observation of editorial convention and readers' convenience; he desired always to make clear to them both the nature of the metre and the articulation of differing metres. Accordingly he used both single and double-length indenting (e.g. *Cyc.* 608–23, *Andr.* 465–94)—and sometimes extended line-beginnings to the left, giving the impression of triple indenting (e.g. *Hec.* 169, 172; 195 = 214; *Pho.* 302–54). Even after this explanation in Murray's Vol. III, Pearson at least was not convinced of its soundness (Pearson 1912, 158). In fact Murray maintained his method in his editions of Aeschylus, creating fresh disquiet at the Press (e.g. 'triple' out- and in-setting at *Supp.* 40–175, *Sept.* 109–49; cf. Section IV below at n. 54).

There were aspects of the work which Murray did not greatly like, as he admitted. First, there was his equivocal attitude to the hard work of first-hand collation, both strenuous (above) and rewarding, but also frustrating. For example, he was dissatisfied with others' study, and his own, of the relationship between two famous manuscripts in Italy (L and the uncertainly dependent P), which was complicated by the multiple and successive corrections in the first of them. Wecklein regarded his own solution as closing the issue (1902, col. 933); Murray however returned to it from his Vol. I (pp. vi–vii) in his Vol. II and again in Vol. III (where he wrote, 'if it had been possible to go back to the Italian mss., I would have tried for a better differentiation of the correcting hands of ms. L' (Murray 1909a, p. iii).[32] Second, there was his reluctance to verify the attribution of conjectures, already remarked. Third, he had a certain dislike

[32] I have not found that this remark was picked up explicitly by either A. Turyn or G. Zuntz in their studies of the problem: Turyn 1957, 222–58, Zuntz 1965.

for reading others' scholarship, especially in German (testimony of Jane Harrison, cited at Wilamowitz-Moellendorff 1991, 73 n. 315). Fourth, Murray referred eventually to his 'disgusting task', a remark apparently made as he neared the completion of his Vol. 3 (letter to R. W. Chapman of 11 Aug. 1908 (GM 397), cited by F. J. West 1984, 85). Although Murray's edition sold extremely well, and was reprinted many times, he did no further work of revision after the second edition of his Vol. III in 1913; here he made a few changes in response to criticism; in Vol. II he made more substantial corrections and improvements in both its second edition of 1908 and third of 1913; Vol. I appears never to have been revised. I have not been able to verify the statement in D. Wilson 1987, 394 that in 1941 Murray 'was revising . . . his text of Euripides'.[33]

A frequently used criterion of an editor's improvement upon his predecessors is the extent, and quality, of his own claimed corrections and new conjectures upon the text.[34] I have done a swift count of Murray's claimed corrections, whether alterations to the text, improved punctuation (including his notorious supposition of 'breaks in sense' such as *Alc.* 198, 1124, *Hipp.* 99, *Supp.* 45, *HF* 575, *El.*. 671–81 (six examples), Tro. 711–23 (three), 1226), revision or addition of voice-parts, particularly of semi-choruses, or revisions in the analysis and setting out of lyrics, all of which he signalled usually by *scripsi, correxi, (partes) distribui*: my total is 210 such 'corrections' printed in his edited text. I have counted also his conjectures which are confined to the apparatus, and signalled most often by *fortasse, malim, possis (-es)*: my total is 249. Such counts are very unreliable, given their inherent imprecision and any counter's individual subjectivity, but also the often incomplete and inaccurate

[33] Unless Wilson made a slip, putting 'Euripides' for 'Aeschylus'. Wilson gives no source—but he had completed his manuscript only as far as the year 1935 at his death, and the rest of the book was put together from his notes by his widow Elizabeth: see her Preface, D. Wilson 1987, p. ix.

[34] Not less true tests are his corrections of other editors' reports of mss. readings, and his new defences of the mss. tradition. Murray could offer few of the first, but see his implicit corrections in the apparatus for example at *Supp.* 402, 435, *Herc.* 1172, *Ion* 39, 386, 545, 676, 780 (all of these in his Vol. II, into which he could begin to feed his collations of 1903). He did sometimes claim the second, for example at *Ion* 691–2, *Tro.* 565–6, *El.* 719, 1107–8, *IA* 627, if to the disbelief of his few reviewers (see below).

documentation of corrections or conjectures by earlier editors;[35] in Euripides this is despite the marvellous industry of Wecklein in the appendices and addenda et corrigenda attached to his major edition.[36] Then there is the value of these claims to later editors. I first did one brief check for *Medea*: of five 'corrections' only one is mentioned in his 1992 Teubner edition by H. Van Looy (line 1255), and of thirteen conjectures also only one (1077); not one is mentioned by Diggle (1984).[37] Then I checked the adoption of Murray's 'corrections' in the whole of Diggle's Vol. II (Diggle 1981): he puts into his text (Diggle's order of plays), *Supplices* 1 out of Murray's 14; *Electra* 3/9;*Hercules* 2/9; *Troades* 5/20; *Iphigenia in Tauris* 2/18; *Ion* 2/14; of conjectures confined to Murray's apparatus Diggle mentions in his own only: *Supplices* 1 out of Murray's 17; *Electra* 3/10; *Hercules* 4/13; *Troades* 5/16; *Iphigenia in Tauris* 2/12; *Ion* 0/13.

Murray himself was clear and open that the credit for his first volume was due mainly to Wilamowitz, stating that 'I make more mistakes than most people! And I may be disgracing myself by some uncorrected asininity!'[38] Despite Wilamowitz' doubts of Murray's

[35] My figures for Murray's claims in the 19 plays, in the order of Murray's text, are: (Vol. I) *Cyclops* 10 'corrections'/9 'conjectures'; *Alcestis* 13/8; *Medea* 5/13; *Heraclidae* 8/14; *Hippolytus* 15/10; *Andromacha* 7/26; *Hecuba* 7/10; (Vol. II) *Supplices* 14/17; *Hercules* 9/13; *Ion* 14/13; *Troiades* 20/16; *Electra* 9/10; *Iphigenia Taurica* 18/12; (Vol. III) *Helena* 19/17; *Phoenissae* 8/7; *Orestes* 8/8; *Bacchae* 6/10; *Iphigenia Aulidensis* 12/32; *Rhesus* 8/4. The figures are generally a little higher for the plays which depend upon the single Florentine ms. L; but the high number of conjectures in *Andromacha* is surprising.

[36] Dawe 1990, 377–8 totals original corrections and conjectures made by scholars of Greek tragedy from the 16th cent. to the present. Reiterating his earlier caution (Dawe 1985) about the unreliability of attributions and therefore of counts, Dawe totals 88 actual original proposals for Murray in his Vol. III, where my count of his claims was 139; and for all three volumes 270, where my count was 459. Subsequently see e.g. Diggle 1994a, 518–23, and the appendixes to the individual editions published by Teubner (see the end of this Section).

[37] For Diggle's judgement in the round of Murray's edition see the end of this Section. I myself made some scattered evaluative comparisons between Murray's and Diggle's editions of Euripides in my reviews of Diggle's first two volumes: vol. 2 (1981) at *Classical Review* 34 (1984) 9–15; vol. 1 (1984) at *Classical Review* 36 (1986) 17–24.

[38] GM Adds. 2, a letter of Murray to W. Archer of 2 July 1901, cited by D. Wilson 1987, 116 n. 17. After the remarkable tribute in the closing words of the Praefatio to Vol. I (Murray 1902a, p. xi), he did not modify his expression of supreme indebtedness to Wilamowitz in his later two volumes: Murray 1904, second unnumbered page; Murray 1909a, p. vii (once again the closing words of the Praefatio).

scholarship (beginning of this Section), he gave the published edition his general approval—he could hardly do otherwise—and wrote to the Press with anxiety that it might not be promoted well enough in Germany.[39] When it came to reviews there were extraordinarily few.[40] Murray expected (and received) bad reviews by Wecklein; the only review at home came after the entire edition was complete, but it was as authoritative as any could have been at that time in Britain, by A. C. Pearson, who had himself published good annotated editions of *Helen* (1903), *Heraclidae* (1907), and *Phoenissae* (1909) (Pearson 1912). It may be useful to summarize both Wecklein and Pearson here.

Wecklein (1902), reviewing Vol. I, was as mean-spirited as Wilamowitz had forecast.[41] He categorized Murray's faults, illustrating each with many examples, but especially his failure to understand his text, and the connection of its ideas, thoroughly, for this is the first duty of a textual critic (cols. 929–30); then came Murray's lack of feeling for Euripides' language and style (931–2), and his incomprehensible or aimless alterations to the text while many obvious corrections or

[39] Revealed in an internal Press note from Charles Cannan to H. Frowde, dated 31 Jan. 1905, cited by F. J. West 1984, 118.

[40] S. Lambrino, *Bibliographie de l'antiquité classique, 1896–1914*, 1 (Paris, 1951), 199 lists four reviews for Vol. I, most prominently by Wecklein himself (1902); two for Vol. II, and two for Vol. III, one again by Wecklein (1911) and the other by Pearson (Pearson 1912). There were to be similarly few reviews for Murray's *Aeschylus* (see Section IV). I cannot explain this paucity of reviews, in either the early or the mid-20th cent.: there were journals enough to print them. It is remarkable that Murray received no reviews at all, for either his *Euripides* or his *Aeschylus*, in the *Journal of Hellenic Studies*.

[41] Letter 22 in Wilamowitz-Moellendorff 1991, 62, of 14 June 1904, cited by F. J. West 1984, 118. Wecklein's review of vol. 1 (Wecklein 1902), and that of vol. 3 (Wecklein 1911), conformed with his usual dismissive hostility towards other editors of Euripides and Aeschylus: so for example towards the Budé editor of Aeschylus, P. Mazon, in *Berliner Philologische Wochenschrift* 46 (1926) cols. 114–15, and the Loeb editor, H. W. Smyth, ibid. cols. 769–70. It is interesting to contrast a British reviewer of Wecklein's *Euripides*, the able scholar E. B. England (for whom see Todd 2004, 1.290–1): evaluating Wecklein's Vol. II.2 *Supplices* and Vol. II.4 *Heraclidae* at *Classical Review* 15 (1901) 54–8, England combined exemplary politeness with exemplary firmness: 'excellent work . . . thoroughness and accuracy of the new collations . . . editor's learning and judgement . . . the question (however) whether . . . the editor has not allowed himself too free a hand . . . replacing, not the bad by the good, but the good by what he holds to be better . . . has not the editor been rather too partial, *seeing that this is a standard edition*, to his own suggestions?' The italics are mine: England was writing before Murray published his first volume.

emendations went unmentioned (933); his deficiency in the fundamental task of evaluating manuscripts and his ignorance of the latest scholarship upon them (933–4). In sum, Wecklein judged the edition to be a step backward (935); and he repeated these criticisms throughout his review of Vol. III (1911). He allowed Murray a few possibly correct conjectures in (1902), remarking that it was exactly those which Murray had put into his text which were unusable; the only thing he praised was the handy and pleasing get-up of the volumes (1911, col. 257).[42] It was indeed a mean-spirited evaluation. Pearson's review of Vol. III was more balanced, as one would expect from so level-headed a critic. Commending Murray's labour in 'verifying his own collations and those of others', and his apparatus as 'reasonable in compass' and judicious in content, he judges the edition 'undoubtedly the most convenient that exists' (Pearson 1912, 155). Then, however, he makes similar complaints to Wecklein's about the inaccurate attribution of conjectures, giving a very long list of examples, and about Murray's refusal to accept obvious and established remedies, while nevertheless praising a number of 'attractive and ingenious corrections'.[43]

[42] Wecklein 1902 named as successful in Murray's Vol. I the conjectures at *Heracl.* 289, 597, 747, *Andr.* 723, *Med.* 209, *Hec.* 478, 901; of these seven, only *Andr.* 723 is mentioned in his apparatus by Diggle. Wecklein (ibid., 931) was hard too on Murray's 'paraphrases': I noted above that on *Med.* 214–26, and Wecklein wrote of it (translated) 'One may say that no word of this stands in the text.' (One is reminded of similar complaints about Murray's translations: see Bowra 1966, 218, cf. Morwood 2005, p. xi.). For other paraphrases, see for example Murray's *Heracl.* 1018–19, *Ion* 1266–81, *IT* 98, *IA* 627.

It appears that Murray was the first to introduce such paraphrases, and also occasional translations or illustrative comparisons, to the apparatus of the Oxford Classical Texts, for I have found none, at least in other Greek ones, earlier than or contemporary with Murray's (Aeschylus, Antoninus, Apollonius Rhodius, Aristophanes, Aristotle ('Ethics' and 'Poetics'), Demosthenes, Homer, Xenophon), until H. Diels later composed the generous apparatus of his Theophrastus ('Characters') in 1909. The innovation was most commendable, continued in Aeschylus by Murray, and followed in its general style by Diggle for his Euripides (Diggle 1981, 1984, 1994b).

[43] *Hel.* 196, 372, 866, 1387; *Pho.* 793, 1714; *Bacch.* 294; *IA* 234, 385, 590; *Rhes.* 256, 849; of these twelve, Diggle puts *Hel.* 196 and *IA* 385 into his text, and mentions *Pho.* 1714 and *Bacch.* 294 in his apparatus. Murray reacted by writing to Pearson rather defensively, much in the vein of his letters over the years to the officers of the Press (his letter is cited by F. J. West 1984, 120; I have been unable to locate it). He wrote that he was 'shocked at the... inaccuracies of which I appear to be guilty'. He apologized over the false attributions, in words which recall his earlier defences and

The best testimony to Murray's edition, however, was its durability, worldwide. Usage established that it was serviceable, for the great part dependable and sensible, and certainly better than any other, so that it justly lasted so long as the standard. It was reprinted for almost all the famous 'red-back' Oxford Clarendon Press commentaries on individual plays between 1938 and 1971 (see n. 6). There were some authoritative general appraisals of Murray's whole edition up to the 1980s, first by R. Kannicht in 1969 (n. 29 above). Then H. Lloyd-Jones wrote: 'his Euripides has remained the best edition for more than half a century, and many things in it reveal the exquisite feeling for Greek that we know from his memorable versions' (Lloyd-Jones 1982, 20); (Murray lacked the necessary training in sound scholarship but was) 'a subtle and ingenious textual critic; indeed, his main fault lies in an excess of these qualities, fostered by the disastrous influence of the clever but sophistic... Verrall' (on whom see above, n. 20) (ibid., 201); here and at 209–10 Lloyd-Jones was evaluating Murray's ingenuity both in defending the manuscripts and in conjecturing for their improvement. Above all there was the judgement of the Oxford editor who eventually superseded Murray, J. Diggle, who praised the edition for showing general good judgement and usefully reporting the best of earlier scholarship (Diggle 1984, p. x: noted by Easterling 1997, 113 n. 2). Diggle recognized its mostly derivative and variably adequate reports of manuscript readings, but marked its superiority nevertheless in this respect to the Budé edition, begun in 1923 but not completed until 2004, and often also to the Teubner editions of individual plays, with almost always a different editor for each, published over thirty years until the 1990s.

excuses (see e.g. n. 26 above): 'I never took much trouble to find out who had really proposed a particular conjecture first.... As to manuscript readings, I may sometimes be right against Wecklein' (see e.g. the main text at n. 32).... 'I am only too conscious that great press of work during volume 3 and which prevented volume 4 may have led me into many bad slips.' His 'volume 4' was to have contained the fragments: see n. 16 above.

IV THE OXFORD *AESCHYLUS*

The early history of this edition is much harder to trace than for Euripides; again, documents which would have been especially revealing seem no longer to exist. The fullest general account is given by F. J. West 1984, 224–5; D. Wilson 1987, 320–1 is briefer (see n. 33). The first suggestion to Murray that he should replace Sidgwick's Oxford *Aeschylus* (1899) was from Charles Cannan at the Press in 1915; Sidgwick had from the beginning acknowledged his edition as weak and unconfident work.[44] Two further requests came from Cannan's successor R. W. Chapman in 1919, when Sidgwick's edition had finally sold out; but in 1921 Chapman was 'not in a hurry'; an internal Press document written by Chapman in 1922 says of Murray's *Aeschylus* 'that it is a revision of Sidgwick's now obsolete edition and may (underlined) never come along'.[45] Although Murray is recorded on 5 August 1930 as 'raging' to do Aeschylus,[46] there is then apparently a gap in the correspondence preserved both in the Press files and in the Gilbert Murray Papers until 1935, when Murray is negotiating the contents of the volume and intending to omit the fragments (which Sidgwick had included in his edition). In that year he can tell Chapman that he has finished a draft of the apparatus; and Kenneth Sisam of the Press writes to him that it had been agreed 'that it would be better to get out Aeschylus, and leave the fragments for some later time, if ever'. Yet early in 1936 Murray sent Chapman a note accompanying finished copy for the edition.[47]

[44] Cannan: a letter of 8 June 1915, GM 397. Sidgwick's admission was in a letter to Murray of 25 June 1898, GM 168: see my entry for Sidgwick in Todd 2004, 3.893 and cf. n. 12 above. Sidgwick's principal shortcoming as editor was his adherence wherever possible to the single most authoritative ms., a mode of textual editing already discredited in Germany by the mid-19th cent.

[45] Respectively Chapman to Murray of 19 Aug. (in which he discouragingly writes 'Edit Aeschylus and die!') and 21 Aug. 1919, and of 3 Feb. 1921, all in GM 397.

[46] M. I. Henderson 1960, 146; she does not identity the correspondent. 'Raging' is cited by F. J. West 1984, 224.

[47] Murray to Chapman of 29 Mar. 1935 and 6 Sept. 1935; Sisam to Murray of 30 Sept. 1935; Murray to Chapman of 1 Feb. 1936; all in GM 398.

It is not evident why Murray agreed to edit Aeschylus so few as six years after completing his Euripides in 1909 (see however D. Wilson 1987, 116); but that he took a further twenty years to finish the edition is explicable from his heavy involvement with 'peace work' and the new League of Nations.[48] There is nevertheless a puzzle here: Murray began his academic career conventionally with a desire to edit texts, including Euripides, and agreed, naturally enough, to undertake the poet for Oxford rather than for his own series; but although he wearied of an editor's work, he soon agreed to return to it. Possibly he had an underlying motive, an act of duty to his mentor and friend Arthur Sidgwick, whose early Oxford edition of Aeschylus had been unsatisfactory (see n. 44). For a number of reasons there can be only speculation about the initial project, and its timing. The scholarly circumstances were favourable, in that Wilamowitz had in 1914 published his major edition, establishing the basis for any sound future work on the poet's text, upon which Murray could readily rely; and unfavourable, in that World War I had begun and Wilamowitz, who had so helped the Euripides, could hardly be invited again to begin correspondence, let alone 'cooperation'. There is however just a scrap of evidence that Murray might have asked Wilamowitz' advice about Aeschylus, even in 1915, during the War, and actually before Cannan's formal invitation to Murray of that year.[49] It seems likely that Murray began to study his text carefully, and to draft material, only after the War had ended, for throughout the 1920s and early 1930s he was beginning to publish his translations of individual plays; and he was following for Aeschylus his practice with Euripides of preparing his edition as he translated.[50]

The manuscript base for Aeschylus is much more slender than that for Euripides, but for this edition Murray nevertheless did no

[48] For Murray's energetic life in these years see M. I. Henderson 1960, 106–15, F. J. West 1984, 143–208, and D. Wilson 1987, 217–310.

[49] Wilamowitz replied to a now lost letter of Murray on 22 Mar. 1915 (no. 57 in Wilamowitz-Moellendorff 1991, 115–17): (translated) 'Aeschylus has rather vanished from my mind'. Why otherwise should Wilamowitz write this at that time?

[50] F. J. West 1984, 224, cf. above at n. 30. The translated *Agamemnon* appeared in 1920, *Choephori* 1923, *Eumenides* 1925, *Suppliants* 1930, *Prometheus* 1931 (Murray held the arguments over its authenticity to be inconclusive: Murray 1937, p. ix); *Seven against Thebes* 1935. *Persians* followed the completed critical edition, in 1939. The plays of the *Oresteia* came out together in 1928, with a second edition in 1946; all seven plays were reprinted in one volume in 1952.

original collating, or evaluation of the evidence, at all. He was therefore dependent even more heavily for his report of manuscript readings upon his predecessors than he had been for Euripides; but in doubtful places he at least used the facsimile of the supremely important Medicean manuscript in Florence (M): Praefatio p. v. He is open about this, and scaled his derivative reports of manuscripts midway between those in Wilamowitz' major edition of 1914 and the much thinner ones of P. Mazon in the Budé edition and of H. Weir Smyth in the Loeb edition, both of the 1920s.[51] He admits also to not having been able to examine all he would have wished of the scholarly literature upon Aeschylus (Murray 1937, p. v). On pp. vii ff. he sets out briefly his view of his text-critical task, one which recalls his approach to Euripides ('Plus interpretationis etc.', cited above: Section III at n. 32): he believes Aeschylus' text not corrupt enough to create despair among editors, arguing chiefly from the surviving accuracy of lyric responsion, the occasional superior readings to be found in ancient citations, and the singularity of Aeschylus' diction (which too many critics had tried to regularize by the false application of Attic standards). He illustrates his belief that the chief causes of mistakes were transcription from uncial to minuscule, but also corrupted verse-order or actors' interpolations. His confidence in the text's quality was not shared by his readers.

[51] Murray gave Chapman at the Press his opinion that Wilamowitz had contributed most work on Aeschylus, but 'his actual text seems to me not nearly so good as either Mazon's or Weir Smyth's': letter of 6 Sept. 1935: GM 398. This opinion is not expressed in the edition itself. Wecklein had dismissively reviewed both Mazon's and Smyth's editions as inadequate and faulty (see n. 41 above). The *Gnomon* reviewer of them both, G. Meyer, 4 (1928) 364–72, wrote in the same way as Wecklein of Mazon's (comparing it unfavourably with Wilamowitz' major and minor editions of 1914: Wecklein would not even mention Wilamowitz: see my n. 18), but praised Smyth's for accuracy and reliability while regretting its conservatism. It was this quality in both Mazon and Smyth which would have appealed to Murray. In contrast with Meyer, A. C. Pearson, *Classical Review* 41 (1927) 323–5, judged that Mazon's 'text challenges comparison with that of Wilamowitz'; he commended Mazon's discussion of the ms. tradition, and the principles of his apparatus. Pearson's judgement largely repeated that of 'A.W.M.' (A. W. Mair?), *Journal of Hellenic Studies* 42 (1922) 112–14. Murray's copy of Wilamowitz' major edition survives in the Sackler Library at Oxford. It has many in-text alterations and annotations (but very few original conjectures) in various inks and pencils; it appears to be Murray's earliest work when making his own text. His notes are much more numerous in the plays other than those of the *Oresteia*.

His failure to engage closely enough with manuscript evidence caused him greater difficulty with a formidable scholar no less fierce in expectation than Wilamowitz had been over Euripides, Eduard Fraenkel (a pupil of Wilamowitz); and Fraenkel was himself in Oxford from late 1934, not at the safe distance of the postal services. It was Fraenkel's exacting work upon Murray's draft and proofs that led to the 'tough genesis' of the 1937 first edition.[52] Other helpers are named on p. x of the Praefatio, who, Murray states with some poignancy, took the place of those whom he thanked for his Euripides, now all dead (see above, Section III). Fraenkel closes the list, with the most explicit acknowledgement, after D. S. Robertson, L. Radermacher, E. Lobel, and E. A. Barber: '(Fraenkel) whose tireless intellect and acumen, in a close reading of the proofs, freed me and my book from many faults'.

The edition was badly received, especially in Oxford. There was the absence of new and personal collations. Murray was thought too ready to defend the manuscripts from correction or conjecture. His attribution of others' conjectures was too often wrong, and his own were usually unconvincing. There were too many misprints. Some local criticism was due to Murray's suspected (and subsequently confirmed) recommendation of E. R. Dodds, and not any internal aspirant, as his successor in the Regius Chair of Greek in 1936 (see n. 6). The mere fact of Murray's recent retirement may have prompted a fitting silence about the Aeschylus rather than open

[52] The phrase is that of M. I. Henderson 1960, 146, citing Murray's plaintive 'Fraenkel treats me with some severity'; cf. F. J. West 1964, 224. Fraenkel fled from Germany to Britain late in 1934, and was soon appointed to the Corpus Chair of Latin at Oxford. A few of Murray's responses to Fraenkel's criticisms survive from the years 1936–7 in the Fraenkel Papers in the Corpus Christi College Archive, but not the proofs; the letters relate to *Ag.* 1299–end and *Supp.* 364–end. Similarly, only a few of Fraenkel's letters to Murray are preserved in the Gilbert Murray Papers. Fraenkel apologized to Murray for being 'peremptory': letter of 13 Mar. 1936 (GM 67), cited by D. Wilson 1987, 321 n. 38.

As to Fraenkel's marked proofs: there has been word in Oxford that some had been preserved in the former Ashmolean Museum Library (now the Sackler Library). A search in late 2005 in that Library, among the Gilbert Murray Papers, and in the libraries of both Corpus Christi College and (so Malcolm Davies told me) St John's College (Murray's college as an undergraduate), revealed nothing. M. Davies 2006, 14 says that to those who like himself had seen them, Murray's description of Fraenkel's severity is an 'ironic understatement'.

criticism; and the disappointed aspirants, together with some other Oxford critics, had in fact already contributed fully to a presentation volume in Murray's honour (Bailey et al. 1936). There were even fewer reviews than for the three-volume Euripides. I have found only three, two of them mere notices, but one which listed and illustrated the faults set out above.[53] The revision of the first edition of 1937 in the second of 1955 appears better documented than Murray's initial work upon Aeschylus. I am not quite clear why in his mid-eighties, he agreed to, or felt that he must, go back to Aeschylus. Murray was however well aware of the volume's defects. The need for a second edition was felt by the Press, and not only because copies of the first were becoming exhausted by 1950 (in fact there were two further reprintings, in 1951 and 1953). Did the Press so respect Murray's now great eminence that the invitation was inevitable? The first suggestion was for a photographic reprint with corrections; but a letter of P. J. Spicer to Murray in 1951 refers to 'your new edition', and a further one in 1954 writes of the 'protracted process of revising your Aeschylus . . . likely we shall find it economical of time and money to reset the whole thing in preference to trying to tinker with the plates.' Spicer suggests 'reconsidering the arrangement of the lyrical passages, which so far as I know differs from continental practice and may fairly be said to be unique. If we are going to the trouble of resetting, we would like the edition to be as perfect as it can be made, provided that this will not entail much further delay in the timetable, so that the new edition could stand unchanged for a number of years.'[54] Murray received particular help from Paul Maas, with whom he had been in contact since 1909 (also see n. 31), and whose welcome as a refugee in Oxford in 1939 Murray ensured

[53] W. E. Muir, *Classical Review*, 52 (1938) 173–4. Also: P. Chantraine, *Revue de Philologie*, 13 (1937) 68, who drew attention mostly to Murray's new conjectures, and R. C. Flickinger (not a textual scholar), *Classical Philology*, 34 (1939) 401, who judged inexpertly that the edition made considerable progress. M. Davies 2006, 14 observes that it has achieved 'virtually iconic status in the world of scholarship' for its failings; cf. Lloyd-Jones 1982, 209: '(it) has little that is new and good to set against its marked perversity and inaccuracy'.

[54] Letters successively of D. Davin of 31 Aug. 1950 ('photographic reprint'), and Spicer on 18 July 1951 and 4 Jan. 1954, all in GM 398. There had been a much earlier letter of K. Sisam to Murray of 3 Mar. 1941, suggesting that 'corrections . . . be made when opportunity offers'. For Murray's individual 'arrangement of the lyrical passages' see Section III above, at n. 31.

(Lloyd-Jones 1982, 213, 216, and 1991, 210; F. J. West 1984, 225). Other helpers were E. R. Dodds, E. Lobel, and in a small way D. L. Page (evidently now reconciled to Murray); Murray thanks all these in his Praefatio. As with the first edition, however, very little correspondence between them survives, and also none of the proofs (or any manuscript) which Murray again showed Fraenkel; who however gets no acknowledgement in the edition.[55] Despite this help, Murray described the volume only as an updating, with little that was new; nevertheless, he hoped that it really was an 'editio emendatior' (p. v). In fact the edition was freshly set, although with little change to its distinctive setting-out of the lyrics (of which Murray gave no explanation whatever in either edition: contrast his behaviour in Vol. III of his Euripides, for which again see Section III at n. 31 above; also n. 61). For 1955 Murray expanded his description and evaluation of the manuscripts only slightly (see below), but he now included the fragments of the tetralogies associated with the plays outside the *Oresteia.* In his Praefatio he was reluctant to follow the general inference from the new Oxyrhynchus Papyrus 2256 fr. 3 (published in 1952) that *Supplices* was not Aeschylus' earliest surviving play; instead, he suggested that its mode of recording the play's performance was anomalous, and might well have related to an occasion or revival outside Athens.

The second edition of 1955 was reissued in 1957, after the Press warned Murray that stocks were low; he was asked to sanction a list of corrigenda to put at the end (P. J. Spicer to Murray, 11 Mar. 1957: GM 398). About the same time, the Press's C. H. Roberts wrote to Murray, 'I hear the Aeschylus is again in the melting pot; I shall look forward to see what transformation takes place this time' (Roberts to Murray, 4 Mar. 1957: GM 398). Roberts is referring to a proposed third edition, on which Murray and Maas had started work early that year, possibly by themselves. They were joined briefly by

[55] There are four very brief letters from Murray to Fraenkel in the Corpus Christi Archive, three written shortly before the second edition's publication in 1955, and one before its corrected reissue of 1957. Some postcards and notes from Maas to Murray are in GM 102 and 104, many with detailed comment on particular passages. Of the four letters from Murray to Fraenkel from 1953–6 in the Corpus Archive, only the last short letter of 17 Aug. 1936 bears on the text of Aeschylus.

H. Lloyd-Jones, before Murray died on 20 May 1957, and no further work appears to have been done.[56]

Opinion of the Aeschylus hardly changed even after the improved second edition: it was still further behind the progress of manuscript studies; too many weaknesses of critical method remained. Fraenkel had not even mentioned the first edition in the Preface, in the chapter 'Some Editions and Commentaries', and the Index to his *Agamemnon* (Fraenkel 1950). The next Oxford editor of Aeschylus, D. L. Page (1972), gave even the second edition no mention in his Praefatio (nor had he when he 'supplied' the Greek text and apparatus for J. D. Denniston and D. L. Page, *Aeschylus, Agamemnon*, Oxford, 1957: see Page's Praefatio, p. vi). M. L. West referred to Murray only once in the Praefatio to his Teubner edition of 1990, and in order to criticize him (and Page before him) for renumbering lines transposed in the lyrics (p. liii n. 21). Before Page and West, there had been a devastating critique of the edition's obsolete manuscript base and methodology by R. D. Dawe in his *Collation and Investigation ot the Manuscripts of Aeschylus* (Dawe 1964, 7–10; cf. Dawe 1965, 6). The second edition, like the first, was barely noticed by journals.[57]

I return to Fraenkel. His annotated proofs of Murray's Aeschylus (of either or both editions) may be lost, but what he was willing to publish in comment on Murray's work may be found occasionally in the Commentary to his *Agamemnon* (Fraenkel 1950). There is nevertheless some quite detailed evidence of his opinion of the first edition of 1937. His lecture notes upon the *Oresteia* (the trilogy comprising *Agamemnon, Choephori*, and *Eumenides*) for Oxford undergraduates of the wartime academic year 1942–3 survive; there are over 230 closely written quarto pages.[58] On the basis of the *Agamemnon* and

[56] See the account by Lloyd-Jones 1991, 210–11, who states that 'the notes (for the third edition) may be found . . . in the Bodleian Library.' Apart from a few letters and notes to Murray by Lloyd-Jones himself (GM 112), I have not located any working papers.

[57] E. Des Places, *Antiquité Classique* 25 (1956) 158 and a mere three sentences (anonymous: the editors?) in *Greece & Rome* 2 (1955) 133. The two major British reviewing journals, *Classical Review* and *Journal of Hellenic Studies*, ignored the volume.

[58] Box 14 of the Fraenkel Papers. The lectures were advertised in the *Oxford University Magazine* 72 (1941–2) 589 under the name of E. R. Dodds, Regius Professor of Greek (n. 6 above); Fraenkel took them over when Dodds went at short notice on a government cultural mission to China (see Dodds 1977, 141, 144–59). I have not found that Fraenkel repeated the lectures.

of these lecture notes, I have tried to establish what effect if any Fraenkel may have had on Murray's second edition of 1955. I counted perhaps six original conjectures by Fraenkel in his *Agamemnon*, at 308, 426, 1389, 1595, 1664, 1673, of which he put only the last two in his text; Murray reports none of them, although he must surely have studied the edition (nor, however, did D. L. Page (1972) report them; M. L. West (1990) reported only 1389). The lecture notes concentrate on textual and linguistic exposition, but there are many extended discussions of the plays and their issues, particularly for *Eumenides*, in the style of the long excursions in the published *Agamemnon*. Fraenkel began the lectures by stating that Murray's 1937 edition would be the base-text. I have looked at the notes for the lines in *Choephori* and *Eumenides* where Murray claimed original corrections and conjectures, and where Fraenkel evaluated them for the undergraduates, often in forceful language. He dismisses Murray at *Cho.* 61 ('Very bad' and 'still worse' to make a corresponding change at *Eum.* 518),[59] 145–6, 544, 573–4 ('absolutely impossible'), 624ff. (628), 1019 ('objectionable'), *Eum.* 188, 259 ('unjustified metrical transposition', as at 372–3, 784, *Cho.* 442), 358 ('impossible'), 360 ('Aeschylus could not have written anything of the sort'), 477, 523, 931; he ignores Murray at *Cho.* 74, 78–81, 109, 243, 698–9, *Eum.* 45, 95, 240, 266, 430, 479, 593, 670, 779 (attributed to 'a friend of Verrall' in Murray's second edition), 858, 912. Murray repeated all of his 1937 corrections and conjectures in 1955, except at *Cho.* 628, *Eum.* 479, 931, and the metrical transpositions at *Cho.* 442, *Eum.* 259, 372–3, 784 (where Paul Maas probably guided him). If Fraenkel communicated his doubts about these passages to Murray for the 1955 revision, they were almost totally ignored—or did he not communicate them at all?[60] If so, why not, given that the two exchanged correspondence?

I have conducted a second evaluative comparison, on the basis of the very corrupt choral ode *Cho.* 783–837 (so corrupt that Fraenkel

[59] M. L. West (1990) puts the conjecture at *Cho.* 61 into his text, but under the name of K. O. Müller, and lodges that at *Eum.* 518 in his apparatus.

[60] Of Murray's other suggestions in these two plays Page (1972) put just *Eum.* 188 and 931 in his text; M. L. West (1990) put 259 and 784 (the metrical transpositions) in his text, and the conjecture at 593 in his apparatus.

in his lectures offered the undergraduates no notes at all, perhaps summarizing the content as he did expressly but very briefly for the hardly less corrupt following ode 935–72). Here Murray in 1937 intervened in the text at 787, 798, 822, 829, 833, 834, 837, and conjectured at 815–16, 836; in 1955 he kept his change at 798 but attributed it (correctly) to Ahrens, introduced a new 'correction' at 815, abandoned that at 822, but retained the rest. D. L. Page (1972) accepted Murray's change at 829 (but attributed it to Tucker; in fact Blaydes was first with it), and also at 837; his edited text differs from Murray's in over 25 places (and his report of the manuscripts at 783, 795, 805, 807, 823, 826). Reprinting Page's 1972 text for his commentary on the play, A. F. Garvie (Oxford, 1986) accepted only Murray's 798, which Page had mentioned. M. L. West (1990) printed the change in 829 (but attributed it to Bourdelot, following Dawe 1965), and made no other mention of Murray for the whole ode.[61] If nothing else, these two sets of comparison reveal in Murray a much less good sense of his author's due than for Euripides, and the same reluctance to verify attribution of conjectures; his own 'corrections' and conjectures have been very roughly treated indeed.

V SUMMARY

Expert judges, obituarists, and biographers uniformly conveyed their disappointment that in textual criticism and editing, traditionally the highest form of Greek scholarship, Murray's achievement did not fulfil his early promise; on the other hand he produced important and in part still valuable or stimulating works of interpretation both

[61] Murray's claimed corrections and conjectures in this ode were indeed original to him at 787, 833, 834, and 837, according to Dawe (1965); but Dawe shows that thirty or so of Murray's claims to originality in Aeschylus were incorrect, disqualifying him for example at *Cho.* 243, 573, 628, 829, 846, *Eum.* 45, 95, 430, 523, 593: Dawe 1965, 5. In a later study Dawe allowed Murray only 14 of his original claims to originality in the whole of Aeschylus (Dawe 1990). The Introduction in Dawe 1965 is a bracing read on the age-long problems of attributing conjectures correctly (compare Murray's statement in Vol. 1 of his Euripides, p. x, cited in my Section III above, at n. 26), and on the implications for valuing them (or not) depending upon the 'greatness' of the name.

academic and general (see Griffith's chapter in this volume). To the British public, and indeed to the world, he became well known for his translations for the stage, and in the second half of his life for his tireless devotion to a liberal and pacific internationalism. In retirement from the University he was a national eminence, a generous source of experience, wisdom and hospitality. Academe's disappointment in Murray is expressed starkly by West, writing primarily of the Aeschylus: 'Notwithstanding his remarkable facility in Greek, Murray as an editor remained an amateur' (F. J. West 1984, 224). The judgement is a little unfair, perhaps, to what Murray may have felt was practicable for him with Aeschylus in the 1930s, let alone the 1950s; and the word 'remained' implies that the Euripides was as flawed as the Aeschylus. It was not (see the end of Section III).

It is invidious to select from the many appreciations of Murray's Greek scholarship, but I note what seem to me the best founded, first by three men with close personal knowledge of him as well as high competence to judge his work. E. R. Dodds (pupil, protégé, successor, and friend) in his obituary (Dodds 1957, 476 = Dodds 1960, 15–16), wrote with balanced detachment on the 'disappointment' felt over Murray's scholarship, to be set against his 'essential personal gift' of being able to 'relive, and cause others to relive, an ancient piece of human experience' (again, note the title of Murray's presentation volume *Greek Poetry and Life* (Bailey et al. 1936)). A similar assessment was made by Maurice Bowra: 'It was idle, and worse, to expect him to conform to the demands of humdrum scholarship, for that would have wasted his superb gift for teaching and interpreting Greek' (Bowra 1966, 221). Then J. A. K. Thomson (literary colleague and friend: see B. McManus' chapter in this volume) in his obituary had admitted the deficiencies of both the *Euripides* and the *Aeschylus* (and of Murray's own perception of the latter's failure), while offering a general assessment of his scholarship (Thomson 1957, 262, 267, 268–70). Lastly, there are two later and particularly authoritative opinions from scholars prominent in Murray's own favourite field of Greek studies, the poetic texts: Lloyd-Jones 1982, 195–214, especially at 199–204, 209–10, with a brief personal reminiscence at 212–13, cf. 19–20 (I have cited Lloyd-Jones at the end of Section III);

and R. L. Fowler, with carefully different judgements of the Euripides and Aeschylus (Fowler 1990, 324, 328).[62]

In sum, disappointment among scholars; but these same scholars and all other judges emphasize the quite extraordinary breadth of Murray's whole achievement, of which his Greek editions were only a part. This volume commemorates that breadth above all.

[62] Note too the chapter 'The Classical Scholar: An Assessment': D. Wilson 1987, 193–203. For general appreciations of Murray see Dodds 1957 = Dodds 1960; Isobel Henderson (Murray's literary executor) in M. I. Henderson 1960, especially 143–6, and in the *Dictionary of National Biography* (M. I. Henderson 1971); Stray 2004a; R. B. Todd in Todd 2004, 2.688–94. The last two offer the most useful and up-to-date bibliographies.

6

Gilbert Murray's Translations of Greek Tragedy

James Morwood

On a celebrated evening in 1901 at Newnham College, Cambridge, Gilbert Murray read excerpts from Euripides' *Hippolytus*, the first of his translations of Greek tragedy, in his famously beautiful speaking voice (on which see D. Wilson 1987, 105). The effect on his audience was electrifying. He ended by reciting what remains his most famous lyric, his version of lines 732–75 which contains the much-loved invocation of 'The Apple-tree, the singing and the gold', and Bertrand Russell wrote to Murray, 'I learnt it by heart immediately, & it has been in my head ever since.' When he read the whole translation, Russell's enthusiasm remained undimmed. He pronounced his encounter with it 'a wonderful experience, & one which I have found almost overwhelming' and expressed the feeling that it 'is to be placed in the very small list of truly great English poems'.[1] Such effusive outpourings were by no means evanescent. As late as 1940 Murray's admiring friend Bernard Shaw remarked of his translations that they alone were likely to survive from the revolutionary burst of London playwriting through which he had lived.[2]

[1] Letter of 26 Feb. 1901: Russell Archives, McMaster University, RA 1 710.053565. I am indebted to William Bruneau for sending me a copy of the correspondence between Russell and Murray about the translations.

[2] F. J. West 1984, 100: a remarkable and, as it has proved, wildly mistaken judgement.

Murray's *Hippolytus* was staged at the Lyric Theatre in London by the distinguished theatre manager Granville Barker in May 1904. On 2 June, the translator wrote to Russell of this inauguration of his West End career, 'I am receiving some ecstatic letters and seeing ecstatic newspaper articles here and there, now that for the moment there is a kind of "boom" in Euripides' (Russell Archives, RA 1 710.053496). In point of fact, the production was well rather than ecstatically received, though Granville Barker declaimed the messenger speech 'in a wildly exciting fashion' (F. J. West 1984, 89), sending a lady in the pit into hysterics and requiring her to be conducted sobbing from the house.[3] The success was sufficient for the play to be staged again later in 1904 (the hysterical lady dates from the revival) and then in 1916. But, as Dennis Kennedy comments, 'the Greek plays never could achieve the popularity of Shaw or some of the realist pieces at the Court. Yet,' as he goes on to remark, 'they achieved a sizeable matinee audience, and a persistent one' (Kennedy 1985, 50).

To Russell, as no doubt to the majority of the Lyric Theatre audience, Euripides' *Hippolytus* had previously been altogether unknown, and a key aspect of Murray's achievement was that his translations served as a channel, conveying the overwhelming power of this and other Greek tragedies to modern theatre-going audiences[4] in the same way that Chapman's Homer unlocked the greatest of Greek poets for Keats. In a brilliant book, Edith Hall and Fiona Macintosh have shown that after 1660 Greek tragedy had never been very distant from the professional London theatre; but it had always appeared in highly adapted forms (Hall and Macintosh 2005). According to Maurice Bowra, Murray's translations are astonishingly

[3] *Pall Mall Gazette*, 19 Oct. 1904, 11; *Daily Graphic*, 19 Oct. 1904, 266: both quoted in Kennedy 1985, 44.

[4] *Trojan Women* followed in 1905, *Electra* in 1906, *Medea* in 1907, and *Bacchae* in 1908. One should probably pass over his *Oedipus the King*, which was staged in a celebrated Max Reinhardt production (imported from Munich via Berlin and Vienna) at Covent Garden in 1912. Murray's text was adapted by W. L. Courtney to conform with Hugo von Hofmannsthal's translation (or rather his 'arrangement for the modern stage'). This meant that the choral passages were savagely cut back. It may also have involved the preservation of such changes by Hofmannsthal to Sophocles' text as his causing Polybus and Merope simply to lie when Oedipus asks them whether he is their son (Sophocles makes them give an evasive answer). (This change is noted by Peter Riemer: *Bryn Mawr Classical Review*, 1999.11.22.)

close to the Greek. There will, of course, be very different opinions on what the word 'close' means (Bowra 1966, 217). They certainly contain adornments plastered on by the translator, some of them notorious (Morwood 2005, pp. x–xi). Bowra gives us Murray's defence of these. 'In his view, English, after centuries of hard use, had lost the freshness which survived in Greek, and he tried to compensate for this by providing an emphasis which the Greek does not possess and does not need' (Bowra 1966, 218). Such 'emphases' are, in fact, few and far between. To illustrate what Bowra and Murray are talking about, we need look no further than the well-known line referred to in my opening paragraph. Murray's version of *Hippolytus* 742–3 reads:

> To the strand of the Daughters of the Sunset,
> The Apple-tree, the singing and the gold...

The literal meaning is: 'And I wish I could make my way to where the apples grow, to the shore of the Hesperides, the songstresses...' The fine phrase 'Daughters of the Sunset' is a justifiable substitute for 'Hesperides', the nymphs of the West, and, if it is complained that Murray has imported the 'gold', the apples that the nymphs guarded were certainly golden. Here we have imaginative translation, responsive to the original but not strait-jacketed by it. It is surely true to say that, in his desire to capture not only the spirit but also—allowing for the somewhat elastic bounds of his poetic sensibility—the letter of the original, Murray brought Greek tragedy to the professional twentieth-century stage with an altogether unprecedented textual authenticity.

The word 'professional' cannot be too strongly stressed. Previously productions of Greek tragedy that aimed at authenticity had been largely the province of amateurs, especially students. Indeed, even when Murray's translations were being produced with a considerable success in the West End, there remained a groundswell of opinion that the true Euripides was to be found in the performances in Greek by schoolboys at Bradfield in Berkshire. The celebrated critic and essayist Max Beerbohm was a leading proponent of this view (Hall and Macintosh 2005, 495). Early in 1906 an unsettled Murray wrote to William Archer, the famous critic and translator of Ibsen, that 'that phrase about the superiority of Bradfield seems to be running like the measles through cultural circles' (D. Wilson 1987, 107). 'Of course,' he goes on to remark, 'if this point of view is right, my whole work as scholar and translator is useless. I am trying to understand the plays more closely and thoroughly and to help English readers to do so.' He was eager to break the monopoly of esoteric productions involving adolescent boys speaking Ancient Greek and staged for the enjoyment (or should I say pretended enjoyment?) of a smugly self-congratulatory coterie. This conflict between the professionals and the boys reminds me of the Elizabethan War of the Theatres, so vividly evoked in Act 3 of *Hamlet* in which the tragedians of the city have been forced to go on tour. Their popularity in town has been taken over by the 'little eyases' [young hawks], the Children of the Chapel, who began to act at the Blackfriars theatre towards the end of 1600.

But Murray was wrong to be worried that any comparable fate might befall his translations. The Bradfield tradition continues, though some may feel that it has lost its way. At its best, it offered an important theatrical experiment aimed at exploring the ancient plays in conditions which approached those of their original performance. It has certainly made its contribution to dramaturgical scholarship. However, Murray's dramatic world revolved around the greatest professional actors and directors of his day, aided by the technical resources of the commercial theatre. It was they who brought to life his at times indifferent poetry and responded fully to its most splendid flights. Sybil Thorndike attributed the effectiveness of the translations on stage above all to the 'beauty and clarity of Murray's verse and its dramatic "speakableness"'.[5] If much of that beauty and clarity and speakableness was in reality attributable to her and her fellow actors, the fact is that they made Murray sing. The translator and his actors were able to establish Greek tragedy in the professional theatre on both sides of the Atlantic, and it has remained firmly entrenched there ever since.

The importance of Murray's translations in the modern reception of Greek tragedy is beyond doubt. However, to stress that fact may be to beg the question of their quality. To put the matter simply, are they any good? One particularly remarkable feature of them has perhaps

[5] Thorndike and Casson 1960, 153. She was writing specifically of the *Hippolytus* translation.

very little to do with their literary quality, but then, of course, there are many other aspects that contribute effectiveness to theatrical texts. Murray was the first—and possibly the last—translator to be highly conscious of the differences between Euripides' dramatic strategies in the original plays.

This seems to me a matter of major importance. While the term 'Shakespearean' has connotations of breadth, depth, and universality, 'Euripidean' suggests something altogether more limited. Yet why on earth should a great dramatist wish to say the same sort of thing in the same way over and over again?

It is perhaps easiest to show what I mean by posing the question, 'Why did Euripides write the *Trojan Women* in 415 BC when he had already dealt with a very similar situation, that of displaced captive women embarking on a life of servitude, in his *Hecuba* of some ten years earlier?' The answer is surely the simple one, that he has something very different to say. While *Hecuba*, complete with its Elizabethan/Jacobean ghost, is a grisly revenge play tracing the chilling extinction of humanity in its heroine—she is to be transformed into a dog after its action is over—, *Trojan Women*, the most heart-rending of anti-war plays, shows the ultimate victory of the human spirit as Hecuba and her female compatriots overcome appalling circumstances and stagger off to the ships and their future. One could extend this kind of distinguishing analysis to all eighteen surviving Euripides plays. And this despite the fact that Aristophanes' Aeschylus in one of the funniest scenes in *Frogs* parodies his Prologues as all starting in exactly the same way!

No doubt Murray was not enough of a poet to create a different tone for the individual plays of the individual dramatists. In any case, his models, Swinburne for the choruses and William Morris for the rhyming couplets of the dialogue (F. J. West 1984, 98), are so pervasively present in his writing that they stifle any possibility of the expression of a strong personal voice with a range of registers. Yet we must remember Bowra's comment about his closeness to the Greek text. The Swinburnean wash overlaying the lyrics and the at times inert poetic diction of the Morris-style couplets may frequently be short on poetic vitality, but in performance they appear to have been remarkably efficient in communicating the tragedies' literal meaning, a major component of their particular flavour.

Furthermore, Murray can militate against the identikit nature of his translations by suggesting very strongly in his Introductions the line that he feels the director should take. In his *Trojan Women* preface he invokes the Athenians' horrific war crime against Melos—what he calls 'the great crucial crime of the [Peloponnesian] war'[6]—in order to colour the presentation of this play. As he points to history, he evokes the Boer War, in ways that Edith Hall and Fiona Macintosh have analysed (Hall and Macintosh 2005, 508–11). The horror of war, the nightmare of that great British invention, the concentration camp, and the plight of captives and refugees at all times and everywhere merge to form a kind of ground-bass that adds depth and resonance to Murray's text.

In *Electra* he points to the brilliant delineation of the characters. Invoking Ibsen as a point of reference for the play's psychology, he writes that Euripides 'seeks real people. And few attentive readers of this play can doubt that he has found them.' Of Electra herself he declares, 'There is, perhaps, no woman's character in the range of Greek drama so profoundly studied. Not Aeschylus' Clytemnestra, not Phaedra, not Medea.' (Since we shall later be considering part of Murray's *The Wife of Heracles*, it may be worth remarking that his title for Sophocles' *Trachiniae* (literally, *Women of Trachis*) is a telling one. His Introduction deals above all with the extraordinarily contrasted delineations of Deianira and her brutal husband.)

As for *Medea*, Hall and Macintosh show convincingly how Murray's translation, staged at the Savoy Theatre in 1907, 'was deliberately performed against the upsurge of public interest in the movement for women's suffrage', the aims of which Murray had supported since 1889 (Hall and Macintosh 2005, 511–13). We should be particularly grateful to them for their analysis since this is not an aspect which Murray deals with in his Introduction. There he is very sensitively alive to the aspects of the play which make Medea a decidedly surprising role model for the suffragettes. On the other hand, his introductory note to *Bacchae* (in point of fact, placed after the translation) insists on a religious, ritualistic and anthropological reading of the play. What he has to say reflects the discussions of the

[6] All the quotations from the Euripides introductions can be found in Murray 2005.

Cambridge Ritualists, one of them in particular, as he acknowledges elsewhere when he observes, 'On points of ancient religion, I have had the great advantage of frequent consultation with Miss J. E. Harrison.'[7] In my view, this approach led Murray far closer to the heart of the play than Colin Teevan penetrated in his version written for the National Theatre exactly a hundred years later. The totality of Murray's introductions and translations is what counts. Just as his friend Bernard Shaw made enormous use of his prefaces and stage directions, so Murray dressed the bare bones of his versions in a commentary that memorably fixed their uniqueness and originality on the modern stage.

It might have been possible to bring this discussion to an end on this positive note were it not for the denunciation of the translations by one of the greatest twentieth-century poets, T. S. Eliot, in his 1920 essay, 'Euripides and Professor Murray'. Viewing the translations not as dramatic poems but as poetry *tout court*, Eliot remarks that 'Greek poetry will never have the slightest vitalizing effect upon English poetry if it can only appear masquerading as a vulgar debasement of the eminently personal idiom of Swinburne... [I]t is because Professor Murray has no creative instinct that he leaves Euripides quite dead.'[8] I have argued elsewhere that Eliot's broadside should be seen not so much as an attack on Murray but rather as the personal manifesto of a poet who some twenty years later was himself to bring Greek tragedy to the West End stage in a totally different way.[9] Even so, it is surely legitimate to concur with Eliot's judgement in considering the rhyming couplets in the 'episodes' (the non-choric passages that carry the action forward). On the printed page there is indeed something dead about their archaic, high-flown diction and their relentless sameness. The fact, however, remains that actors such as Granville Barker and Sybil Thorndike could breathe profoundly affecting life into them on the stage. Whatever their weaknesses as poetry, they certainly enabled Euripides to communicate with a

[7] Murray, *Euripides Translated into English Rhyming Verse* (London, 1902), p. vii. Harrison had designed the statues of Cyprus and Artemis for the 1904 *Hippolytus*.

[8] Eliot 1951, 61, 64; cf. the discussion in Ackerman 1986.

[9] Morwood 2005, pp. ix–x. Eliot's *The Family Reunion* (1939) and *The Elder Statesman* (1958) are versions of Aeschylus' *Choephori* and Sophocles' *Oedipus at Colonus* respectively.

modern audience, at times, as in the case of Barker's 1904 *Hippolytus* messenger, knocking it for six. It may be that they still could.[10]

And even if one judges on purely poetic criteria, Eliot's onslaught seems decidedly wide of the mark when it is applied to Murray's lyric passages. While at one level of his thinking he viewed himself as a poet,[11] at another he was altogether less aspirational, writing to Bertrand Russell that 'all authors—in different degrees, but all enormously—fail to convey their meaning. And translators, being less good writers and having a harder task, fail even more deplorably.'[12] It could well be that his very lack of an individual poetic voice, his determination, so deplored by Eliot, to dye his lyrics in conventionally Swinburnian colours, made him all the more eager to try to capture at least some of the nuance and tone of what he was translating.

At the London conference at which most of the papers in this volume were first delivered, we conducted an experiment in which we compared a Murray translation of a choral passage from each of the three Attic dramatists with the original Greek and, in two cases, with a modern translation. The results were instructive.[13] In Murray's version of the great lyrics in Aeschylus' *Persians* where the Chorus summon up the Ghost of Darius (634–80), we found considerable incantatory power. The Ionic *a minore* rhythms (∪∪ – –) of the original find an echo in Murray's Ionic lines, and Aeschylus' Persian and Phoenician words and extrametrical cries are represented with scholarship, imagination, and dramatic power. A twentieth-century sergeant major

[10] In March 2003 a showcase production of Murray's translation of Sophocles' *Antigone* was staged at the Royal Academy of Dramatic Arts in London, directed by Nona Shepphard. It was pronounced a success.

[11] F. J. West 1984, 98. Burian sums up the matter thus:

> In the preface to Murray's first volume of translations, the stated aim is 'to put before English readers a translation of some very beautiful poetry', and poetry remains his chief concern: 'the groundwork of careful translation once laid, I have thought no more of anything but the poetry.' Murray's emphasis on 'poetic beauties' reflects a sincere desire to convey, as well as the meaning of the words, the emotive power of the Greek text to a wide audience. For Murray this meant freeing his translations from the constraints of the strictly literal in favour of his own conception of the 'spirit' of the original. (Burian 2000, 982)

[12] Letter of 2 Mar. 1901: Russell Archives, RA 1 710.053565.

[13] I am very grateful to David Raeburn for his participation in this experiment. His readings were highly illuminating and much enjoyed.

makes an unfortunate entry in the 'rise and shine' of l. 661! But overall this Chorus struck us as grand and exotic, a strong and convincing passage of dramatic writing. I quote Murray's version of ll. 647–71:

> As ye loved him, love his grave-mound, where the old kind thoughts abide,
> Aïdôneus [i.e. Hades], thou Upraiser, Aïdôneus, be his guide,
> Where a King stalketh lonely to the light.
> Dâryâsha![14]
>
> In the madness of lost battles never wasted he our youth;
> They had named him 'God in Counsel', and God counselled him in truth,
> For his hand upon the helm steered aright.
> Dâryâsha![15]
>
> O our Ba'al,[16] ancient Ba'al, be thou near!
> On the crest of this thy grave-mound, Oh, appear!
> Let the crocus-golden sandal give a sign;
> Let the High King's tiara rise and shine;
> Thou our Father, thou undarkened, hear, Oh hear!
> Ba'alênu![17]
>
> A thing meet for lamentation and strange woe,
> O thou Master of our Masters, hear and know;
> For a darkness as of death is overhead,
> And the youth of all our people lieth dead,
> Thou our Father, thou undarkened, far below.
> Ba'alênu![18]

Moving on to the Chorus in Sophocles' *Trachiniae* which describes the fight between the river god Achelous and Heracles over Deianira (498–530), we admired the direct, sinewy translation of the passage describing the conflict as well as the poignant version of the final stanza communicating the pitiful isolation of the woman as she awaits the outcome. Any apparent additions worked together with,

[14] Based on the Persian name for Darius.

[15] The repetition of the Persian-based word stands for the exclamation ἠέ.

[16] Aeschylus' Greek word βαλλήν may derive from the Phoenician honorary title used by Murray here.

[17] The adaptation of the Phoenician word stands for the exclamation ἠέ.

[18] The repetition of the Phoenician-based word stands for the exclamation οἴ.

not in opposition to, the original. For example, Murray's 'like a star' in l. 524 is his own phrase, laying stress on Deianira's solitude and remoteness.[19] And generally we were impressed by Murray's truth to the Greek. Here is his version of 517–30:

All was a thud of fists, a deadly whirr
Of arrows, clash of wild-beast horn on horn
Grapples of writhing trunks, brows battle-torn
    And one over mastering groan;

While tender, beautiful, afar,
On the clear hillside, like a star,
Sitting she waits till it be known
Which brawler grasps her for his own.
As of a child that I had borne
I speak; that soft eye, battle-won,
Pitiful waiting, and then gone,
A young lamb suddenly alone,
    Motherless and forlorn!

Finally we looked at his version of the terrifying Chorus from Euripides' *Bacchae* in which the bacchantes call upon their fellows on the mountain and on their god to destroy Pentheus (977–1023). Murray had taken the bold decision to try to preserve the wildly exciting dochmiac rhythm of the original (basically ∪ – – ∪ –, with frequent resolution), and while his 'few simple licences' with the metre[20] put something of a damper on the febrile energy of the Greek, his version has genuine vigour and urgent momentum. Repetition and alliteration are strongly effective, and the use of rhyme is a crucial structuring element. We felt that the translator had achieved considerable, if inevitably partial, success with one of the most extraordinarily powerful passages in Greek tragedy.[21] Here is the opening:

O hounds raging and blind,
    Up by the mountain road,

[19] Presumably the phrase was suggested by the fact that the Greek epithet used of the hill can mean not only 'seen from afar', 'distant', and 'giving a distant view' but 'far-shining' too.

[20] Murray's note on l. 976.

[21] There were a number of experiments made with the presentation of the choruses. Should they be chanted or sung or simply recited, as Murray preferred (Thorndike 1960, 163)?

Sprites of the maddened mind,
  To the wild Maids of God;
Fill with your rage their eyes,
  Rage at the rage unblest,
Watching in woman's guise,
  The spy upon God's Possessed.

Who shall be first, to mark
  Eyes in the rock that spy,
Eyes in the pine-tree dark—
  Is it his mother?—and cry:
'Lo, what is this that comes,
  Haunting, troubling still,
Even in our heights, our homes,
  The wild Maids of the Hill?
What flesh bare this child?
  Never on woman's breast
Changeling so evil smiled;
  Man is he not, but Beast!
Lion-shape of the wild,
  Gorgon-breed of the waste!'

Hither, for doom and deed!
  Hither with lifted sword,
  Justice, Wrath of the Lord,
Come in our visible need!
Smite till the throat shall bleed,
Smite till the heart shall bleed,
Him the tyrannous, lawless, Godless, Echîon's earthborn seed!

Murray the translator was certainly speaking out loud and clear to a group assembled in a bomb-torn London in July 2005. Earlier in the conference Mick Morris had played a tape of Murray reading his version of the halcyon chorus from Euripides' *Iphigenia among the Taurians* (1089ff.), a passage which his granddaughter Ann Paludan assured us was a personal favourite of his. I quote the opening lines of this passage:

Bird of the sea rocks, of the bursting spray,
  O halcyon bird,
That wheelest crying, crying, on thy way;
Who knoweth grief can read the tale of thee:
One love long lost, one song for ever heard
  And wings that sweep the sea.

By any standards this is fine and poignant writing. The note of eternal sadness is sounded in the largely monosyllabic simplicity, the pathetic repetitions, the evocative pictorial quality, and the eloquent handling of rhythm and rhyme.

Even so, I must end by insisting that in a dramatic text words by themselves are not enough. The knocking at the gate is a vital, overwhelmingly powerful feature of *Macbeth* (2.2,3); the stage direction '[he] holds her by the hand silent' contributes to *Coriolanus* one of its most shattering moments (5.3.183). Murray clearly had a true instinct for the theatre and involved himself in the staging of his versions, winning the respect of the directors and actors alike. He found himself looking beyond the script to everything that was happening on the stage. He kept an eye on the whole dramatic picture. This is especially evident from his stage directions. Two examples must stand for many. In a copy of his Euripides' *Electra*,[22] he has written, presumably in the course of rehearsals, 'beating the ground' beside the protagonist's name at line 682, making explicit what can be inferred from 678. It is an arresting effect.[23] Probably the most striking and viscerally thrilling instance of his unscrambling a stage direction from the text occurs at line 1327 of *The Trojan Women* when the Greek trumpet blows. This is the moment, cued by Talthybius at 1266–8, for Hecuba and the women of Troy to rise to their feet and walk to the ships. The trumpet call releases them from their tragic past and sends them to an uncertain future. It unlocks the play, allowing it to end. Modern editors have simply failed to notice it. But Murray, the instinctive man of the theatre as well as the first Oxford Classical Texts editor of Euripides, makes it ring out to stunning effect.[24] This is one of the great sound effects of the world's theatre, and it was the translator who rediscovered it for modern audiences. That is a notable part of a notable achievement.

[22] In the Archive of Performances of Greek and Roman Drama at Oxford University.

[23] It is reproduced with extraordinary power in Michael Cacoyannis' film of the play (1962).

[24] 'The Greek trumpet sounds'. A tape of a 1946 Val Gielgud production for the BBC with Thorndike as Hecuba is held by the Oxford archive (see n. 29). The conclusion was played at the London Murray conference.

7

From the Court to the National: The Theatrical Legacy of Gilbert Murray's *Bacchae*

Fiona Macintosh

Gilbert Murray's involvement in the Court Theatre from 1904 to 1907 enabled him to play a significant role in the shaping of modern British theatre. His translation of the *Hippolytus* had been staged by Granville Barker in May 1904 at the Lyric; and when Barker learned that the leaseholder of the Court was keen to produce Greek plays on a regular basis, he arranged for the production to transfer there in the October. The *Hippolytus* was the first of numerous productions of Murray's translations of Euripides' tragedies to be performed at the Court Theatre in Sloane Square; and the production inaugurated a vibrant performance history of Murray's translations that was to last for the next four decades.[1]

Small though the Court Theatre was, it none the less succeeded in ushering British theatre into the modern world. Under the Vedrenne–Barker management, the Court had an intensely international outlook and orientation.[2] This was the case both on account

Thanks to the following for their comments and very helfpul criticism of earlier drafts of this chapter: Edith Hall, Lorna Hardwick, and the staff and students of Reading University Classics Department. I am most grateful also to my colleague, Amanda Wrigley, and to Colin Harris in the Bodleian Library for help in accessing the Murray papers.

[1] For a general overview of Murray's involvement in the theatre, see Wilson 1987 and Hall & Macintosh 2005, 488–520. For a listing of the productions of his plays, see APGRD Database (accessible at *www.apgrd.ox.ac.uk*), edited and maintained by Amanda Wrigley.

[2] For the Court Theatre at this time, see Kennedy (1985).

of the eclectic choice of plays (New drama, ancient drama, and foreign plays) and because the Court was in many ways the London outpost of the most dynamic theatre in the English-speaking world at that time, Ireland's newly inaugurated national theatre, the Abbey in Dublin.

Murray was a staunch supporter of the Court in its early years, together with a collection of Fabians, feminists and avant-garde theatre practitioners; and his support, like that provided by his close friend and collaborator, George Bernard Shaw, did not just take the form of supplying plays for performance. Murray also offered considerable financial support on occasion to this daring enterprise (Kennedy 1985, 24). And just as Shaw's work met with new audiences through Barker's productions of his plays, so Murray's translations, with Barker's mediation, introduced the same people to Euripides at the special matinee performances. Whatever the shortcomings of certain aspects of the *Hippolytus* at the Court, it was generally considered a success; and when it was revived in 1906, the advertisement in the popular pictorial weekly, the *Bystander*, insisted: 'You will like it without any necessity of posing as an earnest student of the drama' (*The Bystander*, 11 Apr. 1906, 72). Greek tragedy, thanks to the combined efforts of Murray and Barker, had finally moved from the private to the public theatre; and Euripides, in particular, was now truly 'popular'.

Ancient and modern plays were deemed equally accessible and relevant by the Court management: each was discussed interchangeably and benefited from the perspective afforded by the other. And if the London venue for this new flowering of international drama was in Sloane Square, the rural retreat around Churt, Hindhead and Haslemere in Surrey—where Murray, Shaw and Barker all had houses for a time—provided further opportunity for the fruitful interchange of ideas and energy.

Perhaps the most important result of this potent collaboration between classical scholar, playwright and theatre director came in 1905 with *Major Barbara*, the first play written for the new theatre. When the text was published that year, it became clear how much the New Drama was benefiting from the matinee performances of the ancient plays, as Shaw chose to make his debt to the leading expert on classical drama clear in the epigraph to his play:

NB The Euripidean verses in the second act of *MB* are not by me, nor even directly by Euripides. They are by Professor Gilbert Murray, whose English version of *The Bacchae* came into our dramatic literature with all the impulsive power of an original work shortly before *MB* was begun. The play, indeed, stands indebted to him in more ways than one. (Shaw 1960, xx)

Murray's translation of the *Bacchae* had to wait until 1908 for its première; and even though it never enjoyed a continuous performance history (unlike, say, his translations of *Medea* or *Trojan Women*), the *Bacchae* went on to exert considerable influence on others, for whom it acted as an inspiration for their own creative engagements with Euripides' tragedy. Both Granville Bantock and Vaughan Williams set sections of Murray's *Bacchae* to music.[3] But perhaps the most significant of the creative works indebted to Murray's *Bacchae* after Shaw's *Major Barbara* is the *The Bacchae of Euripides: A Communion Rite* by the Nobel Prize winning Nigerian playwright, Wole Soyinka.

In the published edition of Soyinka's play of 1973, we find in the Author's Acknowledgement the following statement of debt:

A twenty-year rust on my acquaintanceship with classical Greek made it necessary for me to rely heavily on previous translations for this adaptation of *The Bacchae.* Two versions which deserve especial mention, in that I have not hesitated to borrow phrases and even lines from them, are those by Gilbert Murray... and William Arrowsmith. (Soyinka 1973, x)

To my knowledge, no one has paid any particular attention to this avowed debt to either Murray or Arrowsmith. In Murray's case, this is not surprising given the fact that by the 1970s any comment about his influence would have passed without much note. The critical orthodoxy about Murray's translations (prevalent since at least the late 1930s) was based, more or less, upon T. S. Eliot's damning critique in 'Euripides and Mr Murray' (Eliot 1920, reprinted in

[3] Bantock began work on his *Bacchae* before March 1908 (see Sonnenschein to Murray, 7 Mar. 1908; Bantock to Murray, 10 Mar. 1908: GM 13.90–91, 96), but the full work (Overture and 5 choral songs and dances) didn't receive its première until 1945 (see Grove 1980, 2:125). Vaughan Williams' setting is dated 17 Oct. 1911 and was commissioned for a production by Isadora Duncan and her brother, Augustin, that never materialized. See Wilson 1987, 169–70. Talbot Hodge's *The Fawn Song: A Chorus from the Bacchae* (1937) also uses Murray's translation (a copy of which is in GM 430).

Eliot 1951, 59–64). Murray's verse translations, in Eliot's terms, were sub-Swinburnian obstructions which prevented the reader from accessing the Euripidean text. But it wasn't simply scholarly consensus about his verse translations that contributed to his eclipse; it was also Murray's insistence on the ritual origins of Greek drama, and what we now see as his Modernist insistence on the wider applicability of his theory through comparative analyses of Greek and Shakespearean tragedy.[4] The comparative method was scorned by mid-century anthropologists, who denounced the armchair theorizing of their forebears and practised intensive and extensive fieldwork. This new narrow focus was similarly adopted in the literary sphere, where New Critical analysis of discrete texts held sway. But despite New Critical pillorying in the post-war period, Murray's influence was none the less still widely felt beyond the academy and was a deeply formative influence on new generations hungry for the classics.

It is this wide-ranging influence of Murray's *Bacchae* that provides the subject of this chapter—from its various incarnations at the Court in the Edwardian period, to the National Theatre, then still at the Old Vic in London, which commissioned Soyinka's play for performance in 1973. That such markedly different playwrights, Shaw and Soyinka, separated as they are by time and space, should have been fired by Murray's reading is somewhat surprising. With its three-act structure and marked shifts in location, Shaw's play is a much looser adaptation than Soyinka's, which merely interpolates a prologue, a dumb-show and provides a startling new ending in place of the lacunous Euripidean exodos. In both plays, the lexical appropriations of Murray's text are evident; but more important for this discussion are the ways in which Murray's text and his commentary on the *Bacchae* have informed both versions.

Both Shaw and Soyinka respond to Murray's text after enthusiastic encounters with *The Birth of Tragedy*; and there is no doubt that the Nietzschean echoes in Murray's work make his *Bacchae* of immediate interest to them. Although Murray's introductory essay was written before he had developed the most Nietzschean of his theories—his highly influential thesis concerning the hypothetical ritual sequence

[4] e.g. Murray's essay, 'Hamlet and Orestes' (1914), reprinted in Murray 1927c, 205–40.

that is said to underpin the plays (see Parker and Griffith, in this volume)—in his discussion of Dionysus in the introductory essay and commentary, there are striking and important parallels with *The Birth of Tragedy*. Murray himself had good reasons to be reticent about his reading of the controversial German classical scholar—any such acknowledgement would have precipitated a rift with his much respected colleague, Wilamowitz.[5]

For both Shaw and Soyinka, by contrast, Nietzsche was a frequent and publicly acknowledged source of reference. When Shaw was working on *The Perfect Wagnerite* (1898), an interpretation of Wagner's Ring-Cycle, he was living down the road from Murray in Surrey; and in 1903 Shaw spoke of Schopenhauer and Nietzsche as being 'among the writers whose peculiar sense of the world I recognise as more or less akin to my own'.[6] Soyinka's debts to Nietzsche are generally explicit and well-attested and they appear throughout his critical writings. In his earliest published essay, 'The Fourth Stage: Through the Mysteries of Ogun to the origin of Yoruba tragedy', to which he cross-refers in the Introduction to his *Bacchae*, Soyinka explains: 'Our course to the heart of the Yoruba Mysteries leads by its own ironic truths through the light of Nietzsche and the Phrygian deity'.[7]

What both Nietzsche and Murray provided for the playwrights, and what the dramatists themselves were seeking to replicate in their own work, were radical synthesizing ideas. Nietzsche's Modernist concern with unity focused ultimately on the metaphysical level, but it reached its fullest instantiation in the aesthetic sphere, in Greek tragedy. For Murray, the ideals of coherence and unity were equally important (see Parker's chapter) and were central to his conception of the *Bacchae*: aesthetically through the yoking of thought and feeling in the poetry, but also politically and universally through the communion afforded by the Dionysiac religion

[5] Wilamowitz was author of the first devastating review of *The Birth of Tragedy*, which guaranteed Nietzsche's ostracism from the classical establishment. See Silk and Stern 1981, 95–107.

[6] Holroyd 1988–92, 2. 3–4; and for the quotation, see Shaw Papers, British Library, 1931: f. xxviii.

[7] Soyinka 1976, 140. An earlier version appeared in Jefferson 1969, 119–34.

between disparate peoples and between animal, human, and divine. Indeed, it is this added political dimension in Murray's reading of the *Bacchae* which was to make it so appealing to both Shaw and Soyinka.

MURRAY'S *BACCHAE* AND *MAJOR BARBARA*

When Murray read a selection of his translations in 1901 at a Fabian Society meeting, Shaw was so overwhelmed that he urged Murray to seek immediate publication (West 1984, 72). In 1902 Murray's translations of the *Hippolytus, Bacchae,* and *Frogs* were published as the third volume in the pioneering series edited by George Warr, which combined translation with an introduction and commentary. Murray's experience in preparing lectures for his students during his time as Professor of Greek at Glasgow from 1889 had led him to share with both Lewis Campbell and George Warr a concern for the need of the wide availability of good translations (Hall and Macintosh 2005, 430–486). Following his retirement on the grounds of ill-health from the Glasgow chair in 1899, Murray was to spend the next five years making Euripides' plays available to a range of different audiences: to scholars (through his Oxford Classical Text of the plays) (Easterling 1997); to readers without Greek (through his published translations); and eventually, through the productions of his translations on the professional stage, to a theatre-going public throughout Britain and the English-speaking world.

It was Murray's translation of and commentary on the *Bacchae* in the 1902 collection that impressed Shaw most. Here Shaw found a play (in Murray's reading) that explored religious experiences and questions of moral identity in terms remarkably similar to his own. For both Murray and Shaw, with their shared Irish background, religion could never be considered independent of politics; and through his acquaintance with Murray's *Bacchae,* Shaw discovered how classical scholarship could illuminate twentieth-century political concerns.

In the Introductory Essay to the 1902 volume, Murray concluded that the main message of Euripides' *Bacchae* was that:

The kingdom of Heaven is within you - here and now. You have but to accept it and live with it—not obscure it by striving and hating and looking in the wrong place. (Murray 1902b, lxvi)

The play, according to Murray, was offering a simple, liberating message that the godhead is within you. Murray, it should be recalled, was writing against the nineteenth-century view of Dionysus as a kind of proto-Christ with Euripides, the life-long atheist, now recanting at the end of his life. But Murray was also writing in contradistinction to contemporary readings of the play (by Wilamowitz, Verrall and Norwood) that hailed Pentheus as the embodiment of reason duped by the mountebank, Dionysus. Murray's Pentheus, by contrast, is 'the ordinary hot-tempered and narrowly practical tyrant' (ibid., lvii). The Chorus, Murray insists, do not proffer 'words of a raving Bacchante, but of a gentle and deeply musing philosopher' (ibid., lviii); and in the refrain in the third stasimon, it is less revenge than the state of freedom afforded by Dionyus that is deemed the highest of 'men's endeavour', which Murray chooses to highlight in his translation:

What else is Wisdom! What of man's endeavour
Or God's high grace, so lovely and so great?
To stand from fear set free, to breathe and wait;
To hold a hand uplifted over Hate;
And shall not Loveliness be loved for ever?

(Murray 1902b, 125–6 (= Murray 1909a, *Bacch.* 877–881, 897–901). Cf. Dodds 1944 and Seaford 2001 *ad.loc.*)

In Murray's Introductory Essay, we find an interesting collocation of Dionysus, the pagan ('the God of all high emotion, inspiration, intoxication') with Dionysus, the proto-Christ ('He has given man Wine, which is his Blood and a religious symbol').[8] Although it is clearly Murray's teetotalism that prevents him from resisting the nineteenth-century Christianizing tendencies of his subject entirely, much of what Murray has to say about Dionysus is new and very close to the discussions of the Cambridge Ritualists and Jane Harrison's work in particular. Whilst the content is clearly in line with

[8] Murray 1902b, lix. Cf. Easterling 1997, to whose close reading I am indebted in the next couple of sentences.

developments in Cambridge, the terminology on occasions shows a surprising similarity to discussion much further afield. When Murray states that '...he [Dionysus] gave to the Purified a mystic Joy, surpassing in intensity that of man, the joy of a god or a free wild animal' (Murray 1902b, lix-lx), it is the Nietzschean echo that resounds through his words. Although Nietzsche deliberately omits overt reference to the *Bacchae* in the *The Birth of Tragedy*—it would have confounded his argument to have to admit to the centrality to his thesis of a play by his *bête noire* (Silk and Stern 1981, 258–263)—he draws heavily on its imagery in chapter 1. And whilst Harrison is gratefully acknowledged by Murray in his Preface ('On points of ancient religion I have had the great advantage of frequent consultation with Miss J. E. Harrison': Murray 1902b, vii), any debt to Nietzsche, as we have heard, would have to go unacknowledged.

The understated Nietzschean echoes in Murray's reading of the *Bacchae* would have been both obvious and exciting to Shaw; and Murray's liberating interpretation of the play struck a particularly strong chord in Shaw for whom the only solution to society's ills was to rely on strident action—the Shavian socialist must be a realist and grapple with reality, rather than resort to idealized visions of that reality. That Murray had translated a play about religion, if not just any conventional 'religious' play, was of especial interest to Shaw. Equally importantly, Murray had found a religion that had a 'strong hold over the emotions of the common people' (Murray 1902b, 166). The Fabian socialist could only have warmed to a religion 'which includes democracy...It implies that trust in the "simple man" which is so characteristic of most idealists and reformers. It implies the doctrine of Equality—a doctrine essentially religious and mystical, continually disproved in every fresh sense in which it can be formulated, and yet remaining one of the living faiths of men' (ibid., lxiv–lxv).

In his conclusion to the Preface to *Major Barbara*, Shaw writes: 'At present there is not a single credible established religion in the world. That is perhaps the most stupendous fact in the whole world' (Shaw 1960, 49). Like the *Bacchae*, Shaw's play explores one recent 'alternative' to the established religions; and as with the *Bacchae*, which Murray had shown contained 'real and heartfelt glorification of Dionysus' (Murray 1902b, lvii), Shaw's treatment of the Salvation Army in *Major Barbara* is not without sympathy and respect. He was not the first to recognize the links between the Army of Christ founded by William Booth in 1878 and the Dionysiac cult of ancient Greece. In 1894, Mary E. Coleridge had observed:

> There is much more real religion in the *Bacchae* of Euripides [than, for example, in the *Life of Dr Pusey*], which is simply glorious—a sort of Greek Salvation Army business, all drums and cymbals and ecstasy... There's no real tipsiness as far as I can make out. The Hallelujah lasses get drunk on the wine of the spirit, not the wine of the grape.[9]

That Shaw was not alone in making these connections makes his own case in the preface that much more topical and convincing; but unlike Coleridge, Shaw is not just interested in the 'ecstatic' affinities. For him, it is the political parallels that he had gleaned through Murray's translation that matter. Although at the end of Shaw's play, the Army of Christ is shown ultimately to be no different from the established religions Shaw so vehemently rejected, he is at pains to stress its apparent links with the ancient cult of Dionysus.

In its populist appeal, and even in its militant fight against poverty, the Salvation Army resembles the tyrants' religion that came to unsettle the orthodoxy of the oligarchs in the archaic Greek world. The tambourines, trumpets and drums carried by the soldiers of Christ as they process through the East End of London are clearly seen by Shaw to be akin to the trappings of the dancing Maenads of ancient Greece. Cusins (the Murray figure), the collector of religions, explains to Undershaft in Act II:

> It is the army of joy, of love, of courage... It picks the waster out of the public house and makes a man of him: it finds a worm wriggling in a back kitchen, and lo! a woman! Men and women of rank too, sons and daughters of the Highest. It takes the poor professor of Greek, the most artificial and self-suppressed of human creatures, from his meal of roots, and lets loose the rhapsodist in him; reveals the true worship of Dionysos to him; sends him down the public street drumming dithyrambs. (Shaw 1960, 93–4)

Like the Dionysiac faith in Murray's translation ('No grudge hath he of the great/ No scorn of the mean estate... / The simple nameless herd of Humanity/ Hath deeds and faith that are truth enough for me!': Murray 1902b, 98 (= Murray 1909a, E.*Bacch.* 421–32)), the

[9] Coleridge 1910, 233. I am indebted to Isobel Hurst for this reference.

gospel of the Army is in some senses the great leveller, a truly democratic religion. But although Shaw himself was genuinely moved by the Army's bands and singing, he is at pains to emphasize its political shortcomings. As with the mystery cults at the end of the fifth century BC, the army's gospel merely provides an escape from the evils of reality, blunting the insurrectionary tendencies amongst the masses with the promise, not of a heaven on earth, but bliss in eternity. What had attracted Shaw to the Dionysiac—the message that 'The kingdom of Heaven is within you'—is not ultimately to be found through the Salvation Army. As Shaw says in the Preface of 1906, the Army will very soon lose its radical edge and join the ranks of other established churches.

For the true modern counterpart to Dionysus—Murray's cold, savage and inhuman god (Murray 1902, liv–lvi)—Shaw found the brazen capitalist, arms manufacturer, Andrew Undershaft. Like Dionysus, Undershaft—the underminer, the mineshaft—defies normal categories and boundaries. In addition to his obvious resemblance to the Nietzschean Übermensch, the destructive/creative entrepreneur had numerous real-life models as well, the two most notable being Alfred Nobel (patentee of dynamite in 1867, who subsequently endowed the Peace Prize in 1901), and Friedrich Alfred Krupp (the Prussian cannon-king, whose paternalistic welfare system for workers in Essen was admired world-wide, but who some thirty years on was to be a prominent Nazi sympathizer). The Greek god, Dionysus, embodied Shaw's concept of the Life-force: energy without morality; a potential for both good or evil, depending on what its recipient decides to do with it. We create, as Pentheus does to some extent, either a god or a devil in accordance with how we use the divine energy, or the Life-force. And Undershaft's chilling amorality makes him the modern embodiment of that energy.

Like the *Bacchae*, *Major Barbara* is in this sense a play about the contrasts and contradictions inherent in certain religious experiences. For Shaw, for whom means are often starkly at odds with ends (for example he maintained that socialism could be secured through arch individualism; liberation, very often as here, through mass destruction), the Dionysiac experience became a kind of metaphysical equivalent of the Shavian dialectic. Like Murray in the 1902 Introductory Essay, Shaw would have found Pentheus' position untenable; and in accordance with Shavian dialectics, it was much more important to find a serious contender to meet the Dionysiac force. Cusins (the Murray-figure) is no Pentheus; instead, from Act III onwards, he is regularly referred to as Euripides by Undershaft.[10] What Shaw is offering us at the end of his play, it would seem, is his own version of another play in the 1902 volume, Aristophanes' *Frogs.* And with the *Bacchae* lying behind its first two acts, and the *Frogs* behind its third, *Major Barbara* becomes a tribute to the 1902 volume.

In the Shavian rewrite of the *Frogs* in the third act, Euripides wins the argument against Dionysus/Undershaft. And when Cusins and Undershaft's daughter, Barbara are left alone together towards the end of the play we see the extent of their victory: Cusins's strength is revealed in his realization that 'all power is spiritual', and that power for good necessarily entails the power for evil as well (Shaw 1960, 150); and Barbara espouses the essence of the Dionysiac message when she proclaims that 'There is no wicked side: life is all one' (ibid., 151). Their way of life, Barbara declares, is on the category-defying Dionysiac path, 'through the raising of hell to heaven and of man to God, through the unveiling of an eternal light in the Valley of The Shadow' (ibid., 152). Perivale St Andrews, the hell on earth, will become with their guidance a heaven on earth: death will not be an end in itself, but a way towards a new, better way of life. The message that Murray found in the *Bacchae,* that 'The kingdom of Heaven is within you', will be revealed through the tutelage of Cusins and Barbara. If Perivale St Andrews and its inhabitants are to undergo a rebirth of the kind that Murray and his fellow Cambridge Ritualists found in the Dionysiac religion, Cusins's rebirth as the new Undershaft represents the victory of the new Year Daemon over his predecessor.

That Cusins and Barbara will successfully rise to the challenge set by Undershaft to make war on war by taking over the cannonworks, and that they will run it according to their own principles, seems certain. Undershaft might think he still sets the agenda when he has the last word and orders Euripides to start work at six the following morning, but the silence of Cusins is surely one of

[10] For a detailed discussion of the plot's relationship to the *Bacchae,* see Hall and Macintosh 2005, 503–8.

hopeful dissent rather than silent submission (Shaw 1960, 183). Undershaft, like Dionysus, may well remain powerful and diabolical in human terms until the end of the play, but the combined strengths of Cusins and Barbara (Mind and Spirit respectively) have guaranteed that the wildness of Dionysus has now been held in check, as it was through institutions and rituals during the fifth century BC in Athens.

MURRAY'S *BACCHAE* IN PERFORMANCE

If Shaw's *Major Barbara* captured the spirit and much of the content of Murray's *Bacchae*, this was not the case with the première of the translation at the Court Theatre in November 1908. The director was not Barker, but his earlier mentor, the great pioneer of Shakespearean productions, William Poel. It may well be the marked affinities between Shaw's play and the Euripidean tragedy that explain Barker's apparent neglect of Murray's text.[11] Even if Barker was reluctant to stage the *Bacchae*, his wife Lillah McCarthy was not. Having been prevented by Vedrenne from starring in her husband's productions,[12] when her husband was away in Ireland she took the opportunity to ask Poel to stage Murray's *Bacchae* with herself as Dionysus.

Lillah McCarthy was not alone in wanting to see a production of the *Bacchae* in 1908. At the beginning of the year, Murray had been in correspondence with the actress Edith Wynne Matthison suggesting that sections of the play would 'read very well' for public recitation during her imminent tour to the States (Murray to Wynne Matthison, 22 Jan. 1908: GM 13.57). In March, the dancer Maud Allan caused a great stir with her wild Bacchic reels at The Palace Theatre; and the same month Professor E. A. Sonnenschein asked Murray whether the

11 *Hippolytus* (Oct. 1904) and *Trojan Women* (April 1905) had already been staged before the première of *Major Barbara* (Nov. 1905). Barker went on to direct Murray's *Electra* (Jan. and March 1906), revived *Hippolytus* (March 1906) and produced the *Medea* (Oct. 1907), all before Poel's *Bacchae* in November 1908. See Hall and Macintosh 2005, 488–520.

12 J. E. Vedrenne to Murray, 22 July 1907: GM 12.127.

Bacchae would be a suitable play to stage at the October Classical Association meeting in Birmingham. Sonnenschein recommended the Birmingham-based composer Granville Bantock for the music, because Bantock had already begun working on a larger operatic version of the *Bacchae* using Murray's text as libretto.[13]

Whilst none of these projects ever materialized, Poel was enthusiastic and spent time in the British Museum researching his project. Even though he tells Murray that he thinks it unlikely he would find any scholar who would endorse his own view that Euripides was essentially making fun of Bacchus 'up his sleeve',[14] this Verrall-esque reading of the play had only just been recently restated by Gilbert Norwood in *The Riddle of the Bacchae*, where Dionysus becomes a target for Euripidean contempt.[15] Poel had admired Murray's *Hippolytus*, but found his translations generally, and his *Bacchae* in particular, distinctly non-dramatic. He agreed to the project only on the condition that Murray allow him to take certain liberties with his translation: 'to take out classical illusions [sic] that only scholars would understand—which would leave really the story bold and bare so as to accentuate the satire' (Poel to Murray (dictated letter), 7 Oct. 1908: GM 14.2–3). Murray gallantly entered into a lively exchange of views with Poel about the play (he was, of course, a close friend of Verrall); and despite warning from another close friend, the astute drama critic William Archer, to have nothing to do with the production, Murray agreed to some slight changes to his text (Archer to Murray, 14 Oct. 1908: GM 14.21–22).

However, when he eventually saw what Poel had done, not just to his translation but above all to the text of Euripides, he refused to allow the production to run beyond the first two matinées. The chorus consisted of four 'stately' Maenads, who moved only once from the sides of the proscenium during the two-hour production, and whose function was to chant the 'more solemn passages and to

[13] For Maud Allan and Greek tragedy, see Hall and Macintosh 2005, 548–54. For Bantock's *Bacchae*, see Sonnenschein to Murray, 7 Mar. 1908: GM 13.90–1.

[14] Poel to Murray (dictated letter), 7 Oct. 1908: GM 14.2–3.

[15] Norwood 1908. Verrall's 'Essay on Bacchants' had already been written, but was not published until 1910, although his study *Euripides the Rationalist: A Study in the History of Art and Religion*, which represented his general thesis, had appeared in 1895.

strike the note of inevitable fate'. They were matched by three coryphées, who danced and sang 'the gayer chorus speeches' (Poel to Murray, 25 Oct. 1908: GM 14.212–13). But it was not simply the division of the chorus or the highly static nature of the production that concerned Murray; he was irked primarily by Poel's Verrall-esque reading of the play, which had led to the removal of all mysticism surrounding Dionysus (what Poel felt were the Euripidean 'digressions') and had reduced Euripides' 'Mystery Play' (Murray 1902b, liv) to a 'rational' satire *tout court.*

When Poel writes to Murray of his proposed changes to the ending of the play, he refers to the differences between 'modern' and 'ancient' audiences; and it is here that we can glean the fundamental differences between their two readings (Poel to Murray, 20 Sept. 1908: GM 13.226). For Poel, it is imperative to register the shock, the horror and the anger of the chorus in the final scene of the play, by 'circular' movement in the action; above all, the movement served to deflect attention from the all 'too painful an incident' of the display of Pentheus' mutilated body, which Euripides has mistakenly offered his audience 'in cold blood' (ibid.). 'The play would have to end in a whirl', he added a few weeks later (Poel to Murray, 7 Oct. 1908: GM 14.3). For Murray, in the Introductory Essay of 1902, the silence of the Maenads at the end of the play is central to its meaning (Murray 1902, lvi). The power for good and evil that is inherent in the Dionysiac religion is only fully grasped through the silence of the Chorus. Poel, we infer, had completely failed to grasp the ritual significance of the play's final scene.

If the conclusion to Poel's *Bacchae* introduced stage business where Murray felt none was needed, the rest demanded very un-Bacchic stillness, like 'a Greek vase full of repose, dignity and grace' (Poel to Murray, 25 Oct. 1908: GM 14.213). Poel maintained that the 'pagan pitilessness of it all' had to be grasped 'through the brain, and not through the eye' (ibid.). That such a disjunction of the senses was fundamentally at odds with Murray's own ideas about art is amply evidenced by a comment in his essay of 1912, 'What English poetry may still learn from Greek'. Here Murray insists that thought and instinctive emotion should be one in poetry, although thought, in his view, tends to predominate in modern poetry (Murray 1912e, 672-3: copy in GM 441.7). In the *Bacchae*, by contrast, the Greek yoking of thought and feeling to which English poetry should aspire is amply exemplifed. Murray goes on to cite the following lines from the first messenger speech in his own translation as an example of what he calls the 'oneness of Greece', which all poetry should seek to emulate:

> ... And all the mountain felt,
> And worshipped with them; and the wild things knelt
> And ramped and gloried...
> (Murray 1902b, 116 (= Murray 1909a, *Bacch.* 726–727)

Whilst Murray's identification of Greek 'oneness' has a decidely Arnoldian ring, and whilst its roots lie ultimately in Romantic Hellenism, its link to the Dionysiac is pure Nietzsche. What is significant, however, about Murray's 'oneness' is that it relates to both religion and poetry. Indeed, there is a sense in which poetry is for Murray, the agnostic, a kind of surrogate religion. Poetry, he writes in 1927, is

> a thing that unites rather than separates... It is a common worship wherein all servants of the Muses labour, a common service wherein each can help another, and wherein a 'thing of beauty' lives on and is a 'joy for ever', on one condition only, that it is still studied and loved and understood.
> (Murray 1927a, 160-1. For further comment on this lecture, see Griffith in this volume)

Even though Shaw's version of the *Bacchae* had accommodated 'feeling' in its sympathetic portrayal of the Salvation Army, in the final scene of this Drama of Ideas emotion is eschewed altogether in favour of a typically Shavian non-corporeal ideal unity of Mind and Spirit in the persons of Cusins and Barbara. Poel's production of the play, by contrast, had deliberately omited the emotional dimension entirely, in what Murray would have seen as a very modern preoccupation with ratiocination alone. It was not until 1973, in Soyinka's version, that we find a *Bacchae* that seeks to combine thought with feeling within a highly ritualized context.[16]

[16] Richard Schechner's *Dionysus in 69* (Performing Garage, New York 1968) makes much use of ritual, but its concern with ritual is more academic than 'felt'. The same is true of Grüber's *Bakchen* (Schaubühnen am Halleschen Ufer, Berlin 1974). For comment on these milestone productions, see Zeitlin 2004, 47–75 and Fischer-Lichte 2004, 332–44.

SOYINKA'S *BACCHAE* AT THE NATIONAL THEATRE

When Soyinka comes to translate the contents of the first messenger speech, which Murray singled out as combining the poetic requisite of thought and feeling, he responds intuitively to its contents. He renders the lines cited by Murray as follows:

> Everything
> The very mountain seemed to sway to that one beat
> A beat like the hearts of a thousand men in unison.
> The beasts moved with them, they seemed
> Touched by a savage divinity. (Soyinka 1973, 60)

Even though neither Murray nor Soyinka is able to convey the extraordinarily potent compactness of the Greek (Murray's translation tails off into 'and the wilderness | Was filled with moving voices and dim stress'), here in Soyinka's version the formal aspects of the verse—the enjambment, sibilance, repetition, and half-rhyme and the alliterative plosives—none the less serve to reinforce the sense of Dionysiac unity.

Indeed the contents of the first messenger speech appear to infuse the whole first part of Soyinka's play. Listen to the highly charged and percussive language of the prologue:

> A seed of Zeus was sown in Semele my mother earth, here on this spot. It has burgeoned through the cragged rocks of far Afghanistan, burst the banks of fertile Tmolous, sprung oases through the red-eyed sands of Arabia; flowered in hill and gorge of dark Ethiopia. It pounds in the blood and breasts of my wild-haired women, long companions on this journey home through Phrygia and the isles of Crete. It beats on the walls of Thebes, bringing vengeance on all who deny holy origin and call my mother—slut. (ibid., 2)

Here with these lines from the prologue the audience shares in the energy and the intensity—and with the sharply bathetic conclusion, also the contradictions—that the Dionysiac religion ushers in its wake.

But it is not simply Soyinka's ability to yoke thought and feeling that makes his play so intensely true to Euripides' tragedy. It is also because he is able to draw on the striking parallels between Yoruba and ancient Greek culture. Soyinka has written extensively about the ties between the Greek and Yoruba pantheons, and more particularly about the ties between Ogun, the Yoruba god of iron whose powers include creativity, war and liberation, and the Greek god of contradictions, Dionysus (Soyinka 1976, 13–31, 140–60). Dionysus' followers carry the *thyrsus*, Ogun's carry the willow pole bedecked with palm fronds; Dionysiac rites culminate in the rending of a live quarry *(sparagmos)*, similarly the rites of Ogun culminate in the tearing apart of a live dog. When he was commissioned to write a version of Euripides' *Bacchae*, therefore, the transposition from Thebes to a Yoruba context was easy and natural. For Soyinka, it is the affinities between peoples which matter; and in his version of Euripides' *Bacchae*, he insists that the chorus of slaves be ethnically mixed: what unites them is their servitude, not their ethnic roots. And just as the Greeks celebrated a god of enormous contradictory powers, so did his grandparents.[17]

In his Introduction to *The Bacchae of Euripides*, we find, alongside references to W. K. C. Guthrie, E. R. Dodds and George Thomson (Soyinka 1973, viii–x), undiluted Murray intermixed with Nietzschean flavouring. For example, Soyinka's insistence that the worship of Dionysus affords the 'release[. . . of] the pent-up frustrated energy of all the down-trodden' is strikingly evocative of Murray's consistent desire to emphasize that the wisdom of ordinary people lies at the heart of the Dionysiac religion.[18] For Soyinka, Euripidean tragedy is (à la Murray) a sharp, but perforce veiled, critique of the 'subhuman' behaviour of the Olympians, at a time when overt criticism risked serious reprisal (Soyinka 1973, vi–xii; Murray 1897, 266, 268–9). And when Soyinka explains the underlying pattern of Euripides' *Bacchae*, the voices of Nietzsche and Murray come together:

[17] See Soyinka's interview with James Gibbs in Jeyifo 2001, 68–115. Soyinka significantly resisted the French movement of négritude—the Francophone movement led by the Senegalese poet and president Leopold Sere Senghor, which advocated black African identity divorced from European rationalism (Soyinka famously retorted: 'A tiger does not proclaim its tigritude'). As the Malawian critic Msiska has pointed out, Soyinka is in many ways the precursor of the 'hybridity' proclaimed by post-colonial critics like Homi Bhabha. See Msiska (1998), 5–7.

[18] Cf. Murray 1902b, 166: 'This religion, very primitive and barbarous, but possessing a strong hold over the emotions of the common people'; and 'No grudge hath he of the great/ No scorn of the mean estate . . . / The simple nameless herd of Humanity/ Hath deeds and faith that are truth enough for me!'

> I see *The Bacchae*, finally, as a prodigious barbaric banquet, an insightful manifestation of the universal need of man to match himself against Nature. The more than hinted-at cannibalism corresponds to the periodic needs of humans to swill, gorge and copulate on a scale as huge as Nature's on her monstrous cycle of regeneration. The ritual sublimated, or expressive, is both social therapy and reaffirmation of group solidarity, a hankering back to the origins and formation of guilds and phratries. Man re-affirms his indebtedness to earth, dedicates himself to the demands of continuity and invokes the energies of productivity. Re-absorbed within the communal psyche he provokes the resources of Nature; he is in turn replenished for the cyclic drain in his fragile individual potency. (Soyinka 1973, xi–xii)

Behind Soyinka's assessment of the ritual structure at the heart of Euripides' play, we detect Murray's account of the ancient rite of the Year Daemon as the controlling tragic principle alongside Nietzsche's insistence on the continuity and power of Dionysiac collective unity.

Like Shaw before him, Soyinka has also responded instinctively to Murray's liberatory message in the *Bacchae*. In Soyinka's play, this is made explicit from the opening scene, when Dionysus is immediately recognized by the Slave Leader as saviour. 'Welcome the new god . . . We are no longer alone', the Slave Leader urges his fellow slaves (Soyinka 1973, 7), emphasizing that Dionysus' strength lies in his capacity to unite the dispossessed. But although Soyinka's Thebes is on the brink of insurrection, the disparate group of slaves fear the consequences of resistance. Soyinka's Pentheus (not unlike Murray's reading of the Euripidean protagonist) presides tyrannically over the state. Here the tyranny is made explicit in the opening scene, where skeletons of crucified slaves line the path taken by the citizens of Thebes as they join the ritual procession, designed to enact the passing of the old year and the rebirth of the new. The procession, we gather, will culminate in the death by flogging of the ritual (usually but not, this year, enslaved) scapegoat. Now with the return of Dionysus, the liberator, subtle changes to the ritual occur: dying Thebes is represented not by the traditional slave but by Tiresias (who has elected himself as victim in order to defuse the political tension), and who in the opening scene is miraculously saved from death by the timely arrival of Dionysus. (Soyinka 1973, 5–7.)

Murray's quasi-Christian and pagan Dionysus is recalled in Soyinka's liturgical choral greeting of the god:

Blessed are they who know the mysteries of god
Blessed all who hallow their life in worship of god
Whom the spirit of god possesses, who are one
With earth, leaves and vine in the holy body of god. (ibid., 16.)

Soyinka's Slave Leader—as Murray explains—now reminds the chorus of slaves (who are distinct here from the chorus of Maenads also on stage) that the Dionysiac godhead is in them:

Seek him in your breasts with love, within
Your hidden veins, in the quiet murmur of your blood
Seek him in the marrow, in wombstone, he is fount of life...
A bud on the autumn bough, he blossoms in you
His green essence fills your womb of earth. (ibid., 21)

Later, when Pentheus lashes out at the slave who had initially been marked out as the Spirit of the Old Year before Tiresias' intervention, the tyrant meets with a new sharper resistance from all the slaves and from their Leader in particular, who proclaims: 'Dionysus shall avenge this profanity / I live to witness / The feast of the vengeance of joy' (ibid., 38). A horrified Pentheus realizes the implications of this new-found solidarity between the slaves, and the stage directions add that the Slave Leader 'bows his head suddenly and intones, the others repeating each line after him, as if this is a practised liturgy...':

...And this is what this day we celebrate
Our feet at the dance are the feet of men
Grape-pressing, grain-winnowing, our joy
Is the great joy of union with mother earth
And the end of separation between man and man. (ibid., 3)

In the final scene of the play, Soyinka provides 'a new resolution in the symbolic extension of ritual powers, but only such as we have already encountered with the Bacchantes on the mountain side' (ibid., xi). Instead of the Euripidean epiphanic Dionysus, who pronounces banishment for the survivors of the royal house of Thebes, we witness onstage a scene of fecundity that recalls the one reported by the herdsman in the first messenger speech, when we heard how one of the Maenads had

Tapped a rock and... out of that rock
Spouts—water! Clear, spring water, fresh as dew.
Another drove her fennel in the ground and, where
The earth was wounded—another spring! But this time—
Wine! A wine-spring! Two women on their knees
Scrape the soil with fingers and out flows
Milk, creamier than the morning yield from a champion cow. (ibid., 59)

First, however, we hear Tiresias' explanation to Kadmos of the horror that has taken place in the second scene on the mountain, which deliberately echoes in the minor key the harmony of that earlier cornucopia:

O Kadmos, it was a cause beyond madness, this
Scattering of his flesh to the seven winds, the rain
Of blood that streamed out endlessly to soak
Our land. Remember when I said, Kadmos, we seem to be
Upon sheer rockface, yet moisture oozes up at every
Step. Blood, you replied, blood. His blood
Is everywhere. The leaves of Kithairon have turned red with it. (ibid., 97)

But then the mood changes—as swiftly as it did on the mountains when the Maenads spied the intruders; and we witness the collocation of opposites that lies at the heart of the Dionysiac religion. As Agave is about to lift the head of Pentheus down from the stake upon which she had earlier mounted it in tragic frenzy, the head becomes incandescent and spurts forth red jets of what seems at first blood, but soon is understood to be wine. The celebrants 'Slowly, dreamlike... all move towards the fountain, cup their hands and drink.' But it is left to Agave to 'tilt... her head backwards to let a jet flush full in her face and flush her mouth' (ibid., 97). Here in the final moments of Soyinka's play, we see Murray's Dionysus, the proto-Christ ('He has given man Wine, which is his Blood and a religious symbol': Murray 1902, lix), fully incarnated on the stage in the 'Communion Rite' referred to in Soyinka's subtitle.

It was this final scene, above all, that caused huge controversy at the National Theatre in 1973.[19] But this was really hardly surprising. Soyinka was offering his audiences a very different *Bacchae* from those

[19] For comment, see Goff 2005, 73–88.

family-centred, psychologizing readings of Euripides' play that were popular at the time.[20] Soyinka too had been reading Murray, whose translations had fallen from fashion; and he had absorbed absolutely, moreover, Murray's ritual reading of tragedy, at a time when it was deemed by some to be mildly eccentric but by others to be wholly heretical. But now that ritual readings of ancient drama have gained wider currency—thanks notably to the work of Burkert, Zimmerman and Seaford[21]—the extent of the theatrical legacy of Murray's *Bacchae* can be fully acknowledged.

[20] e.g. Maureen Duffy's *Rites* (National Theatre, 1969).

[21] Burkert 1966, 1972, 1987; Zimmerman 1991, 1992; and Seaford 1994, 1996.

8

Gilbert Murray and A. E. Housman

Malcolm Davies

Of Murray and Housman it has been said that, in the 1920s and 1930s, 'to younger men, two opposing principles seemed to be personified' in them (M. I. Henderson 1960, 142); and their capacity for provoking meditation upon the very nature of scholarship has not ceased with their deaths. In the first place, they have much in common: both students at St John's College, Oxford, in the last quarter of the nineteenth century, and later honorary fellows of the same institution; both professors, of Latin or Greek, at Oxford or Cambridge; both recipients of an offer of the Order of Merit (declined in Housman's case, accepted in Murray's). One could go on. But their careers and characters also supply much in the way of antithetical contrast. Murray's brilliant undergraduate years, littered with prizes, culminated in his appointment as Professor of Greek in Glasgow at the age of 23. Housman's failure to win any University prizes, and his even more spectacular failure at the Finals examination known as 'Greats', followed by the years at the galley (if one may so term a youth divided between the Patent Office and the British Museum Library), set off all the more effectively his ultimate academic triumphs in the decades at Cambridge. The two men knew each other and corresponded by

For a different attempt (from a different angle) to compare and contrast these two scholars see my *Housman and Murray: A Syncrisis* (M. Davies 2006), a lecture originally delivered as part of the 450th anniversary celebrations of the Oxford college at which they were both undergraduates. In what follows I have tried to avoid excessive overlap with that earlier piece.

letter. Only Housman's contributions to this exchange have survived,[1] but one sees clearly therein his awareness of the differences in attitudes to scholarship and life by which the two were divided, and his eagerness to emphasize them. Again one could go on; but I bring this introductory paragraph to a close with an obvious ploy. Both men's achievements were known to Wilamowitz, Germany's greatest classical scholar (though only Murray met and corresponded with him), and of Housman he declared, towards the end of their lives, 'We Germans... pronounce him to be the greatest living authority on both Latin and Greek in the English-speaking world' (see M. Davies 2006, 14; cf. Diggle 2007). Of Murray he had earlier remarked, 'He writes almost pure nonsense; a pupil of Verrall', and 'I take Murray seriously only as a poet. So much as I have read of the Homer book can rank only in the category poetry' (Wilamowitz-Moellendorff 1991, 6). Since Wilamowitz entertained a deep reverence for the poet's vocation, the remark is less damning than it may initially appear. And in fact Murray's book on Homer, with its ingenious attempt to find comparative material in the Old Testament, may rank as forerunner of that study of the Ancient Near East's influence upon Greece which is the most striking development of classical studies during the last fifty years or so.[2] But Wilamowitz here rates Housman above Murray even as a Greek scholar, a verdict that is perfectly compatible with James Diggle's recent magisterial survey of Housman's achievements as a critic of Greek literature, especially Greek tragedy (Diggle 2007). The casual way in which Murray privately spoke of Housman as an editor of Manilius, placing him in a trio also including Robinson Ellis and Garrod (M. Davies 2006, 11f.), does not, perhaps, suggest he grasped the distinctive features that set Housman apart as a scholar.

One wonders whether Wilamowitz's verdict on Murray may not also have been Housman's opinion too. In their exchange of letters Housman was courtesy itself, for instance, as regards the second

[1] See the new edition of Housman's letters by Archie Burnett (Housman 2007): index s.v. 'Murray'.

[2] One would expect the minds of poets to have picked this up more readily than others, and it is symptomatic that Hugo von Hofmannsthal should have told the producer of his adaptation of Sophocles' *Electra* to think in terms of the orient: see Hofmannsthal 1997, 379.

volume of Murray's Oxford Classical Text of Euripides, writing to him on 4 November 1904 (Housman 2007, I. 167) that 'it is much the pleasantest edition and clearest apparatus to use', admittedly a rather ambivalent statement in the mouth of this critic,[3] and proceeding 'I have been looking through the earlier part of the *Heracles* in general agreement with your selection of readings. Turning over the pages at random, it strikes me that Verrall has exerted a baleful influence: e.g. < τί > at *Suppl.* 149 is what I should call a perfectly impossible reading. Why didn't Porson make this conjecture? ... when one at this date makes a conjecture of this sort one ought to do it with one's hair standing on end and one's knees giving way beneath one; because the odds are a hundred to one that it is a conjecture which our betters were withheld from making by their superior tact'. And we find him telling Murray that 'with your command of language and metre you are really a noble example of ἐγκράτεια, in that you don't produce volumes of original poetry' (letter of 13 Oct. 1903: Housman 2007, I. 157). His genuine feelings may be more discernible in a review he wrote of the inaugural lecture delivered (but not published) by Murray's predecessor as Professor of Greek at Oxford, Ingram Bywater: 'it is the business-like performance of a good scholar who did not aspire to be an indifferent man of letters, and readers who wish to hear about the Greek spirit may leave it alone' (Housman 1920). C. M. Bowra is not the only reader to have concluded that 'this is all too clearly aimed at Murray' (Bowra 1966, 221).

A similar contrast may be cited between Housman's compliments to Murray on his appointment as Professor of Greek at Oxford (letter of 17 Oct. 1908: Housman 2007, II. 226–7) and his earlier letter to Grant Richards opining that his addressee's uncle 'Herbert Richards ought to' be appointed (27 June 1908: Housman 2007, II. 222–3). This

[3] The words are strikingly reminiscent of the opening sentences that constitute the sinister calm, the lull before the storm, at the start of one of Housman's most devastating reviews (published the year before this letter to Murray) of another OCT, this time by S. G. Owen:

> 'this edition of Persius and Juvenal is certainly the handiest in existence. The paper and binding are good, the print is excellently clear, the notes, by the omission of unimportant variants, are rendered not only briefer than Mr Buecheler's but plainer and easier to use, and the whole is executed with sufficient accuracy of detail.' (Housman 1903b)

opinion, if investigated, transpires to be eloquent as to Murray and Housman's divergent views of scholarship. For that this was no casually thrown out remark or indirect compliment to his publisher is shown by a letter written about ten years later (19 Feb. 1916) to the same addressee (Housman 2007, l. 355): 'I am very sorry indeed to see in the paper today the sudden death of your uncle—though I suppose it was not altogether sudden, as it took place in the Ackland Home. When I saw him last, at your house, he seemed full of sturdiness. There are far too few severe and thorough scholars of his sort.'

In an earlier handling of Housman's preference for Richards over Murray as a Greek scholar (M. Davies 2006, 10), I fear I allowed myself to treat Herbert Richards as something of a figure of fun—which is easily done. Apart from the apparently absurd self-importance of his juvenile (in every sense) letter to Karl Marx, written during 1871 in his capacity as 'secretary of the Oxford Republican Club', there is the issue of his behaviour in 'the Great Wadham Row' of 1879. This event, beginning with 'scenes of wild anarchy' in the days following upon Eights week, saw undergraduates attack 'the room of a don known as "Unbelieving Dick", who fled across the quad in his nightshirt'.[4] The radicalism evinced by his letter to Marx seems also to be reflected in the sobriquet just cited.

Years later, in 1913, Richards was considered for the Wardenship of Wadham against J. B. Wells, commentator upon Herodotus and on this occasion the successful candidate. Wells wrote privately that Richards would have been a disastrous appointment, since he lacked both humanity and approachability. It was not, then, an individual particularly predisposed towards Richards who, as seems likely, was author both of the obituary in the *Oxford Magazine* reprinted in the *Wadham College Gazette* and of the obituary which the latter published on the immediately preceding pages.[5] In terms reminiscent of Housman's he speaks in the first of 'the great Greek scholar, whose decisions in matters of criticism were received even in Germany, as

[4] See C. S. L. Davies 1979 ('the story that the whole College was sent down in 1880 is one of the more cherished pieces of Wadham folklore'), quoting the account in Gribble 1910.

[5] 'In memoriam: H. P. Richards', *Wadham College Gazette* 56 (Hilary Term 1916) 395–7, reprinted from *Oxford Magazine* 34 (25 Feb. 1916), 211–12; editorial, *Wadham College Gazette*, ibid., 385–7. I owe this information and the attribution of both the relevant obituaries to the Wadham College archivist, C. S. L. Davies.

"the last words" that settled the question', and quotes a colleague on 'the best Greek scholar of his time... of his scholarship scholars must speak; for all scholars knew it and many feared it'. In the latter he says that 'probably there was no contemporary British scholar whose emendations were received with such respect by the learned of Europe and America... Since the death of Professor Bywater, [he] was probably without dispute the first of English Greek scholars, and it was rather hard that his work never received any University recognition.' If one is looking for contrasts between Housman and Herbert Richards on the one side and Murray on the other, one may recall at this juncture the latter's verdict on Bywater in a letter to a friend: 'Bywater, I suppose, knows that this is so' [that 'there are really life and poetry and things that move one in ancient literature'], but I doubt if he can make anyone else know it' (M. I. Henderson 1960, 127). Richards' work is explored further in the Appendix to this chapter.

I have touched elsewhere on the contrasting conceptions of scholarship entertained (explicitly and implicitly) by Murray and Housman. The issue of popularization of ancient literature, especially in the shape of performable translations, is of obvious relevance here, and there is an interesting letter on this topic (25 Oct. 1904: Housman 2007, ll. 166–7) from Housman to Murray inspired by the former's visit to the Royal Court Theatre, London, to see the latter's rendering of Euripides' *Hippolytus* ('though I can't say that witnessing the play gave me as much pleasure as reading it, it did give me pleasure and indeed excitement'). Murray was far better known for his renderings into English of ancient literature than Housman, but very near the beginning of his scholarly career the latter did produce three translations, one from each of the Attic tragedians, for his Oxford friend A. W. Pollard's anthology *Odes from the Greek Dramatists* (Pollard 1890). The passages were Aeschylus' *Seven against Thebes* 848–60, Sophocles' *Oedipus at Colonus* 1212–48, and Euripides' *Alcestis* 962–1005. The Sophoclean passage is a masterpiece of rendition excelled only by its author's own 'The snows are fled away' (Horace *Odes* 4.7) from near the end of his life.[6] It is both

[6] On this translation see, e.g., the remarks of Wilkinson 1974, 44–5. For the famous occasion of Housman's reading out of Horace's Ode, 'the most beautiful poem' from antiquity, followed by his own rendering, and then precipitately leaving the lecture room, see e.g. the account preserved in G. Richards 1941, 289.

appropriate and moving that Housman's literary and scholarly existence should be thus rounded with poetry clearly evoked by an apparent coincidence between the ancient poet's and his own pessimistic outlook on life. As for the Euripidean version, over forty years after its first publication, Housman wrote to W. R. Agard (22 Mar. 1933: Housman 2007, 2.326) giving permission to reprint what he called 'my Swinburnian translation from Euripides'. Since Murray's translations of the same dramatist were notoriously denounced by T. S. Eliot as 'a vulgar debasement of the eminently personal idiom of Swinburne' that 'blurs the Greek lyric to the fluid haze of Swinburne' (Eliot 1920; cf. M. Davies 2006, 16), it is interesting to find Housman making this confession. Interesting too that, almost simultaneously with Eliot's denunciation, Housman, in a review of two volumes of *The Cambridge History of English Literature* (Housman 1917), makes a similar point though more allusively:

> In the sixties it seemed indeed as if there had arisen a band of writers to launch poetry on a new career; but time showed that they were cruising in a backwater, not finding a channel for the main stream, and in twenty years all heart had gone out of the enterprise. The fashions of that interlude are already so antique that Mr Gilbert Murray can adopt them for his rendering of Euripides; and there they now receive academic approbation, which is the second death.

As with the notice of Bywater's posthumously printed inaugural, one finds here again that tension between private praise delivered to Murray's face (Housman had written to him, as we have seen, complimenting his renderings of Euripides' *Hippolytus* and *Bacchae* for their 'command of language and metre') and the decidedly more ambivalent attitude expressed publicly and rather gratuitously in a review not directly connected with Murray at all.

Also relevant is Murray's translation into Greek elegiacs of an original poem by Housman (*Fancy's Knell*), with its exquisite modulation of the last line (Smith and Toynbee 1960, 121). And though it does not count as a translation, one may appropriately end this section with a reference to the introductory Latin elegiacs which Housman composed to stand at the beginning of his edition of the first book of Manilius' *Astronomica* (Housman 1903a). When Murray was asked implicitly about the poetic merit of Manilius, he replied that there were 'beautiful phrases and passages in Manilius—perhaps nothing quite so good as' Housman's own dedicatory elegiacs (M. Davies 2006, 18). This reads like a typical donnish joke; but that Murray's admiration was more deeply rooted is shown by his verdict that 'it was the only modern Latin verse he had read that might have come from the lips of a classical poet' (Goold 2000, 143). Deep emotion certainly underlies the lines—Edmund Wilson's translation of the couplets into English (Ricks 1988, 253–4), specifically the English of Housman's own poetry, makes an apt point, though it reads too like pastiche—which with characteristic irony were dedicated *sodali meo M. I. Iackson, harum litterarum contemptori*. As for Murray, not many will ever have agreed with Wilfrid Scawen Blunt's verdict (confided to his diary) that Murray was 'worth ten of [W. B. Yeats] as a poet' or that he deserved to be appointed Poet Laureate (Blunt 1919, 2.103, 390).

If we compare and contrast the two men's spontaneous and unrehearsed responses to masterpieces of contemporary literature, Housman notoriously (though inadvertently) did Richards a bad turn and cut him off from a much-needed financial windfall by arguing him out of commissioning a translation into English of Proust's *A la recherche du temps perdu*: a letter of 9 Oct. 1919 (Housman 2007, l. 418) warns that 'an English translation would not sell, and... could not be really satisfactory, as the merit of the French is in great part a matter of diction and vocabulary'). Nor was his response to Gerard Manley Hopkins—in effect a 'contemporary' poet—any more impressive. Writing to Robert Bridges on 30 December 1918 he observed (Housman 2007, ll. 396–7) that 'the faults which you very fairly and judiciously set forth [in your Introduction] thrust themselves more upon my notice... here is a lesser than Keats doing much more [violence upon the English language].... His manner strikes me as deliberately adopted to compensate by strangeness for the lack of pure merit.' Admittedly, as late as the 1920s and 1930s it was still the case that, as Q. D. Leavis put it, 'to value highly the poems of Hopkins was another way to incur academic odium' (Leavis 1943, 14). But one may still wish that Housman had been able to surmount this barrier. It is of course some such failure that T. S. Eliot attributed to Murray's translations of Euripides in his famous denunciation.

Murray, by contrast, seems to have appreciated pretty instantly the impact of Hugo von Hofmannsthal's adaptation of Sophocles' *Electra*. The Austrian poet's friend Count Harry Kessler was introduced to Murray in Bernard Shaw's company on 29 January 1908 and wrote back to Hofmannsthal the following day: 'he spoke with great admiration of your *Elektra*, which he found "extraordinarily fine" and "really more primitive than Sophocles".[7] Since he is Professor of Greek at Oxford or Cambridge his verdict is of great interest and value'. One may smile at Kessler's characteristic aristocrat's indifference as to precisely where Murray professed[8] (he is writing—*natürlich*—from 'Hotel Cecil, Strand, WC'), but the opinion preserved is certainly an index of independent judgement at a time when the excessive and second-hand idealizing of Sophocles was leading many in England to denounce Hofmannsthal's 'perversion' of the Greek original.[9]

Both men were resistant to chauvinism. Murray's *ODNB* entry (Stray 2004) identifies him right at the beginning as 'Classical scholar and Internationalist' and one may recall his reaction to dispraise of 'the Germans' by T. W. Allen, who in the Preface (dated May 1923) to his book *Homer: The Origins and the Transmission* (Allen 1924) had written thus:

It is not to overlook their merits and service in the collection and arrangement of material, and their capacity for soul-destroying and sometimes futile labour... Recent events [i.e. World War I] have shown how erroneous German psychology, the intuition of the feelings of other nations, is... Their

[7] 'Er sprach mit grosser Bewunderung von deiner Elektra, die "extraordinarily fine" and "really more primitive than Sophokles". Da Gilbert Murray Professor der griechischen Literatur in Oxford oder Cambridge ist, so ist das Urteil interessant und wertvoll' (30 Jan. 1908: Hofmannsthal 1968, 170 = Hofmannsthal 1997, 432).

[8] This is no reason for Hilde Burger to confer a knighthood on Murray in her note ad loc. in her edition of the letters (Hofmannsthal 1968, 509: 'Sir George Gilbert Aimé Murray'); an error taken over by Matthias Mayer's corresponding note in the *Kritische Ausgabe* (Hofmannsthal 1997, 432 n. 69). For Murray's refusal of the honour, see D. Wilson 1987, 193.

[9] See my remarks in M. Davies 1999a. For less tolerant contemporary reactions to Hofmannsthal's adaptation (and then to his libretto for Strauss's opera), see M. Davies 1999b. These less tolerant reactions were influenced by the nineteenth century's idealization of Sophocles, an idealization not shared by Murray. See Griffith's chapter in this volume, Easterling 1997, 119–21, and in general Uhlig 2003, 133ff.

principles are a *trompe-l'oeil*, their methodology a rigmarole. We have suffered too long under them.

Such remarks evoked from Murray the notable rebuke (as the last sentence of his notice of the work in the *Classical Review*), 'We feel bound to add that Mr. Allen's tone towards German and Austrian scholars will be regretted by those who value the courtesies of intellectual life' (Murray 1925b, 73).

Even Wilamowitz, in the eulogy cited above, automatically assumed that Housman was 'a rabid Germanophobe', a charge which Housman denied in this specific case. In his famous talk on 'The Application of Thought to Textual Criticism' (Housman 1922), he wrote:

Patriotism . . . in the sphere of the intellect . . . is an unmitigated nuisance. I do not know which cuts the worse figure: a German scholar encouraging his countrymen to believe that 'wir Deutsche' have nothing to learn from foreigners, or an Englishman demonstrating the unity of Homer by sneers at 'Teutonic professors', who are supposed by his audience to have goggle eyes behind large spectacles, and ragged moustaches saturated in lager beer, and consequently to be incapable of forming literary judgements.

But clearly the misconception about Germanophobia derives from Housman's memorable polemic.

By chance, Murray's notice of Allen's *Homer* was immediately followed in the pages of the *Classical Review* by J. T. Sheppard's notice of the third edition of Murray's own *Rise of the Greek Epic* (Murray 1924)—a notice which in turn ends with observations regarding *tone*: 'however keen the controversy, he remembers always the urbanity, the courtesy,—the *Aidos*—which should be, but is not, always shown to one another by the students of "humanities"' (Sheppard 1925, 74). Writing from Cambridge in the mid-1920s, Sheppard may have had Housman in mind as antithesis to the desiderated ideal. The controversy has a long history: 'What profit is it', Jeremiah Markland had already asked in 1763, 'if an education in letters, instead of making us, as it professes to, gentle, upright, simple, frank, modest and kindly towards all men, renders us fierce, virulent, cunning, arrogant, malignant and implacable towards all who presume to differ from us even in trifles?'[10] He doubtless had Bentley in mind. Housman himself may well have been thinking of this passage when he observed in his inaugural lecture at University College London in 1892 that

> the classics cannot be said to have succeeded altogether in transforming and beautifying Milton's inner nature. They did not sweeten his naturally disagreeable temper; they did not enable him to conduct controversy with urbanity or even with decency. . . . It appears that upon the majority of mankind the classics cannot be said to exert the transforming influence which is claimed for them. (Carter 1961, 10)

One may further quote a more recent scholar's summation of Murray's character: 'He was a stranger to academic pettiness; . . . the kind of person humanistic scholarship ought to produce but so rarely does, for all its fine talk' (Fowler 1990, 329).

In fact, Murray occasionally allowed himself to move in the direction of a more swashbuckling style. The opening paragraph of his review of Allen's aforementioned volume is a case in point:

> His method of argument reminds one of the accused in some recent murder cases. . . . He now admits facts that are notoriously proved, and bases his case on the things about which there is no evidence. He was seen in the company of the deceased up to 11.50 p.m.; he was seen burying the body at twelve midnight; but in the intervening ten minutes, when he was not seen, he assures us that the most amazing things happened. (Murray 1925b, 71)

However, one senses that his heart was not really in it; and when he came to write a notice of Allen's superficially impressive three-volume *editio maior* of the *Iliad* (Allen 1931), all reservations flew out of the window, to be replaced by a tone of near-servile veneration: 'This is a book before which a critic must take off his hat and stand in respectful silence. It is almost incredible that such a vast mass of minute and highly skilled research should be the work of one man' (Murray 1932, 12). In reality, the respect is utterly out of place, as is

[10] In his edition of Euripides' *Supplices*:

> 'quo enim eruditionis nomen si barbarorum animos retineamus? . . . quid prodest si pro mitibus, probis, simplicibus, ingenuis, modestis, benevolis erga omnes homines, quales promittit litterata institutio, ea nos dimittit feroces, maledicos, versutos, malignos, implacabiles omnibus qui a nobis dissentire ausi fuerint, etiam in nugis?' (Markland 1763, p. iv)

the claim, following hard on its heels, that Allen's collation supplies 'a complete and trustworthy account of all the minuscule MSS of the *Iliad* from the ninth or tenth centuries onwards'. On the contrary, as an expert has more accurately said of Allen, though

> even the Germans were impressed by his energy, it is now quite certain that they should not have been.... In recent years scholars wishing to test and build upon Allen's results relating to both epics have found a state of affairs which can only excite dismay. There is so much inaccuracy in what Allen states about the readings of the manuscripts that one cannot rely on him at all.... It can only be thought surprising that the weakness in Allen's work was not exposed sooner... Allen had claimed... that he had collated more than 100 manuscripts of the *Iliad*. The most elementary calculation proves that his boast cannot be taken literally. He had been at work some 10 years, so that on average he would have had to collate 10 manuscripts every year. But collation is a very slow business, and to collate a copy of the *Iliad* in a month would be quite an achievement if one had nothing else to do. (N. G. Wilson 1990, 316)

And so on. A reminder, surely, that courtesy and urbanity are not invariably the best tools when evaluating a work of classical scholarship.

The continuing appeal of the contrast between Housman and Murray can be seen, for instance, in Hugh Lloyd-Jones's inaugural lecture *Greek Studies in Modern Oxford*:

> A good edition of Manilius will retain much of its value fifty years later; a book like *Five Stages of Greek Religion* will be largely out of date. Does this mean that Housman was right to dismiss Murray as one who could have been a good scholar, but preferred to be an indifferent man of letters? My answer would be a thousand times no. (Lloyd-Jones 1982, 28)

Indeed, Lloyd-Jones elsewhere made the point that the books which most powerfully determined his own devotion to Greek studies were by Murray (ibid., 212). This may serve as a useful reminder that both Housman and Murray, different though their conceptions of scholarship may have been, were both capable of work that could *inspire*: one thinks of the last paragraph of the Preface to Dodds's commentary on Euripides' *Bacchae* (Dodds 1944, vii), or of Shackleton Bailey's declaration that the reading of Housman's *Manilius* was 'the most memorable intellectual experience of' his life (N. Page 1998, 175).

But this is to talk merely of the relatively circumscribed world of classical scholarship. Beyond their 'works', the life and character of both men has exerted a fascination—and sometimes even an influence—on individuals far removed from their purely professional fields.[11] One may finally be tempted to take refuge in Lord Blake's conclusion to his contrasting of Gladstone and Disraeli: 'Perhaps we should end as we began with Lord Granville [writing to Queen Victoria]: "Lord Beaconsfield and Mr. Gladstone are men of extraordinary ability", and leave it at that' (Blake 1998, 70). But this would be too easy an exit. For, as we have seen, the two men do seem to personify different attitudes to life and learning. Over several decades now, Housman's model has dominated and served as a powerful incentive to professionalism. But of each it could be said that he was, though in a very different way and in different areas, a crucial modernizer of English classical studies.[12]

[11] In the Italian general election of 2006, Romano Prodi, the ultimately victorious leader of the centre-left coalition, lambasted the incumbent prime minister as a man who 'clings to data in the way a drunkard clings to a lamp-post—not for illumination but to keep him standing up'. Housman would have been surprised, though perhaps gratified, to learn that one of his best-known *bon mots* (about 'gentlemen who use MSS as drunkards use lamp-posts, not to light their way, but to dissimulate their instability') had, at whatever remove, been thus drawn into the political arena of the Mediterranean.

[12] For Murray as, along with Frazer, Jane Harrison, Farnell, and Marett, one of 'the most remarkable modernisers of English classical studies', see A. Momigliano, *Nono Contributo alla Storia degli Studi Classici e del mondo antico* (Roma 1992), 599.

APPENDIX

Herbert Richards

Since there is no *DNB* entry for Herbert Richards, and Housman has paid him the compliment—extravagant or not—of preference to Murray, it is not irrelevant to investigate his scholarly achievements further. This is all the more desirable since one suspects a covert self-portrait lurking beneath the words 'severe and thorough' used by Housman in his letter to Herbert Richards' nephew. It is no coincidence that E. J. Kenney's obituary of D. R. Shackleton Bailey (described by another colleague as the classical scholar 'least unlike' Housman) should have used, in its opening sentence, the self-same phrase of both scholars (Kenney 2006; for 'the least unlike' see Lloyd-Jones 1982, 182).

Herbert Richards' scholarly monument takes the form of three volumes of reprinted articles—decidedly unusual for British classical scholars of the time, as opposed to Germany, where such *Kleine Schriften* were a familiar phenomenon. The availability of his nephew's London publishing firm is a partial but not total explanation (and it represents a further contrast with Murray, who published several books proper, but strikingly few articles in classical journals). The volumes were substantial too: *Notes on Xenophon and Others* (H. Richards 1907), amounting to over 350 closely-printed quarto pages, *Aristophanes and Others* (H. Richards 1909) to almost 400, and *Platonica* (H. Richards 1911) again to over 350.

If one selects the middle one of these three volumes from which to cull a few representative emendations, one soon notes that an editor who knows his business has cause to cite the best of them, at least in the *apparatus criticus.* Taking M. L. West, then, as an uncontroversial instance of 'an editor who knows his business',[1] we see that in the *apparatus criticus* to his Teubner edition of the *Anacreontea* (M. L. West 1984) he quotes, for instance, at 33.9 Richards' κατὰ μευ

[1] It may, however, be noted that M. L. West only cites (1974, 151; 1984, p. xxv; 1990, 380) by original publication in the relevant classical journal, without adding references to the reprint in H. Richards 1909. He thus misses Richards' (not particularly convincing) εἰκὸς δ' ὑπάρχειν for οἶκοςδ' ὑπάρχει at Aesch. *Ag.* 961 and ἂν γράψειεν for ἀντρέψειεν, ibid. 1328.

σκεδαῖς (for σχίσας) ὀνείρους, at 34.8 σὺ δὲ φίλτατος (for φιλία) γεωργῶι, though West prefers his own φείδεαι γεωργῶν, and at 37.11 ἐθέλοντος δὲ φιλῆσαι Richard's δ' ἐκφιλῆσαι. Likewise, towards the end of the 'Unlisted emendations (18th–20th centuries)' which stands as Appendix IV to his *Studies in Aeschylus* (M. L. West 1990) and supplements the similar lists of Wecklein and Dawe, West adds on p. 400 for *PV* 1030f. ὡς ὅ δ'οὐ πεπλασμένος | ὁ κόμπος, ἀλλὰ καὶ λίαν εἰρημένος Richards' suggestion ὡρισμένος. Finally, at Tyrtaeus 5.4 Richards' ἀμφ'αὐτῆι for ἀμφ'αὐτήν is mentioned in the *app. crit.*, and at Theognis 96, M. L. West actually places in the text Richards' λεῖα (unmentioned in Young's Teubner edition) for the MSS' λώια or λῶστα, supporting it at M. L. West 1974, 151. One may also note that Richards' φρενοῦντες for φρονοῦντας at Eur. *Hipp.* 115 was convincingly supported by Lloyd-Jones 1965, 166, though unmentioned in the editions of Barrett or Diggle.

One may further note at Aristophanes *Acharnians* 68f. Richards' παρὰ [τῶν] Καϋστρίων | πεδίων (διὰ [τῶν] Bentley) which is rightly cited in the apparatus, rightly not preferred to Bentley's solution, and rightly restored to Meineke in Olson's edition: see his discussion of the solutions advanced (Olson 2002, 92). At Sophocles *OT* 772 Dawe commends (1973, 243) and puts in the text of his Teubner edition (Dawe 1996) Richards' κἀμείνονι for καὶ μείζονι (*vid. contra* Lloyd-Jones and N. G. Wilson 1990, 97). Richards also produced (reprinted as an Appendix to H. Richards 1907) a number of emendations in Latin literature, and S. J. Harrison informs me that he and M. D. Reeve find convincing Richards' *dominae* (for *geminas*) *deorum ad aures nova nuntia referens* at Catullus 63.75 (H. Richards 1895, 305 = H. Richards 1907, 323): *deorum* is impossible of a single specific deity (whence Goold's *deae* (Munro) *tum*) and *geminas* has no point (the set phrase *geminae aures* at *Culex* 150 etc. cited in defence could on the contrary be a source of corruption). Cf. *deum mater* of Cybele at Lucretius 2.598 etc.

Finally, the volume just cited opens with several emendations to the text of Xenophon's *Oeconomicus*, so one may observe that in the edition which prefaces Sarah B. Pomeroy's 'social and historical commentary' thereon (Pomeroy 1994), one conjecture by Richards is promoted to the text and several cited in the apparatus (some being there reassigned to their original author).

9

'*Macte nova virtute, puer!*': Gilbert Murray as Mentor and Friend to J. A. K. Thomson

Barbara F. McManus

'I find myself awfully tired and ninety-ish. You are becoming a popular author, with your Penguin Aristotle and all the classical influence books. Macte nova virtute, puer!' (20 Mar. 1956: GM 175.228).[1] Gilbert Murray wrote these words to James Alexander Kerr Thomson (hereafter referred to as J. A. K.) to compliment him on the publication in 1955 of his translation and commentary on *The Ethics of Aristotle* as a Penguin Classic, as well as on Thomson's four books on classical influences on English Literature.[2] Murray's choice of this quotation from *Aeneid* 9.641 incorporates many layers of irony. In its original context, Apollo commends Aeneas' son Ascanius for killing one of the enemy with an arrow: 'Blessings on your new valour, boy!' Thus Murray is putting himself in the position of a god congratulating an untried boy on his first accomplishment. Since Murray had both inspired and actively promoted Thomson's work for over forty years, his choice of the role of Apollo had some justification, though at the age of 77 Thomson was hardly a boy, and these books were the culmination of a lifetime of classical scholarship and teaching. Moreover, Apollo praises Ascanius for following in his own footsteps, while Thomson's

[1] GM = Bodleian Library, Oxford, MSS Gilbert Murray, with box and folio number.

[2] Thomson's four books on this subject, all published by Allen & Unwin, were *The Classical Background of English Literature* (1948), *Classical Influences on English Poetry* (1951), *Shakespeare and the Classics* (1952), and *Classical Influences on English Prose* (1955).

nova virtus has drawn him outside Murray's shadow into a new initiative which Thomson himself has launched and is continuing to develop without his mentor's help. The unexpressed second part of the quotation, *sic itur ad astra* ('that is the path to the stars'), suggests Murray's belief that Thomson's new work is at last bringing him some measure of fame and public recognition, with perhaps a hint of wistful regret at the incipient waning of Murray's own star. This last is the deepest irony of all; far from shining brightly in the scholar's heaven, Thomson's name has become so dim that very few classicists even remember who he was.

Gilbert Murray devoted a considerable amount of time and energy to mentoring younger scholars; any modern reassessment of the man should include information about this important aspect of his contribution to Classics. Murray's mentoring relationship with J. A. K. Thomson is significant not only for its extent and duration, but especially for its transformation into the closest personal friendship that Murray had with another classicist. This relationship was recognized at the time (witness the British Academy's choice of Thomson to write Murray's obituary for *Proceedings*) but is today virtually unknown and previously unchronicled. None of the biographies or biographical articles about Murray devotes more than a few paragraphs to Thomson, if indeed he is mentioned at all.[3] This article will draw upon the long and remarkably unguarded correspondence between the two men to examine such questions as what led Murray to become a lifetime patron and promoter of Thomson and his work, why he ultimately drew Thomson into the sanctum of his personal life, and what this relationship reveals about Murray's ideals, personal judgments, and sense of fun.

Murray first became aware of Thomson through an unsolicited letter in 1908, one of many that Murray received from strangers wanting his advice, help, or attention. It is hard to imagine that

[3] West describes Thomson as 'an old friend and frequent holiday companion' (F. J. West 1984, 236), summarizes their relationship in a paragraph, and briefly quotes from a few of their letters. Wilson quotes from the British Academy obituary and some of the later letters and states that Thomson was 'perhaps the man who knew Murray best' (D. Wilson 1987, 394), but he never explains the relationship or says anything about Thomson himself. Stray echoes Wilson's assessment that Thomson knew Murray 'better than most' and quotes once from the obituary (Stray 2004a, 917); the other biographers ignore Thomson completely.

such letters were not an annoying incursion on the time of an already very busy man, but Murray always responded with politeness and sometimes, as in this case, the initial contact led to a mentoring relationship. Thomson's letter began rather awkwardly: 'I have been reading your book on "The Rise of the Greek Epic"—which you will perhaps take as a sufficient justification for my writing to you.' He went on to criticize Matthew Arnold's contention that Homer's 'grand style' argued against the theory of a composite Homer, maintaining that 'the style of Homer, incomparable as it is, is not an individual style.... It is like the style of the Scottish ballads in this respect, that it is everywhere the same and everywhere (when the subject is a great one) at the level of that subject.' Thomson ended the letter with a characteristically self-deprecating comment: 'Will you excuse the unavoidable egotism of all this?' (12 Feb. 1908: GM 171.1–3). Murray sent a one-paragraph response several months later, commenting that Thomson made a point that was 'well worth working out and stating carefully.... If I were less busy I would write more fully' (13 Oct. 1908: GM 171.4). This encouraged Thomson to identify himself as an Oxford graduate and Greek Assistant to John Burnet at the University of St Andrews and to continue the correspondence. After Murray sent him a copy of the second edition of *The Rise of the Greek Epic*, Thomson asked whether he could call on Murray when he was next in Oxford, and they met for the first time in 1911. At this meeting Murray must have seen something more than a young scholar with anti-unitarian views on Homer, because the two began to exchange more frequent letters on Homer, and Murray's letters show a more personal interest in Thomson's situation and prospects.

At the end of 1911, in response to a request from Murray, Thomson wrote this rather dispirited reply:

> I shall be very happy to let you know from time to time how my work is progressing—if I can get it to progress. The immediate future, however, is quite obscure to me.... I may be driven from the possibility of doing effective work on Homer at all.... I am afraid this reads rather like an appeal. I do not want you to think that.... And perhaps I am exaggerating the difficulties of the situation. (21 Dec. 1911: GM 171.31–2)

Despite Thomson's disclaimer, it is clear that Murray recognized the element of appeal in Thomson's note, for he now began to play the role of patron as well as mentor to Thomson, encouraging him to submit an article to the *Classical Review* and to begin a monograph on the *Odyssey*. When Murray found out that Thomson's teaching position would conclude in the spring of 1913 and he had no immediate prospects of further employment in Greek, he asked Thomson to detail his academic accomplishments and send him copies of any testimonials he had. Thomson recounted with pride his achievements as a student at Aberdeen, from which he had graduated with first-class honours and the Fullerton Scholarship for the best Classic, but was obviously embarrassed to admit that he had earned only second-class honours in Mods and Greats while at Oxford: 'Probably the least affected thing to say about it is that I may not have done myself justice' (3 June 1912: GM 171.37–8). More significantly, Murray read and critiqued Thomson's *Odyssey* manuscript and solicited Jane Ellen Harrison's help as well:

> Miss Harrison seems to be fully as much pleased with your Odyssey studies as I was. They really are ~~remarkable~~ [word crossed out] quite out of the way. Your two points about the similes and about HOMEREUSAI, throw a flood of light on the questions at issue at the very start. Now what is to be done next?
>
> I wrote some time ago to the Clarendon Press to tell them about the book, and had a friendly answer from Cannan. So I think if you send it to them it will get due consideration—unless of course they send it to some hostile critic to read. But probably they would send it to me, or take my word for it, and accept it if Bywater approves. (27 Dec. 1912: GM 171.49)

Both Murray and Harrison helped shepherd Thomson's work through revisions and proofs until it was finally published in 1914 as *Studies in the Odyssey*. This level of aid is unusual in a mentoring relationship, even for a favourite former student, and highly unusual in a relationship that had begun with an unsolicited letter from a stranger, as Thomson's preface recognizes: 'My debt is especially great to Professor Murray and Miss Harrison, to whom, and above all to Professor Murray, I owe more than I can acknowledge in detail, more, indeed, than could be expressed in a mere reckoning of obligations' (Thomson 1914, p. x). It is not surprising that reviewers hostile to Harrison's work and to the associated work of Murray wrote negatively of Thomson's book. The most virulent reviewer,

Thomas William Allen,[4] used his review in the *Journal of Hellenic Studies* to attack Murray and Harrison. Allen had applied for the Regius Professorship of Greek at Oxford and lost the post to Gilbert Murray; he may also have known about Murray's prominent role in getting the Clarendon Press to publish the book:

> Mr. Thomson, who sails under the colours of Miss Harrison and Professor Murray, ... has chosen a theory which has spent its force, and developed it, I am afraid, without judgment or self-criticism. He has constructed a flimsy building on a foundation of sand. Instead of gathering passages and references and so increasing this freak-literature, he would have better spent his time considering the validity of his teachers' premisses. I do not think the Press of my University should have accepted this book. (Allen 1914, 335)

In January of 1915, Murray suggested that Allen & Unwin, the firm which published his translations, should contact Thomson about the book of essays he was preparing, thus initiating a life-long association between Thomson and this press. Perhaps Murray felt that Allen & Unwin would be a more suitable publisher than the Clarendon Press for Thomson's style of writing. One could theorize that this move helped to direct the course of Thomson's subsequent publications, but if so, it was a gentle push in a direction Thomson was already heading. As Thomson wrote Allen & Unwin: 'I am trying in all my work now to popularise scholarship as far as possible—pretty much on the lines of Professor Gilbert Murray and Mr F. M. Cornford and others' (26 Jan. 1915: Allen & Unwin Papers, 209). Thomson shrewdly asked Murray to write an introduction for his new book, an invitation that Murray tactfully tried to refuse: 'After all you are not an unknown beginner; you are the author of 'Studies in the Odyssey', and grown up, so that I incline to thinking that it might be a mistake to get an introduction' (29 Jan. 1915: GM 171.135). But Thomson was insistent, and Murray apparently decided to use the introduction as an opportunity to muse on his view of 'the proper aims' of classical scholarship. He opens with a clever comeback at T. W. Allen that segues gracefully into a compliment to Thomson and a reassurance that Murray himself was once in the same position:

[4] For more information on Allen, see Calder 2004; Francis West also discusses Allen's application for the Regius Chair (F. J. West 1984, 128).

> When Mr. Thomson's fine Studies in the Odyssey appeared, I happened to notice one solemn reviewer who, after four lines of earnest misdescription, concluded by expressing his grief that any University had published such a book.... Meditating on the point of view disclosed, I remembered that exactly the same thing had been said about one of my own early books.... There is nothing odd in this. It is only one more reminder to us old and established scholars to keep our minds as alert as we can, and not grow stiff and deaf in our favourite orthodoxies. But the incident made me try to think why I had derived so much pleasure and instruction from a book which other students appeared whole-heartedly to despise.

Murray reflects that classical scholars tend to confine themselves to 'safe ground'—questions relating to lexica, syntax, and scholia—but ignore the questions that matter most: 'What does this poem mean?... What is there fine about it?... How did it come to be what it is?... From the semantic point of view the central fact to grasp is that to understand Greek literature, you must be able to understand literature, and that you cannot understand literature without using your imagination.' In praising Thomson's methods in this book, Murray is also describing his own methods:

> If a scholar... tries really to feel the meaning and the connotations of every important word, if he faces each familiar thought or practice until it seems strange and then tries to trace the path by which such strange things became natural and inevitable; then, if he has the requisite equipment of learning and imagination and sensitiveness, he is sure to produce work of real beauty and value, and equally sure to leave much of his work uncertain and inconclusive and his full purpose unachieved. (Murray 1915e, pp. ix–xiii)

In 1917, Murray made the first of several attempts to secure a university position for Thomson, writing Thomson that Harvard had asked him to suggest a young man for a year's lectureship to replace a faculty member who had just died. Murray helped Thomson collect testimonials, including one from Jane Ellen Harrison, and sent them all to Herbert Weir Smyth, Professor of Greek at Harvard, along with his own letter recommending Thomson. This is a personal letter to a man he knows, not a testimonial, and it is worth quoting in full for what it tells us about Murray's opinion of his protégé:

I have pleasure in sending you some opinions about J. A. K. Thomson, including one or two reviews of his last book.

You will see that he has the power of raising great enthusiasm, and that among very competent judges. And naturally there are many people who think him capable of every intellectual crime and go about wishing he was dead.

His technical scholarship is perfectly safe and exact. He is also methodical and businesslike and has been a successful examiner of provincial and Scottish Universities for many years. I mention this to show that his great imaginative and literary gifts have not had a bad influence on the severer side of his mind.

Personally he is a quiet modest and rather reserved man. Not impressive, in the ordinary sense, but I should say decidedly rather attractive. Younger men, of the intellectual sort, admire him greatly, and no one could dislike him on personal grounds. Character etc. all that can be desired. The only point on which I should feel at all doubtful would be his power to impress the ordinary man and make his teaching popular in the current sense.

I ought to add that I think him a scholar of quite extraordinary brilliance and promise. If you do not take him he will be snapped up by Oxford or Cambridge in a few years. Indeed it will be a real loss to England, and to me personally if he goes to Harvard; but I think the change and encouragement would do him good and bring some relief from his present harness. (3 Feb. 1917: GM 171.194–5)

This letter, taken together with Murray's introduction to *The Greek Tradition*, presents some important clues about the reasons why Murray took such a keen interest in promoting Thomson's career. Murray seems to have identified (perhaps unconsciously) with Thomson, viewing him as a younger version of himself but without the remarkable success that Murray achieved at Oxford and beyond. Hence Thomson's difficulties also triggered Murray's well-known sympathy for the underdog. As an Australian and a Scot, both were outsiders in the British class system and had experienced 'the misery...of being peculiar and not standardized', as Murray put it in *An Unfinished Autobiography* (Murray 1960, 56). Both had lost fathers and been partly raised by mothers without economic means; both had been scholarship students at Oxford. When Murray describes himself as a young man striking people as 'over-serious and over-enthusiastic' (ibid., 97), his description would apply equally well to the person one can recreate from Thomson's letters. Neither man was physically impressive 'in the ordinary sense', but 'decidedly rather attractive' to younger men 'of the intellectual sort'. Both based their scholarship on 'great imaginative and literary gifts'.

There is no reason to suppose that Murray was exaggerating or misrepresenting his true opinion when he claims, 'I think him a scholar of quite extraordinary brilliance and promise.' Although contemporary classicists may not rate J. A. K. Thomson's scholarship highly (if they remember him at all), it is very clear from the correspondence that Gilbert Murray did. For example, he wrote Thomson that he had read *Greeks and Barbarians* 'with real delight':

> It is so exceedingly well written; and I get to feel more and more that you cannot expound classical literature unless you write well. You have first to see the subtleties and then make other people see them; and that needs literary power. (23 Aug. 1921: GM 172.19–20)

In a letter recommending Thomson for a position in Amsterdam Murray stated, 'He seems to me to stand out among all our younger scholars for a unique combination of learning and literary insight', and when the position fell through he wrote Thomson:

> I should have liked you to be appointed both on international grounds and because you might have spread in Europe that artistic and aesthetic conception of scholarship which seems almost non-existent there and rare enough in this country. Otherwise I cannot help feeling selfishly rather glad that you are remaining here. (6 Dec. 1922: GM 172.99; 172.46–7)

After Thomson completed the year's position at Harvard that he had obtained with Murray's help, growing financial difficulties prompted him to accept another temporary position in America as a sabbatical replacement at Bryn Mawr in 1921–2. This year produced long letters between Thomson and Murray reflecting on the nature of scholarship. These letters reveal the growing understanding between the two men and shed some light on the transformation of their relationship from a mentor-discipleship to a friendship. Thomson opens the discussion in the fall of 1921 in very personal terms:

> The temptation is great of writing to somebody who understands.... There is a growing doubt in my own mind as to what exactly I am after. For I cannot help treating scholarship as an art, and who am

I to say to really scientific scholars 'Now watch me building on your foundations!' It must be very irritating.

Take for instance the matter of literary criticism.... What's the use of a man's scholarship if it merely ends in the sort of inarticulate grunt of admiration which is all the average scholar can utter about the writer to whom he has devoted years of labour?... And yet if you or I suggest to him what he might say, he naturally feels rather sore on the point; at least he will probably listen to you; but he is jolly well not going to listen to me! (27 Sept. 1921: GM 172.23–4)

Murray's reply to this is quite illuminating:

There is another letter of yours... about taste and style in literature, and how little they seem to be generated by pure scholarship. Certainly Jebb had only a good commonplace style, and ditto judgement. And so with most savants, in classics or other subjects. If I felt more confidence about the future of education in general and classical edn [sic] in particular, I should say that a group of us—you and I and Livingstone and Zimmern and Cornford and J E H and Robinson of Eton and some others in England—had a very good chance of establishing a style of scholarship which consisted essentially in the perception of beauty, and to some extent in the representation of it. As it is I do not feel able to prophesy but we still have a chance (the special danger that I see is the growing belief of the uneducated and stupid man that he is 'it', exactly right, and that all superior ability or character or learning is actually a disqualification for life). (4 Dec. 1921: GM 172.27–9)[5]

Note that Thomson highlights his own lack of eminence and distance from Murray while simultaneously asserting a kinship of aims and understanding. Murray, on the other hand, tactfully ignores their difference in status and matter-of-factly includes Thomson in his circle of right-minded scholars.

As his year at Bryn Mawr came to a close, Thomson was again faced with unemployment, and he described his goals in a letter to Murray: 'I care very little, comparatively speaking, about salary or

[5] For Richard Winn Livingstone, see Stray 2004b; for Alfred Eckhard Zimmern, see Stapleton, this volume. Since there was no classicist at Eton named Robinson during the relevant period, Christopher Stray has suggested to me that Murray may have inadvertently substituted Eton for Winchester when thinking of Cyril Edward Robinson, who taught at Winchester from 1909 to 1945. Robinson's books included *The Days of Alkibiades* (1916); *The Genius of the Greek Drama: Three Plays, Being the Agamemnon of Aeschylus, the Antigone of Sophocles, & the Medea of Euripides, Rendered and Adapted* (1921); and *A History of Greece* (1929).

official dignity if any sort of humane or gentlemanlike post should happen to present itself' (26 Aug. 1921: GM 172.21–2). Murray had twice mentioned that he would like to get Thomson a position at Oxford but did not see any immediate opportunity: 'I want greatly to get you back here in some capacity or other. Of course the prospects are not good, owing to the slump in classical teaching; but the slump in classical scholars is quite as great' (23 Aug. 1921: GM 172.19–20). However, he recommended Thomson for two openings at other English universities, one at Leeds and one created by W. C. F. Walters' retirement from the Chair of Classics at King's College London. The letters in the Murray papers show very clearly that Murray's efforts were decisive in securing the London post for Thomson. The three external experts for London were Albert C. Clark of Oxford, James S. Reid of Cambridge, and Gilbert Murray himself. Thomson was in something of a dilemma about Leeds, since they wanted him to appear before the Appointments Committee several months before the decision was due to be made at London. Sir Ernest Barker, Principal of King's College, asked Murray to telegraph Thomson to come to his house before going to Leeds: 'I could probably settle the matter with him in advance, if I can be sure of the support of you and Clark and Reid. I can carry all my colleagues here' (27 Feb. 1923: GM 172.90). After the visit, he wrote Murray that he had persuaded Thomson not to go to Leeds at all, since the odds of election to King's College were '100 to 1 in his favour' because of Murray's support (28 Feb. 1923: GM 172.91). As a result, Thomson now owed Murray the greatest debt of all, a 'humane and gentlemanlike post' that gave him both financial and professional security. Although Murray was often generous with his time and advice in mentoring other scholars, the degree of help he provided to Thomson was extraordinary.

By 1926, a strong bond of friendship and trust had formed between Murray and Thomson. In preparation for his trip to the United States to assume the Charles Eliot Norton Chair of Poetry at Harvard, Murray had made a new will, and he wrote Thomson that he had named him as his literary executor: 'It will involve looking through unpublished papers and letters and deciding about publication &c. I thought you would be the person who covered most completely the same ground and had the same outlook. In fine, you are the person I should most like to act with Toynbee' (22 Sept. 1926: GM 172.168). At this time Murray also invited Thomson to join him on his summer holiday. Their first shared trip was in 1927 to the Swiss Alps, where they enjoyed hiking and mountain climbing, and this remained their preferred destination. In 1928 Lieutenant-Colonel Charles Archer, brother of the playwright and critic William Archer, joined them in Switzerland, and from this point on the three men formed the core of an annual holiday group. Archer died in 1941, and after the war Murray and Thomson shared a summer holiday in places closer to home, usually in Wales, until Murray's death; in the last few years they were joined by Barbara Hammond, widow of Murray's friend Lawrence Hammond, and Murray's current secretary. In fact, a little more than a month before he died Murray wrote Thomson urging him to come to Yatscombe for their holiday since he was no longer able to manage a hotel. This pattern of behavior, supported of course by the letters, provides strong evidence that Murray had deep personal affection for Thomson and preferred his companionship to that of many more distinguished men. As Murray put it one year when a railway strike prevented Thomson from joining him, 'This holiday is not itself without you. And there is nobody who could take your place' (1 June 1955: GM 175.199).

In his obituary article for the British Academy, Thomson referred to these shared trips to Switzerland to demonstrate that Murray was not 'a physical weakling': 'He would spring across crevasses and cut steps in the *séracs* in a way which astonished and alarmed a much younger man' (1957: 246–7). Thomson suggests here that he was not quite as fearless, but Murray described him in a letter to Grace Macurdy as 'a man of great courage and steady nerve': 'I remember his falling on a glacier and dislocating his thumb badly. He just insisted on my setting it by pulling it out with great violence, while he merely said "thank-you" and walked on' (16 April 1941: GM 157.182).[6] This incident apparently made a great impression on Murray, for he referred to it again in a later letter to Thomson:

[6] Grace Harriet Macurdy, Professor of Greek at Vassar College in the United States from 1893 to 1937, had a long-standing friendship with both Murray and Thomson; see McManus 2007.

I have been imitating you in your errors if not in your virtues. I slipt on some ice and fell on my hand and cut it and dislocated one finger. Then, remembering you, I pulled it hard and slipped the joint in again quite neatly. No pain to speak of at the time but violent pain that night, which made me wonder if you had had a much worse time than you let me know at the Rieder Furka.—People who wish to tumble about ought to do so when young, not put it off. (25 Nov. 1943: GM 174.153)

The shared exhilaration and physical exploits of these Switzerland trips cemented the friendship between Murray and Thomson, so that when Archer was no longer able to join them as the war approached, Murray playfully wrote to Thomson, 'I rather wish we could get an additional companion, someone young and juicy' (5 July 1939: GM 173.235). The ease and informality of the letters testify to their close companionship, with first-name salutations, homely details such as what books they should bring to read aloud together, and jesting references to that fact that Thomson once paid Murray's hotel bill because he had forgotten to do so before he left.

When Murray announced that he would retire in 1936, Thomson at last had a chance to do something for the man to whom he owed so much, and he worked unstintingly to get the *Essays in Honour of Gilbert Murray* (Thomson and Toynbee 1936) in print. Although he enlisted the aid of Arnold Toynbee, Thomson was the driving force behind this collection, which he envisioned as 'a rather remarkable demonstration of the position that [Murray] holds in the intellectual and political life of the present day as well as in the regard of those who have enjoyed his friendship' (typed circular enlisting contributions to the volume, September 1933: Allen & Unwin Papers, 44.4). It is likely that this collection touched Murray more than the Oxford volume of classical essays in his honour (Bailey et al. 1936) because of its more personal nature and wide-ranging scope. Thomson knew better than most what would truly please Murray; for example, he later wrote Sir Stanley Unwin criticizing the purposes of the fund being established in honour of Murray's ninetieth birthday as 'too vague and wide.... My own idea would be to found something like the Reith Lectures on the B. B. C. I am sure Murray would like that better' (12 Nov. 1955: Allen & Unwin Papers, 697.22).

In his obituary, Thomson described Murray as 'a modern Stoic... with a sense of humour' and also as 'a Victorian Liberal'

(Thomson 1957, 256–7). Both terms could equally describe Thomson, a fact which helps to explain why Murray so enjoyed the company of his friend. Murray frequently teased Thomson about being a Victorian at heart: 'I am doing a broadcast talk on the Last 25 Years after the news on Tuesday, the 11th. I give it the title "How It Strikes a Victorian". So I expect large and warm agreement from you' (6 Nov. 1946: GM 174.249). Thomson's moral stance and sense of humour perfectly matched Murray's; for example, during World War II he wrote Murray, 'Approximately nine pounds of Mr. Gladstone (whose statue in the Strand was hit by a bomb) flew through the air and crashed precisely into my room at King's College. The Librarian says it was to express his disapproval of my views on the Homeric Question. I say it was to take refuge with a kindred spirit' (15 Oct. 1940: GM 174.28).

At the outbreak of this war a rather odd exchange between the two men reveals an unusual aspect of their shared 'Stoicism'. The disheartening news from the front prompted Thomson to make this proposal:

> Personally I would rather kill myself than be taken to a concentration camp; I do not even think I could bear to see the orgies of cruelty to other people. Scholars like us are so helpless at such a time; the only protest we can make is a moral and spiritual one—the gesture of the Roman Stoics. Even that is not an easy thing, unless one has some convenient drug or weapon, and I have none.... But it seems to me that, if you and I and Archer... had some common policy and perhaps pool our resources in the form of some sleeping potion, we should be a moral support to each other. Of course it might be impossible for us to meet, but the sense of loneliness would be mitigated.
>
> Of course you will not take this letter any more seriously than the war news warrants. If you look a danger squarely in the face it often passes by. (24 May 1940: GM 174.5–6)

Murray's response reveals his supreme tact and empathy for his friend's concerns. Without exactly agreeing to the proposal, he conveys his understanding of Thomson's feelings. He begins by describing the 'warmly appreciative reply' he sent to an appeal he had just received from the Euthanasia Society. He then answers Thomson's question about method, stating that a doctor he knew had told him that '6 dials would be fatal' (Dial was the proprietary name for the barbiturate allobarbital). 'However,' he cautions, 'one would have to wait for a situation in which (1) one could be no help to others or to the national effort; (2) one was really in the power of the enemy, or just about to be so.' Finally, he defuses the situation with humour which indirectly suggests that the danger of invasion may be exaggerated. Referring to a recent fire at his house, he writes, 'Whether it was [the British fascist leader] Oswald Mosley, or the Nuns opposite, who obviously came down on parachutes, or the 1000 learned Germans said to be in Oxford, who did it we cannot yet say' (26 May 1940: GM 174.7). Murray's grasp of his friend's feeling of isolation and need for something that would give him a sense of control may have arisen from the memory of an incident from his own childhood, or perhaps his later account of this childhood incident was coloured by his discussion with Thomson here. In his *Autobiography*, Murray describes his nine-year-old self, totally miserable at a boarding school, deciding on 'the simple old Stoic conception'; he says that he determined to hang himself, 'and the feeling of relief, of mastery over circumstances, which the thought of my plan gave me, made me really a good bit happier than I had been before' (Murray 1960, 62).

The correspondence between Murray and Thomson spans nearly fifty years and deserves further study. Because of their closeness, Murray expressed his opinions very candidly on many different subjects. An illustrative case in point is provided by their correspondence on Jane Ellen Harrison. Early on Thomson had suggested a *Festschrift* in her honour:

> An idea occurred to me recently about Miss Harrison. Would it be at all feasible for her friends to get up a book of contributions 'presented' to her... I think she would like that, and I believe there would be no difficulty in finding the contributors. (15 Feb. 1923: GM 172.80–3)

Murray is probably the only person who could have brought such a project to fruition, and there is no doubt that this would have pleased Harrison. However, Murray never responded to the suggestion, although Thomson brought it up again in a subsequent letter. Much later, when Jessie Stewart was organizing a celebration of the centenary of Harrison's birth, she enlisted the help of Thomson and Murray, who mused, 'I also am a good deal puzzled as to what part I shall take in the celebration of Jane Harrison's centenary. She very much deserves a celebration, and I was very fond of her. But the form of celebration is a difficulty' (19 Aug. 1950: GM 175.36). He eventually agreed to present a BBC talk during the festival, acknowledging that he 'owed a very great deal to her' (7 Dec. 1950: GM 175.49). He then proposed that Thomson write an article about the movement led by Harrison:

Mrs. Stewart, of Cambridge, has just been here bringing a mass of Jane Harrison's letters to Lady Mary and me, and some to Verrall. There are also lots to Cornford. I don't think that they are quite worth publishing as a book, particularly because those to me, much the most numerous, are nearly all about points of scholarship and my answers have been destroyed. But I think a quite interesting article might be written on a certain movement in Greek studies, represented principally by J. E. H. and me, and Cornford, together with your early Homeric work. Typical points would be: first, Farnell, in his great book on Greek religion, starts with the Olympian gods as if they were definite persons and formed the foundation. Prolegomena completely destroyed that approach. Again, the history of Greek philosophy before Cornford consisted largely of the views of particular philosophers. Religion to Philosophy put all that on a different basis. My work, I suppose, was partly the traditional book in place of the quarrel between Unitarians and Separatists, the attempt to get at the real meaning of and poetry of Euripides as against a sort of accepted convention, and perhaps a rather friendly welcome to anthropology. Anyhow, the movement is a real one and J. E. H. played a very important part in it. I wonder if you would be inclined to write, for the C. Q. or the J. H. S., an article? A set of these letters and perhaps some that one could get from Mrs Cornford would form the basis of it. You are, among scholars outside the particular circle, the one that gave the most sympathy and general understanding to the movement. (14 Feb. 1951: GM 175.52)

Thomson did not ultimately write such an article, but he did give Jessie Stewart some good advice about publishing Harrison's letters:

I have read many of the letters and they are so personal and vivid that, merely as letters, I think they might make a hit, provided the personal touches were kept in untouched and as much of the technical scholarship left out as was compatible with intelligibility. Mrs Stewart says she has got just the opposite advice from Cambridge dons. But, hang it all, Jane was a genius and they are only a passing phenomenon. The world has a right to her letters—or the best of them. So I am inclined to say 'Publish and be damned'. (6 Mar. 1951: GM 175.55)

Murray's reply indicates that he had altered his original feelings about the letters in response to Thomson's perspective, and also that he may have been reflecting on how he himself would be perceived fifty years after his death:

> The Cambridge people on the whole disapproved of the letters and at any rate wanted the personal parts severely removed. One can see their point of view, and I was inclined to agree with it; but I'm not at all sure that you are not really right. You will be able to tell better when you have read more of the letters. The thing that may make them really interesting is her character, and impulsive statements, and even indiscretions. Wissenschaftlich points will be stale by now. It is a frightfully difficult thing to know what is worth remembering or preserving for posterity in the mass of anybody's remains, and probably the judgment of fifty years hence will be quite different from that of the present. (8 Mar. 1951: GM 175.56)

Exchanges such as this provide valuable insights into Murray's own perception, late in his life, of Jane Ellen Harrison, the movement now called Cambridge Ritualism, and the part he himself played in it—subjects that are still under debate. For example, in *The Invention of Jane Ellen Harrison*, Mary Beard argues that the 'thriving scholarly industry' epitomized by the conference and volume *The Cambridge Ritualists Reconsidered* (Calder 1991; see particularly Ackerman 1991a) mistakenly concretizes shared ideas and friendships into a 'group' or 'movement'. She maintains that it was Jessie Stewart 'who first chose to turn the productive encounters of Harrison and friends into a much more formal "group of which Jane was the forerunner in age and inspiration."' The 1952 and 1953 letters from Murray to Stewart usually adduced in support of the concept of a movement, she argues, were actually prompted by Stewart's draft chapter on 'The Group', although 'even if it had not been put into his head, he *might* have put it in very much those terms himself; we do not know' (Beard 2000, 116–18). Anyone who has studied the Murray–Thomson correspondence, however, does know. Murray's letter to Thomson of 7 December 1950, quoted above, shows that Murray did in fact use exactly those terms before Stewart had sent her chapter to him ('a certain movement in Greek studies, represented principally by J. E. H. and me, and Cornford . . . the movement is a real one and J. E. H. played a very important part in it'). Indeed, it is more likely that Stewart's chapter was influenced by Murray's concept of a group than vice versa, since Murray had asked Thomson to give that letter to Stewart (16 Feb. 1951: GM 175.54). These letters do not, of course, disprove Beard's main point, but they do provide independent evidence of what Murray was thinking in the 1950s.[7]

Thomson's friendship with Murray continued after he retired from King's College and moved to Scotland, despite the fact that Thomson was emerging from Murray's shadow with his classical influence books. Thomson was ahead of other classical scholars in perceiving the need for books analysing English literature's debt to classical literature. This work drew upon his strengths—broad knowledge not only of classical but also of English literature, clarity of style, ability to reach and engage the non-specialist reader. Murray was genuinely pleased by Thomson's success, as the quotation which opens this article indicates. On a holiday in Wales, he wrote Janet Spens, whom he had taught at Glasgow and who was currently an English tutor at Lady Mary Hall in Oxford, 'Here we are, JAK and I.... JAK overflowing with abstruse knowledge of English literature, which you could criticise and cope with better than I' (7 June 1953: GM 169.143). Murray had previously proposed Thomson for fellowship in the British Academy without success, but he now drew on Thomson's classical influences work for one last try in 1954. This time the votes were there, but Murray wrote Thomson with chagrin that the Academy had notified him of new rules requiring that Ordinary Fellowship not go to anyone over 74; Thomson had turned 74 only nine months before the vote (27 Feb. 1954: GM 175.152).

Episodes like this happened frequently, reminding Thomson of the immense disparity between his lack of professional recognition and Murray's fame, but Thomson alludes only once in the letters to the

[7] As Beard points out, no archives are 'neutral... who saves what, and why, always counts' (Beard 2000, 157–8). For the Murray papers, however, *everything* was saved, apparently under the influence of Lady Mary Murray, and the Murray–Thomson letters do not reflect the kind of loaded choices that make the Harrison archive so difficult. Beard herself occasionally makes judgements that go beyond her sources, as when she interprets a remark Thomson made about Murray in a 1955 letter to Stewart: 'Thomson reassures Stewart with the comforting thought that the old man no longer had a mind of his own' (Beard 2000, 204–5 n. 30). The content and tone of the Murray–Thomson correspondence in the last years of their lives indicate quite clearly that Thomson never held such an opinion and Murray never warranted it.

envy that he must have occasionally experienced. When thanking Murray for sending him a copy of *The Classical Tradition in Poetry* Thomson wrote:

No one else, I believe, could write such a book and I have read it with almost complete agreement and extreme pleasure mixed with a little jealous depression at the thought that there seems to be no reason why, after you, I should write about literature at all. (27 Nov. 1927: GM 172.217–18)

Murray's esteem and affection for him must have ameliorated Thomson's sense of the gulf between their achievements in the eyes of the world. Within their friendship, at least, they were equals. Thomson's last communication to Murray writes an eloquent coda to their relationship. He had copied out a poem by the Scottish Victorian writer John Gibson Lockhart:

It is an old belief
    That on some solemn shore,
Beyond the sphere of grief,
    Dear friends shall part no more.

Beyond the sphere of time,
    And sin, and Fate's control,
Serene in ageless prime
    Of body and of soul.

This faith I fain would keep;
    That hope I'll ne'er forego.
Eternal be the sleep,
    Unless to waken so.

Below the poem he wrote, 'Dear Gilbert, You probably know these lines. They were sent by Lockhart to Carlyle, who remembered them to the end of his life. If you are familiar with them, at any rate you will know why I sent them' (GM 175.264).[8] This letter epitomizes the tenor of their friendship; at the end of their lives, Thomson expresses his deep affection for Murray only elliptically and indirectly, through a literary allusion to the friendship of other intellectuals. Since Thomson was so well read, he may also have had in mind H. Rider Haggard's reference to this poem, which had been sent to him by his

[8] The letter is undated, but a reference to the third edition of Murray's *History of Ancient Greek Literature* indicates it was written in late 1956 or early 1957.

dying friend Andrew Lang. In any case, Haggard's words directly express the emotion that Thomson only alludes to obliquely: 'And so to Andrew Lang, among men my best friend perhaps, and the one with whom I was most entirely in tune, farewell for a while' (Haggard 1926, ii.80).

10

Gilbert Murray, Bertrand Russell, and the Theory and Practice of Politics

William Bruneau

Gilbert Murray and Bertrand Russell met in February 1901 at Newnham College, Cambridge, where Murray was giving a reading of part of his translation of the *Hippolytus* of Euripides. Russell was cousin to Murray's wife, Lady Mary Howard, and had known of Murray's classical studies and research on that account. Now they began an epistolary friendship that lasted until Murray's death in 1957.[1] Because Russell travelled across the world and taught only occasionally at Cambridge, while Murray spent most of his teaching life at Oxford, face-to-face meetings were infrequent. Their letters helped to keep the connection lively and productive.

Russell wrote in 1951 to the Philosophical Society of Great Britain,

> [Murray] and I have not always agreed on public issues, but we have, I think, throughout whatever divergences on this or that question been conscious of

[1] Although there was a family tie, Murray and Russell had also in common their educational background, the privileged social groupings from which they came, and a fondness for art and literature. Philip Ironside argues (Ironside 1996) that there was a 'sub-class' of reform-minded aristocrats (as was Russell) and 'near-aristocrats' (as was Gilbert Murray, married into an aristocratic family) who, before the Great War, were intermittently Liberal or Fabian. Their Liberalism and Fabianism were not always consistent with their own social-economic interests—but this argues for the strength of the principles that drove these men, and helped them to overcome the prudential calculations 'typical of their class'. Ironside summarizes all of this by saying simply that Murray and Russell were socially and intellectually tied by common membership in a 'liberal aristocracy'.

a deep underlying agreement on fundamentals. . . . As growing darkness descends upon the world, stars shine more brightly, and of these stars Gilbert Murray is among those of the first magnitude.[2]

Murray replied in a typically considerate typewritten note:

I was greatly touched by the letter you wrote to the Philosophic Society Dinner about our fifty years of close friendship. It is, I think, quite true about the fundamental agreement; I always feel it—and am proud of it.[3]

On *what*, exactly, did these men have fundamental agreement? After all, their 'divergences' were energetic and substantial. Murray supported British war aims from 3 August 1914, whereas Russell ferociously opposed them. Murray was a life-long proponent of international order, as embodied eventually in the League of Nations and then in the United Nations. About the League, particularly, Russell was highly sceptical. These were not just differences of taste or preference, not the disagreements one might have after a long walk and a cup of hot tea.[4]

LIBERALISM IN PRACTICE AND IN THEORY

There are two ways of seeing how the Murray–Russell friendship continued and flourished despite occasional political differences. There is, first, the matter of their 'fundamental' liberalism.

[2] Typescript of Bertrand Russell's 'Message' to the Philosophical Society of Great Britain, 11 Sept. 1951, in the Bertrand Russell Archives [hereafter RA], McMaster University, Hamilton, Canada; part of the text appears also in Bertrand Russell, 'A Fifty-Six Year Friendship': Smith and Toynbee 1960, 211.

[3] Ms letter, RA 3 071J, Gilbert Murray [Oxford]/Bertrand Russell [Richmond, Surrey], 12 Sept. 1951. In a charming aside, Murray added that

I preferred you to other philosophers because, while they mostly tried to prove some horrible conclusion—like Hobbes, Hegel, Marx &c, you were, I believed, content if you could really prove that $2 + 2 = 4$, and that conclusion, though sad, was at least bearable ('To think that two and two are four, And never five or three, The heart of man has long been sore, And long is like to be.')

[4] This is not to underplay or underestimate Murray's and Russell's similarities of background. On that similarity, see D. Wilson 1987, 96–7. Their link through Mary Murray was a tie by marriage, not by blood, but it was reinforced by the further connections that came through activity in the English literary community.

As life-long agnostics, as respecters of individual rights, and as writers of prose that would appeal broadly to general readers and scholars alike, Russell and Murray displayed a broadly liberal outlook. It was a world-view reminiscent of Voltaire's, just one of the eighteenth-century figures to whom Murray and Russell gave admiring attention.

If liberals prized equality and social justice, then Murray and Russell were *systematically liberal*.[5] For twenty years, both were members of the Liberal Party, although only Murray would retain that membership through his adult life.[6] Their religious doubts, their humanism, their internationalism,[7] all made them liberals. If there was 'fundamental agreement' it was on these points, but not these only.

Second, the correspondence between the two, along with their published output, suggest they agreed fundamentally about 'philosophy', understood broadly. On ethical theory, on their views of instinct (especially as it affected political behaviour), and in their suspicions of an over-powerful or overweening state (Russia came to mind), Murray found Russell's work helpful. Their letters show how far Murray's and Russell's liberality and underlying philosophical agreement could stand up to the pressures of social–political upheaval.

The letters are a good place to start in a reassessment of Murray as liberal and philosopher, and of the Murray–Russell relation itself. They run to just under 100,000 words of text.[8] In the opening letter, dated 1 June 1900, Russell (aged 28) offers polite congratulations

[5] For a brief and typically allusive introduction to the history and meaning of lower-case 'l' liberalism, see Russell 1947b; Russell 1946, 577–83, on 'Philosophical Liberalism'.

[6] Russell left the Liberal Party in 1914 with the opening of the War. He joined the Labour Party in 1922, immediately presenting himself in Chelsea in the general election of that year. See Moorehead 1992, 353.

[7] On the relation of individual to state, for Murray see D. Wilson 1987, 236–43; for Russell, see Russell 1961 (an excerpt from Russell 1932).

[8] W. A. Bruneau and R. Wodell (eds.), *The Murray–Russell Letters, 1900–1956*, forthcoming. Nearly all the letters are catalogued in BRACERS, the computerized record of correspondence to and from Bertrand Russell maintained by Kenneth Blackwell, Russell Archivist, McMaster University, Hamilton, Canada, available at http://www.mcmaster. ca/ russdocs/russell.htm. A small minority of letters appear in the catalogue and finding aids for the Murray Papers, Bodleian Library, Oxford University.

to Murray (by then 34) for a recently published essay on 'The Exploitation of Inferior Races in Ancient and Modern Times'.[9] In the background of this early correspondence was the Boer War, and in the foreground, the morality of the Empire—indentured labour,[10] mercantilism, and militarism. Murray and Russell both wanted Britain to retreat from its acquisitive stance in the world. In 1900, Russell remarked how happy he was to read Murray's essay in proof, and that 'I have found hardly any criticism to make' (Russell to Murray, Friday's Hill, Haslemere, Surrey, 1 June 1900, RA 1 710.053564). The essay was a straightforward argument for human rights and for equality, and in 1900, neither Murray nor Russell could see the sense of denying anyone his or her rights.

For almost ten years, until 1910, their correspondence dealt mainly with literary and philosophical matters. From 1910 to 1914, politics proper (women's rights, Home Rule, workers' rights) took centre stage. In these fifteen years, more than at any later time in the exchange with Russell, Murray revealed his ethics, epistemology, and theory of history.

The letters begin with discussions of Murray's experiments in the English verse translation of Greek drama, and deal with Russell's professional work as a philosopher.[11]

In 1901, Russell writes of Murray's translation of the *Hippolytus*:[12]

> I have now read the Hippolytus.... Your tragedy fulfils perfectly—so it seems to me—the purpose of bringing out whatever is noble and beautiful

[9] Murray's essay 'The Exploitation of Inferior Races in Ancient and Modern Times' (Murray 1900a) appeared in Hirst et al. 1900. The other entries were 'Imperialism and Finance' by Francis Wrigley Hirst (1873–1953) and 'Colonial and Foreign Policy' by John L. Hammond (1872–1949). Hammond's biographer for the *Oxford Dictionary of National Biography*, Stewart A. Weaver, describes this book as 'a lonely protest in the name of reason against the imperialist excesses of the age'. A facsimile edition was issued by Routledge/Thoemmes Press in 1998.

[10] On indentured labour, Indian and Chinese immigration to South Africa, and the Boer War, see Shannon 1974, 336, 360–2.

[11] On Murray's translations as an historical problem, see Morwood 2005. For Russell's philosophical output in the period, see Slater 1994.

[12] This is the period of Russell's famous 'conversion experience', a permanent development in his mental life. His willingness to contemplate a nearly pantheist and emotionally complex 'mysticism' is, once again, close to Murray's religious views—agnostic, inquisitive, and anxious to ensure the survival of civilization—first against the horrors of materialism and greed, then against the horrors of violence and death in world war.

in sorrow; and to those of us who are without a religion, this is the only consolation of which the spectacle of the world cannot deprive us. (Russell to Murray, Downing College, Cambridge, 26 Feb. 1901, RA 1 710.053565)

A month later, Murray writes to comment on Russell's latest work on ordinal and temporal series, and on the logic of relations:

The second is tremendously exciting. The part I could best follow was the criticism of Lotze.... Also about 'points'; I don't understand what you mean by the very interesting suggestion that they may have other qualities which we can't see.... I think your argument for absolute Time very strong; indeed practically convincing to me. (Murray to Russell, Barford, 24 Mar. 1901, RA 1 710.053449)

Murray and Russell implicitly agreed in these first letters to say freely what each was up to in his professional capacity, the one literary, the other philosophical. Within two years, the discussion moved away from explicit problems of methodology, as though Murray and Russell tacitly acknowledged one another's intellectual limits, and no longer wanted to try to reconcile their different stances on logic.

Murray could still write in 1902, without hesitation, about his utilitarian ethics, claiming that Mill was 'very near the truth'. Russell's reply, extensive and constructively critical, might be read as showing impatience with Murray's philosophical amateurism:

Our differences seem to spring from the fact that you are a utilitarian, whereas I judge pleasure and pain to be of small importance compared to knowledge, the appreciation and contemplation of beauty, and a certain intrinsic excellence of mind which, apart from its practical effects, appears to me to deserve the name of virtue. What I want to discover is, whether you too do not hold moral principles not deducible from utilitarianism, and therefore inconsistent with it. (Russell to Murray, 3 Apr. 1902, RA 1 710.053567)

Russell's discussion, in a closely argued five-page letter, is technically and conceptually demanding. Murray's reply is revealingly brief. He makes a list of standard claims for and against Utilitarianism, writing in a way that 'shop assistants' would understand, and puts a question:

Well, what is the real criterion [of the Good], if it is not Happiness or Utility? I don't think we know. I believe very strongly that—how shall I put it?—there is always a great deal in our minds, conscious and semi-conscious, which is beyond our analysis. (Murray to Russell, 5 Apr. 1902, RA 1 710.053452)

Murray here asserts his right as a literary person to stand his ground, to make aesthetic and moral claims, including psychological grounds (the 'semi-conscious')—but to leave difficult formal-logical matters to Russell. By the same token, Russell defers to his good friend Murray on most questions of Greek accidence or religious history. It was a compromise that kept the friendship steady, but to say this is not to deny either Murray's philosophical power or Russell's knowledge of classical languages and literatures (Lenz 1987–8).

The Murray–Russell compromise lasted well. Among its early fruits was Russell's successful *The Problems of Philosophy* (Russell 1912). In 1911, Murray had become editor-in-chief of the Home University Library, a scheme for the general education of the English-speaking literary masses, in all the arts and sciences. Russell was among the first authors whom Murray approached (D. Wilson 1987, 190–1), first for a book on mathematics for the millions, and then (when Russell demurred), a book on philosophy for 'shop assistants':

I am writing my book for your series and have written more than half of it. I find, however, that one or two things are happening to it which you may not desire. In the first place, it deals almost entirely with theory of knowledge, only occasionally arriving at metaphysics through theory of knowledge. This seems difficult to avoid owing to the exclusion of religion & ethics. In the second place, I find that, quite contrary to my intention, it is an exposition of my own views, not an impartial account of what is thought by various philosophers. I found it impossible to write interestingly or freely or with conviction, where I was not trying to persuade the reader to agree with me. In the third place, I find that after the first few chapters, it grows rather difficult. It remains quite easily intelligible, without trouble to any educated man, however little he may know about philosophy; but it would be difficult for a shop assistant, unless he were unusually intelligent. I hardly know myself whether it is too difficult or not. If it is, I must rewrite it.[13]

Murray wrote to tell Russell, when the manuscript came to the editor's desk (on time, as Russell's manuscripts always did), that

[13] Russell to Murray, Malvern (a hotel where Russell was writing half his book in a couple of weeks), 12 July 1911.

the book was 'exactly what was wanted'. Its literary quality pleased Murray 'enormously', its original arguments pleased the philosophers, and its sales pleased Williams & Norgate.

In reassessing Murray's intellectual history and development, it is well worth noting his part in the commissioning and publication of Russell's 'shop assistants' book', and dozens more books authored in the next forty years by an international roster. To this, we add Murray's later turns at philosophy, or rather applied philosophy, in his 1938 Hibbert Lectures on *Liberality and Cvilization* (Murray 1938) and again in 1954, three broadcast lectures on *Hellenism and the Modern World* (Murray 1954). In short, Murray may have 'deferred' to his philosophical friend (or should we say friends, since Murray was well acquainted with many British and continental philosophical luminaries), but he did not stop doing philosophy.

THE WAR AND THE LEAGUE: MURRAY AND RUSSELL AT ODDS

We return to Murray's and Russell's differences. They were at odds mainly on two practical questions, each resting on principles we have met in the correspondence and in Murray's and Russell's published works.

The first was, of course, the question of British participation in World War I. Britain entered the war on 4 August 1914. More than a half-century later, in 1955, Murray recalled that he

> signed a letter against Britain joining the war, then doubted, and was finally convinced the other way by Grey's speech on August 3rd [1914].[14]

[14] Murray [Oxford] to [Penrhyndeudraeth, Merioneth], 26 Aug. 1955. RA 3 071 I. Murray in 1955 thought that 'the effects would have been less disastrous if we had stayed out and allowed Germany to become complete master of Western Europe, on more or less equal terms with U.S.A. and Russia.' This late change of opinion has to be understood in the light of the Cold War and the threat of nuclear annihilation, which made almost any option preferable to armed conflict.

The letter to which Murray refers may have been the 'Declaration of British Neutrality in Case of War between the Powers' of 27 July 1914, described in passing in F. J. West 1984, 144. Murray cannot have meant the famous 'Writers' Manifesto' published soon afterward in *The Times*, 18 Sept. 1914, which was a firm declaration of support for British war aims. Cf. D. Wilson 1987, 219.

By contrast, Bertrand Russell was an anti-conscription spokesman after 1914 and, for his pains, eventually an inmate of Brixton Prison from 1 May to 14 September 1918.[15] Russell ran afoul of the Defence of the Realm Act, as he was judged to have weakened the British war effort.

But while Russell gave anti-war and anti-conscription talks, Murray was travelling in the United States to encourage American intervention, and in Scandinavia to advance British war interests. His lectures and publications may well have been read as widely as Russell's, perhaps even more so. The Murray–Russell difference was real and was widely remarked at the time.

After the war, Murray and Russell again differed, this time on the value of a League of Nations. Murray was committed to it in theory and in practice, whereas Russell thought a League built on Wilsonian principle would distract from the 'real work' of building a world government. Russell wanted a world system where national boundaries and national sovereignty would have less and less force and would finally disappear altogether. Murray took the gradualist line, believing that old habits of aggression and possession die hard, and that those habits would weaken only through vigorous public diplomacy, and then through great international cooperative institutions.

Were I writing this as a Norse saga, I would introduce now the figures of Russell the Impatient and Murray the Calm. Through all the excitements of the first half of the twentieth century, Murray and Russell corresponded and met and collaborated. Their letters show how similar were their theories of morality, human psychology, and the State. Murray's and Russell's ethics of fairness and non-violence, their mildly Freudian view of the unconscious, and their scepticism about the claims of the State—all these brought our two activists to the point of consensus . . . but not quite. On matters of principle,

[15] Russell was by 12 Jan. 1918 no longer Chairman of the No-Conscription Fellowship [NCF]. Even so, he was sentenced on 9 Feb. 1918 to six months' imprisonment for undermining the war effort, as he had published an article in the NCF *Tribunal*, no. 90 (3 Jan. 1918), 1, recommending acceptance of a German peace offer, but also asserting that a future American garrison would suppress workers' rights in Britain as they had done in the USA before and during the War. For Lloyd George, this was the last straw, and Russell was prosecuted.

Russell's logical apparatus took him further and faster than Murray the Calm would go. Murray wrote energetically and at length in support of Sir Edward Grey's foreign policy, and campaigned to ensure public opinion would be united in the great fight.[16] Russell wrote just as energetically against armed intervention in Europe, for a unilateral British declaration of peace, and against Sir Edward.[17]

In October 1914, in Oxford Pamphlet No. 18, Murray wrote that 'we were right to declare war against Germany', and that Britain occupied the moral high ground in the conflict.[18] Russell by Christmas 1914 was regularly claiming that all warring states were equally to be condemned. Here is Murray writing for a general, literate audience:

> From the point of view of one who really believes that great nations ought to behave to one another as scrupulously and honourably as ordinary, law-abiding men, no Power in Europe, or out of it, is quite blameless. They all have ambitions; they all, to some extent, use spies; they all, within limits, try to outwit each other; in their diplomatic dealings they rely not only on the claims of good sense and justice, but ultimately, no doubt, on the threat of possible force. But as a matter of degree, Germany does all these things more than other Powers. In her diplomacy, force comes at once to the front; international justice is hardly mentioned.[19]

There was no name-calling between the two. Even in 1915, after Murray had written a book-length justification of Britain's declaration of war, and after Russell had published his equally substantial and contrary reply, the two old friends showed they could yet be reasonable about war and peace. Reasonable or no, Murray made it plain that in his mind, the German leadership and people were

16 Murray 1915c. There is a reliable account of Murray's pro-War activity in F. J. West 1984, 144–75.

17 Russell 1915, reprinted in his *Collected Papers*: Russell 1988, 214–80.

18 Murray 1917a, 20.

19 Murray 1914b; Murray 1917a, 33. *How Can War...?* was first published as the eighteenth of eighty-seven Oxford Pamphlets. The Oxford Pamphlets were one arm of the British government's War Propaganda Bureau, headquartered in Wellington House from 1914. Charles Masterman headed the office, and with the help of secretly recruited, but well-reputed British writers and academics, arranged for the publication of more than 1,160 pamphlets, at several large publishing houses (Oxford University Press being one) between late summer 1914 and September 1918.

power-mad. He remained stubborn on the point until the 1919 Peace Conference.[20]

We should not be too much distracted by rare displays of temper and stubbornness.[21] Across decades, Murray helped Russell—encouraging him to write, giving him money and moral support, consistently assuming the best of Russell as politician and as philosopher. Most famously, Murray worked behind the scenes to reverse the denial of a lectureship to Russell by Trinity College, Cambridge, and later, in 1918, to reduce the severity of Russell's imprisonment; these actions were far more typical of the relation between the two than was their 1915 tiff, or later differences between them as the League faltered in the run-up to World War II.

THE HERD INSTINCT AND WHAT TO DO ABOUT IT

Now, in the midst of the Great War, Russell saw the herd instinct as a dangerous force, a force stronger than Murray thought it. Russell took a Manichean view, arguing that human beings were driven either by constructive instincts and motives or by destructive ones.[22] He believed a thoroughgoing worldwide commitment to peace and socialism would 'dispose' people to choose the good.

[20] Murray 1915c; Russell 1915.

[21] A year after publishing his Oxford Pamphlet, Murray's humane scepticism was again in the ascendant. He accepted the broad lines of official government policy, but also acknowledged the case against war. His October 1915 address to the Congress of Free Churches, 'Ethical Problems of the War', included remarks Russell might have made:

> 'the loss of these young Germans is also a great and terrible loss to humanity. It seems almost trivial... to think too much of our monetary losses; of the fact that we have spent 1595 millions and that we are throwing money away at the rate of nearly five millions a day.... Just think of all our schemes of reform and how they are blown to the four winds—schemes of social improvement, of industrial improvement; a scheme like Lord Haldane's great education scheme [which] would cost nearly as much as half a week of the war!' (Murray 1917a, 79–80)

[22] Michael Potter, 'Russell's Integrated Emotivism', unpublished paper, Annual Meeting of the Bertrand Russell Society, Hamilton, Canada, 15 May 2005; see also Potter 2006.

That position led Russell to offer practical advice on education, schooling, marriage, morals, and property-sharing, all to be reformed so that constructive instinct would prevail. Russell's version of 'reform' was thoroughgoing and, by prevailing standards, extreme. To make a child happy and reasonable, for example, Russell thought it necessary to make its schooling wholly free, free of irrational and superstitious curriculum and pedagogy, and free in the positive sense (children ought to do much as they pleased, provided they harmed neither themselves nor others, and provided they learned to reason well, on the evidence, and not on the say-so of tradition). With extensive and intensive reforms like that in education, nationalism would weaken, cooperation increase, and armed conflict cease to be attractive.

On his side, Murray saw the dangers of instinctive motivation, the 'herd instinct' and its effects on crowds (Murray, 'Herd Instinct and the War', *Atlantic Monthly* 115 (1915), 830–39, repr. in Murray 1917a, 46–66). But although he knew and read numerous psychologists in his long academic career, Murray did not develop a systematic psychological theory to guide his political practice. His psychology was consistent, but must be inferred from his arguments about war, peace, and politics. For Murray, the deep roots of behaviour might be instinctual, but to this position he would add a further, complicating point. For him, instinct had several possible forms. It might be aesthetic, religious, strictly biological, or communal. Each helped to account for behaviour, and each should be considered in choosing one's politics, one's approach to education, or one's attitude to religion. Murray was willing to contemplate a range of psychic phenomena and to experiment with them (see Lowe's chapter in this volume).

In cyclic fashion, Murray's views of psychology take us once again to his ethics and epistemology—and to Russell's. In 1947, Russell gave a BBC talk on 'The Faith of a Rationalist', laying out a credo whose roots went back more than thirty years (Russell 1947a):

When I try to discover what are the original sources of my opinions, both practical and theoretical, I find that most of them spring ultimately from admiration for two qualities—kindly feeling and veracity. To begin with kindly feeling: most of the social and political evils of the world arise through absence of sympathy and presence of hatred, envy, or fear. . . . If I am asked 'Why do you believe this?' I should not appeal to any supernatural authority, but only to the general wish for happiness.

The philosopher Michael Potter (see n. 20) recently showed how this position is consistent with an emotivist ethics, with a pragmatic view of habit and sentiment, and with the desire of all human beings for happiness—leading to a type of universalizability reminiscent of Spinozistic ethics (Stevenson 1970). Russell thought the good life was 'one inspired by love and guided by knowledge', a view relying on universal and maximally compossible desire (a phrase straight from the shadowy vineyards of philosophical logic) to know things, to love others, and thus to be guided in everyday life. The upshots are peace, security, and the satisfaction of many desires. The ethic relies heavily on the impulse (not clearly explained in Russell) to compassionate activity, and on agreement that our own and others' growth not be thwarted.

Ten years earlier, Gilbert Murray, in his talks on *Liberality and Civilization*, had reminded his listeners that the history of liberalism had roots in Antiquity. It had not the apparatus of formal logic and theory, as Russell's ethics did, and yet . . .

Murray began with the argument that people, if they are to be fully realized beings, must not be in the grip of passion, prejudice, and fear. He moved on to claim that freedom requires liberation of another kind—that is, liberation from the struggle merely to survive, so that one has leisure to create—and no further need to hate or to destroy.

We have got beyond the point where to be a bloody Protestant, or a blinded Papist, or a follower of the 'false Mahound,' was necessarily to be a villain. We have now to remember to feel the same tolerance towards Capitalist and Proletarian, Fascist and Communist. . . . [O]ne of the most certain things in the world is the moral law. Justice, good faith, kindness, temperance, courage are things recognized and admired in the earliest ages of man as well as the latest. . . . Against injustice, falsehood, bad faith, cruelty, and the denial of the human conscience, Liberality stands unshakably firm: for there the centre of its religion is touched. (Murray 1938, 24–5)

Murray insists freedom is causally and conditionally linked ($p \rightarrow q$) to tolerance and kindness. If you are free to speak your mind, your free speech will lead to reasoned thought, and the combined force of free speech and reasoned thought gives us society. There can be no room for dogma, for limits on speech, but there must be *unlimited* room for the respect we give to other persons, and an unwavering determination never to see them as 'other'. Liberality must be for everyone, not just the wealthy, and not just *men.* The aim must be to rise above national communities to see the towers and streets of the One Great City, to be citizens of the world.

Marx and Hitler were therefore wrong (Murray opined) in their practical and moral reasoning, for people are capable of being moved to political action by ideals of civility and civilization—not just by money, economic interest, or the desire for oppressive power (Murray 1938, *passim*, but esp. 20, 30, 45). In his late book, *Hellenism and the Modern World*, Murray's examples and cases (the UN, the WHO, UNRRA, the 'better' post-colonial governments of the Third World) illustrate the point that humans are at their best when in that One Great City (Murray 1954, 58), when they see the reasonableness of population control, the necessity of honesty among judges, the fair treatment of prisoners—in short, when they are Hellenized (on a well informed twentieth-century understanding of Hellas, of course).[23]

At first or even second look, there is no unbridgeable gap between these two outlooks. But there *is some difference*, and as so often, the devil is in that detail. Despite broad agreement on the meaning of liberalism, civility, and *polis*, Murray and Russell were not at one when it came to methods in politics, in philosophy, or to literary–expository technique.

Some of the variance in 'method' that set Murray and Russell apart could be considered effects of habit and character. A straightforward example would be the two men's attitudes to the administration of associations and organizations. Murray had considerably more patience for administrative work than Russell. This difference

[23] Francis West (F. J. West 1984, 176–251) makes effectively and persuasively the point that Murray read back into his Hellenic studies a set of twentieth-century questions and preoccupations. See also West's ' "Ghosts Can Not Speak Until They Have Drunk Blood": A. E. Housman and Gilbert Murray as Donors', paper read to Staff Seminar, Schools of Social Science and Humanities, Deakin University (Geelong, Vic., Australia) Aug. 1982, esp. p. 11, on Murray's almost wholly modern premises as a translator and interpreter of Euripides.

became especially noticeable as they entered middle and old age. By 1937, Murray had worked for two decades in leadership roles in the League of Nations Union and its predecessor organizations.

Murray was a gradualist reformer, a co-operator, a practitioner of communication (and in every form of institutional speech), a negotiator and a greaser-of-wheels—aiming always to popularize and to realize in practice a related family of ideas from ethics, psychology, intellectual history, and classical literature. This *combination* of motives and theories best explains (to take but one example from the 1930s) his campaign for the League of Nations Union's peace ballot in 1935–6. By now Murray and the great public had begun to see that Hitler and Mussolini were more dangerous to civilization than Britons who favoured rearmament (M. Ceadel 1980). But that fact need not distract us from the point or the methods of Murray in the case of the Peace Ballot.

Russell, on the other hand, impatient and driven by the mere logic of his conceptions, saw first the Union of Democratic Control (in 1915), then the League of Nations (after 1919) as weak and impractical vehicles for opposition.[24] His 1936 book *Which Way to Peace?* adopted a near-complete pacifism, accepting that some wars may be justified, but only if they are for the sake of saving the whole of civilization. Russell had accepted since 1915 (Russell 1916, a series of lectures given in autumn 1915) the idea of a world government supplied with an international military force whose size would grow even as the nationalist ambitions of the 'old world' declined. But that idea accorded ill with recent history, for Russell saw that the League had little clout, most especially that it had allowed the Abyssinian disaster. It was thus now almost beneath Russell's contempt. Without the United States, struck by the departures of Germany, Italy, and Japan, and weakened by the dithering of the United Kingdom and France, the League seemed to Russell a waste of time.

[24] Ryan 1988, 58, 145. Ryan connects Russell's political theory, strategy, and practice to his ethics, his views of history, his private views on his family's history (including his notion that to be a Russell entailed a life of tough-minded, confrontational campaigning for reform), and his theory of instinctive motivation in politics.

DEMOCRACY AND UTILITY

Yet Russell's argument in 1936 had a familiar utilitarian cast. Like Murray, he held that civilization *was* at stake, that international tensions must be defused, but he arrived at an anti-Murrayian conclusion: that this defusing should be done at a stroke through a British renunciation of arms. Russell's central theme remained that war was inconsistent with the civilizing work of sensible persons.

Murray's thinking about the herd, the herd mentality, and the necessity of a strong commitment to reason and kindliness differ only in tone from Russell's. For Russell saw a strong relationship between 'individual psychology and social and political events' (Ryan 1988, 72–3). Reason was nearly powerless against impulse and desire.[25] But as there are 'good' and 'bad' impulses, the point is to detect 'good' impulses, and to encourage them. The redirection of destructive impulse, and the encouragement of creative work and life, made eminent sense to Murray.

If the outbreak of war was shocking and surprising in 1914, how much greater a shock it was in 1945 to hear of the explosion of atomic bombs over Hiroshima and Nagasaki. American attacks on these two mainly civilian targets occurred in Murray's eightieth and Russell's seventy-sixth years of life. As usual, Russell responded with speed and full-out energy to the crisis, understanding immediately the dangers of nuclear proliferation.[26] To judge by the Murray–Russell correspondence, Murray deferred once again to Russell, leaving the fight for disarmament to the younger man (!). In the 1940s and early 1950s, Murray worried far more about the fair treatment of displaced Germans, about the best way to give the United Nations a clear and strong mandate the world, and then about the drabness of post-war social life in Britain. Of principles, of the bomb, and large questions of war and peace Murray wrote in 1955—a prescient document replete with strong hints about 'principles' and what to do about them:

25 *Pace* Ryan, who exaggerates the power of impulse in Russell's political thought. See Baldwin 2003, esp. 441–3, for a discussion of Russell's views in 1921 on behaviourism, belief, and sentiment.

26 For a convenient summary of Russell's view on nuclear disarmament and world government, see Russell 1954, repr. in Bone 2003, 33–7.

I am a good deal more disgusted than you are with the excesses of democracy, the sort of newspapers and amusements that the demos really likes; the absurdity of universal suffrage, including women's suffrage, in India, and apparently in every place that can kick over the traces. No doubt on the whole the people of this country are much better off than they used to be, though I do regret the change from a liberalism which aimed at enlightenment and justice to a Labour movement that aims at the welfare of one (admittedly very large) class, with a good deal of hostility against other classes. No doubt the hydrogen bomb makes a real world war much less likely, but I think it is a long time since it has been so impossible to find real peace anywhere. Also, many great religions are likely to be re-barbarised and there is real danger that the Moslem world may unite against the West.

Lord Carlisle [Murray's father-in-law, George James Howard, 9th Earl of Carlisle (1843–1911)] used sometimes to say that he didn't believe in any general principles except the precepts that his nurse used to give him when he was a child, e.g. that he mustn't tell stories, and mustn't bite his sister. Experience had taught him that these were true. Evidently he had the blood of governesses in him somewhere. (Ms letter, Murray (Oxford) to Russell (Richmond), 16 Sept. 1955. RA 3 071L)

11

Gilbert Murray and International Politics

Martin Ceadel

Possessing the intellect and energy he did, not to mention the classical education, Murray developed a formidable grip on many aspects of international politics. Yet he did so not as a policy wonk but as an ideologue. An illustration is provided by his treatment of Persia in the influential vindication of British foreign policy which he published in 1915 with a progressive audience in mind. Having read 'a certain number of book and articles' and 'some thousands of official despatches', he admitted that he was unable to see his 'way clear through the almost maddening complexities, sometimes tragic and sometimes grotesque' of this topic. Even so, he was persuaded that the policy of the British foreign secretary towards it, as towards his other areas of responsibility, had been 'a prudent, a peaceful, and a liberal-minded' one. This was all Murray really needed to know: he was happy to concede that from their respective viewpoints both Persian nationalists and British imperialists 'have a right to attack and denounce Sir Edward Grey for his policy in Persia'; but for him the only relevant consideration was that 'Liberals, as far as I can see, have no right' (Murray 1915c, 83–4, 101–2). For Murray, therefore, ideology served as an adequate road map of international politics: detailed topographical understanding was in the last resort unnecessary. I shall therefore approach Murray's views on this subject through his Liberalism. Murray was somewhat unusual in deriving this largely from a combination of youthful sensitivities and Hellenic studies; and these derivations had some implications for the way he applied it. Moreover, like many of his contemporaries, at different stages in his life he favoured different strands within Liberalism, moving from Gladstonism, to radicalism, to Asquithism, and in old age to a Liberalism so conservative as almost not to qualify as such. But at the height of his personal influence, the era of the two World Wars, he was a pillar of Liberal orthodoxy; and in consequence his views on international politics were archetypal rather than distinctive.

Here I self-indulgently intrude a personal anecdote. My eeriest moment in three and a half decades of research came while revisiting the Murray papers[1] in the Bodleian Library for this essay. I stumbled across a letter written to him on 14 June 1941 by my late father, E. B. Ceadel, then a classics finalist at Christ's College, Cambridge. Aged 20 years and 4 months, he had recently published the second of three articles in the *Classical Quarterly* written while he was an undergraduate, the first of which had appeared when he was only a few months past his nineteenth birthday (E. B. Ceadel 1940, 1941a, 1941b). With characteristic generosity Murray had written to congratulate him on his metrical analysis of Euripides' verse, even though it called into question some of his own datings of Euripides' plays. Indeed, he conceded that his own long-held view of *Electra* 'may be merely a subjective fancy. Certainly the metrical statistics are against me' (E. B. Ceadel to Murray, 14 June 1941; Murray to E. B. Ceadel, 20 June 1941 (copy): GM).

This anecdote suggests that even in Murray's lifetime his scholarship was facing challenges, and that he was gracious in acknowledging this. As an academic, despite a phenomenal appetite for work, he had preferred imaginative thinking to the technical grind, finding even the collation of the texts of his beloved Euripides a 'disgusting task'—a telling, even if jocular, epithet quoted by Francis West (F. J. West 1984, 118). As a teacher, despite his diligence, he was no Stakhanovite: he lasted only four years, broken into two spells, as a fellow of New College, even though during the second his teaching load was only 'two hours a week in each of two terms' (ibid., 112); after he moved to his first chair, 'his record of illness and absence over his near decade at Glasgow was... deplorable', in the words of Sir Duncan Wilson, owing to his 'career as an invalid'; and half-way

[1] Bodleian Library, Oxford, MSS Gilbert Murray, cited as GM in notes and text.

through his tenure of his second chair he managed the notable achievement for that place and time of provoking an Oxford vice-chancellor to inquire whether he was pulling his weight, though he responded honourably by surrendering part of his salary (D. Wilson 1987, 64, 301–2). By contrast, when drudging for political causes he discovered boundless reserves of physical resilience and good cheer. In particular, the erstwhile valetudinarian was able, apparently with minimal physical and mental stress, to commute once or twice a week to London and chair endless committees for the League of Nations Union over almost two decades, until his colleagues, worried at his declining physical powers, eased him out. In addition, he travelled to Geneva for meetings of the League Assembly and later the Committee of Intellectual Co-operation. This active internationalism was all the more remarkable for the fact that unlike his theatrical ventures, for which he also showed considerable energy, it lacked the attraction of alluring actresses.

What made Murray a top-rank figure was his political contribution. In the early years of the twentieth century he was a radical intellectual of some significance. In 1914–15 he was transformed into the leading Liberal apologist for British intervention in the First World War. And from 1918 he was, along with Lord Robert Cecil, one of the 'two British civic monks', as Salvador de Madariaga memorably termed them (Smith and Toynbee 1960, 178), who for a quarter of a century were synonymous with the League of Nations Union. Generally known as the LNU, this was the most remarkable voluntary association of its time, collecting more than 400,000 annual membership subscriptions at its peak in 1931 and conducting a remarkable private referendum on attitudes to the League and disarmament, the Peace Ballot of 1934–5. Though the LNU declined after 1936, and its successor from 1946, the United Nations Association, was to prove but a pale shadow, Murray remained devoted to the internationalist cause until well into the 1950s.

Thus Murray not only edited, taught, translated, and dramatized Hellenism: he identified it with the principal progressive creed of his day. His son-in-law Arnold Toynbee, whose *Surveys of International Affairs* for Chatham House provided him much of his foreign information in the interwar period, famously pointed out that

> liberalism was the link between his public work and his scholarship. He identified both the Hellenic genius and the modern Western genius with the liberal spirit, and so identified them with each other. This was the master idea that gave unity to all his pursuits and inspiration to each of them, and this idea had shone out in him from the start. (Smith and Toynbee 1960, 212)

Of course, Murray was not the only classically trained academic to promote a Hellenizing Liberalism; but the personal style and social connections with which he did so gave him the greatest public influence.

Murray's political creed had been built up in layers that bonded cohesively together. Its bedrock was a double sensitivity nurtured by his Australian childhood. The cruelty of schoolmates had taught him to abhor the ill-treatment of animals, so that when justifying British intervention in the First World War he specifically, and in my experience uniquely, acknowledged the suffering which this was bringing not only to soldiers but to horses and other dumb animals (Murray 1914b, 5; Murray 1915b, 5). And his father's drinking away of his health and wealth had converted him to near-teetotalism. Additional layers of Liberalism were added by the intellectual and educational climate he discovered in Britain. He was brought by his widowed mother to the old country in 1877, when he was 11 and Gladstone was limbering up for his Midlothian campaign; and he was sent to Merchant Taylors' School where he discovered Hellenism, which he was to define in his inaugural lecture at Glasgow as 'that peculiar way of looking at things, that extraordinary shrewdness and knowledge of the world, that child-like impulsiveness for wild hopes and idealism' (cited in D. Wilson 1987, 44). Hellenism also provided him with the high moral tone that others achieved through the religious observance he never managed. By the time he went to St John's College, Oxford, in 1884 he was an avowed Liberal. While an undergraduate, moreover, his political creed was given a final veneer through meeting the formidable Whig chatelaine of Castle Howard, the Countess of Carlisle, and soon afterwards marrying her daughter Lady Mary Howard. As a result of this uplifting into the high-minded Liberal aristocracy he was in Wilson's shrewd phrase 'trained to support the favourite causes of Lady Carlisle and of his wife' (D. Wilson 1987, 61), including votes for women and home rule for Ireland.

Murray's Liberalism was thus a matter of sensibility as much as of philosophical doctrine: it was to a considerable extent an aesthetic repudiation of the cruelty, befuddlement, mindlessness, crassness, and chauvinism that were all too commonly associated with Toryism. Wilson noted that the fact that Murray and his wife both 'disapproved of luxurious living and practised the simple life' was 'highly relevant to their political attitudes'. These attitudes 'tended to be anti-establishment'; yet in Murray's particular case his radical 'feelings were complicated by a certain relish for his position of friend and adviser to at least the classically educated leaders of the Establishment' (ibid., 184). Indeed, the particular character of Murray's Liberalism disposed him to suspend his critical faculties in respect of those whom he credited with similarly good taste. For example, as chairman of the LNU's executive committee in 1929 he was to inform the future Conservative prime minister Harold Macmillan, then a left-wing Tory, that he would be very sorry to lose him from the committee not only 'because you so much strengthen the progressive Conservative wing' but also 'because I feel, or imagine I feel, a certain Hellenic atmosphere in your presence' (Murray to Macmillan, 11 Feb. 1929 (copy): GM). A more worrying consequence of a Liberalism based on fastidiousness and Hellenism could, however, be a disgust for the less civilized. There is a hint of this in Murray's perception of a 'rather large proportion of small dark Latin nations' at the League of Nations Assembly in 1921 (Murray to Smuts, 8 Oct. 1921, cited in Stray 2004), and more than a hint in his chilling defence of America's and Australia's restrictive immigration policies seven years later: 'Populations which breed like flies to the limit of subsistence, and then die like flies when the weather changes, can never build up a standard of life or character worthy of the dignity of man' (Murray 1929b, 166).

Even so, Murray equated Liberalism with rationality, being capable unselfconsciously of writing a sentence that began: 'As a Liberal and a reasonable man I. . . .' (Murray 1915c, 101). This identification made him unusually secure in his political allegiance: though politically ecumenical, as shown in his close cooperation with the maverick Tory Lord Robert Cecil and his signing of the progressive 'Next Five

Years' manifesto in the 1930s, he did not waver from his commitment to the Liberal Party until it reached the nadir of its electoral fortunes, and he entered the twilight of his life, in the 1950s. He was never tempted to jump on the Labour bandwagon, as even his wife did in 1924; but nor did he backslide into Conservatism via support for coalition or national governments, as many anti-socialist Liberals did in the period between 1915 and 1945. Peter Clarke's account of progressives responding to the rise of socialism and labourism identifies him as one of the small group for whom the preservation of a Liberal affiliation 'was sacred ground'. Michael Freeden's study of interwar liberalism does the same, and even presents him as neutral in respect of a second-choice affiliation, his preferences seeming to be 'delicately poised between the more humane side of conservatism and treading the downward path of a democracy out of control' (Clarke 1978, 200, 276; Freeden 1986, 215). The serenity of Murray's Liberalism and his indifference towards alternatives must help to explain why the liveliest of his children turned to Communism, Catholicism, or Bohemianism.

The Murrays' youthful Liberalism did not go down well in the Conservative atmosphere of Glasgow University whose professoriat he joined in 1889 as a precocious 23-year-old; but he kept up his political spirits by writing regular letters to his mother-in-law that reveal sound Gladstonian instincts: in 1896, for example, he was 'furious' about the Salisbury government's inactivity over Turkish atrocities in Armenia (Murray to Rosalind, Lady Carlisle, 15 Jan. 1896: GM). After he resigned his Glasgow chair on grounds of ill-health in March 1899 to live for some years in Surrey as an independent man of letters, his opposition to the South African War placed him among the 'pro-Boers' who constituted a minority even within his own party. Another of their number, J. A. Hobson, sent him the proofs of his radical classic *Imperialism: A Study* (Hobson 1902) to comment on. Murray was generally admiring, but queried its 'view that class government makes for the antagonism of nations'. Hobson explained in reply that Britain's imperfect democracy gave too much influence to 'a confederacy of business forces' and encouraged a 'spirited foreign policy' as a distraction from domestic discontents (Hobson to Murray, 31 July, 4 Aug., 17 Aug. 1902; Murray to Rosalind, Lady Carlisle, 26 Sept. 1902: GM). Murray's failure to be persuaded by Hobson's thesis was an early sign that his mature Liberalism was to be of the mainstream kind that identified international anarchy as the main cause of war, in contrast with the developing conviction of the Liberal Party's radical wing that the problem was a lack of democratic control over elites and vested interests.

Murray's sense of isolation during the Boer War helped to kill any lingering idea that, having left his chair, he might take up a political career. Moreover, after he returned to academic life at Oxford, first as a Classics fellow at New College in 1905 and then as Regius Professor of Greek at Christ Church from 1908, his support for women's suffrage and sympathy for the emergent labour movement placed him among the more radical of the supporters of the Campbell-Bannerman and Asquith governments. Although his political interests at this time were primarily domestic, he played a role in the creation on 4 February 1914 of an Oxford War and Peace Society to support the work of Norman Angell, whose recent book *The Great Illusion* had argued the neo-Cobdenite case that because of financial interdependence a great power could not gain from military success. Angell was duly grateful; and the two men got to know each other in the spring of 1914.[2] It was therefore reasonable for Murray to claim soon afterwards: 'We Radicals had always worked for peace, for conciliation, for mutual understanding' (Murray 1915b, 10). And it was no surprise on the outbreak of the First World War that he initially opposed British intervention, signing the manifesto of the short-lived and ineffective British Neutrality Committee organized by J. A. Hobson, Graham Wallas, and other radicals.

However, in the defining moment of his political career, Murray attended the House of Commons on 3 August to hear the foreign secretary, Sir Edward Grey, explain the Liberal government's position. Grey's ill-prepared performance proved unexpectedly persuasive, for a reason which the historian Cameron Hazlehurst neatly put his finger on: 'The one massive virtue of Grey's speech was its stumbling manner, mistaken this time, as so often before, for

[2] *War & Peace* (March 1914), 179. Angell to Murray, 8 May [not 'March' as Angell originally typed before making an almost illegible correction, and which is where the Bodleian has chronologically placed it] and 19 June 1914: GM.

honesty. Here was a man, it seemed, who had struggled for peace' (Hazlehurst 1971, 46). Murray was one of those taken in: he evidently felt sympathy for a fastidious Oxonian statesman from an old Whig family struggling to do the right thing. What thus separated Murray from those radicals who maintained their neutralism and suspicion of secret diplomacy and formed the Union of Democratic Control was as much a difference of temperament as an alternative reading of international politics. Murray was temperamentally disposed to trust certain members of the Liberal establishment, whereas the likes of E. D. Morel, Arthur Ponsonby, and Bertrand Russell were not. He thus metamorphosed from radical to Asquithean in the course of an afternoon, accepting the constraining realities of governmental responsibility, particularly in foreign policy, though not to the extent of later swallowing the ultra-realist, fight-to-a-finish Liberalism associated with Lloyd George after he replaced Asquith as prime minister.

Murray's trustfulness towards the Asquith ministry of 1908–16 not only caused him to abandon neutralism: it led to his becoming an apologist for Grey. He wrote two pamphlets for the *Oxford Pamphlets 1914* series that constituted Oxford University Press's patriotic service. The first, *How Can War Ever Be Right?*, was designed to appeal to Liberals, even those of a radical persuasion: to establish his credentials with such a readership he claimed to 'have spoken and presided at more meetings than I can remember for peace and arbitration and the promotion of international friendship', reminded his readers of his opposition to the South African war, and insisted that he had put more 'intense feeling' into his translation of Euripides' *Trojan Women*, 'the first great denunciation of war in European literature', than into any of his other work. Interestingly in view of his later support for a league of nations, he refused in justifying British intervention to 'lay any stress on the hopes which we may entertain for the building up of a better Europe after the war'. This, and his moderate tone, indicated his tacit disapproval of the 'war that will end war' rhetoric and combative style of other pro-war propagandists such as H. G. Wells. Nor did Murray depend on the moralistic justification for war provided by German violation of Belgian neutrality. He insisted that British security 'would have been terribly endangered by the presence of Germany in a conqueror's mood at Ostend and Zeebrugge, not to speak of Dunkirk and Calais' so that 'mere self-preservation' would have justified fighting. In other words, he argued, 'our interest coincides with our honour'. That he went out of his way explicitly to endorse 'one of the old optimistic beliefs of nineteenth-century Liberalism ... that a nation's duty generally does coincide with its interest' indicated a self-conscious ideological orthodoxy (Murray 1914b, 3, 21–2).

His second pamphlet, *Thoughts on the War*, must however have worried his intended audience. In it he included the candid admission:

> For my own part, I find that I do desperately desire to hear of German dreadnoughts sunk in the North Sea. Mines are treacherous engines of death, but I should be only too glad to help in laying a mine for them. When I see one day that 20,000 Germans have been killed in such-and-such an engagement, and next day that it was only 2,000, I am sorry.

Moreover, in response to radical disapproval of siding with Tsarist Russia, Murray did not simply offer the geopolitical argument that it was a necessary counter-weight to Germany but somewhat implausibly claimed to be 'glad and proud' to have it as an ally, and to be helping the country 'of Turgenev and Tolstoy, the Russia of many artists and many martyrs, to work out its destiny and freedom'. He also invoked the prospect of post-war improvement, which he had previously disdained. He insisted that a peace conference would be an advance on the one which followed the Napoleonic Wars because, in place of Castlereagh 'we shall send from England someone like Mr Asquith or Sir Edward Grey, with ten times more progressive and liberal feeling and ten times more insight and understanding'. Anticipating Woodrow Wilson's belief in national self-determination as the basis of a new European settlement, he suggested that 'in general we must try to arrange, even at considerable cost, that territory goes with nationality'; and he for the first time acknowledged the case for an international organization, noting that 'we need a permanent Concert, perhaps a permanent common council' (Murray 1914c, 7, 12–14, 17).

The pinnacle of Murray's career as an apologist was his publication in the summer of 1915 of a 126-page response to the radical critique, encapsulated particularly in Union of Democratic Control pamphlets by his former pupil at Glasgow the journalist H. N. Brailsford and his friend Bertrand Russell. As Murray satirically summarized it, this critique held that 'the central enemy of the human race is Sir Edward Grey'. Though not deeply researched, *The Foreign Policy of Sir Edward Grey*, published by Oxford's academic imprint, the Clarendon Press, was at least all Murray's own work, unlike Russell's subsequent rejoinder, which relied on the able research assistance of Irene Cooper-Willis. Murray's comparative advantage lay in his judicious tone and style of argument. He thus began by acknowledging that there was 'no harm whatever, there is rather credit, in an Englishman trying hard to make his countrymen realize the case for Germany', before insisting that any such defence of Germany 'must of course be subjected to criticism just as much as a vehement pro-British statement'. He concluded confidently that Grey's policy in the ten days leading to British intervention was 'exactly right', and offered almost as ringing an endorsement of his policy since taking office in December 1905. He also criticized a key assumption made by Grey's radical critics: the 'full ideal' of democratic control of foreign policy was 'utterly impracticable'; and although 'a general interest in and understanding of Foreign Affairs would doubtless produce a healthier tone in the nation generally', it would 'not have had the slightest effect in averting or delaying the present war' (Murray 1915c, 6–8, 34, 124).

These activities as an apologist delayed Murray's emergence as an internationalist. He did not take a leading role in the early campaign for a league of nations. It was the Cambridge political scientist Goldsworthy Lowes Dickinson who created the committee to draft the first blueprint for an international organization; and it was the former Ambassador in Washington Lord Bryce who chaired it. Murray did not join, though he was sent its initial draft proposals in February 1915, and annotated them sceptically (D. Wilson 1987, 246). Moreover, it was the Liberal MP Aneurin Williams who played the key role in founding the League of Nations Society in May 1915; and although Murray was invited to a preparatory meeting (Mrs W. Rea to Murray, 12 Feb. [1915]: GM), there is no evidence that he either attended it or took any part in the society until 1917. Indeed, during the first two years of the war Murray was something of a refusenik in respect of anything that publicly implied lack of confidence in the government: he declined either to participate in a Fabian committee on internationalism, or to review Norman Angell's updated version of *The Great Illusion*, or again to sign a draft statement by British progressives in response to a manifesto issued by the German Social Democratic Party.[3] It was not surprising that Russell strongly disapproved of his behaviour at this time and in his rejoinder to *The Foreign Policy of Sir Edward Grey* Russell accused him of having written it 'under the tutelage of the Foreign Office' (Russell 1915, 2).[4]

Murray's transition from apologist to internationalist was a three-stage process. The first began in 1916 when conscription was introduced. Despite remarkably generous legislative provisions for conscientious objection, which allowed local tribunals both to grant exemption from service of any kind and to recognize non-religious beliefs as conscientious, a hard core of objectors had their claims rejected. This was partly because the tribunals applied the law in a restrictive way, but also because more objectors than expected sought complete exemption—an absolutist stance encouraged by the No-Conscription Fellowship, a socialist–pacifist body in which Bertrand Russell took a leading role. Rejected objectors were forcibly inducted into the army; and when in some cases they refused to obey orders, they were subjected to military punishment. Murray, anxious to square conscription with Liberal principles, used his influence in official circles to suggest a new procedure whereby objectors would be placed under civil rather than military authority if they accepted alternative service. On 16 April he complained to Russell: 'I find on pleading for the C.O.s that the pitch is terribly queered by the resolution of your N.C.F. Convention rejecting any form of alternative service', but received an implacable reply from Russell defending the absolutist stance and even claiming: 'The sacrifice of the C.O.'s is immensely greater than that of men at the front' (Murray to Russell, 16 Apr. 1916 (copy); Russell to Murray, 17 Apr. 1916: GM).

[3] Wilson 1987, 246. The invitation to review Angell's *Prussianism and its Destruction* for *War & Peace* came in a letter from Gerald Shove of 6 Jan. 1915: GM. His refusal can be inferred from the fact that the book was later reviewed by a staff writer. H. Wright to GM, 3 and 6 Aug. 1915: GM.

[4] On being corrected, Russell apologized for giving the 'wrong impression', but commented: 'I certainly thought you had more to do with them.': Russell to Murray, 28 Dec. 1915: GM.

Undeterred, Murray lunched with Asquith on 30 April, and urged him to improve the treatment of objectors. In May, moreover, he again interceded with the prime minister, this time over the fate of a group of rejected objectors who had been sent to the Western Front where disobedience to army orders might lead to their being shot as deserters (Rae 1970, 128, 152–5, 215). This taking up the cause of conscientious objectors showed he had ceased to be an unconditional fan of the way the war was being prosecuted.

The second stage of Murray's transition from apologist to internationalist came after Lloyd George became prime minister in December 1916. Asquith retained the leadership of the Liberal Party yet moved into a quasi-oppositional role. (Neville Chamberlain was to manage a similar predicament much better in 1940: he served on under Churchill before dying promptly so that his successor could become party leader.) Though a Liberal and former pro-Boer, Lloyd George was, as a Welshman, a member of a small, dark nation; and he also lacked a classical education. These deficiencies were compounded by the fact that he replaced Grey as foreign secretary with the Conservative former prime minister Balfour. Antipathy to the Lloyd George ministry pushed a number of ex-Liberals towards the Labour Party, which drew increasingly close to the Union of Democratic Control during the last year and a half of the war. But Murray was one of those who in Clarke's words 'were able to translate this antipathy into an admiration for Asquith' (Clarke 1978, 195). In consequence of his lack of trust in those who now directed the war effort, Murray became less shy of associating with the peace movement. When, following American entry into the war in April 1917 under a President committed to its cause, the League of Nations Society began to hold public meetings and expand its membership, Murray accepted a vice-presidency. Admittedly, he took no active role in the society, which may help to explain the inaccuracy of his recollection in old age that it had 'contained a good many real pacifists': in reality, the League of Nations Society had from the outset favoured the equipping of a league of nations with military sanctions.[5] At the end of June 1917, he contributed a preface to a

[5] Wilson gives his date of joining as November 1916, but the notepaper in use a year later had his name typed in as an obviously recent addition: see, for example, A. Williams to Murray, 29 Oct. 1917: GM. M. Ceadel 2000, 207.

book outlining the plight of imprisoned absolutists, which appeared over the name of the mother of the saintly Quaker pacifist Stephen Hobhouse, but was in fact ghost-written by Bertrand Russell. Murray's preface showed that he had become more irritated by the authorities than by the absolutists: after noting that two military officials had told him that they favoured shooting selected conscientious objectors, he insisted that 'the worst point of the whole miserable business' was 'that the great majority of ordinary decent people who have come into personal contact with the treatment of the objectors by the Tribunals and the War Office find themselves angered and embittered against the Government of the country at a time when it needs all their support' (Monk 1996, 500; Hobhouse 1917, pp. viii, xiii). In addition, when Lord Lansdowne, who had been foreign secretary when the *Entente cordiale* had been established, called for peace negotiations in a famous letter to the *Daily Telegraph* on 29 November 1917, Murray supported him to such an extent that the Foreign Office withdrew its unofficial sponsorship of a planned visit to the United States (M. Ceadel 2000, 231–2; D. Wilson 1987, 249–51; Hibbert to Murray, 10 and 18 June 1918: GM). And he also interceded on Russell's behalf when, ironically just at the point of giving up his pacifist work to return to philosophy, he was prosecuted early in 1918 and eventually imprisoned for sedition.[6]

The final stage of Murray's emergence as an internationalist occurred in the late spring and early summer of 1918. By that time Wilson's support and America's holding of the military balance had turned a league of nations from a progressive dream into a realistic possibility, though many progressives were pursuing radical or even, given the Bolshevik revolution, socialist alternatives. Murray wrote a pamphlet, *The League of Nations and the Democratic Idea*, which insisted that 'in most wars of recent times you could find as much war-frenzy in the Jingo mob as in the most plutocratic club or drawing room'. He insisted that a league, created by linking together existing arbitration agreements, was a practical possibility. In consequence: 'The principle that will solve the problem of war is not Democracy but Internationalism' (Murray 1918b, 12, 23, 28).[7] His

[6] For Russell's gratitude, see his letter to Murray, 15 Feb. 1918: GM.

[7] This book was reviewed in the *Times Literary Supplement*, 25 July 1918, 351.

conversion to the league idea coincided with that of a hard-headed group, led by David Davies, a millionaire industrialist and Liberal MP who had formerly been a member of Lloyd George's private secretariat. Accepting the inevitability of a league, this group wanted one created as soon as possible on the basis of Britain's existing alliance against Germany. Davies tried to win over the League of Nations Society at its annual meeting on 14 June 1918; but most of its members feared that such a league would turn into a mechanism for permanently discriminating against Germany, so in the exultant words of Virginia Woolf, the novelist, who attended with her husband Leonard, the Fabian Society's leading expert on international government, the 'jingoes were defeated by the cranks' (Woolf 1977, 157–8). Within a week of this rebuff an infuriated Davies had launched his own rival, the League of Free Nations Association. Murray became a key part of his new association. He was one of five people who attended the provisional executive committee meeting of the League of Free Nations Association on 24 June, the others being Davies, another Liberal MP Charles McCurdy, a leading journalist J. A. Spender, and H. G. Wells; and he was appointed as its chairman. Moreover, one of his closest friends, William Archer, was hired as the salaried director of its research committee. At the same time Murray approached the government's leading League enthusiast, Lord Robert Cecil, who on 27 June expressed willingness to talk to him about the subject (Cecil to Murray, 27 June 1918: GM).

It was odd that Murray was drawn into the league-of-nations movement in the slipstream of David Davies, who was closer to Lloyd George than to Asquith, as Lady Mary Murray pointed out, and was also obsessional rather than Hellenistic (D. Wilson 1987, 253). But he found his metier as a direct result. Davies's lavish funding placed the League of Free Nations Association at such an advantage over the League of Nations Society that after only a few weeks of rivalry the latter in effect sued for peace. In October 1918, just ahead of the armistice which was to give the league cause its great opportunity, the two organizations officially completed a merger, as the League of Nations Union (or LNU), with Grey as its president, though because the League of Free Nations Association had the premises and paid staff it looked as if it had achieved a takeover of the older body. That the LNU soon established its own identity was to a considerable extent due to Murray, who became the first chairman of its executive committee. Ideologically, he was well placed to unite the movement: though coming into the LNU as one of David Davies's 'jingoes', as Virginia Woolf had called them, he was at one with the 'cranks' in his distaste for Lloyd George's going to the country on a 'programme of frantic war passion' in December 1918. Indeed, he even claimed that Lloyd George was at that time in a position 'to choose between plain good and plain evil. And he chose, deliberately, evil' (Murray 1921b, 11). Evil evidently paid the bigger dividend, however: Lloyd George's coalition won the general election; and the Asquithians were humiliated, Murray himself going down to the first of six thumping defeats in eleven years in the unwinnable constituency made up of Oxford graduates.

He proved much more successful as the LNU's chairman than as a Liberal candidate. He was able to bring the full force of his intellect, intuition, and charm to bear on the often outspoken individuals inherited from the two precursor bodies: Charles McCurdy was soon apologizing to him for 'extravagant expression' at one meeting (McCurdy to Murray, 17 Jan. 1919: GM). In addition, as the LNU's historian has recognized, Murray 'skilfully played the role of moderator and arbiter at . . . the Union's headquarters, answering countless letters and revolving staffing and financial problems' (Birn 1981, 22). He even staged a special series of matinees of the *Trojan Women* at the Old Vic in October 1919, with Sybil Thorndike as Hecuba, to raise money for the LNU, thereby bringing his Hellenic, dramatic, and liberal–internationalist interests into a happy convergence (D. Wilson 1987, 297–8).

Perhaps Murray's greatest service to the LNU was his playing second fiddle to Lord Robert Cecil. He demoted himself to vice-chairman in June 1919 when Cecil returned from the Paris peace conference after helping to create the League of Nations. Cecil was available to move into the chair of the LNU's executive committee because he had resigned from the government when the disestablishment of the Anglican church in Wales, suspended for the duration of the war, came into effect. At the time of this resignation he was at the peak of his prestige: indeed, with the Asquithean Liberals in crisis, Cecil was talked of as a leader of the new party that might be formed to oppose the Lloyd George coalition. In the LNU he could, as a political heavyweight, hold David Davies in check, and, as a Tory grandee, give it an all-party rather than a merely left-wing appeal. He was also bold enough to insist that the LNU be more than an educational body: it should also put pressure on governments. His inspirational leadership was thus of inestimable value, particularly in the early 1920s, when the LNU was struggling to establish itself. It was not until the second half of that decade that the LNU took root in civil society.

Even so, Cecil could be headstrong: although some of his impulses paid off handsomely, as did the Peace Ballot, others turned out to be demoralizing distractions, as did his insistence that the LNU support the International Peace Campaign, a popular-front inititative launched by the Comintern in France in 1935. He could also be petulant, threatening resignation if he seemed unlikely to get his own way. Murray managed his senior partner with great skill, to some extent restraining him—hence de Madariaga's remark that 'Cecil was rather the motor and Murray the brake'—whilst always remaining loyal. He deferred to Cecil's political judgement since he was still an active politician. Cecil served as a Conservative cabinet minister in 1923, being replaced by Murray as chairman of the executive committee and becoming co-president of the LNU with Grey instead. He did the same in 1924–7, before resigning as a dramatic protest against his colleagues' reluctance to disarm. And he advised the Labour government of 1929–31. Murray's deference was made easier by ideological affinity: for all his inherited Toryism, Cecil was very close to Liberalism in his approach to international relations.

Celebrating their remarkably quarrel-free relationship after almost two decades, Murray observed to Cecil that 'on political matters I naturally tended to accept your guidance but I never had the feeling of yielding against my judgement' (Murray to Cecil, 29 Apr. 1938, cited in Birn 1981, 22). Undoubtedly the extent to which he accepted Cecil's political guidance restricted his capacity to express his own independent views on international politics. For example, there are signs that, like progressive opinion generally in the early 1920s, he was critical of French policy, writing in 1921, for example: 'France cannot quite yet escape from her war psychology' (Murray 1921b, 119). But Cecil was of the opinion that reassuring rather than criticizing the French offered the better chance of inducing them to disarm. This tactic was probably wise, but became very unpopular when France occupied the Ruhr in 1923 to extract reparations that it was owed. As Wilson has shown, in order to minimize dissent within the LNU Murray made some policy concessions to members who wanted it to show more sympathy for the Germans (D. Wilson 1987, 300–1). But, as far as he could, he kept to Cecil's approach; and it is hard to know how far he would have liked to tilt towards Germany. Thus when in the spring of 1939 Murray identified 'ungenerous treatment of the Weimar Republic' as a cause of the current crisis, he not only blamed 'the unreasonableness of France and the Little Entente' but also acknowledged 'our British unwillingness to give the firm assurances that would have made them reasonable' (Murray, 'A League of Nations: The First Experiment (1939)', in Murray 1948, 71).

Cecil also insisted that the LNU support the League as it had been constituted, rather than undermine it from the outset by calling for its reform as many radicals and socialists wanted to do out of disappointment at its limited supranationalism and association with a vindictive peace. Murray was very willing to present the League in the best possible light. He understood the modesty both of the demands it made on national sovereignty and of its provisions for what would later be called collective security. Indeed, he acknowledged that it 'leaves its members almost as free as if they were outside' and that its 'true weapon is not force but publicity' (Murray 1921b, 118). But he did not bemoan the League's lack of military muscle, unlike David Davies who spent most of the interwar period calling for it to be equipped with an international police force, consisting mainly of aircraft. Indeed, in a pamphlet of 1920 that skilfully analysed the Covenant of the League of Nations, Murray argued:

> A League always in arms coercing would-be war-makers would be a League in the last stage of collapse. A successful League will be one which by securing international justice, by removing oppression and fears of oppression, and by spreading the habit of general confidence and security, shall make large armies and navies gradually disappear and reduce even the police forces of the world to a minimum. (Murray 1920, 19)

Murray could accept a League of modest powers because he regarded a cooperative ethos as being at least as important as international machinery. That is why he was so upset by Lloyd George's illiberalism. Thus although his 1921 book *The Problem of Foreign Policy* identified the League as the solution to all international problems, it implied in a telling passage that a return to Asquithean attitudes was a more fundamental requirement: 'We need in foreign policy and home policy a higher standard than we had before, the standard implied by the League of Nations in international affairs and the ideal of Co-operation in domestic affairs. But the first thing is to recover our wholesome tradition' (Murray 1921b, 6–7). Murray was of the same opinion after Lloyd George left office in 1922. His Halley Stewart lectures of 1928 defended the League's Covenant as 'on the whole a wonderfully successful instrument, flexible, comprehensive, and exactly directed to the main evil it was desired to cure', but expressed dismay at the inability of political leaders to 'see steadily beyond the limits of the old "sovereign independent state".' As a result:

> Many of those who have watched international policies closely for the last ten years come away with the same impression: that the average present-day government does not yet realize how small and transient are the gains, how large and enduring the losses, that result from small failures in moral courage and the lack of complete honesty. It is a lesson which good business firms had learnt generations ago. (Murray 1929b, 131, 134)

This criticism of state sovereignty and complimentary allusion to capitalism, taken with the identification in the same lectures of 'the liberation of international trade' as the most vital material question facing Europe, and an explicit celebration of 'the age of Nineteenth-Century Liberalism' (Murray 1929b, 160, 170), indicated how self-consciously conformist Murray's Liberalism remained, and therefore how generic his internationalism was. Indeed, this is how he is treated in the authoritative volume on interwar 'idealism' edited by David Long and Peter Wilson in 1995: he is mentioned a few times as a representative figure, in one case explicitly as 'an exemplar' (Long and Wilson 1995, 304), but is not one of the ten thinkers to whom an individual essay is devoted.

Being archetypal, Murray's thinking about international security went through exactly the same four stages as that of the LNU as it tried to cope with the opportunities and challenges of the interwar years and the Second World War.

First, in the relatively fair weather of the 1920s, when it was keen to encourage general disarmament, the LNU implied that the League would get its way by moral rather than military pressure. Murray thus argued in 1928 that the League's

normal sanction is the public opinion of the world; its most effective weapon publicity. You cannot punish a nation; you cannot even coerce by force any moderately strong nation. But you can exert a very strong pressure on even the strongest by simply putting a question to its representatives at the Assembly, or at one of the permanent Commissions, and publishing its reply. (Murray 1929b, 131)

Secondly, after Japan seized Manchuria in September 1931, in defiance of world opinion, the LNU had to accept that, in Murray's words it had been guilty during the 1920s 'of not grasping firmly this nettle of security' (Murray to Allen, 18 Feb. 1933 (copy): GM). David Davies urged it to accept an international air force, creating the New Commonwealth Society in 1932 to argue this case. However, the LNU considered Davies's proposal, and indeed an emphasis on military sanctions more generally, too divisive, and found it expedient to argue instead that economic pressure would usually suffice. Murray went along with this fudge, explaining to a leading League enthusiast in the Labour Party, Philip Noel Baker, in 1933: 'We are having a grave and deep-seated difference in the L.N.U. about the [International] Air Force... and I think we must concentrate on (1) the need of sanctions and (2) the efficacy of diplomatic, financial and economic sanctions' (Murray to Noel Baker, 2 Apr. 1933 (copy): GM). This reassuring argument ensured the success of the Peace Ballot of 1934–5 by presenting collective security as a means of upholding international law and order without actually risking war.

Thirdly, however, the triple crisis of 1936—in which Hitler remilitarized the Rhineland, Mussolini completed his conquest of Abyssinia in defiance of (albeit mild) economic sanctions imposed by the League, and Franco rebelled in Spain—made it clear that 'collective security' entailed both rearmament and alliances even though, paradoxically, it had been to oppose policies of this kind that the league-of-nations movement was launched in the first place. Many LNU supporters turned away from collective security and embraced 'peaceful change' or even pacifism. But the LNU leadership, including Murray, resolutely continued to support collective security even though its military implications were clear. Indeed, the LNU co-opted Winston Churchill on to its executive committee, though he preferred to accept the presidency of David Davies's New Commonwealth Society instead. Murray was fully aware of the irony of the LNU's new Churchillianism, pointing out to Cecil in December 1937: 'We are no longer a peace party, opposing a Jingo party, we are a "League and Collective Security" party opposing pacifists, isolationists, pro-Germans, etc. We are actually for a "spirited foreign policy".' And in a simultaneous memorandum to his executive committee he observed that the LNU had

> lost the support of great numbers who no longer believe in collective security: e.g. the pure Pacifists, most Conservatives, and many influential writers and teachers who used to support us, such as the Lothian group, Sir J. Fischer Williams, and all the holders of the special League of Nations Professorships, Zimmern, Manning, Carr and their numerous pupils. (cited in M. Ceadel 2000, 368)

Fourthly, after Hitler's seizure of Prague in March 1939 made war virtually inevitable, the LNU had for several years to fight on two fronts: against the new school of realists led by E. H. Carr, whose influential book *The Twenty Years' Crisis* (Carr 1939) accused internationalists of neglecting the factor of power in international relations, and also against the ultra-idealists of the briefly fashionable Federal Union movement, who rejected a mere confederation such as the League of Nations and its successor the United Nations and dreamed instead of a federation of the democracies. In response to Carr's charge, Murray privately admitted to Cecil: 'In the early years... I myself did not take the obligation to make war against an aggressor very seriously' (Murray to Cecil, 22 Aug. 1939 (copy): GM); but he strongly defended the LNU's subsequent record. In response to the challenge from the Federal Union, Murray—from 1938 a co-president rather than chairman of the executive committee—remained actively loyal to the LNU, and from 1946 for several years was strongly supportive of the United Nations Association, of which he was again a co-president.

However, his life-long serenity was beginning to desert him. His preface to his 1948 collection of essays, *From League to U.N.*, expressed dismay at the 'disease', of which Carr's work was 'an early symptom', infecting 'those sections of British opinion, on the extreme left and extreme right, who hate the whole liberal tradition which is the result of our long security and peace' (Murray 1948, 7). Moreover, in the 1950s, as he entered his mid-eighties and his wife slipped into dementia, even his own Liberalism became to some extent compromised. He voted Conservative for the first time in the 1950 general election, though he persuaded himself that this was the best way to promote his old political creed given the institutional decline of the Liberal Party (D. Wilson 1987, 391). Although not so carried away by anti-Communism as some former internationalists in the early Cold War, he became increasingly worried about the changing balance of civilization as Asia and Africa increased their representation in the system of states. As with his increasing sense that the executive committee of the United Nations Association consisted of mediocrities (F. J. West 1984, 243), his Hellenism seemed to have turned sour. Most notoriously, in the last year of his life he moved back from being an internationalist to being an apologist, this time for the Conservative prime minister Sir Anthony Eden, whose Suez intervention of 1956 he endorsed as 'a daring attempt to stop the "anti-West" conspiracy of Nasser's usurpation'. In addition to supporting Eden on international-order grounds, he turned against the United Nations. Publicly, he warned that its increasing 'egalitarianism', as former colonies joined the organization on becoming independent, carried a 'real danger that not merely the British Empire but the whole "Western" or "Christian" civilisation will become of less and less account' (*Sunday Times*, 16 Dec. 1956, cited in Clarke 1978, 289). Privately, he disparaged the new members of the United Nations as 'nearly all of them uncivilized, Asiatic, Arabic or South American nations with a violent anti-west prejudice or anti-civilisation majority' (cited in D. Wilson 1987, 393).

Murray's sharpness of expression and his attentiveness to contemporary events thus survived until his final coma in early 1957, even though, sadly, his Liberalism, which for virtually all his adult life had guided his intelligent and energetic engagement with international politics, did not quite do the same.

12

Retrieving Cosmos: Gilbert Murray's Thought on International Relations

Peter Wilson

This chapter takes a retrospective look at the international political thought of Gilbert Murray, ninety years after his first substantial work on the subject was published (1915c), and nearly sixty years after his last (1948). Of course, no retrospective, whether in the art world or in the world of political thought, can be neutral. It inevitably comes from a particular perspective. The perspective in this case is that of a student of the history of early mid-twentieth-century international thought; of someone who has been involved in the revision of how this important period in international thinking has been received in the discipline of International Relations (IR); of someone who has written a number of critical reassessments of E. H. Carr's contribution to IR (e.g. P. Wilson 2000), and a detailed study of Murray's League of Nations Union colleague, Leonard Woolf (P. Wilson 2003); but someone who holds Carr's *The Twenty Years' Crisis* (Carr 1939) in high esteem, despite its flaws, and is opposed to its outright rejection as an account of the 'first phase' of IR theorizing. It was *The Twenty Years' Crisis* that branded interwar internationalism (to which Murray was a prominent contributor) as the utopian (and therefore deeply flawed) phase of IR thought. Only recently, spurred on by the dramatic changes in the international landscape following the end of the Cold War, has this characterization been challenged (Long and Wilson 1995; P. Wilson 1998; Schmidt 1998; Ashworth 1999, 1–21).

Most importantly this retrospective is from someone who has been schooled within that broad body of thinking known as the English school of IR (Dunne 1998; Buzan 2004; Linklater and Suganami 2006), and whose outlook within it can be described as 'pluralism plus'. States are the most important actors in international relations (Jackson and James 1993, 3–25, 346–67). Their relations are sufficiently orderly and mutually influential to describe them in terms of an international society (Bull 1977; James 1986; P. Wilson 2004). But this society is 'practical' rather than 'purposive' (Nardin 1983). Its rules are mainly concerned with peaceful coexistence, not the achievement of common goals (Bull 1977, 67–71, 86–93). Collective action to achieve common goals, while growing, is still limited compared to well-ordered domestic societies. This is due to the political, economic, and cultural diversity of this society. Common goals have proved hard to define, at least with precision. Even our most hallowed international documents have large margins of discretion built in to them concerning how they are to be interpreted. Agreement on the collective use of force to achieve common goals has proved particularly elusive (Jackson 2000, 16–22, 249–93).

Arguably we have witnessed in the last 100 years a revolution in the use of force in international relations. From a situation in which the resort to arms by independent sovereign states was always legitimate, we have moved to one where the resort to arms is heavily circumscribed. International law now tolerates the use of force on only two grounds: enforcement action under Chapter VII of the UN Charter by the Security Council; and individual and collective self-defence (Hurrell 2005). But agreement on the legitimacy of wars of self-defence disguises some hefty disagreement between states. There exists little agreement on what constitutes self-defence. States have purposefully kept the concept extremely elastic. Sometimes it suits them to define it narrowly, sometimes broadly. The Bush Doctrine asserts a right of preventive war. But this is not a right that extends to all members of international society. Rather it is a special right born of the special circumstances of the 9/11 terrorist attacks, and the requirements of the War on Terror. It is a special right of the US. Self-defence, under current US doctrine, does not begin at the water's edge, but anywhere in the world where armed anti-American fanaticism has taken root (Dunn 2006).

The argument that a permissive right of humanitarian intervention is evolving is a strong one. This would provide a third ground for the legitimate use of force. If it becomes firmly established this would be evidence that international society is becoming more purposive, more 'solidarist' in nature and less 'pluralist' (Wheeler 2000, 11–13, 21–52). But the matter is still deeply controversial. The only thing that can be said with confidence is that the majority of members of international society are now prepared to tolerate the use of force to prevent the most egregious violations of human rights. But too many states are too hesitant, they have too many reservations, to suggest that a fully fledged right already exists. Hence 'pluralism plus'. There are thin solidarist elements in international society. They may in time become thicker and stronger. At the moment they are brittle.

I have spelt out at some length the perspective from which I see Murray, so as not to give the false impression that the following assessment of his IR thought is neutral or objective. In brief, this perspective is conservative, but far from anti-liberal.

RESTORING GOOD FAITH IN INTERNATIONAL RELATIONS

What did Gilbert Murray stand for in international relations? In broad terms he stood for honesty, sincerity, good faith, honourable dealings, openness, fairness, reason, the rule of law, mutual trust, discussion, moderation, cooperation, concern for the welfare of others, and commitment to the 'high and remote' motive of the general good over the 'low and immediate' (Murray 1929b, 180) motive of national self-interest. It might be said that he wanted to inject into international affairs the values, manners, and code of conduct of the nineteenth-century English gentleman. Not a bad thing in abstract terms, it might be added. But not a good strategy in the age of Lenin, Stalin, Mussolini, and Hitler. Indeed this was at the core of Carr's critique of Murray and his ilk. It was not that their ideas and values were wrong, but that they had become inappropriate, dangerously so, in a world that had moved on to new forms of economic, social, and political organization. The nineteenth-century order policed by Britain's benign hegemony was dead. Attempts to recreate it were doomed to failure. They represented, indeed, little more than an ideology the function of which was to sustain an international order beneficial to certain countries and certain classes long after the material conditions for its existence had broken down (Carr 1939, 81–112, 287–397).

There can be no doubting Gilbert Murray's devotion to the cause of international peace, nor the tirelessness of his practical work for the League of Nations, the League of Nations Union, the International Committee for Intellectual Co-operation (ICIC), and the Council for Education in World Citizenship (CEWC). The public spiritedness that motivated Murray was truly impressive. He was a man of high ideals and fine personal qualities. But the intellectual foundations on which his work was based are less sound. Indeed I have read no other interwar thinker to whom Carr's most severe criticisms more apply.

Yet there are many positives in Murray's IR thought and acknowledgement of them is long overdue. Due to the success of Carr's critique and the dominance of Realist thinking during the Cold War the positives from this period of writing have been, until recently, almost totally ignored. (Realism is the doctrine, sceptical of the role of law and morality in restraining state behaviour, that stresses the importance of power and self-help, and the immutability of the international anarchy. It is associated in modern times with the names of Carr, Hans Morgenthau, and Kenneth Waltz, a large part of whose work was a reaction to the liberal 'idealism' or 'utopianism' of Murray's era. See e.g. Donnelly 2000; Haslam 2002; M. Williams 2005.) It is true that Murray does not provide much for the modern theorist of international relations to get his teeth into. Contemporary theorists skilled at mining past thought for usable materials—an Andrew Linklater (e.g. 2000), a Ken Booth (e.g. 1990), or a Barry Buzan (e.g. 2004)—will not find Murray a useful resource. There is much in Murray's IR works, however, that the modern student of the international scene will find stimulating, illuminating, or surprising.

Most surprising is Murray's repeated assertion that struggle in social life is unavoidable. He was fond of Aristotle's observation: 'We toil for the sake of leisure, we make war for the sake of peace'

(Murray 1929b, 14). Fighting and killing was an essential part of life on earth. Man sustained himself by eating other animals or else by eating their food. 'Life is not based on peace but on an unrelenting murderous struggle' (ibid., 16). But in human societies the struggle became less murderous as Man became more civilized. The law 'Kill-to-live' was gradually suffused and penetrated by another: 'Co-operate-to-live' (ibid., 17, citing Prince Kropotkin's *Mutual Aid*). This was the normal upward road of civilization. But the growth of civilization did not mean an end to strife. 'Strife', Murray said, 'is integral to life. You cannot fully have life without it' (ibid., 18). 'If Peace is to mean repose, or an absence of effort and striving,' he continued, 'we do not want it perpetual. It is a rather dangerous drug, a thing to be taken in very small doses' (ibid.).

This runs contrary to the conventional image of the interwar idealist as the purveyor of easy truths about cooperation and the existence of a natural harmony of interests. There is no evidence to suggest that Murray believed in such a harmony. Cosmos—a settled, coherent, rational order—had to be fought for. The achievement of Cosmos was not possible without struggle. But this did not mean that force and violence were inevitable. Though strife and conflict were a 'permanent necessity in life' (ibid., 24), as civilization advanced the quality of strife changed. Peaceful striving replaced violent striving. This process was well established in Western society. The challenge now was to extend it to the societies of the East and to the international society of nations. Indeed this latter task had now become vital. In the modern, industrial, highly interdependent, nationalistic age, violent striving, unlike in previous ages, had become incompatible with civilization.

One finds in Murray's writings one of the earliest uses of the term 'international community' (1929b, 86), of 'crimes against humanity' (ibid., 89), and of 'terrorism' (1921b, 88–9), using the latter to describe the extreme bullying and gangster tactics of Lenin, Mussolini, and Hitler. One also finds many prescient remarks and observations. He correctly predicted that the Soviet Union would collapse because of its inability to compete with the liberal West in providing the good life for its citizens. In the 1920s he contended that no foreign power was capable of conquering Soviet Russia, and every attack by a foreign power tended, counterproductively, to unite the whole Russian people under its existing rulers. East and West were locked in a struggle for life; a struggle between 'two special systems and two religions'. The victor would not be the one most successful in terms of deception, repression, or propaganda, but the one that best provided what its people, and other peoples around the world, wanted. Murray was convinced that communist rule in Russia could not be permanent. 'If the Western nations can solve their economic troubles, maintain the peace, and progressively remove the worst discontents in their people,' he presciently asserted, 'the Western system is bound to win' (1929b, 54–7).

Murray also recognized the tension between democracy and the achievement of world order. Implicit in much of what Murray says is the liberal belief that democracies are more pacific than authoritarian states. But he also correctly noted that democracy can impede international agreement, even the observance of international law. Democratic statesmen have to keep a constant eye on domestic opinion. Not keeping public opinion on board can have dire domestic political consequences. Sometimes they act not out of right but in order to bolster their popularity. Sometimes they are dissuaded from taking the right course of action, even from honouring international obligations, because of the unpopularity of such moves at home. Sometimes they pander to powerful interests or attend only to the complaints of the noisiest or most troublesome elements in society. At all times the press feeds a patriotic public with national prejudice and jingoism, making it exceptionally difficult for a politician publicly to take an impartial or critical view of his own country's position. In addition, governments can seldom afford to be generous or far seeing in international negotiations for fear of being accused by opposition parties of betraying national interests (Murray 1929b, 59–62, 125–6, 190–1). In these and other ways (e.g. Murray 1948, 38–9, 68–9) democracy could get in the way of reaching complex international agreements, and in the way of their consistent implementation. It also made statesmanship, acting for the good of the world as a whole and taking the long, broad view rather than the short and narrow, an activity fraught with difficulty.

Yet it was an activity that the world desperately needed. Many peoples around the world had been ravaged by war, they had become habituated to cruelty, they had terrible wrongs to avenge, and their minds had been poisoned by an endless stream of hate-propaganda. Woodrow Wilson pledged peace with justice, but for them justice did not mean mercy and reconciliation, but cold-blooded revenge. They desperately needed someone to save them from themselves. Murray repeatedly emphasized the importance of leadership: the importance of the sincere and courageous man 'with a gift for leading' who could save people from their worst passions and their meanest instincts (Murray 1929b, 133–4; 1921b, 10–16, 30–59). The world had such a man in President Wilson, but the severe stroke he suffered in September 1919, and the failure of the US Senate to ratify the Versailles Treaty, effectively removed him from the world scene. David Lloyd George possessed the intelligence and humanity to step into the breach, but when the time came he proved 'curiously destitute of generous ambition' and 'incapable of thinking greatly', exploiting the psychology of hatred and violence generated by the War rather than seeking to repair it (Murray 1921b, 10–14).

Leadership had little chance of succeeding, however, in the absence of greater education on peace, the League, and internationalism. In true Athenian fashion, citizenship and education for Murray went hand in hand. True, the duty to educate could no longer be left in the hands of the citizen himself. It had now passed to society as a whole. But education remained an elemental ingredient of any effectively functioning society, and with the onset of modern industrial civilization it had become even more so. Without the ability to think disinterestedly, without some capability for independent thought, the citizen was not fitted to carry out his social duties, not the least to take a constructive part in political life. Reasonable political views could not be expected from the uneducated (Murray 1925c, 691–4).

The same logic applied to international society. The good life internationally was not possible unless its varied peoples had a tolerable knowledge of world affairs. Hence Murray's indefatigable work for ICIC and the Council for Education in World Citizenship, his enthusiasm for non-nationalist education (especially the non-nationalist teaching of history), his support for student exchange schemes, and for regular meetings of the 'Higher Schools of International Politics' (Murray 1929b, 193–7; 1948, 5–6). Hence also his work in the League Assembly and the League of Nations Union to promote education in the principles and practice of the League, and to promote international cooperation as the 'normal method of civilization' (Murray 1929b, 194). An interest in and understanding of foreign affairs was part of the 'natural equipment of intelligent democracy' (Murray 1915c, 124). The prospects for peace, cooperation, and the other great goals for which the League stood were forlorn without them.

On a more mundane level there is much that can be learned from Murray's account of particular events. He demonstrates, for example, the extent to which, and the clever ways in which, the major Western powers hedged their commitment to the Briand–Kellogg Pact of 1928. This agreement, which committed its parties to renounce war as an instrument of national policy, is seen in IR as one of the great totems of interwar idealist thinking. Murray provides a cool and sceptical analysis of it, stressing the British desire for 'flexibility', particularly with regard to its Empire and contiguous areas, and the American desire to maintain its special privileges under the Monroe Doctrine. In their letter of acceptance, which Murray notes was a long time in coming, the British government declared that there were 'certain regions of the world the welfare and integrity of which constitutes a special and vital interest for our peace and safety'. Interference in these regions from without 'could not be suffered'. Great Britain accepted the pact, therefore, only on the understanding that her freedom of action with regard to these regions was in no way compromised. But the British government showed no inclination to specify where these regions were situated. Nor was it inclined to specify what might constitute 'interference'. The terms of Britain's acceptance in effect knocked a huge hole in the treaty. Her pledge in effect became: 'I solemnly promise to renounce war as an instrument of national policy, unless anything happens which I do not like in certain parts of the world which happen to interest me' (Murray 1929b, 140–4).

The American position fared no better. Being unfamiliar with debates in the League, American opinion tended to regard the distinction between aggressive and defensive war as so much European hair-splitting. Yet when pressed on the issue the US Secretary of State, Frank Kellogg, while insisting that the treaty renounced war without qualification, added that no treaty could ever abolish the sacred and inalienable right of self-defence. He then championed an understanding of self-defence that was far more permissive than anything contained in the League Covenant. In effect, he said, each nation must be the judge in its own case. 'It alone is competent to decide whether circumstances require recourse to war in self-defence' (Kellogg, quoted in Murray 1929b, 140). As with the British reservation, this interpretation effectively undermined any credibility that the Briand–Kellogg Pact had. Before the eyes of the world, states could piously renounce war as an instrument of national policy, but then use it as an instrument of national policy under the veil of self-defence.

This analysis would not be out of place in *The Twenty Years' Crisis*, and it is surprising that no mention of it is made in the pages of this great book. Of course, Carr may have been unaware of this particular piece of analysis, though he was certainly familiar with other Murray contributions (see e.g. Carr 1939, 14, 252, 264). The fact remains, however, that to have one of the most prominent 'utopians' sceptically analysing one of the great totems of utopian thought would not have suited Professor Carr's purpose. Nor may Carr have felt inclined to cite favourably someone who had conspired with Lord Davies, President of the University College of Wales, Aberystwyth, to block Carr's appointment, in 1936, to the Woodrow Wilson Chair, and later similarly conspired to have him removed (B. Porter 2002, 80–84, 90–93).

One further positive feature of Murray's work on international relations merits special note: his simple, clear, humane writing style. This stands in stark contrast to the mechanical and bombastic style that dominates the pages of today's social science journals. There is not a single obfuscating passage in the whole of Murray's IR writing. In their desire to be scientific and novel, and as a result of the ever-greater specialization in the academic world, modern social scientists are rapidly losing their ability to convey their ideas in simple, accessible, humane terms. Parsimony, humility, and clarity are trading at a huge discount in today's social-scientific world. A definite retreat, as Murray might have put it, from civilization.

HELLENISM AND LIBERALITY

'Liberalism is what the world needs both at home and abroad'. So wrote Murray during the relatively calm years of the 1920s (Murray 1925c, 697). Yet from today's perspective many of the stances Murray took in domestic and international politics do not strike one as especially liberal. He was a staunch defender of the British Empire, believing it to be a great source of progress as well as stability in world politics (Murray 1900a; Morefield 2005, 101–35, 213–30). He distrusted the 'small dark Latin nations' the representatives of which he encountered in alarmingly large numbers during his days in the League Assembly (F. J. West 1984, 190). He had a low opinion of the common man and popular tastes, and feared many aspects of the democratization of society. He was against drink and sexual permissiveness. He was suspicious of human rights and vocally anti-egalitarian (e.g. Murray 1925c, 689, 694). He feared the rise of those nations that 'bred like flies' (Murray 1929b, 166) the incidence of which he equated with moral weakness. He unabashedly supported continued Anglo-Saxon hegemony in world politics. One of his last acts as a public figure was to support Eden over Suez, writing an article in the *Sunday Times* under the title 'Shadow of Barbarism' (16 Dec. 1956).

To understand the stances Murray took in politics one has to understand the two mutually supporting pillars of his moral, philosophical, and political outlook: Hellenism and liberality. As his son-in-law and fellow internationalist Arnold Toynbee astutely observed, Murray 'identified both the Hellenic genius and the modern Western genius with the liberal spirit, and so identified them with each other. This was the master idea that gave unity to all his pursuits and inspiration to each of them' (Toynbee 1960, 212). Significantly, Murray preferred to talk not of liberalism but of liberality. The word liberalism was too closely associated with the Liberal Party, and while he was a lifelong member of that party, Murray's instincts were bi-partisan. He hated extreme partisanship in any form. He hated the exaggeration, the misrepresentation, and the tribalism that were characteristic of the two-party system. The word liberalism also suggested the existence of a definite doctrine or set of principles. Murray doubted whether such a doctrine or set of principles existed. Rather, liberalism was a temper, a spirit, or an attitude of mind. John Morley once told him that when Gladstone wanted to get the measure of a man he would ask: 'Is he a man of real Liberality?' (Murray 1938, 16). This appealed to Murray's ecumenicalism as it implied that good men, men of real Liberality, could be found in all the major political parties.

The notion of liberality also enabled Murray to downplay the traditional liberal emphasis on individual liberty. Following Mill he believed that liberty did not mean licence. For the mass of men complete liberty was a destructive principle. Only the noblest men in society, those possessed of considerable powers of self-discipline and self-denial, could enjoy it unfettered. Yet individual liberty, especially the freedoms of conscience and speech, was a vital ingredient of civilization. But it had to be contained within a framework of law. The rule of law was, practically, the condition of freedom.

The basic attitude of liberality was to 'get free from the forces that blind us' (Murray 1925c, 682). These forces included prejudice, ignorance, self-interest, and the passions of class and nation. The man of liberality hated injustice, cruelty, vulgarity, and vice. He hated everything that enslaves human beings, believing in the intimate connection between reason, enlightenment, and progress. To this list Murray sometimes added scepticism. This was the natural result of true enlightenment. The true liberal might believe passionately in something, but he was always aware that he might be wrong. Murray was fond of Cromwell's plea to his Council: 'I beseech you in the bowels of Christ to remember that it is possible you may be mistaken' (Murray 1938, 22).

But above all else liberality meant concern for the common good. It meant putting to one side private and class interests and doing what was right for the whole community. Here, as elsewhere, his ideas were shaped and moulded by his understanding of classical Greece. Individual freedom and loyalty to one's family or clan were tremendously important, but not at the cost of disservice to the *polis*. Indeed, individual freedom meant having sufficient security, wealth, and leisure to be able to contribute to the well-being of the *polis*. Individuality and service to the community went hand in hand.

Murray's Hellenism informed his political outlook in other ways. It informed his elevation of the spiritual aspects of society over the mere material; his commitment to simplicity and frugality, and of giving more than taking; his respect for law and his understanding of freedom as living in accord with just laws; his dedication to the search for truth and the promotion of justice; his corresponding faith in reason and rejection of all forms of relativism; his faith in the power of human imagination and human effort to create new possibilities and new paths of creative endeavour; his belief in the role of superior civilizations as the engine of progress; and his belief in universal fellowship in the unfettered pursuit of *arêtê*: perhaps the ultimate gift of the Greeks to the world (Murray 1921c; 1954).

RETRIEVING COSMOS

Murray's basic outlook on twentieth-century international relations was that of a late Victorian middle-class intellectual, and one whose instincts were essentially aristocratic. The nineteenth century, he believed, had been one of great progress in virtually all domains: social, economic, scientific, cultural, political, even ethical. The Victorians, in their practical, empirical way had built an impressive Cosmos. It was an ordered, coherent world that, while far from perfect, was good and getting better. But it had one great flaw. It left untouched the international anarchy. While government within the state had become progressively more refined, representative, and effective, in relations between states it remained wholly absent. Despite the great changes that had occurred in the nineteenth century, the great technological changes and the rapid growth in international trade, methods for the conduct of international relations remained more or less untouched. There were no regular procedures for the settlement of international disputes. No world court to settle international legal disputes. No regular system of international conferences. No communal method for deterring or punishing the lawbreaker. States remained judge and jury of their own cause (Murray 1929b, 48–58, 190–1; 1938, 60–2; 1948, 18–22, 42–6, 137–9).

The result was World War I and the onset of Chaos. The chief task, therefore, was to restore the Cosmos enjoyed by the Victorians. And this could only be done by rectifying the chief fault of that Cosmos: its laissez-faire approach to international political relations. Hence Murray's dedication to the League, and all the nostrums associated with it: the rule of international law, collective security, disarmament, the peaceful settlement of disputes, conference diplomacy, and organized social, economic, technical, and intellectual cooperation.

MURRAY AND IR: SOME CRITICAL FAILINGS

One initial problem with Murray's thinking is that he does not provide us with a means of knowing whether the period we happen to live in is one of Cosmos or Chaos. The alliteration is nice, but the distinction is too stark. Are not all but the most static or dynamic periods of history comprised of both elements, to some or other degree, varying according to issue-area, and from region to region? Was the Cold War a period of Cosmos or Chaos? It was a period in which superpower war was avoided, in which Europe and Japan recovered economically and politically to a remarkable degree, but in which many regions had to endure terrible Chaos. The post-Cold War period is generally regarded to be one of Chaos, but the world has been freed from the fear of a nuclear confrontation between the superpowers, and many parts of the world have enjoyed unparalleled economic growth and domestic political liberalization. In addition, does a distinction need to be made between good forms of Chaos and bad forms? Globalization has brought Chaos in the form of the disturbance of many customs, habits, traditions, and practices. But is it not an agent of opportunity, prosperity, and modernization? Many think so (e.g. Bhagwati 2004; Friedman 1999).

Murray's eulogy of the nineteenth-century order is that of the comfortable, British, middle-class benefactor of that order. His Cosmos is predominantly an Anglo-Saxon Cosmos. Murray seems to have been little aware of the contingency and ethnocentrism of his position. His Cosmos is not a Cosmos but a sense of Cosmos from those in a privileged position. Things looked very different from Ireland, India, China, South Africa, Tasmania, or the West Indies (to name some areas where Anglo-Saxon atrocities occurred). Indeed, one of the striking features of Murray's writing on world politics, sixty or more years on, is just how unabashed and uncritical he was in asserting not only the rightfulness of Anglo-Saxon predominance, but its ongoing desirability (Murray 1925c, 688–9; 1929b, 162–7; 1948, 120–4). This stands in stark contrast to his call for disinterestedness in world politics and constitutes a considerable intellectual failing on his part.

This Anglo-centric and uncritical stance taken by Murray undermines the credibility of much of what he has to say. He was dedicated to the League and gave unswerving support to its Covenant, in particular to Articles 10, 11, and 16 dedicated to the maintenance of peace. But his constant assertion of the importance of law, order, and peace, is vulnerable to the charge first made by Carr that these were the special interests of the status quo Powers and classes. Revisionist Powers and disadvantaged classes held quite a different view. Though Murray presented them as abstract and universal principles, peace, law, and order were not, to use Carr's famous words, 'principles at all, but the unconscious reflexions of national policy based on a particular interpretation of national interest at a particular time' (Carr 1939, 111). Murray's repeated, and no doubt genuine, calls for fairness and sacrifice of immediate interests sound hollow in the absence of a much more critical analysis of the nature of the order that the League and its Covenant were designed to defend. It is revealing that while staunchly defending the 'status quo' articles of the Covenant, Murray spent much less time examining Article 19 and the concept of peaceful change (see e.g. Murray 1929b, 81, 115–19; 1948, 80–1). This stands in stark contrast to two of the shrewder analysts of international relations in Britain during this period: Carr and C. A. W. Manning (Carr 1939, 264–84; Manning 1937; P. Wilson 2004).

There are a number of related weaknesses in Murray's analysis that are fairly typical of the period. First, he failed to examine critically the concept of aggression so central to both the League and the UN. The evidence suggests he regarded it as an unambiguous, cut and dried concept providing a firm foundation for the new League order (see e.g. Murray 1929b, 67–97; 1948, 65–83). He declared in 1938 that '[t]here has never yet been the slightest difficulty in determining the aggressor' (Murray 1938, 64). But in 1931–2 the League encountered considerable difficulties in ascertaining the precise nature of Japanese military action in the Chinese province of Manchuria. While the Lytton Commission, set up by the League Council to investigate the crisis, eventually found against Japan, it did so in cautious terms. It acknowledged, for example, that Japan enjoyed 'extensive economic and administrative privileges' in the province and had the right to maintain 15,000 troops there to guard the South

Manchurian Railway. It also acknowledged that the Japanese officers at the scene of the initial incident (an explosion on or near the railway) may have believed they were acting in self-defence. Significantly, the Lytton Commission was not set up until three months after the outbreak of hostilities, it took seven months to report, the League Council took a further two months to consider the report, and the Assembly a further three. For a variety of both contingent and systemic international factors, along with some deep domestic ones, the major states were in no hurry to take strong action. The Assembly adopted the report in full in February 1933 (a full seventeen months after the initial incident) but did not call for economic or military sanctions under Article 16. It contented itself with an affirmation of Chinese sovereignty over the province, a call on member-states not to recognize the new state of Manchukuo (declared by Japan a year earlier), and an appeal to the protagonists to work for a peaceful settlement of their differences. Murray was partly right to say that the episode revealed a dearth of public-spiritedness or sense of corporate duty on the part of the major League Powers (Murray 1948, 75). But it also revealed that they had a keen appreciation of certain realities, not least the limits of their effective power in the region. In addition it showed that in the heat of an international crisis the process of determining the aggressor is fraught with difficulty, and one in which narrow political considerations (*contra* Murray's ideal Platonic world) will always play a big part (Walters 1952, 465–99; Henig 1973, 91–116; Northedge 1986, 137–64).

Subsequent analysts have demonstrated that aggression is anything but clear-cut (e.g. Stone 1958; Claude 1962, 195–8; Aron 1966, 121–4). Murray was content to conceive aggression in terms of the state that dealt the first blow. But political, technological, and strategic developments had already by Murray's time rendered such a simple concept obsolete. State sponsorship of non-state violence, fifth columns, malicious propaganda, economic warfare, hostile armament, all made the determination of acts of aggression a highly partial affair. Add to this the advantage given to the offensive of new highly mobile land and air technologies and it would not be extreme to say that Murray's concept was already dead in the water by the 1920s. He described 'coercing the peace-breaker' as the 'ultimate question' of international relations (Murray 1929b, 86). Yet along with doubts over the ease with which the peace-breaker can be identified, it may be doubted whether this is, in fact, the ultimate question (and indeed in the multi-layered world of international life whether it makes sense to talk of ultimate questions). Might it be better not to coerce a minor peace-breaker in order to keep her 'on side' in the struggle against a potential major peace-breaker? This is precisely what the principal League Powers elected to do, albeit vacillatingly, in response to Italian aggression in Abyssinia in 1935–6. In this case the identity of the aggressor was clear. Far less clear, given the geo-political circumstances of the time, in particular the rising threat from a resurgent and militant Germany, was that full implementation of Article 16 of the Covenant was the right course of action.

Second, in response to aggression Murray set great store by the pressure of 'world public opinion' and economic sanctions. But the former is an even more nebulous concept than aggression (see e.g. Morgenthau 1978, 264–75). Murray, following his good friend and League of Nations colleague, Robert Cecil, placed far too much reliance on it (Murray 1929b, 131–2, 221–2; 1948, 136, 155, 173). While he several times noted the power of modern state propaganda and the news media to manipulate the truth (e.g. 1948, 54–5), he nowhere analysed the implications of this for the 'sanction' of 'world public opinion'. He also took it for granted that the economic weapon could be the 'silent, deadly weapon' that President Wilson said it could (ibid., 74). He recognized that to be effective any imposition of economic sanctions would need to be universally observed (1929b, 92–3). But he failed to appreciate the tremendous difficulty in achieving this. He also failed to see that sanctions not only presented 'distribution of costs' problems but a problem of 'absolute costs'. States will rarely be prepared to jeopardize their own economies unless a vital interest is at stake. Murray embraced the platitude that 'peace is indivisible'. Therefore a breach of the peace was always and everywhere a threat to the vital interests of peace-loving nations. But peace proved to be highly divisible in 1931, 1935, and 1936. Aggressive acts committed in China, Abyssinia, and Spain during those years were deemed by the League Powers not to be threats to their vital interests.

As a last resort Murray backed collective security. He did not face squarely, however, the dilemma that lies at the heart of this concept. Collective security is needed because war has become intolerable. But collective security involves the threat of war in order to deter it. If deterrence fails, collective security brings about the very act it is designed to prevent (Claude 1962, 150–204; Hurrell 1992). As with Leonard Woolf and other League enthusiasts (see P. Wilson 2003, 70–1), Murray got around this by calling the use of force by the community not 'war' but something else, e.g. collective defence, enforcement action, coercion against the law-breaker, action to defend the Covenant, etc. But this is a semantic not a substantive solution. Moreover it is one based on an unconscious application of a straightforward 'domestic analogy'. This holds aggression in international society to be analogous to violent crime in domestic society, and therefore action to stop it not as a similar act of violence but police action. There are all sorts of problems with this kind of reasoning, as Suganami has skilfully shown (Suganami 1989). Not least, it is based on the assumption that the central task of government is the enforcement of the law against miscreant individuals, when in fact it is the management and conciliation of conflict between large and powerful groups (ibid., 165–96). Police action is usually effective in the first case, but often ineffective, even counter-productive, in the second.

Third, Murray stood foursquare behind Article 8 of the Covenant committing member-states to the reduction of national armaments to 'the lowest point consistent with national safety, and the enforcement by common action of international obligations'. He favoured 'all-round disarmament', and the Grotian view (Bull 1966) that arms should only be employed by and for the community as a whole (Murray 1929b, 90–1; 1948, 37–8, 79–80, 159–60). But again in common with Woolf, he did not show how 'all-round disarmament' could be made compatible with extensive collective security obligations. A level of armaments consistent with national safety and the enforcement by common action of international obligations is not necessarily a low level. It might be a very high level. The drafters of the Covenant knew what they were doing! There is a complex strategic conundrum here that Murray does not begin to explore.

POWER, THE STATE, APPEASEMENT, AND WAR

There are a number of more general problems with Murray's thinking. For instance, nowhere does he analyse power, its nature in international politics, and the subtle ways in which its employment, actual or potential, often shapes international outcomes. The term 'balance of power' does not even appear in his three principal IR writings. He seems little concerned with states' strategic interests. He seems to regard such concerns as an anachronism or an aberration. But unwittingly in his various texts he provides plenty of evidence to the contrary. His general theoretical assertions leave no place for strategic or balance of power concerns. The concrete cases he considers, however, from the Moroccan Crisis to the Great Game in central Asia to the protection of minorities under the League, leave no doubt that such concerns remained an important part of the international equation (Murray 1915c, 60–77, 86–93; 1929b, 123–4).

Secondly, he frequently calls on states to be more public-spirited, more *communitaire*. Yet he does not seriously analyse the nature of the state, nor the community to which they supposedly belong. In his own writings he provides ample evidence that the state is not constituted to be public-spirited or *communitaire*. Seriously lacking here is a sociological account of inter-group behaviour and the institutional requirements for reasonably ordered and stable coexistence. Indeed he has no sociology of the place of war, law, diplomacy, and the Great Powers in international society: no account, that is, of the social functions they serve, their effectiveness, and the ways in which they are mutually dependent. As a result Murray's strictures on these matters come across as extemporary. They may suit his purpose at a particular time, but their cogency is limited for not being part of a broader systemic understanding of international relations or a consistent philosophy. It was largely in reaction to this major shortcoming in the thinking of Murray and his fellow liberal internationalists that the first generation of scholars of the English school developed their sociological account of international society, providing an ontology of that society and a deep account of its formal structure (Manning 1962; James 1973; Bull 1977; Wight 1991). This was a major intellectual advance and gave analytical rigour, conceptual precision, and historical perspective to a field hitherto dominated by gifted amateurs such as Murray and lacking in these vital respects.

Thirdly, and more empirically, while consistently supporting the collective security provisions of the Covenant, there is no question that his constant references to the increasing horrors of war, the illegitimacy of its unilateral use, and how another war would be disastrous for Britain (e.g. Murray 1929b, 137, 232–5) contributed to the psychological foundations of appeasement. The revisionist view that Murray and his kind were the real realists in the 1930s, not Carr and his fellow appeasers (Ashworth 1999, 118–21), can therefore be questioned. It is true that Murray and his fellow liberal internationalists did not aid and abet appeasement. They took a strong line against the dictators and consistently supported the implementation of the counter-aggression and collective security provisions of the Covenant. But by then, in the mid-1930s, the damage was already done. By constantly talking peace, decrying the horror of war, and not frankly accepting that full implementation of the Covenant meant war, in all its ugliness, they engaged in a kind of psychological disarmament. In the 1920s and early 1930s they helped to undermine the psychological conditions that would have made a tough response to the aggressions of the later 1930s possible (see e.g. Murray 1929b, 226; 1948 [1934], 37, 43, 53). While Carr underestimated the reality of Hitler's ideological fervour and the threat that his Reich posed (P. Wilson 2000, 186, 196), Murray underestimated the reality of the balance of power, and the place of force, both uni-lateral and multi-lateral, in its maintenance. They both, therefore, lacked realism in some key respects.

Fourthly, Murray acknowledged in the 1940s that the League had failed. But why had it failed? Murray's answer was simply that the Covenant had not been faithfully carried out. But why not? Because of the lack, he said, of public spirit and a sense of international public duty (see e.g. Murray 1929b, 104, 108–9; 1948, 65–76). But why were these things lacking? All too often Murray's analysis falls short of a deeper explanation of the sources and motivations of state behaviour. It too frequently concentrates on what states did not have but should have had rather than on what they actually had.

Finally, when it came to the causes of war, Murray was self-consciously a 'third image' man (Waltz 1959). He located the cause of war unequivocally at the level of the international system. When less self-consciously concerned with war, however, he often implies that the second image is very important (e.g. 1929b, 218; 1948, 87–90, 103–6, 186–7) and on occasion the first image (e.g. 1915c, 57; 1948, 11, 87–90). That is, he locates the fundamental cause of war at all three levels of the nature of man, the nature of (some, authoritarian or totalitarian) states, and the nature (anarchic) of the international system. There is nothing necessarily wrong in combining the three levels. But applying Waltz's typology brings home the lack of system in Murray's analysis. Despite his hatred of war and his deep desire to eradicate it he nowhere attempts to analyse it systematically. A curious fact when one thinks about it.

CONCLUSION: MURRAY'S LEGACY TO THE FIELD OF IR

It might be said that the thrust of this retrospective is unfair. I have judged Murray as an international relations theorist. But while Murray played an important role in the establishment of IR, and while he worked closely with several early IR professors (Sir Alfred Zimmern especially), he was not an IR professor himself, and certainly no theorist in today's sense. But this will not do. In Martin Wight's sense he certainly was a theorist (Wight 1991, 1). He conducted no detailed empirical research into international relations. He relied for his information, apart from the normal media channels, on the reports of the various committees on which he sat, on official League publications, and on conversations with colleagues and eminent acquaintances from around the world. His writing on international questions is of a general, theoretical, kind. He sought to capture something of the political world as a whole. He was concerned not with this or that state but the international firmament of states. He was concerned not with the foreign policy of this or that country but the principles of foreign policy. It is true that he was more an advocate than an analyst, and concerned above all about Britain and Britain's place in the world. Yet, to the extent that he was engaged in a debate about how states and other significant actors behave in international relations, and how they ought to behave, he can be regarded as a theorist. True, he was an amateur theorist. But for a latter-day Athenian this was no insult, and in the 1920s and 1930s most theorists were amateurs. His trade was the generation and evaluation of general propositions about international relations. This is impeccably the trade of the IR theorist (Bull 1972, 30).

The post-Cold War era has been kind to Murray's legacy. The UN has started to become the kind of forum for international discussion that its architects envisioned. Its specialized agencies play an increasing role in fostering cooperation and implementing common policies in the areas of health, education, the environment, trade, economic development, the relief of refugees, and the protection of individual rights. War between the advanced industrial countries has become unthinkable. Conference diplomacy is a regular feature of international life. Discussion of international issues at various levels has never been so intense or so frequent. The level of education on international issues and knowledge of them in the wider public has grown remarkably. So many of the things Murray worked for have become an established part of international life. Yet war continues, states remain reluctant to discard their sovereignty, steps towards substantial disarmament remain few and far between, Great Power politics not the UN remains the principal managerial mechanism in international politics, and collective security in the way Murray envisaged it has proved to be a chimera.

So what is Murray's legacy to the field of IR? First, it is to have identified in an age of growing interdependence and technological advancement the need for far-reaching international cooperation on a number of fronts. Secondly, it is to have emphasized that international cooperation is always difficult and always entails the sacrifice of some immediate national interest. In this respect Murray was not an idealist but a realist. International agreement requires compromise, and the path of compromise is often difficult, requiring considerable moral and intellectual courage, especially in a world still fiercely nationalistic. Thirdly, it is to have recognized the importance of statesmanship in breaking the vicious circle of national jealousy and competitiveness, thereby putting international relationships on a more civilized and cooperative footing and creating the conditions for some kind of Cosmos. Fourthly, it is to have highlighted the importance of education in world citizenship, or at least the importance of an education with an international focus. How can the necessary compromises and sacrifices be made unless people understand why they are necessary? And unless they have an appreciation of the complex relationship between the good of the parts and the good of the whole? In this respect, statesmanship and international education go hand in hand. As with democracy and freedom at the national level, they are the essential and mutually supporting pillars of progress.

On the negative side of the balance sheet, however, Murray overestimated the power of international public opinion. He overestimated the extent to which the world needed move away from traditional practices of diplomacy. He underestimated the difficulties of achieving any degree of permanent disarmament, and also the size of the gap between Truth and cynical propaganda, and the various gradations of partial truth and partial falsehood that lie in-between. He overestimated the need of putting an end to the international anarchy, and the ease with which this could be done. He underestimated the difficulties attendant on the collective use of force. He underestimated too, in classic imperial fashion, the degree of cultural heterogeneity in the world and the implications of this heterogeneity for his favoured cosmological model.

Hedley Bull's conclusion that the works of pre-Carr IR writers are worth reading now 'only for the light they throw on the presuppositions and preoccupations of their place and time' is true in the main (Bull 1972, 34). But some of their preoccupations and presuppositions are still ours. And it is always salutary to revisit civilized books and civilized minds.

13

The Classicist as Liberal Intellectual: Gilbert Murray and Alfred Eckhard Zimmern

Julia Stapleton

Throughout his life Gilbert Murray was an evangelist for civilization and what he termed 'liberality' against the multiple forces of darkness by which his age seemed increasingly beset. This endeavour was premised upon a persistent belief in Hellenism as the mainspring of human progress, despite the decline of Greek as a universal exemplar within the academic curriculum (Stray 1998, ch. 8). But in using his authority well outside the bounds of his position as Regius Professor of Greek at Oxford to further the Hellenist cause, Murray was by no means isolated. In the context of a university that had been fired by a mission of public service under the influence of Benjamin Jowett and other reformers from the 1860s onwards, Murray found strong support for his presence on the national and world stage among a younger generation of classicists. One such protégé was A. E. Zimmern (1879–1957). Like Murray, Zimmern actively sought to transform public life in accordance with the

I am very grateful to the British Academy for a Small Research Grant which helped to finance this research, and to Chris Stray for excellent editorial support throughout. I am also grateful to Stefan Collini, Peter Mandler, and Robert Todd for their helpful comments on earlier drafts. Paul Millett and John Toye kindly allowed me to read their hitherto unpublished papers on Zimmern (see Millett 2007; Toye and Toye, 2007). I would like to acknowledge, too, the assistance of Colin Harris and Oliver House at the Modern Manuscripts Reading Room of the Bodleian Library, Oxford.

Hellenist watchwords of knowledge, truth, justice, wisdom, goodness, beauty, and harmony. Like Murray, too, he attempted to shape the 'modern' subjects that were developing in British universities at the turn of the twentieth century in the same mould of Classics that had formed the bedrock of his own education. Finally, he was at one with Murray in emphasizing the close affinity between the spirit of ancient Greece and liberalism in the largest sense, including but going well beyond Liberal Party policy. This is not to suggest that Hellenism in Britain presented a united front on all questions religious, political, and philosophical; it did not, as we shall see. Nevertheless, its residual strength was such that it succeeded in shoring up intellectual liberalism of a distinctively late-Victorian kind well beyond the death of political liberalism after 1914.[1]

This chapter considers Murray's conception of Hellenism in relation to the vicissitudes of twentieth-century liberalism, both political and intellectual, and explores his tireless work on its behalf. It examines his early influence on classical scholarship at Oxford and the wider pursuit of cultural and political improvement to which he believed Classics was inextricably tied. The chapter analyses the quarters of society in which Murray and Zimmern sought to spread the Hellenist message as they understood it, and the extent of their success. It further emphasizes Murray's growing attachment to the historic English nation as a facet of his later conservatism that has been overlooked. Finally, it sets Murray's enhanced cultural pessimism during the interwar period in the context of the decline of a particular type of 'public intellectual'[2] in Britain: the liberal intellectual, whose role it was to cultivate selflessly liberal habits of mind throughout Britain and beyond, and in increasingly adverse climates of opinion that nonetheless exposed the limits of Murray's liberalism, at least.

[1] For a view of intellectual liberalism as less robust but which underestimates Murray's wider cultural rather than narrowly political mission on its behalf, see Bentley 1977, 172; Freeden 1986, 13, 215–16.

[2] After Stefan Collini's definitive *Absent Minds: Intellectuals in Britain*, it will not be possible to see the qualifying term 'public' as anything other than 'constitutive' of the meaning of the intellectual in a cultural sense (Collini 2006, 50).

MURRAY AND THE HELLENIST MISSION IN TWENTIETH-CENTURY BRITAIN

Murray's burning sense of mission on behalf of Hellenism emerged early on in his career as a classicist turned liberal intellectual. While he developed Radical convictions at school, it was only at Oxford under the inspiration of Arthur Sidgwick that the potential for an alliance between classical scholarship and liberalism became clear to him (Smith and Toynbee 1960, 86). He was further convinced of the importance of pressing both Classics and liberalism into the service of widespread cultural uplift during his ten-year sojourn at the University of Glasgow as a young professor of Greek. Although not best pleased by his success in securing the appointment in July 1889 he accepted out of a strong sense of duty to strengthen the intellectual vocation in Britain. This is clear in the bitter statement of regret he sent to his undergraduate friend and life-long associate, H. A. L. Fisher, when Fisher was passed over for the first Glasgow chair in History five years later in favour of Richard Lodge. The letter was full of contempt for an institution which, in Murray's view, had opted for 'safeness' in reaction to the recent appointment of Henry Jones to the chair in Moral Philosophy; Jones had been deemed 'not entirely "safe"'. The loss was wholly that of the University, Murray informed his friend. It had

> taken a turning step which marks the low path on which it desires to walk. I personally have lost even more. I shall not only miss your companionship which would have made a vast difference in this unillumined place, but I also am made to feel that the goal at which this body on the whole aims is one with which I have little sympathy, and that such hopes as I have had of the standard being raised and a really intellectual society being formed in the University are over-sanguine.[3]

Nevertheless, Murray continued to believe that he was usefully employed in Glasgow, even without Fisher's reinforcement. In the early years of his career he was moved by a fervent conviction that the universities *outside* Oxford and Cambridge formed the nucleus of

[3] Murray to Fisher, 5 July 1894, Bodleian Library, Oxford, MS Fisher 54.39–40.

a new class of intellectuals. As he informed one such audience at Aberystwyth in 1909, this class was developing out of an unprecedented thirst for 'higher knowledge' among those who 'formerly either despised it or had no hope of it'. It was inseparable from the movement in adult education that was bearing fruit in the University Extension movement, the Workers' Educational Association (WEA), 'many dozens of polytechnics, Athenaeums, institutes, reading unions', and so forth.[4] It embraced other voluntary groups active in the cause of education for citizenship such as the Civic and Moral Education League which Murray addressed in August 1919 (Murray 1919, referred to by Wallace 1988, 109). This new intellectual class was Murray's most cherished constituency, and one upon which he pinned all his hopes for freedom, truth, and progress; it was to this class that he looked for the disinterested perspectives on public affairs that were increasingly being eroded by cheap, popular literature and newspapers. The old, elite universities had dissociated themselves from reform since the Renaissance and the Reformation, all effort towards improvement subsequently having been independent of their influence. While they harboured many devoted scholars, willing to renounce material success for the more rewarding and important work of scholarship, they were burdened by their aristocratic and Anglican past.[5] Murray had a nasty suspicion that many of those who had enjoyed the privilege of an education in Classics at the ancient universities were unmoved by its central ideals and values. On one occasion he berated successive governments in Britain for failing to support the League of Nations' Committee of Intellectual Co-operation. He emphasized that the ministers involved—Classicists to a man—were 'badly tainted with the virus of intellect' themselves. He was particularly dismayed by rumours of a minute in a government file, 'Intellectual co-operation all rot'.[6]

The case which Murray put to audiences such as the one he addressed at Aberystwyth was that the study of Greek embraced far

[4] Murray, 'Wherewith Shall it be Salted', *The Sociological Review*, 2 (1909) [Murray 1909b], 260–61. The biblical title of the address (Luke 14: 26–35) is revealing.

[5] Murray 1909b, 262, 264.

[6] Murray, letter to *The Times*, 25 Sept. 1936, p. 10; on Murray's striking sense of personal shame and regret in failing to advance the cause of Intellectual Co-operation in Britain, see Murray 1948, 4–6.

more than the learning of the Greek language; it extended to the poetry, literature, and politics of Greece, which brought the language to life and in turn stimulated a 'living interest in the world'. As such it should not be the exclusive preserve of a privileged class to which its members were condemned whatever their intellectual interests; instead Greek should be made available to all those who were capable of grasping its wider historical and cultural significance. He conveyed this outlook on Classics and the humanities more widely to the Salt Schools, Shipley, in his presidential address in January 1917. The address itself is indicative of his concern to help set the tone of the embryonic system of secondary education while working for Herbert Fisher at the Board of Education (D. Wilson 1987, 230–1). Such schooling should aspire to the intellectual and moral standards of the best public schools, not the level of 'the average vulgar man'; at the same time it was necessary to guard against the monopolization of education by the few in the 'one-sided pursuit of internal culture without any reference to the world of fellow-men'.[7] He reiterated the point to an audience of school teachers in his capacity as President of the Teachers' Guild in the same month: 'Allow the Oxford science man to dispense with Greek if he wishes, and at the same time allow the Hellenistically-minded boy or girl in an average secondary school to have a fair chance of learning it'.[8] This was a pitch for the campaign at Oxford to abolish compulsory Greek for all students, which Murray supported ardently in the interests of the subject's continued vitality (D. Wilson 1987, 151–2, 258–60). The campaign reached a successful conclusion in March 1920, followed shortly after by a similar move at Cambridge. However, it was not matched by any increase in provision for the teaching of Greek in schools, in spite of Murray's efforts to persuade the government otherwise (Stray 1998, 265–70).

Against all such odds, Murray was seeking to ensure the wide diffusion of the Greek legacy. This would throw into sharp relief

[7] Murray, 'An Educated Nation', 8 Jan. 1917, Bodleian Library, Oxford, MS Gilbert Murray (hereafter GM) 391.10.

[8] Murray, 'An Educated Nation', Conference of Educational Associations, University of London, Jan. 1917: GM 441.14, p. 7. In this address he singled out Charterhouse, the Manchester Grammar School, and Winchester as worthy models for secondary schooling more widely.

the spiritual needs of the modern age and obstacles to their fulfilment. His liberal perception of those needs are evident in his scholarly work before the First World War at three levels. First, what he identified in *The Rise of the Greek Epic* (1907) as the 'spirit of upward striving in man' (Murray 1907b, 23) at the heart of early Greek poetry resonated with the continuing concern in British liberalism for the cultivation of character throughout society, as a result of the legacy of Mill. That spirit consisted of

> both feeling the value and wonder of life, and being desirous to make it a better thing: and further, with that purpose in view, as combining a spirit of intense enjoyment with a tempering wisdom, going into seas of experience steered by Sôphrosynê. (Murray 1907b, 28)

Murray's preoccupation with the early Greek virtue of *Sôphrosynê* was central to what Robert Parker has described elsewhere in this volume as the 'single progressive history' that bound together his otherwise disparate theories of religion, ritual, tradition and reason in ancient Greece. Murray defined *Sôphrosynê* as a 'tempering of dominant emotions by gentler thought' (Murray 1907b, 27–8). That the Greeks failed to erect a permanent barrier against unregenerate humanity only testified to the strength of the forces that opposed the progressive spirit. Echoing prominent liberal thinkers of the later nineteenth century such as Henry Maine, Murray underlined both the fragility and rarity of progress (Murray 1921c, 12–13; cf. Maine 1905, 22–3. For Murray the Greeks were not the dark, sinister pagans they were portrayed as by Christian apologists, anxious for self-vindication; rather, such evils as slavery, homosexuality, human sacrifice, the subjection of women, and sexual promiscuity as existed in Greece were 'remnants of that primaeval slime from which Hellenism was trying to make mankind clean' (Murray 1907b, 16).

A second element of Murray's liberalism is apparent in his conception of the chief instrument of the progressive spirit as the 'man of words' (the type captured in the Greek phrase, *Logios Anêr*) and their proxies: such agents furnished an overarching sense of identity to a society that had been settled by invaders from the north. Their books drew heavily on the history, geography, myths, morals, charms, and oracles of each community, and were forced to 'grow as [their] people grew'. Each recital and reworking was a public event that inculcated self-discipline and a sense of common culture (Murray 1907b, 97). In particular the man of words expurgated the worst pagan practices of the past, not least all that was merely tribal and exclusive and the source of barbaric practices. It was in this creative adaptation of tradition by an advanced literary class that Murray found the seeds of all Hellenic success, and a secure liberal future for his own society, too.

A third liberal strand in Murray's early understanding of the Greek legacy is a deep hostility towards nationalism and patriotism. He was particularly aghast at the patriotism unleashed by the Boer War and its threat to the 'disinterested verdict of civilized Humanity'. He maintained that against such evils only a despised minority of enlightened intellectuals such as himself were on their guard.[9] This animus against nationalist sentiment and its relation to Murray's perception of the need for *Sôphrosynê* and an effective liberal elite is evident in the *Four*, eventually *Five Stages of Greek Religion* delivered initially as lectures in 1912. Here Murray maintained that the progress of ancient Greece was halted by the decay of the self-governing *polis*. While the Homeric Gods had been banished the mind of man had not yet been trained to the 'hard discipline of reasonableness and honesty'. Only Aristotle continued to embody the spirit of Hellenic *Sôphrosynê*; he refused to desert philosophy for religion, unlike the Stoics and Epicureans, for all their merits in placing the inward life above 'things external'. The city (based on reason) never gave way to the Macedonian '*ethnos* or nation' in Aristotle's thought, with all the misguided patriotism (based on emotion) this entailed. But despite the best efforts of the Peripatetics, Aristotle's influence waned. J. B. Bury's conception of a 'failure of nerve' was for Murray crucial to understanding the abandonment of interest in ascertained truth and concomitantly, the welfare of the state, in deference to 'infallible revelation' (Murray 1925a, 163, 144–5, 161, 155).

But the conception of a 'failure of nerve' was no isolated historical moment for Murray; it also framed his approach to the disturbing turn that twentieth-century politics had taken in the interwar period

[9] Murray 1900b, 181–2. For an illuminating account of the 'herd instinct' in *fin de siècle* liberalism more widely, see Gerson 2004.

and beyond. At its root was not a difference of faith but 'Faith' itself—'unquestioning and heroic Faith', which for Murray was tantamount to fanaticism. This was reminiscent of the voice of 'sceptical' rationalists of the eighteenth century such as Hume and Gibbon, the latter of whom Murray quoted directly in the darkest hour of the Second World War. The only effective antidote to faith, fanaticism, and its accompanying persecution was 'liberality', something which 'seeks to learn and understand instead of claiming to know'. No amount of change in economic relations per se would bring an end to war and violence since without liberality, the pursuit of ambition, power, and glory would continue regardless (Murray 1943a, 7–8, 11–12).

THE HOME UNIVERSITY LIBRARY

For Murray, increasingly, the fate of civilization hung firmly in the balance of education, a process by which minds across society would undergo infinite expansion, and ignorance and prejudice be thwarted. As such, he—and Herbert Fisher, together with J. Arthur Thomson of the University of Aberdeen on the science side—were ideal choices as editors for the Home University Library of Modern Knowledge (HUL) launched by the publisher Williams and Norgate in 1910. The scheme was a response to a question posed by Sir George Reid, ex-prime minister of Australia who became first high commissioner in London in that year. He had asked, 'when will a literature be established to satisfy the legitimate intellectual curiosity of Young England?'[10]

In the first notices of the series the publisher actively sought to define and shape the needs of this market; it was not so much identified by age but a 'new generation of readers' who attended polytechnics, working men's colleges, University Extension classes, home reading circles, and literary societies, as well as upper elementary and public schools. What these 'unprivileged' readers were perceived as lacking above all else was short but authoritative and

[10] Notice of the series, 'The Home University Library': GM 403.11–12.

above all, cheap guides to history, philosophy, art, and science in all their various phases and conceptions. Young England had existed hitherto on an exclusive diet of textbooks, supplemented more recently by cheap reprints of literary and philosophical masterpieces. But it deserved better. The 'intelligent working and middle classes' of whom it was composed would, with the aid of the Home University Library, acquire 'some share in the heritage of contemporary culture' they would otherwise be denied by their limited education.[11] The progressive nature of the venture was made clear in an Editors' note found among publicity material: drawing a parallel between the need to re-distribute property and knowledge, they emphasized the new intellectual avenues it would make available to readers, and the equally satisfying 'public spirit' with which distinguished writers had responded to the editors' invitation.[12]

Originally conceived as the 'People's University Library', the Home University Library emphasizes the degree to which autodidact culture had captured the imagination of the intellectual elite at the turn of the century. This marked a shift away from the more exclusive literary and metropolitan circles of thought which its predecessor had primarily served in the last quarter of the nineteenth century (Collini 1991, ch. 1). Wedged between this older generation of scholars who led public and intellectual debate from the citadel of government and the professions on the one hand, and a new generation of academic specialists on the other, Murray and his contemporaries turned their attention to the intellectual underclass. They were ably assisted by enterprising publishers such as Williams and Norgate, who were not slow to perceive a market opportunity. With Murray and Fisher at the head of the venture, the Senior Partner at Williams and Norgate, Geoffrey Williams, was confident that the Library would see off competition from rival schemes such as Jack's 'Peoples Books'.[13] Indeed, when the Director, Home Gordon, visited the Congress of Associated Booksellers in Edinburgh in June 1914,

[11] Ibid. On the flurry of cheap reprints of the classics in the Edwardian era, most notably J. M. Dent's Everyman's Library founded in 1906, see Lewis 2005.

[12] 'Editors' Note', undated: GM 403.156; based on a draft, GM 403.134, with Murray's hand-written comment, 'I think this is admirable'.

[13] Geoffrey Williams to Murray, 1 Dec. 1912, GM 404.171.

the Library was hailed as the most notable development since the last meeting five years ago, with no other book series mentioned.[14]

The great strides forward in working-class self-education most obviously engaged the sympathies of this new breed of scholar. The Cambridge classical scholar and student of Greek philosophy and religion, Francis Cornford, was praised by Murray as a model of intellectual virtue on account of his dedication to the Working Men's college at Cambridge for over forty years and the delivery of some of his best lectures to the WEA.[15] But equally important was the extension of this endeavour towards what Fisher termed 'humble people' more widely,[16] to the clerks and shop assistants who formed the backbone of the new democracy. It was a welcome prospect for scholars who shared the HUL vision, as did the historian, G. M. Trevelyan, who wrote to Murray that he 'rejoic[ed] to think that [the Library] will go forward conquering and to conquer, raising the clerk and the intelligent working man to higher things'.[17] More ambitious still was the prospect of shaping the mind of these classes, not only in England but also in America 'and all the English speaking-world'. While Murray was not responsible for much of the publicity statements about the Library, he (and Fisher) clearly did nothing to challenge advertisements which described the editors as 'winged messengers of a species of knowledge and sympathy that may yet prove more effective in binding together the scattered units of the empire than the cleverest of political schemes.'[18]

Despite poor sales in the United States, the publishers' investment in the scheme paid off handsomely in its initial years, particularly before the First World War. By that time some ninety books had been published and over a million copies sold. Record monthly sales were reached in January 1914 when they exceeded 45,000.[19] This was at a time when booksellers were reporting a severe falling off of demand for books, which affected HUL sales later in the year but not

[14] Gordon to Murray, 8 June 1914: GM 406.29.

[15] Murray 1943b, 430–1. See also the fine chapter on Cornford in Gerson 2004, 173–8.

[16] Draft letter by Fisher to an unspecified author inviting a contribution on 'A History of Non-Conformity': GM 403.125.

[17] G. M. Trevelyan to Murray, 27 Jan. 1912: GM 404.171.

[18] Home University Broadsheet no. 4: GM 404.164–5.

[19] Gordon to Murray, 3 Feb. 1914: GM 406.5.

seriously.[20] Even in wartime, the Library remained buoyant: Geoffrey Williams reported to Murray in September 1915 that orders were received daily for books which were destined for the Front.[21] Sales declined after the war, although the Library remained a profitable arm of Williams and Norgate. But the publishing house was in difficulties and in 1928 the HUL was purchased as a going concern by Thornton and Butterworth. As one of the outgoing Directors commented in informing Murray of this development, the Library's future as a valuable national institution was now secure.[22]

The intellectual conservatism of the autodidact culture on which the Home University Library depended in its pre-war prime has been highlighted recently by Jonathan Rose in a magisterial study (Rose 2001). Rose focuses on the taste of this readership for classic works of literature as the key to their social and intellectual emancipation. However, the HUL organizers conceived these works as of limited educational value by themselves;[23] in their view it was imperative that the cheap reprints of literary classics circulating in this market should be supplemented by the fruits of high scholarship on a wide range of subjects associated with 'civilization'.

The deferential market upon which the HUL was launched is readily apparent in reviews and in the journals and newspapers in which they appeared. These emphasize the Library's early roots in local and provincial as much as national culture more widely.[24] The general response was enthusiastic, and parallels were drawn between the venture and the spirit of improvement abroad among ordinary people. However, one review made clear that the Library's frontier stopped at town bookshops. As the *Manchester Evening News* commented, it was unlikely that the Library would be known in many of the suburban and rural homes in which the paper circulated, although it emphasized the importance of breaking into this territory.[25] Less welcome for the editors and publishers

[20] Williams to Murray, 14 May 1914: GM 406.95.

[21] Williams to Murray, 23 Sept. 1915: GM 406.100.

[22] L. Urwick to Murray, 1 Jan. 1928: GM 407.95.

[23] Home University Library, 'Instructions to Authors': GM 403.158.

[24] Many of these early reviews can be found in MS Myres 88, Bodleian Library, Oxford.

[25] 'Bookland', *Manchester Evening News* (26 Aug. 1912); in MS Myres 88.212.

would have been the critical review of the Library in the monthly journal, *Unity*, serving co-operative and friendly societies: 'The style of more than one of the volumes betrays haste, inattention and carelessness in preparation'.[26] Murray was aware of the problem: as he wrote to J. L. Myres, whose contribution, *The Dawn of History*, in 1911 was exempted from this criticism by the reviewer, 'I have been somewhat disappointed in one or two of the recent volumes'. *The Dawn of History* (no. 29 in the Library) had been a 'great restorative'.[27]

However, the autodidact market was less robust after the war, certainly as served by the HUL. As the editors conceded in an interview with *The Sunday Times* to mark the Library's Silver Jubilee in 1936, the WEA response, in particular, had proved 'patchy'; the volumes were more likely to be found in the houses of HUL contributors such as Edwyn Bevan and John Bailey.[28] Shortly afterwards, the Library faced stiff competition from Pelican, the non-fiction arm of Penguin Books founded by Allen Lane in 1937. A man of the Left with no academic background, Lane sought the diffusion of expert knowledge to laymen in cheap, paperback form. His list was far more political than the HUL's and tapped into the thriving progressivist culture in Britain in the 1930s. Pelican/Penguin's success was a clear indication of the diversification of both readers and intellectual authority by the late 1930s; but also their convergence around a common, more democratic culture.[29] Certainly, Murray seems not to have been approached either in an advisory capacity or as a contributor, despite his manifest interest in the topical subjects of the 'Penguin Specials' in the immediate pre-war years: Spain, Czechoslovakia, and anti-semitism in Germany. By contrast, he had been an obvious choice of author for the projected book on 'great writers of Greece' for Ernest Benn's 'sixpenny library' of paperback

[26] F. Starr, 'The Study Table: Book Notes', *Unity* (10 Oct. 1912): MS Myres 88.213.

[27] Murray to Myres, 8 Sept. 1911: MS Myres 88.43.

[28] GM 409.63. Edwyn Bevan was the author of *Stoics and Sceptics* (Oxford: Oxford University Press, 1913) which greatly influenced Murray; John Cann Bailey was educated in *Literae Humaniores* at New College, Oxford from 1883 to 1887 when Murray was a Fellow and Tutor. He was a literary critic and author of two volumes for the HUL, *Dr Johnson and his Circle* (1914) and *Milton* (1915).

[29] See Lewis 2005, 84–5.

primers established a decade earlier.[30] In 1938 he confessed himself a 'little anxious' about 'all these Penguins and Albatrosses and other birds', although he suggested to Tresham Lever at Thornton and Butterworth that they might be serving a different public than the HUL. He was right; however, that public was growing and the HUL's was shrinking. Lever confirmed a falling off of sales recently, not all of which could be attributed to a decrease in the number of HUL books published in the last year and political problems affecting sales abroad.[31]

There was no fallback for the HUL in other markets, not least in America where the Library had failed to make the headway its original publishers had confidently expected. Despite glowing testimonies to the value of the Library by prominent figures in church and state at the time of its Silver Jubilee,[32] its future lay squarely in academic rather than autodidact circles. Indeed, it was purchased by Oxford University Press in 1941, much to the relief of Murray, who wrote to the new publishing editor, Humphrey Milford, that Fisher and himself had found it difficult to 'keep up the old standard' of late.[33]

The development of the Library over this period well emphasizes its conservative nature, fuelled by the zeal of the editors and many of the contributors for the intellectual progress of the nation from above. Murray's Hellenist mission provided the moving force of the series in its pre-1918 heyday as a beacon of popular literary culture. His own book on *Euripides* was an instant success, and is a clear testimony to his early, Radical faith.[34] However, he never succeeded

[30] John A. Benn to Murray, 26 Oct. 1928: GM 54.163. Murray, as ever, was too busy to oblige.

[31] Murray to Sir Tresham Lever, 28 Jan. 1938: GM 409.140; Lever to Murray, 31 Jan. 1938: GM 409.141. On Albatross Verlag, Toucan Books, and Bluebird Books—all pioneers of paperback publishing in the 1930s—and their influence on Allen Lane, see Lewis 2005, 76–9, 112–13.

[32] *The Home University Library of Modern Knowledge: Silver Jubilee Appreciations*: MS Fisher 147.128.

[33] Gilbert Murray to Humphrey Milford, 28 Mar. 1941: GM 410.2.

[34] Murray 1913. He defended the Sophists against the charge that they were 'dangerous and shallow'. This was only the case 'if we prefer blinkers and custom, subordination and the rod' (p. 50). For sales figures, see Home Gordon to Murray, 19 Nov. 1911: GM 405.181; 6,317 copies in the first few weeks of publication.

in accomplishing the work that he variously projected as ancient Greek literature, a short history of Greece, and Greek civilization. This was despite repeated pleas for some such book from Home Gordon as the only prospect of salvation for the Library in the early 1920s; it was despite, too, a promise of collaboration by J. A. K. Thomson, as well as the opportunity it afforded of persuading the WEA of the need for the continuing study of Greek.[35]

Fortunately, however, the popularization of Hellenism did not depend upon Murray's energies alone; it drew on a broad range of scholarship and pedagogical effort at Oxford, in particular. More exactly, it was New College that constituted what Ernest Barker termed the 'fountain-head of Greek studies and the interpretation of the Greek genius' (Barker 1953, 47). The College's status as such was much enhanced by Murray's connection with it. Among younger classicists at New College whom Murray influenced following his return to Oxford in 1905 was Alfred Eckhard Zimmern—scholar of the college and then lecturer in ancient history, and Fellow and tutor from 1904 to 1909. This context provided the essential stimulation for Zimmern's best known work, *The Greek Commonwealth* (Zimmern 1911). Reviewers were quick to note the similarities with Murray's work in style and content.[36] Indeed, such was the strength of their common Hellenist cause that their friendship survived political and religious differences (the son of a Jewish émigré, Zimmern converted to Christianity as an undergraduate), and conflict in working relationships, such as those concerning Intellectual Co-operation (D. Wilson 1987, 357–9). Zimmern will repay close attention as

[35] Home Gordon to Murray, 9 Oct. and 14 Dec. 1923: GM 406.206, 213. The idea was revived a decade later, but again it went no further: Murray to J. A. K. Thomson, 12 Feb. and 3 Mar. 1932: GM 408.48, 66. Murray proposed other titles, too, one on 'Social Ideals' and another on the League of Nations. These also failed to appear because of pressure of work. On Murray's continuing sense of the need for a book on the 'essential contribution of Greece to civilisation', see Murray to Milford, 22 Sept. 1942: GM 410.109. The nearest the series came to closing the lacuna on Greek history was in 1959, when Arnold J. Toynbee finally delivered the manuscript of a book that Murray had commissioned in 1913–14: *Hellenism: The History of a Civilisation* (Toynbee 1959). For Murray's concerns then about Toynbee's insufficient enthusiasm for Greek achievements, see MacNeill 1989, 46.

[36] 'Imperial Athens', *Times Literary Supplement* (14 Sept. 1911), p. 333; and 'The Golden Age of Athens', *The Nation* (4 Nov. 1911), p. 207.

a liberal intellectual whose fortunes were tied closely to the Hellenist paradigm set by Murray.

ZIMMERN, THE *POLIS*, AND INTERNATIONAL SOCIETY IN THE TWENTIETH CENTURY

In the first decade of the twentieth century Zimmern played a key role in attempts to modernize the curriculum at Oxford and bring the university and the working class into closer proximity.[37] Throughout the first two decades of the twentieth century he believed fervently that it was through close contact with such organizations that Oxford could be roused from its persistent intellectual dormancy. Even more ambitiously—writing after the First World War—he hoped that an alliance between the more progressive elements within Oxford and the WEA would liberate the English national soul from its enslavement to an ideal of 'external success'. Not only the 'redemption' of England but that of the industrialized western world depended on this development; for integral to England's materialist vices was the 'iron law of wages' of which the Germans had merely been 'apt disciples' in their recent pursuit of power and domination (Zimmern 1923, 37).

However, restless and impatient with the slow pace of university reform, Zimmern resigned his fellowship in 1909. After two years of residence at the British School of Athens, where he wrote *The Greek Commonwealth*, he began work as an (unpaid) lecturer in Sociology at the London School of Economics (LSE). He immediately sought to bring the contents of the book to the attention of working-class audiences in London through extra-mural lectures. In one of these lectures Zimmern took as his focus the Greece of the 'ordinary man', not 'individual Greeks, famous poets, philosophers, etc but . . . their public'. The 'everyman' of ancient Greece was a superior specimen of

[37] He was the lead author with R. H. Tawney of the 1908 report entitled *Oxford and Working-Class Education: A Report of a Joint Committee of University and Working-Class Representatives on the Relation of the University to the Higher Education of Workpeople* (London: Oxford University Press, 1908).

humanity, the key to whose uncommon happiness would bear close analysis in furthering social progress in the present.[38]

The decisive factor in Zimmern's appointment at the LSE was Graham Wallas. Wallas had taught Classics to Zimmern at Winchester School before embarking on his career as a social reformer and then as Professor of Politics at the LSE. Wallas's influence is clear in *The Greek Commonwealth.* Subtitled *Politics and Economics in Fifth-Century Athens*, the book utilized new evidence—particularly that of archaeology—to illuminate the 'facts and spirit' of Greek civilization at its best, not in the period of decline to which Plato and Aristotle had left memorable but distorted testimony.[39] In doing so, Zimmern sought to throw into sharp relief the 'senseless greed for more' inherent in British industrial society. Employing Wallas's Darwinian-inspired ideal of equilibrium in human nature, Zimmern stressed his Athenians' unparalleled sense of 'harmony and proportion' evident in their 'art and conduct and institutions'. What drove them to economic activity was merely a realization that wealth was necessary to further the ends of their civilization (Zimmern 1924, 226–7). In its fifth-century prime the city-state offered signal lessons in virtue (especially moderation—that Platonic ideal of *Sôphrosynê* employed by Murray again) and knowledge of humanity, of which he evidently thought all classes in Britain should take stock (Zimmern 1924, 8, 226–7, 122). In a footnote Zimmern hailed Wallas's *Human Nature in Politics* (1908) for attempting 'to do for modern politics what Socrates did for Greek, to explain to our political craftsmen the nature and use of their tools' (Zimmern 1924, 268). In the delicate psychological tissue of the *polis*, Zimmern was particularly struck by 'the plain primaeval emotions of friendship or family' out of which it had grown and which it must on no account disturb. There was more than a hint here of Burke's suggestion that the state was simply the hearth writ large, one of the many 'English' perspectives, and English

[38] Zimmern, 'Syllabus of a Short Course of Four Lectures on *Ancient Greece and Modern Problems*, given under the auspices of the University of London Joint Committee of the Higher Education of Working People' (London: University of London Press, 1911): Bodleian Library, Oxford, MS Zimmern 137. 2–3.

[39] For this he won the praise of the greatest classicist of his day, Ulrich Von Wilamowitz-Moellendorff, who wrote tó Zimmern of the 'spell of a special magic' he had come under in reading the book: see Calder 1989.

Establishment perspectives at that, to have informed *The Greek Commonwealth*.[40] Still, for Zimmern, the triumph of the *polis* over competing ties and loyalties—'the steady crystallization of Greek feeling round the City State'—was a momentous development in human society. It was no mean achievement, either: for Zimmern, as for Murray, progress in this sense was the exception rather than the rule (Zimmern 1924, 81).

With this conception of ancient Greece as a sounding-board for modern society and politics in the throes of democratic change, it is small wonder that Zimmern was quick to dismiss the evolutionary sociology of L. T. Hobhouse, Edward Westermarck, and other sociologists at the LSE. Responding at length to Murray's request that he write a volume on 'Sociology' for the Home University Library, Zimmern expressed his faith in psychology rather than biology (by which, presumably, he meant social evolutionism) as the root of all sociological understanding. Nothing useful could be gleaned from 'assimilating and drawing conclusions from the whole mass of social phenomena since time began'; trust must be placed instead in the power of psychology to 'penetrate into the secrets of the individual consciousness in its social relations with other beings, what is sometimes loosely called the social consciousness.' For this method of 'Interpretation' Zimmern expressed his debt to Murray as much as Wallas. Emphasizing strongly his Edwardian turn of mind, he maintained that 'No doubt the Solomon Islander helps us (if one happens to know him) to understand the hooligan; but the hooligan is close at hand, and I would far sooner trust a scoutmaster than Fraser for the correct interpretation of any of their common phases'.[41]

Zimmern's proposed volume on sociology failed to come off. His plans for a sequel to *The Greek Commonwealth*—variously the 'modern' and 'English' Commonwealth—proved equally abortive, despite

[40] Zimmern 1924, 72. For Zimmern's debt to Burke see also Zimmern 1939, 18–23; and Zimmern 1935, in MS Zimmern 168. In his forthcoming paper, 'Zimmern's *The Greek Commonwealth* Revisited' (Millett 2007), Paul Millett has perceptively noted the 'English Establishment' reference points in *The Greek Commonwealth*: 'public school, collegiate university, cathedral close and London club'.

[41] Zimmern to Murray, 11 Apr. 1911, GM 404.16. ('Fraser' was presumably J. G. Frazer.)

the unique vantage-point he believed he had gained for the human material of such a study as a result of his work for the Board of Education from 1913 to 1916.[42] Nor was he any more successful than Murray and the HUL in persuading the WEA to devote more attention to the 'larger and deeper interests of life' at the expense of the 'economic' subjects with which they seemed to be overly preoccupied (Zimmern 1923, 39). Indeed, his association with the organization ended abruptly in 1922 when he resigned as Honorary Treasurer after clashing with what he termed a 'class-conscious committee'; its members reacted angrily against the subscriptions he had collected from 'middle class sympathisers whom they cursed in their speeches'.[43]

But within a more limited sphere of influence that nevertheless transgressed narrow, academic boundaries Zimmern's 'psychological' approach to social relations proved more successful as the cornerstone of his work as a pioneer of the study of international relations between the wars. With Murray's support, he became the first holder of the David Davies Chair in International Relations at Aberystwyth between 1919 and 1921, and of the Montague Burton Chair at Oxford from 1931 until his retirement in 1944.[44]

As a student of international relations, Zimmern posited an emergent 'international mind' as the interface between local, national, and state minds; by contrast, Murray perceived international unity in terms of an undifferentiated whole. Jeanne Morefield has argued that this difference notwithstanding, the receptiveness of both men to the language of mind (and associated concept of

[42] Zimmern to Oliver Wendell Holmes, 28 Mar. 1913, Harvard Law School Library, MS Holmes 52.6) and Zimmern to Beatrice Webb, 13 May 1924, British Library of Economics and Political Science, MS Webb II.4.h.24.

[43] Zimmern to Horace Kallen, 17 Nov. 1922, YIVO Jewish Institute of Social Research, New York, MS Kallen.

[44] Murray's support may have been crucial in securing the Chair at Aberystwyth, given Murray's close links with Davies in the League of Nations Union: see Martin Ceadel's chapter in this volume. As well as the 'scandal' caused by Zimmern's affair with the wife of another professor, Zimmern's brief stay at Aberystwyth was also influenced by purported resentment at the 'missionary' attitude, which he clearly shared with Murray, towards provincial and working-class culture: see Porter 1972. He was an unsuccessful candidate for the Sir Ernest Cassel Chair in International Relations at the University of London in 1924, much to Murray's astonishment: Murray to Zimmern, 16 May 1924: MS Zimmern 18.59.

'spirit') betrays an unacknowledged debt to the dominant philosophy of Idealism during their formative years at Oxford. It was a debt, moreover, that was deeply implicated in their defence of 'pre-liberal', hierarchical, and patriarchal forms of association: families, nations, and class systems, in particular (Morefield 2005, 130–1, 173). How liberal, then, were these two figures, in the terms set out here?

We have seen that Murray's liberalism echoed strongly the sceptical, 'aristocratic' liberalism of pre-Idealist thinkers such as Maine, Hume, and Gibbon, to say nothing of J. S. Mill, whose influence he openly acknowledged; neither at Oxford nor Glasgow (working alongside Henry Jones) does he seem to have imbibed the metaphysics or the ethics of Idealism. The closest he came was acceptance of the Aristotelian principle that 'politics are really ethics on the great scale', which he saw as the essence of (Gladstonian) Liberalism.[45]

Similarly, the receptiveness of Zimmern to the idea of a 'common mind' at various levels owed more to the close familial, cultural, and national ties he observed in the Mediterranean while writing *The Greek Commonwealth*, than to Idealist influences at Oxford. It certainly led him to reject the 'fictitious', individualist concept of equality that in his view had misguidedly informed the 'Western Republics'. Instead, he favoured a richer ideal of equality as 'fellowship', one which was especially encapsulated in the 'patriarchal system and Gods of the Northern invaders of Greece'. This had triumphed over the 'vaguer and more unfixed traditions' of the population among whom the immigrants settled, not least the Mycenaeans with their matriarchal family organization (Zimmern 1924, 75 n. 1, 77). If he elevated the patriarchal family thus, it was as the instrument of a wider liberal ideal that in his view would not tear society apart. The 'inbred feeling' of fellowship, he wrote, had always found a home 'in common needs and common intercourse, at the springs and the well-heads, the cross-roads and market-places, the temples, shrines, and mosques, of the Middle East' (Zimmern 1924, 62). Again, there are strong Burkean overtones here, notably

[45] See Murray to Barker, 18 Mar. 1939: GM 86.142.

Burke's praise of the corporate 'inns and resting-places' of national life, an aspect of his political thought that became central to nineteenth-century Whig Liberalism.[46]

The influence of Mediterranean culture in shaping Zimmern's communal sympathies, albeit mediated by Burke, was enhanced by his Jewish background. His 'spiritual' conception of nationality was forged in the first instance through the writings of the Jewish philosopher, Ahad Ha-am (Asher Ginzberg) in 1905, as a result of which he rejected Zionism.[47] He applied Ha-am's model of the nation not just to Palestine but to America, too, where the cult of common citizenship seemed to have eclipsed nationality, to the detriment of the human spirit. Needless to say, Zimmern's passionate defence of national communities as the key to a vibrant '*res publica*' went hand in hand with his vehement rejection of the principle of national self-determination as fundamentally at odds with political liberty. In this respect, he remarked in 1917, only the Jewish and the English nation understood the true nature of nationalism as rooted in common culture rather than statehood.[48] Another key influence here was Lord Acton who emphasized the basis of liberty in diversity (Zimmern 1918, 46–7, 72–3). Acton's influence—coupled with that of Burke and Ha-am—casts doubt on any suggestion that Zimmern's liberalism was in tension with his 'pre-liberal' sensitivities, and that it was primarily indebted to Idealism. His liberalism was complex but not incoherent when set in its appropriate historical context.

Zimmern was active in support of the League of Nations, whose outlines he had helped to shape through the Cecil Draft and whose educative arm, the League of Nations Society, he—and Murray—had also been instrumental in founding in 1917.[49] He certainly invested high hopes in the League as an arbiter of world peace. For example, like Murray, he was a staunch defender of the Geneva Protocol in 1925 and critic of the British government for

[46] For the centrality of Burke to nineteenth-century Whig liberalism, see Burrow 1988.

[47] See Zimmern's introduction to Simon 1920.

[48] Zimmern, 'The Passing of Nationality', in Zimmern 1918, 97.

[49] For an illuminating account of the involvement of Zimmern and Murray in the drafting of the Covenant of the League in accordance with their commitment to state sovereignty, see Morefield 2005, 174–87.

refusing to sign.[50] However, as Paul Rich has argued, Zimmern was mostly a 'cautious idealist', a figure who endeavoured to take account of political exigencies in his vision of a new world order.[51] The contrast with Murray is apparent in Murray's review of the only substantial book Zimmern wrote after *The Greek Commonwealth*, his *The League of Nations and the Rule of Law* (1936). It was a book which Murray found disconcerting, not least because it made light of the collapse of the Disarmament conference at the heart of the League's *raison d'être*.[52]

Zimmern's conception of the study of International Relations was shot through with the Hellenic vision by which he and many of his contemporaries had been captivated before the First World War. In his inaugural lecture at Oxford he stressed the importance of 'Hellenizing' the barbarian as a prerequisite of peace, a task for which Oxford was supremely well equipped. The barbarian—in the shape of the anonymous economic forces that currently shaped the world's destiny—must be brought inside the 'polis' of civilized mankind through the knowledge and understanding of 'standards' thus afforded. More than this, however, 'chaos' must be turned into 'cosmos' through the application of the 'philosophic discipline' in politics. This was never more urgent than in the present when

> all over the world, peoples unused to power are tempted to regard the great universal conceptions of justice and liberty as mere emanations of local self-will and to deck out the soul of nationality in the tawdry trappings of tribalism. (Zimmern 1931, 19, 23)

Murray's fear of group closure is much in evidence here, so different, it would have seemed to Zimmern, from the convivial, English ideal of 'fellowship' which, as we have seen, he read back unproblematically into other cultures. Perhaps this critique was a reflection of

50 See Zimmern, 'Europe and the Geneva Protocol', *New Republic* (4 Feb. 1925); see also Murray's letter to the editor, 'A False Step at Geneva', *The Nation & Athenaeum* (18 Oct. 1924), p. 108.

51 Rich 1995, 84–5. Zimmern's conception of the League as 'mere machinery' has been perceptively noted by Toye and Toye (forthcoming).

52 Murray, 'A Lively Book on the League', *Manchester Guardian* (20 Feb. 1936), p. 7. Zimmern reiterated his opposition to disarmament in a paper entitled 'Religion and World Affairs' read to the Industrial Christian Fellowship in 1939. 'Armaments are a symptom not a cause of international unrest', he argued (p. 8): MS Zimmern 169.

Zimmern's experience of a League that had backfired: an organization that had invited the 'peoples' of the world to meet in a spirit of international peace and harmony had only served to encourage the *arrivistes* among nations. As Morefield has argued, Zimmern and Murray emphasized the relationship of nations as one of equality within hierarchy, not least of an imperial kind (Morefield 2005, ch. 3). Murray, in particular, openly embraced England as the driving imperial force for good in the twentieth century, even while Zimmern's faith in his adopted country faltered and was redirected to the United States after the Second World War.[53]

MURRAY, ENGLAND, AND THE PERSISTENCE OF REASON IN HUMAN AFFAIRS

On the occasion of Zimmern's retirement from his Oxford Chair in 1944 and the appointment of E. L. Woodward as his successor, Murray wrote to him expressing his sadness

> that your professorship is over and that your chair will be filled by an ordinary historian without any special faith or inspiration or even interest in the League of Nations movement. There was not anyone who could really fill your place.... Well, I suppose we must say it is the end of an epoch: the age of the Apostles superseded by that of the Church Historians. You had genius and faith, and those qualities cannot be got in the ordinary market.[54]

Zimmern had certainly been passionate in his belief that universities—and scholars such as himself—could alter the bleak climate of international affairs (Stapleton 2001, ch. 5). But Murray was engaged in self-characterization here, too. In the above quotation, he struck the keynote of proselytization—in the cause of liberalism—versus academic specialization that underpinned the particular

[53] See Barker's plea to Zimmern to 'remember England. A good, quiet country, which does its work (or used to do) without too much talking, but does work': Barker to Zimmern, 10 Apr. 1949: MS Zimmern 56.110–11. For Zimmern's pro-Americanism later in life, see Toye and Toye (forthcoming).

[54] Murray to Zimmern, 23 Mar. 1944: MS Zimmern 48.27.

style of intellectual leadership he had established in previous decades.[55] In his inaugural address at University College, Aberystwyth, in 1933 he recalled his pleas to the academic body at Aberystwyth a quarter of a century earlier to promote progress actively through the application of intellect. He also reaffirmed his belief in the strength of civilization, notwithstanding its current travails. He urged his listeners to take seriously the task that lay ahead of resisting the challenge of the dictators to an ordered 'cosmos'—the supreme legacy of the Greeks. It would be strengthened only by 'Law', resting on an 'agreed basis of Justice and Freedom'. His audience had a special responsibility to ensure that, through their 'public action, ... thinking, and ... individual lives', Order was restored.[56] He felt the weight of this obligation the more heavily with the weakening and, in some cases, destruction of the intellectual class elsewhere in Europe. He believed that in some cases it was a fate this class had brought on itself by a 'contempt for bourgeois tastes', proceeding to a 'contempt for citizenly morals and duties' (Murray 1944a, 44). This was a clear indication that in his view, intellectual experimentation had reached its outer limits. The statement is also a reminder of the chasm that existed between intellectual life in Britain and continental Europe following a decade that had promised considerable rapprochement.[57]

Murray was only too conscious that the public would grow weary of his incessant interventions on behalf of justice, peace, and harmony among nations.[58] He thus used indirect as well as direct means of influencing the public and raising its awareness of wrongdoing. For example, he would contact sympathetic newspaper editors about atrocities abroad to which his attention had been drawn. He requested further investigation by the newspapers themselves in the belief that a fair hearing was assured only if his name was

[55] On the 'modernist' challenge to Whiggism in historiography in Britain, and of which Woodward was an exemplar, see Bentley (2005). As is evident with Murray, wider canons of academic scholarship were also affected.

[56] Murray, *The Cult of Violence*, inaugural address given at the opening of the session 1933–4 at Aberystwyth (London: Lovat Dickson, 1934), pp. 19, 23–4.

[57] See Collini, *Absent Minds*, p. 137, for the ways in which the 'discourse about "intellectuals" in Britain could, by the late 1930s, appear to be coming to resemble that found elsewhere in Europe', in contrast to the return of perceptions of intellectual exceptionalism in the following decade.

[58] Murray, letter to *The Times* (14 Oct. 1932), p. 8d.

suppressed.[59] But he never doubted the necessity of the role he had carved out for himself as a scholar of a very public and political kind, not least to the future of liberalism upon which civilization vitally depended. This was evident when he wrote to Fisher of his dismay at his friend's resignation as MP for the Combined English Universities in 1926, having already left office in 1922 to become a 'private member in a small and rather helpless minority'. Murray consoled himself—and Fisher—with the reflection that 'after all, if Liberalism is to be re-built, it must be re-built slowly and thoughtfully, outside Parliament. Jowett and Green and Arthur Sidgwick did probably as much for the liberalism [sic] of our time as most of the practical politicians'.[60] Whether or not the spelling of liberalism in the second sentence without a capital letter was a typographical error, Murray clearly believed that a pervasive liberal frame of mind diffused from above was a precondition of the success of Liberalism proper.

However, Murray's liberalism was taking an increasingly conservative hue, not least because of his growing admiration for his country and what he perceived as its peculiar affinity with the Greek spirit of reason, tolerance, and liberality.[61] During the First World War he had been anxious to keep the cause of Liberal support for the war well apart from the 'simple, old half-animal' patriotism which demanded full retribution for Germany's wrongs. In his view, patriotism conceived thus (and Murray seems not to have been able to understand it in any other way at that time) contradicted every Liberal principle, not least 'Public Right as the law of the civilized

[59] See, for example, Murray to W. P. Crozier (editor of the *Manchester Guardian*), 25 Mar. 1936: GM 76.92. 'Have you seen the account of this pogrom at Pryztyk [from the *Jewish Chronicle*]? I do not much want to write a letter to the press about it, after my review of the *Yellow Spot*, for fear of becoming identified too much with pro-Jewish propaganda, but it is appalling the way this anti-semite pest is spreading under Nazi encouragement'. Crozier duly instructed the paper's Warsaw correspondent to send a despatch immediately; Crozier to Murray, 26 Mar. 1936: GM 76.98. (Murray's review of *The Yellow Spot* was in the *Manchester Guardian* (17 Mar., 1936), p. 7.) See also Murray to Geoffrey Dawson (editor of *The Times*), 27 Sept. 1937 (GM 82.213) about a trial of sixteen anti-fascist intellectuals in Rome. Dawson duly complied with Murray's request that the matter be investigated by the paper's Rome correspondent; Dawson to Murray, 29 Sept. 1937: GM 82.217.

[60] Murray to Fisher, 14 Feb. 1926: MS Fisher 55.90.

[61] Murray, 'Greece and England', a lecture given to the Royal Society of Arts, March 1941, in Murray 1946, 192–212.

world; Freedom for all nations, and for the men and women inside the nations; the deliverance of humanity from the power of the Sword'. For Liberals, he maintained in 1917, England went to war to neutralize a crime; 'mere self-defence' of 'our country and our freedom' was an afterthought (Murray 1917a, 14–19; see also Grainger 1986, 314).

It was an afterthought which, as Martin Ceadel has noted in this volume, rested simply on the duty and interest juncture in nineteenth-century liberalism and had actually provided the basis of Murray's own support for the war initially.[62] As the war proceeded Murray was at his most sensitive to the adverse effect of the 'herd instinct' on individual thought and reason—the propensity to 'glide with the current' as he so contemptuously put it, and to level the field of mere feeling to way below that of the 'average man in normal life'.[63]

Yet in an address to the British Institute of Philosophy in early 1940, Murray abandoned this previous distrust of the 'herd instinct'. While fully alive to the snares of self-deception, he paid striking tribute to the 'herd instinct' of the British in particular, and the nobility of the national character that underlay its generous impulses. He asserted that, on account of a long experience of security and freedom from the evil lessons that 'terror teaches',

> we are still on the whole a singularly good-natured, tolerant people, moderate in our political controversies, and eager to shake hands with old opponents after a fight. Think of the great popular welcomes given to the Boer generals and to Gandhi; the wide popularity even of Hindenburg.

By contrast, the herd instinct in Germany was characterized by a perniciousness in relation to its own members as well as those beyond. Earlier, he had not allowed a word to be said against the German people as a whole, as was the wont of Conservatives.

[62] For the various shifts in Murray's stance during the First World War, from opponent to apologist of the British Government to internationalist—all of which eschewed any express patriotic commitment—see Martin Ceadel's chapter in this volume, 'Gilbert Murray and International Politics'.

[63] Murray, 'Herd Instinct and the War' (1915), in Murray 1918a, 46–66. Murray's concern about the disfigurement of the national psyche under the strain of Great War patriotism is well brought out in Wallace 1988, ch. 6.

Now, he also rallied to England's defence against a mounting hail of fire from abroad in recent years. Such criticism, he believed, often emanated from the impossibly high expectations under which no other nation laboured and to which England had been trained by weighty imperial responsibilities. What instances of aggression there had been in the cause of empire—and in his view they were often exaggerated by those who were ignorant of Indian and colonial history—was a thing of the past.[64]

Murray was also impressed by the concern of a great number of his fellow countrymen for the disturbing course that Germany had taken in the events leading up to war. His chief complaint against Neville Chamberlain in March 1939 before the German invasion of Czechoslovakia was that the Prime Minister had signally failed to make any gesture towards the keen sense of the British people—expressive of the 'moral idealism' at the root of their character—that serious moral issues had been flouted in the pursuit of peace through appeasement.[65] And as Ernest Barker—with whom Murray had clashed inexorably on this issue in the Letters pages of *The Times*—commented in a private letter to Murray subsequently, he went some way in moving the other side.[66] The deluge of correspondence that Murray's intervention precipitated also emphasizes his continued effectiveness as a liberal intellectual.[67]

Clearly, Murray's confidence in the moral instincts of his compatriots and pride in their national character had risen substantially in recent years. This was apparent in his offensive against mounting criticism of Britain from within, as well as without, the interwar tone of which he found disconcerting. In his *Euripides* in 1913 Murray had drawn parallels between his hero and contemporary critics of

[64] Murray, 'Herd Instinct: For Good and Evil', in Hooper 1940, 35, 44–5; and on the German people compare Murray 1917a, 19–20.

[65] Murray, letter to *The Times* (4 Mar. 1939), p. 10.

[66] Barker to Murray, 13 Mar. 1939: GM 86.133. Barker was referring to the *Times* leader of that morning, which applauded Murray's suggestion that Chamberlain, like Baldwin, should have confessed that recent events had 'cost him "bitter humiliation."' For Barker's letters on appeasement, see *The Times* (22 Sept. 1938), p. 11; 6 Mar 1939, p. 15. For Murray's letters to *The Times* during, and after the Munich settlement and their context in the All Souls Foreign Affairs Group of which he was a member, see Aster 2004, 223, 234–5.

[67] Letter to *The Times* (9 Mar. 1939), p. 10.

Victorian society: Euripides, like the assailants of the Victorian age to date, had undermined Periclean Athens on account of its complacency, 'its rush and chivalry and optimism, its unconscious hypocrisy, its failure to think out its problems to the bitter end'. Neither Euripides, nor the Victorian and immediate post-Victorian critics of England, wished to impugn the standards of the age they attacked, merely the failure of their respective societies to push them as far as they would go. They seemed to illustrate the principle that the best traditions make the best rebels (Murray 1913, 15–16).

However, in the interwar period and beyond, Murray saw things in a different, and far more sinister light; the best traditions were not always well served by 'good' rebels. In the Halley Stewart Lectures of 1928 he felt it necessary to stress the impressive extent of the achievements of Victorian England as much as the ideals that had inspired them. Moreover, he praised the Victorians for their clear sense of work that remained undone in the realm of social reform. He emphasized virtues that had been left out of the count earlier and the decline of which seriously imperilled public life in the present—the status which parliament commanded within the nation, especially. He also drew attention to the ability of the late-Victorians to recognize—and learn from—parodies of themselves, for example, in Gilbert and Sullivan operas.[68] He did so not least against the detractors who were increasingly rejecting the ideals of the Victorian age themselves (Murray 1929b, 56, 175). In the Romanes Lectures of 1935 he portrayed the contemporary knife of indictment of the Victorians as having been twisted further than even Shaw, Wells, Tolstoy, and Ibsen had dared at the beginning of the twentieth century; the mood now was of a 'strange despondency, as if our civilization were losing faith in itself'. For Murray, the malaise was epitomized in Auden's poetic drama, *The Dance of Death* (1934). More unnerving still was the tendency of the new critics to write for the pleasure of their own small clique rather than a wider public, thereby going against the grain of the *Logios Anêr.* At the same time, the structure of society was increasingly less able to shoulder the criticism, and be amused by it as it had done earlier, as the international anarchy took hold (Murray 1935,

[68] It may be recalled here that Gilbert Murray was named for W. S. Gilbert.

18, 13). The cynicism of psychoanalysis left him cold, and while he generously speculated on its potential to improve human conduct in the longer term, in the present he could see only its destructive effect upon the 'cosmos of our moral ideas' (Murray 1929b, 56, 175, 188). In the interests of the latter, he defended the teaching of Christianity in state schools against secular humanists on the ground that

> the religious—and what is more—the ethical emotions of the English people are rooted in the Christian writings, especially in the Gospels, some of the Epistles, and books like the *Imitation* and the *Pilgrim's Progress.* The situation must be accepted. (Murray 1944b, 5)

The iron insistence here on 'must' emphasizes Murray's often despairing conception of the 'inherited conglomerates' that formed the bedrock of human society, the shell of which was 'practically unbreakable'. And it was breakable, it seems, only at substantial cost; the great emancipatory movements of the nineteenth century had merely served to generate political extremism in Italy, Germany, and Russia by way of reaction. On the other hand, even after the overthrow of Fascism the future of free thought against the 'rigid orthodoxies' of *themis*, taboo, and superstition was not assured.[69] Murray's ambivalence towards open-ended intellectual inquiry on the one hand, and acceptance of custom on the other, is never more apparent than here. He was certainly susceptible to the myths that sustained the 'inherited conglomerate' of England/Britain. With evident pleasure he read—and re-read—Francis Brett Young's epic poem *The Island*, published in 1944. In a letter to the author he praised it as 'a return to sanity, both in form and content'. He noted the special appeal of two chapters. The first was 'Dead men on Bredon', in which the narrator is overwhelmed by a deep sense of connection to the ancient Britons slaughtered by the invading Roman troops in AD 55. The second was 'On Windmill Down', in which two well-placed devotees of cricket in the village of Hambledon in 1789 express confidence in England's ability to weather the revolutionary storm

[69] Murray, 'Prolegomena to the Study of Ancient Philosophy' (1934), lectures delivered to Greats students published and revised for the postwar world in Murray 1946, 66–7. I am grateful to Robert Todd for this reference.

across the channel. Murray especially approved of the author's searing critique of modern poetry as a betrayal of all that the poem had rightly celebrated in the national past.[70]

As Murray argued after the Second World War, the menacing rejection of old certainties amounted to 'a subject on which not only political Liberals but the great mass of intellectuals and literary England stands in some need of repentence'; at no time was it more necessary to remember the intensity with which Gladstone confessed to feel 'in the very fibre of his being the nobleness of the inheritance that has come down to us and the sacredness of the duty of maintaining it'.[71] England's failure of global nerve, in particular, was not the least unwelcome feature of the postwar world, for Murray, certainly; notoriously, he supported Eden over Suez. The United Nations Declaration of Human Rights intensified Murray's concern for the future of liberalism; it was a statement of 'abstract principles' which detracted from 'an old familiar freedom' embodied in the traditions of Hellenism and Christendom (Murray 1950b, 15). Murray and other Liberals who shared his outlook sought refuge in the Conservative Party from the chill winds of socialism.[72]

Increasingly, the Gladstonian parameters of the work of Murray and others, to say nothing of his increasing identification with historic England, proved too narrow for those who pursued social and intellectual improvement in the middle decades of the twentieth century. For a new generation of scholars and intellectuals who trained or began their training in Classics, democracy, socialism, and the techniques and insights of the social sciences provided the way forward for society. The careers of Richard Crossman and C. A. R. Crosland especially underline this shift, as does that of W. J. M. Mackenzie, a classicist turned political scientist who

[70] Murray to Mrs Brett Young, 17 Feb. 1953, University of Birmingham Library, MS Francis Brett Young 3175–6; on the reception of *The Island* (London: Heinemann, 1944), see Stapleton 2005, 189.

[71] Murray, 'The Meaning of Freedom', in Lord Samuel (ed.), *The Meaning of Freedom*, supplement 7 to *World Liberalism* (1956), based on lectures delivered in 1949: GM 396.7, p. 7.

[72] See the letter to the *Sunday Times* by the critic Desmond MacCarthy, upholding Murray's support for the Conservative Party at the 1951 general election and urging other Liberal readers of the newspaper to follow suit: 21 Oct. 1951, p. 4.

pioneered the study of public administration at the University of Manchester from 1949 until 1966 and transmitted it to a wide, albeit local, audience.[73] Social—and particularly Freudian—psychology seems to have played an especially important part in the anti-liberal reaction that gathered momentum after the First World War, extending even to the Classics profession itself in Murray's successor, E. R. Dodds.[74]

The new forces of social and intellectual change that had been in play for several decades took some time to work themselves out fully; certainly, Murray continued to command public attention in the immediate postwar period, as did his Hellenist contemporaries—Zimmern, Barker, and R. W. Livingstone, all of whom received knighthoods for their contribution to national life. But the dramatic loss of appeal of Hellenism in British intellectual and national culture after 1945 was apparent in Karl Popper's scathing attack on Plato in *The Open Society and its Enemies*.[75] Henceforth, the liberal ideals behind Hellenism, and the guiding role of the liberal intellectual they had reinforced, were on the defensive. Enacting that role and urging others to do likewise had been Murray's primary means of assuaging the cultural pessimism to which he had always been prone. When it ceased to carry conviction among both intellectuals and the public, his despond knew

[73] On Crossman, see the brief entry in Todd 2004. Crosland began his university career at Oxford as a classicist, switching to PPE when his studies resumed after the Second World War. Plausibly, the switch was one factor in his increasing ambivalence concerning direct attempts by the state to 'improve' minds: see J. Nuttall 2003. On Mackenzie, see Kenny 2004.

[74] On Dodds's pessimistic view of the decline of rationalism since fifth-century Greece, the salvation he sought in the theory of the instincts in social psychology, and the contrast this represented with an older classicist such as Barker (steeped in a Christianized view of moral and political philosophy in ancient Greece) see Todd 2006. Dodds' emphasis on social—especially Freudian—psychology as the source of ethics bears close comparison with that of Evan Durbin. On Durbin's early flight from both 'God *and* Gladstone' (my italics), see Brooke 1996, 31.

[75] See Barker's bewildered review, 'From Plato to Marx', in the *Sunday Times*, 9 Dec. 1945, p. 4b. Murray encouraged G. C. Field's proposal to correct 'current misunderstanding and misinterpretation of Plato's philosophical ideas' in a volume for the Home University Library: see Geoffrey Cumberlege to Murray, 6 Aug. 1946 and G. C. Field to Murray, 6 Sept. 1946, GM 411.17, 20; also Field 1949.

few bounds.[76] His increasing sense of alienation from contemporary society underlines the changing patterns of cultural authority integral to the simultaneous decline of both intellectual liberalism and Classics in Britain during the first half of the twentieth century. High-profile intellectuals of a distinctively *liberal* kind were not unknown after Murray's death, the most obvious example being Isaiah Berlin (Ignatieff 1998). But as they lost the single centre of disciplinary gravity that Classics had once provided and as their moral and political philosophies fragmented, they were a mere shadow of their former cultural selves in the heyday of Murray.

[76] See his letter to Veronica Wedgwood, 2 Mar. 1955, inviting her to write a book on 'The Crisis of Democracy' for the Home University Library.

'Democracy has turned into Despotism just as Plato and Aristotle say it may be expected to do, in so many European countries, and while we in the west are all singing its praises and spreading universal suffrage in the most unsuitable places, we are nevertheless conscious of the troubles of proletarian influences, e.g. in McCarthy-ism and colour prejudice in the United States, and the difficulty of getting over old popular prejudices almost everywhere.' (GM 411.234)

Wedgwood seems to have declined.

14

'That Living Voice': Gilbert Murray at the BBC

Mick Morris

'That programme, *The Brains Trust*, made my name well known'. Gilbert Murray[1]

The distinguished historian of Victorian England, G. M. Young, recalled how, as a 14-year-old, he 'was standing on a railway platform one day in the summer of 1896 when a man, certainly not of the aesthetic class (I guessed him to be a Gravesend pilot) opened his paper and exclaimed to a friend "Millais is dead" ' (Young 1937, 146). Such was the fame of the Pre-Raphaelite painter that no further explanation was necessary. I am sure that in 1957 in staff rooms, common rooms, offices, bus stops, and factories here and abroad people would have said 'Murray's dead', and most would have understood. Such was the scale of Murray's fame. Murray was the best known British Greek scholar of his time: other learned men like Richard Jebb, Murray's predecessor at the University of Glasgow, had been knighted and awarded the Order of Merit, but none before had been granted a funeral service in Westminster Abbey, interred near David Garrick and Dr Johnson, attended by a congregation of 1,500 who listened as the Dean of the Abbey recited Ecclesiasticus 44,

[1] A remark recalled by Murray's granddaughter, Ann Paludan, at the conference, 'Reassessing Gilbert Murray', held at the Institute of Classical Studies, London, in July 2005.

'Let us now praise famous men—the Lord hath wrought great glory by them' (Order of Service: GM Add. 11–91).[2]

Why was Murray so well known outside the confines of Oxford? He was of course a man of many parts: scholar, internationalist, and author of the famous green, limp-back translations which sold over 250,000 copies. It is worth pointing out that Murray, along with his great friend George Bernard Shaw, more or less invented the play script that could be read at home as well as performed on stage. Murray's translations of the choruses of Euripides were so popular that Granville Bantock in 1929 set some of them to music: *Five Choral Songs & Dances from the Bacchae of Euripides, With an Accompaniment for Piano or Orchestra* (GM 56.67). He co-edited the Home University Library from 1911 until his death, and for that imprint, produced the one book of his that has survived the test of time best, *Euripides and his Age.*[3] But the answer to the question about fame is, almost certainly, radio broadcasting; and that meant, in Murray's lifetime, the BBC. Murray's friend and fellow classical scholar A. E. Housman was certainly famous, but aloof: Murray was quite literally, to millions of radio listeners, the voice of classical learning.[4]

It is very unfortunate that the standard biography by Duncan Wilson (D. Wilson 1987) pays such perfunctory attention to Murray's broadcasting career: four pages in a book of 400 pages. Murray's connection

[2] GM = Bodleian Library Oxford, MSS Gilbert Murray; nos. refer to boxes and to folios.

[3] Murray 1913; reprinted many times; described by Christopher Collard as a 'brilliant, ageless sketch' (Collard 1981, 37).

[4] One man who recognized the significance of Murray's broadcasting work was his successor in the Oxford Greek chair, E. R. Dodds. After Murray's death in May 1957 the Trustees of the Murray Estate approached friends and colleagues of his to see if they had any correspondence to or from Murray that could be deposited at the Bodleian Library as part of the Murray Papers. Dodds was approached but seems to have demurred; but he immediately contacted the BBC to see what recordings had survived, and whether the BBC would contribute these to the University. This plan seems to have come to nothing: GM Add. 12–31. Although Dodds did not surrender his correspondence to the Trustees, one fascinating letter is to be found in the Murray Papers at the Bodleian Library. On 1 Jan. 1915 the 23-year-old Dodds contacted Murray, asking him about neo-Platonism: 'It was the only (topic) that suggested itself and I wondered what you would think of it—I should like to have something definite to work on in my spare time, even if there was no examination capital to be made out of it' (GM 26.52).

with the BBC began in 1925, with his translation of *Iphigenia in Tauris* which was broadcast from Belfast under the direction of the 25-year-old Tyrone Guthrie: this event is significant as it was the first broadcast by the infant BBC[5] of any Greek tragedy.[6] It could be argued that after 1918 Murray's importance was no longer in the field of technical Greek scholarship—the silence that greeted his Oxford Classical Text of Aeschylus (Murray 1937) was deafening—but in the fields of international affairs and teaching, in the widest sense of the term, for he made every effort to reach out to a wider, lay audience in Britain, Europe and the Empire.

For Murray the mass media of communication were, for all his adult life, the press, the cinema, and the wireless. He embraced them all to promote the two causes closest to his heart, Greek studies and internationalism: for example in March 1932 he made a short trailer for a Gaumont film, *War is Hell* (GM 493.219). Radio has always been a Cinderella figure in reception studies, lacking the glamour of the theatre, cinema, or television. It should be pointed out, however, that while cinema-going in the 1930s and 1940s *was* very popular, people listened to their wireless sets seven days a week. Established in 1922, the BBC, with its single channel, the 'National Service', commanded vast audiences, in large part because of 'the brute force of monopoly'.[7] The phrase is that of John Reith, the BBC's first Director General and the man most closely associated with the establishment of the institution. Reith created a single-channel national radio station, the National Programme, but also with parallel limited regional broadcasting. The terms 'Reith values' and 'Reithian' are used very loosely today to suggest an Arnoldian sense

[5] The British Broadcasting Company Ltd. was established in October 1922; the Belfast station began life in Sept. 1924. The British Broadcasting Corporation was established by Royal Charter on 1 Jan. 1927.

[6] Guthrie, radio playwright and distinguished theatrical director, is a rather neglected figure these days. This is unfortunate, as like Murray he was a crucial figure in the revival of interest in ancient Greek tragedy. 'At Stratford, Ontario, his Oedipus Rex (in 1955) with James Mason would be the first modern production of a Greek play to use full masks, in the way they had been used twenty-four centuries before' (Blakemore 2004, 270–1).

[7] In 1922 there were 22,000 radio licence holders; by 1932 this figure was over 5 million (*Radio Times*, 11 Nov. 1932, 18); by 1946 the figure was 10.7 million (A. Briggs 1985, Appendix C).

of an elitist concentration on high-status culture: 'the best that is known and thought'. It would be much fairer to say that Reith wanted a cultural 'mix' with Greek tragedy rubbing shoulders with popular entertainers.[8]

The BBC was from the start not just a broadcaster but was also forced, by circumstances, to become a publisher, because newspapers refused to print daily programme details; it launched in 1923 the *Radio Times*.[9] This was a weekly publication, appearing on a Friday priced two pence: Reith, a son of the manse, ruled that the week began, at least for the *Radio Times*, on a Sunday; indeed on that day broadcasting began at 3.30pm in order to allow people to attend church. The *Radio Times* contained not just programme details but short features and often superb line illustrations advertising prestige productions; the front-page article, in the early years, was often written by Reith himself.[10] By 1946 it was selling five million copies a week—which suggests a *readership* figure in the region of 15 million. In 1929 Reith launched another weekly, *The Listener*, to capture 'the fugitive word in print'; this was a general arts magazine which also reviewed programmes and published transcripts in part or in whole of important broadcasts given that week. The BBC's Charter prevented it from adopting a particular political stance, so *The Listener* had to remain apolitical. At its peak, in the 1950s, *The Listener*'s circulation reached 150,000; it ceased publication in 1991. Both magazines were important vehicles for promoting and

[8] The commonly accepted image of Reith as a relentlessly gloomy Presbyterian does not quite square with the facts. He was for example a very keen member of the BBC Amateur Dramatic Society, and in the 1936 production of *The Sport of Kings* won praise from the *News Chronicle* (25 May 1936) for his portrayal of the butler.

[9] From its inception the BBC was forbidden to make any news broadcast until 7.30 p.m., when it was assumed that all the day's newspapers would have been sold. This was to change in May 1926 when the General Strike closed down all newspapers and magazines, including the *Radio Times* and *The Listener*, and the broadcaster became the sole provider of national news.

[10] The *Radio Times* employed a distinguished group of artists to illustrate each week's publication but the most important was Eric Fraser (1902–83) who for over 60 years produced some of the most dramatic and beautiful advanced warnings of Murray's plays. What is remarkable is how little time Fraser was given: he received his brief and play synopsis on Friday and the final drawing was to be ready by the following Monday. Perhaps many people who did not listen to the play were affected by the magnificent Fraser drawings. For further information, see Backemeyer 1998, Driver 1981.

recording programmes made by men like Murray. Thus there were three aspects to Murray's work at the BBC: promotion of the programme in the *Radio Times*, the broadcast, and in some cases a reprint thereafter of the text in *The Listener.*

The leading archive of sound recordings in Britain is the British Library Sound Archive: established in 1955, it holds over a million items and is one of the most important collections of its kind in the world. But archives of radio and indeed television broadcasts are notoriously patchy: music, sport, politics, and the monarchy are well represented, but anything else is a lottery. Murray is unique among classical scholars, in that there are over twenty recordings of his broadcasts in their catalogue; in contrast there seems to be no record of any broadcasts being made by some of his noted contemporaries—nothing of Maurice Bowra, J. D. Denniston or, saddest of all, A. E. Housman (and it seems unlikely that the deeply private Housman would ever have consented to become involved with the BBC). This wealth of Murray material testifies to the importance accorded to him by the archival powers at Broadcasting House, from the 1930s onwards. The broadcasts of Murray's that are preserved fall into the following broad categories: schools programmes, performances of his translations, Murray as a panelist, broadcasting on the World Service, and finally, Murray remembering, as almost the last eloquent Victorian alive, friends and places long gone.

But Murray's first appearance in front of the microphone falls into none of these categories, for it took place at the conclusion of one of the most dramatic events of the interwar years, the General Strike of 1926. When the talks between the mine owners and the mining unions broke down, on 4 May the Trades Union Congress called a General Strike. During this strike, no newspapers were published save the TUC's *British Worker* and the government's *British Gazette*: both perceived, correctly, as partisan. The BBC therefore, with its five news bulletins a day, constituted the principal source of trusted, national news. Reith had invited the Prime Minister, Stanley Baldwin, and the Archbishop of Canterbury to speak to the country during the Strike, but had denied any access to the union leaders.[11] When the strike

11 'The strike would certainly have lasted much longer had it not been for us, and all sorts of panic might have come': Reith 1975, 137.

collapsed on 12 May, Reith asked Murray to speak to the nation. Clearly the intention was for Murray to try and bind wounds. He begins his broadcast of 13 May by suggesting why he has been chosen for this task:

I have been asked, I suppose, because I belong to neither side, I have friends, whom I respect and trust on both sides, and I have worked for the League of Nations and international peace. (GM 491.76)

He then considers the TUC's decision to call off the strike:

I think the nation will be grateful to the men who took that step, and to anyone who may have made that step easier to them—Was that defeat? Was it a sign of weakness? For my part I think was a big and generous action, bravely done. I do not believe that by any man who knows what honour is it will be counted a dishonour to have yielded first. It will be counted an act of wisdom and of patriotism.

He studiously avoids any mention of the miners who were still on strike, and were to remain on strike for another six months. Murray's intention is clearly to see the way the strike ended as proof of how civilized nations should behave. He notes 'the discipline, and self-restraint and good humour of the strikers and the police'. The whole short address is an appeal for there not to be any element of triumphalism: 'Let there be no taunts, no shouts of victory'. He goes on to recommend acceptance of the recent Samuel Commission's Report ('an exceptionally able and impartial commission'), which had recommended imposing pay cuts on the miners. He concludes by seeing the major problem as mutual suspicion: 'The cause of half our trouble is mistrust'.

Two things are worth noting about this address: it indicates the unique position Murray occupied in British public life: there is no doubt which side of the argument Murray warmed to, but he was clearly seen by Reith and others as being 'above politics'.[12] The second point to note is the public reaction to this talk: he was inundated with requests to be allowed to reprint his text; which permission he always granted (GM 51.119). When the *Radio Times* reappeared Murray

12 'There was a time—it was when Ramsay MacDonald was Prime Minister—when there was a likelihood that he would be sent to Washington as British Ambassador' (Thomson 1957, 265).

pursued his theme in print, but now he celebrated not only the tolerance and good sense of the British people, but also the vital role the BBC played in British society; and never more so than during the General Strike:

As one listened, and felt that some millions of one's fellow citizens, whatever their opinions, were listening at the same time and getting the same knowledge, one felt comfort in the thought of that living voice which could pass from end to end of the nation and amid the noises of discord make us one. ('Broadcasting the News', *Radio Times*, 28 May 1926, 350)

But it would be very wrong to see Murray as merely an apologist for the status quo. In September of the same year, 1926, the BBC received an urgent message from the GPO, who were in overall charge of telegraphic and telephonic communication in the UK; they were incensed that the *Radio Times* had announced a live broadcast to all stations of a speech by Murray entitled 'The League or Chaos'. They insisted that unless they had sight of the text the programme could not be transmitted. What this correspondence reveals is that it was not the GPO which vetted Murray's words, but the Foreign Office.[13]

The earliest recording of Murray's to survive is a lecture on the *Prometheus* of Aeschylus, made in 1934 and broadcast on the recently created Empire Service.[14] This play was a particular favourite of Murray's; he remembered learning it off by heart while still a pupil at Merchant Taylors' School. Together with Shelley's *Prometheus Unbound*, it became, he said much later, 'a gospel for me in those days'.[15] All that has survived is an extract from a much longer programme, but it does give some insight into Murray's approach to Greek tragedy and students of Greek. This seems to have been a schools broadcast aimed at the students of the Classics in the sixth forms of India, Canada, and Australia.

This morning, gentlemen, we come to the *Prometheus*. The classic stage of the fifth century BC, towards the end of the life of Aeschylus, settled down

[13] BBC Written Archives Centre, Gilbert Murray Talks: 1, 1926–1941. Accession 48531. The correspondence begins on 6 Sept. 1926.

[14] Permission to quote from Murray's BBC broadcasts has been kindly granted by the Corporation, which holds the copyright.

[15] 'The Unfinished Battle', *The Listener* (5 Jan. 1956).

into a fairly uniform convention. There was little or no attempt at what we call 'scenic effect', the background was merely a background. The effect of the drama was left to the actors and the words they spoke. The poet never relied on the stage carpenter for effects of romance or terror. He eschewed use of the *μηχαναί* or machines, and when Euripides in his more romantic plays re-introduced them the comic writers immediately made them a subject for jokes. What is not often realised is that before settling down to this discreet form, tragedy had made much more ambitious experiments. Aeschylus had used *μηχαναί* with much greater boldness than Euripides. Let us look in detail at the dramatic and scenic devices that are implied in the *Prometheus*. In the first place there is a definite attempt, by means of the scenery, of producing an effect of romantic terror. Prometheus is bound to a wild rock at the end of the world; it is a sky-piercing precipice, it is above a tempest-riven gulf, and in the language of the stage the rock is 'practicable': that is, it is really there. And when it is hurled by lightning into the abyss, it really goes. The gigantic figure of the friend of man is crucified against it. How was this done? It seems clear that the thing nailed upon the rock was a wooden structure and not a man. It was motionless, upright, 'not closing eye nor bending knee',[16] *ὀρθοστάδην ἄυπνος, οὐ κάμπτων γόνυ*. When Hephaistos fixes the bonds around his chest, Kratos bids him 'climb down', or at any rate go down, '*χώρει κάτω*', in order to the put the fetters round his ankles. It was fixed in a way not suited for a human being, a wedge of biting adamant is driven through its chest to pin it to the rock, nails or piercing gyves are driven through its feet. And one may notice the magnificent silence when the torturers are present and the still more magnificent burst into speech when left alone. Seen in the light of this hypothesis, nicely suited to the stage conveniences, the actor who went off went into the wooden structure and spoke.

Murray is trying to make a clear link between text and stagecraft to his pupil audience, while not disguising his emotional response to the text. The only other schools broadcast to survive was made in 1937 and is devoted to two plays by Euripides, *Iphigenia in Tauris* and *The Trojan Women*. This broadcast was advertised as being part of a series called 'Talks for Sixth Forms'.

The later plays of Euripides seem to be written with a sense of the horrible cruelty of the world. The love of Athens and Greece remains but has nothing

[16] Murray, as was his habit in broadcasts, was quoting from his own translation (Murray 1931).

warlike about it; it is more a sort of home-sickness for something lost. In the *Iphigenia in Tauris* this longing of the exile for home is the main motive. The scene is laid in the barbarous land of the Taurians; the Greek captives, who form the chorus, help Iphigenia to escape home to Greece but they know as a result they will be left behind in exile for ever. They look at the seabirds, the halcyons, soaring away:

> Bird of the sea rocks, of the bursting spray,
> O halcyon bird,
> That wheelest crying, crying on thy way;
> Who knowest grief can read the tale of thee:
> One love, long lost, one song for ever heard
> And wings that sweep the sea
>
> Sister, I too beside the sea complain,
> A bird that hath no wing.
> Oh, for a kind Greek market-place again,
> For Artemis that healeth woman's pain;
> Here I stand hungering.
> Give me the little hill above the sea,
> The palm of Delos fringed delicately,
> The young sweet laurel and the olive-tree
> Grey-leaved and glimmering;
> O Isle of Leto, Isle of pain and love;
> The Orbed Water and the spell thereof;
> Where still the Swan, minstrel of things to be,
> Doth serve the Muse and sing! (Murray 1910, lines 1088–1104)

That kindly, peaceful Hellas was a thing of the past: all about him now was war and Athens was in the hands of a war-maddened mob. All witnesses agree about this. Then there was one particular deed of cynical cruelty, which is taken by Thucydides as the very type caused by the war and which made Euripides turn in indignant wrath against those who were guiding his country. This was the siege and capture, utterly unprovoked, of the little neutral island of Melos: the massacre of all the men and the enslavement of its women and children. No doubt the people who did it were proud of their glorious victory. The next year Euripides wrote a tragedy on the great victory of the heroic age: the capture of Troy, the massacre of its men and the enslavement of its women and children. This play, *The Trojan Women*, shows what conquest and triumph look like when the excitement of fighting is over and nothing is left but to wait and think. It shows not merely the brutality of war, that's obvious: it shows what a miserable and unsatisfying thing victory is, hideous in the sight of God if there be a God:

How are ye blind,
Ye treaders down of cities, ye that cast
Temples to desolation, and lay waste
Tombs, the untrodden sanctuaries where lie
The ancient dead; yourselves so soon to die!

Listening to this broadcast and knowing the historical context: the collapse of the League of Nations, Nazi Germany rampant, and Spain engaged in an internecine war, it is difficult not to detect a note of passion in Murray's normally unruffled delivery. He was broadcasting to a generation soon to go to war.[17]

In considering the production of Murray's translations, one BBC figure needs to be mentioned: Val Gielgud, brother of Sir John and Production Director of Drama and Variety from 1929 until 1952.[18] He seems to have been the person who urged Murray to allow his translations to be broadcast by the BBC:

> It always pleases me greatly to remember, that I persuaded you to let us include these examples of your work in our broadcast drama output. I am sure that the current success of much verse drama in this country owes in the first instance a very great debt to you.[19]

Gielgud was also convinced of the relevance of Greek tragedy to the political turmoil of 1940:

> I think it is an excellent time now to remind people of the obvious parallels between the Persian Wars and today; and incidentally a shortened version of *The Persians* might well come into the possible (new) series.[20]

[17] Everyone who heard it commented on the beauty of Murray's voice: mellifluous, with a good actor's sense of the rhythm of words, but to some ears at least, with a distinct Oxonian drawl.

[18] Val Gielgud (1900–81) was one of the most flamboyant members of the BBC in the early years. His first post with the BBC was editing the letters page of the *Radio Times*, where as he later admitted he supplied the letters under a variety of pseudonyms. Without any qualifications, he was put in charge of drama and variety: his keen interest in amateur dramatics at the BBC may have aided his career (see n. 7). The one thing he did not lack was confidence: when Ernest Milton fell ill shortly before the 1942 recording of *Medea*, Gielgud promptly took his place, the part of Creon. For further information see Gielgud 1957 and 1965.

[19] BBC Written Archives Centre, Gilbert Murray, Script Writer, 1936–66. ACC 48533, 6 Nov. 1950.

[20] Ibid., 4 Apr. 1940.

Murray himself was not always convinced of the virtues of the BBC classical 'style': 'My main criticism would be of the BBC methods; I always think they over act'.[21] His view was shared by at least one reviewer in *The Times*:

> The broadcast of Hippolytus in the National Programme yesterday evening was an interesting though certainly rash experiment, for the plays of Euripides... come fully alive only on the stage... (and) it seemed one was listening not to a play, but to a poetry reading of nineteenth-century English verse. (*The Times*, 19 Oct. 1936. BBC Written Archives Centre, Press Cuttings, Programmes Box 1.193)

By far the most important part of the Murray archive are the five recordings of his translations: *Rape of the Locks* (1942), *Hippolytus* (1945), *The Trojan Women* (1946), *Frogs* (1947), *Electra* (1948).[22] These plays are important for two reasons: the size of the audiences they reached and the production values they embody. In the 1940s the BBC were claiming that their premiere drama slot, Saturday Night Theatre, was attracting an audience of over ten million listeners (A. Briggs, 1979, 64). The BBC conducted daily polling nationally of 3,000 people and the results produced the (confidential) 'Listening Barometer'.[23] The figures are staggering: for example *Trojan Women* (1946) gained an audience of 450,000.[24] To put that figure into perspective, the National Theatre's largest auditorium, the Olivier, which can accommodate 1,100 people, would need to

[21] Ibid., letter to the BBC producer Peter Watts, 14 Apr. 1953.

[22] It is perhaps worth observing that when Murray's translation of *The Frogs* was broadcast in 1947 on the Third Programme, listeners were given an opportunity, later that evening, to hear scenes spoken in the original Greek (Carpenter 1996, 59). This was not an isolated example of ancient Greek on the Third Programme. On 1 May excerpts from the *Bacchae* were broadcast, the *Radio Times* supplying the line references, and on 14 September 1949 Phillip Vellacott read extracts in Greek from *Iphigenia in Tauris*.

[23] These daily *Barometers* consist of a large spreadsheet based on the questions a panel of 200 interviewers have asked the sample of 3,000. All that day's programmes are listed and percentages are given for the nation as a whole and then a breakdown for six regions: London, West Region, Midlands, North, Wales, and Scotland. The most popular programme invariably tended to be the 9 p.m. news on the Home Service, with over ten million listening—about a third of the adult civilian population.

[24] BBC, Written Archives Centre [see n. 12]. Listening Barometer, Monday 4 Mar. 1946.

secure full houses every day of the week for a year and a half to match that audience. Nor was this play the exception: *Hippolytus*, according to BBC figures, attracted a national audience of 300,000.[25]

These audience figures raise all sorts of questions; for example, did the audience listen with the Murray text to hand? (Nearly every public library would have had multiple copes of these translations.) How were these ancient texts received, to use Martin Esslin's striking phrase, in 'the theatre of the mind'?[26] Did Murray attract such a large audience because of his fame in other areas? Did these audiences feel more comfortable at home with their Greek tragedy, rather than undergoing the more expensive and socially more daunting experience of theatregoing?

Murray himself became very involved in these productions, advising, attending rehearsals, and often appearing in front of the microphone, as in the case of *Frogs*, to provide a brief introduction to the play. The producer was often the BBC's most senior drama producer, Val Gielgud, whose brother John appeared in at least one production (*Trojan Women*). These productions were given added glamour by attracting some of the leading performers of the day: Flora Robson, Leon Quatermaine, Robert Speight and most importantly for Murray, Sybil Thorndike (Thorndike and Casson 1960). Her association with Murray began in 1908, and she famously toured Ireland, South Wales, and the East End of London with a double bill of Murray's translations of *Medea* and *Trojan Women*. These broadcasts are, I believe, little changed in performance terms from the productions at the Lyric and the New Theatre that caused such a stir before the First World War. To us they may sound slow and mannered, but we have no way of knowing what the productions were like that preceded them: one can assume they were slower and even more mannered. At the very least they give an insight into how the most important cultural institution in Britain in the 1940s projected not

[25] BBC, Written Archives Centre [see n. 12]. Listening Barometer, 1 Oct. 1945.

[26] Esslin 1971. Martin Esslin (1918–2002) was a radio producer and writer who worked for the BBC from 1939 to 1977. In the 1960s and 1970s he occupied the very influential post of Head of Radio Drama. On retirement from the Corporation he became Professor of Drama at Stanford University. I am grateful to Amanda Wrigley for drawing my attention to this article. (For her own pioneering work in this field, see Wrigley 2005.)

just an attempt to imitate the dramatic style of ancient theatre, but also its promotion to a mass audience.

But it was one particular BBC programme that made Murray a household name: *The Brains Trust.* This started life on 1 January 1941 as a Variety Department Programme, called at first *Any Questions*, and broadcast on the Forces Network. This programme was based on a very simple format; a panel of experts would, over the 45 minutes of the programme, answer questions sent in by viewers on a postcard. (Postcards were specified to facilitate the speedy processing of the vast numbers of questions sent in.) The regular panel consisted of the biologist Julian Huxley, the philosopher C. E. M. Joad and the retired naval commander A. B. Campbell; to these were added one or two experts appearing on a rotating basis. This rotating panel consisted of the great and good in British intellectual life: Bertrand Russell, Kenneth Clark, Freddie Ayer, Eileen Powell, W. H. Auden, Monsignor Ronnie Knox, Malcolm Sargent and Murray himself. The programme was an immediate and immense success; it attracted an audience of almost (modern day) soap-opera proportions. It soon had twelve million listeners, representing one in three of the adult population, and the programme makers received over 4,000 letters a week (A. Briggs, 1970, 319). The first series ran for eighty-four weeks without interruption, and soon after its creation it was given the prime-time slot on Sunday afternoon.[27] Perhaps something of the flavour of the programme can be conveyed by the following extract; this edition was broadcast on 16 October 1945, the panel consisting of Julian Huxley, the economist Barbara Ward, the Spanish diplomat Salvador de Madariaga, Lord Samuel, and Gilbert Murray. The chairman was, as usual, Donald McCulloch.

Donald McCulloch The next question comes from AC of Edinburgh: 'Do we agree it's not the true function of the university to train anybody for anything?' Huxley?

Julian Huxley Yes, I do agree—

(a few seconds rather stunned silence)

[27] Radio audiences on Sundays were the largest of the week, when most people were not at work and the other great vehicle of mass entertainment, the cinema, was closed. The pattern continues to this day in newspaper sales.

Donald McCulloch Miss Ward?

Barbara Ward Well it seems hardly fair to carry the question on! I quite agree with Dr. Huxley the function of the university is to train minds with a capacity rather than for devoting themselves to particular pursuits. But the important thing is the quality of thinking it creates.

Donald McCulloch Huxley?

Julian Huxley Yes of course it was a flippant and snap remark, but it is true on the other hand that I deprecate the idea in some quarters that there are all sorts of fields it is beneath the dignity of the university in which to enter. There can be and are in existence admirable courses in such fields as journalism, veterinary science and so on and so forth. Many universities in the past thought that such courses were beneath their notice. I think it is fair to say that certainly most and probably all such applied and specialized courses should be post-graduate. That the university in preparation for the main degree should devote itself to more general branches, such as pure science, history, classics and so forth.

Donald McCulloch Any further observations on universities?—I feel that Gilbert Murray more or less invented them. (General laughter)

Gilbert Murray Of course the sentence standing by itself is a little too dogmatic, but certainly I do agree with it, if it means it isn't the business of the university to train people for some particular profession. There is a university I know where there is a School of Journalism—well I don't think that's quite the thing for a university.[28]

(Rather embarrassed silence)

Julian Huxley I'm sorry I thought I just said that it was.

Gilbert Murray No, I don't think you said you were in favour of a definite School of Journalism. You were in favour of a training that might turn out to be later useful for journalism. Well, I don't think it's a good thing to have training for a definite money-making job. You oughtn't to have your mind concentrated on that, you're to

[28] [The foundation of the Reuters Institute for the Study of Journalism at the University of Oxford was announced in June 2006. Ed.]

have the mind of the university concentrated on something a little broader and higher than that.

Julian Huxley Well, I quite agree. But it seems to me in post graduate and specialized diploma work you would not prevent courses in architecture or medicine, would you?

Gilbert Murray Oh, I quite agree.

Julian Huxley Well, these are things you make your money at and I think journalism if properly conducted and confirmed to graduate courses . . .

Gilbert Murray But these are graduate courses?

Julian Huxley Yes, graduate courses.

Lord Samuel You remember the famous Cambridge toast? 'Here's to the Higher Mathematics and may they never be any use to anyone.'

In the same programme the other issues dealt with by the panel were: 'Will the defence of war criminals (at Nuremberg) by British counsel be deemed to be an example of British hypocrisy?' and, by using a quotation from Macaulay, 'The ancient philosophy disdained the useful and thus remained stationary', sent in by a listener, the team were invited to discuss the relevance of philosophy. The latter question gave Murray a chance to exercise his laconic wit, 'The great advantage of being Kant was, you didn't have to spend all your life studying Kant.'[29]

By means of the BBC's Empire Service, established in 1932, Murray could reach the four corners of the world. Thus in 1941, at the height of the blitz, he broadcast on the BBC's Overseas Service a talk entitled *What Has Socrates to Say to Us?*

Well, to begin with let us think about the present world, the society we live in. Some of my friends tell me it is terribly corrupt and wicked and that is why we have wars. Somehow I do not quite believe them. People have always talked like that. There is an ancient Babylonian tablet in the British Museum, dating from about 3000 BC, which starts, if I remember rightly: 'Alas, alas; this modern world is very wicked'. I cannot think that Londoners under the blitz have found themselves particularly materialist and selfish. Yet if society was so bad, the Londoners ought to be about the worst.

[29] *The Brains Trust* transferred to BBC Television in September 1955, but the rather static format did not work so well on the small screen, and by the 1960s it had gone. The format however still survives in a variety of guises.

Another example is a broadcast, *The Hard Road to Peace* of 1946, where Murray was talking to Australasia about the hope represented by the foundation of the United Nations. In his long life Murray had met, due to academic, political, or family connections, many of the great figures of the twentieth century: Asquith, Gandhi, Henry James, Kipling, Virginia Woolf, Einstein, and Marie Curie had all crossed his path. The recollections of these giants became the source for many of his later broadcasts. In one such broadcast, *Glasgow in the 1890s*, Murray recalled what it was like to arrive at Glasgow as a 23-year-old Professor of Greek, and to have to deal with the challenge of the large boisterous Scottish classes; but also to be admitted to one of the intellectual elites of late Victorian Britain.[30] His closest friend on the staff was Andrew Bradley, Professor of English, who when he lectured on Hamlet left his students with the impression that 'he had written the play himself' (*I Remember: Glasgow University in the 1890s*, 4 Mar. 1954; Home Service). But it is Murray's final, major broadcast, *The Unfinished Battle*, that contains perhaps the most moving of all these vignettes. He begins with an ironic comment on his long life:

> My excessively long and fairly industrious life has been devoted to two main enterprises: the teaching of Greek and the building of world peace. A very suitable programme, the cynic might say, to come from that home of lost causes, Oxford.

But this valedictory broadcast covers the whole of Murray's life. He pays a very moving tribute to his wife of over sixty years:

> Castle Howard gave me a wife who seemed the answer to all my ideals and who through good and evil days of a long life has never once failed in courage, never once missed a chance of doing a kindness.

Murray's mind finally goes back to the final collapse of the League of Nations:

> I always remember our last meeting, when war was closing in on us in 1939 and all the frail edifice of peace that the League had built up was being swept away by the flood, how we pledged ourselves to keep peace in our hearts and wait, and waiting ready as soon as the war finished to be ready to re-build the ruins.

[30] Much of the material broadcast can be found in Murray 1960.

A moving and fitting valediction to the world by a man who had devoted so much of his energies over a long life to international understanding.

This chapter has been an attempt to examine an aspect of Murray's career, as a public figure, largely ignored by biographers and critics. More work needs to be done in this area. If the radio broadcasts of his translations were close to being replicas of those Edwardian productions, it is necessary to look at the original theatrical reviews, compare them to the recordings and try to see what it was that made the original performances so new, so different, and so dangerous. Then what needs to be explored is whether there was a preferred type of translation at the BBC, and who made this decision.[31] Why did Murray command such a vast constituency? It was not just Murray's translations that were used but also those by Yeats, MacNeice, and Robert Fitzgerald.

Murray's life was all of a piece throughout: in October 1956, when he was very frail and 90 years old, he made a great plea for those millions who had no voice, the displaced of Europe (*Thoughts on Refugees*, 8 Oct. 1956). All his life, whenever he was asked, Murray always answered the voice of conscience. Fashions change in scholarship, and now no longer do students of ancient Greek beliefs turn immediately to his *Five Stages of Greek Religion* (Murray 1925a), but he had done something remarkable in his translations: 'He was listened to as no classical scholar has been listened to in England before or since' (Thomson 1957, 270). But at the end, at what was virtually, in July 1957, a state funeral, it was very appropriate that Murray's final resting place was marked by the sonorous words of another translator. He did indeed belong to that group of

> Men renowned for their power, giving counsel by their understanding and declaring prophecies: Leaders of the people by their counsels, and by their knowledge of learning meet for the people: Rich men furnished with ability, living peaceably in their habitations. (Ecclesiasticus 44: 12–23; King James version)

[31] The BBC employed readers to vet translations for broadcasting, but the archives reveal very little as to who these individuals were and the nature of their qualifications.

Appendices

1 Translations broadcast by the BBC
2 Other broadcasts for the BBC
3 Broadcasts and articles published in the *Radio Times* and *The Listener*
4 Recordings held at the British Library Sound Archive

Any attempt to create a complete list of all Murray's broadcasts for the BBC faces considerable difficulties. The key resource, the *Radio Times*, provides no annual index to radio programmes in the thirty years of the period in question; the annual cumulated volumes of this weekly periodical amount to well over 2,000 pages. In addition, by the time of Murray's death in 1957 there were seven regional editions of the *Radio Times*. There are also gaps in the BBC's own archives, most notably, and quite understandably, in the war years. The following list has been created using the *Radio Times* 1923–57 (Scottish edition), the Murray Papers deposited at the Bodleian Library, and the records at the BBC's Written Archives Centre at Caversham. The list given in Appendix 1 differs from that provided by Duncan Wilson (D. Wilson 1987, 454), who reports nothing earlier than 1939. On the other hand, he includes broadcasts not listed in the sources I have used; these have been added, and are indicated by an asterisk (*).

Appendix 1

Murray's translations broadcast by the BBC

The recordings of these productions were invariably repeated at least once, often during the same week of initial transmission. Murray himself would on a regular basis supply a brief contextual broadcast introduction to the play in question.

Iphigenia in Tauris, 14 May 1925 (Northern Ireland Service). This first BBC broadcast of a Murray translation was preceded by a musical selection that included Gluck's *Iphigenia in Aulide*, Offenbach's *Orpheus in the Underworld* and Campbell's *Thais and Talmaae.*
Rhesus, 22 August 1926 (National Service)
Electra of Euripides, 16 July 1929 (National Service)

Hippolytus, 18 October 1936 (National Service)
Persians, 16 April 1939 (National Service)
Seven Against Thebes, 25 August 1940 (Home Service)
Alcestis, 30 March 1941 (Home Service)
The Rape of the Locks, a comedy based on fragments of Menander, 28 February 1942 (Home Service)
Medea, 15 April 1942 (Home Service). Extracts from the play, performed by the Old Vic. Company; introduced by Tyrone Guthrie.
Trojan Women, 4 March 1946 (Home Service)
Antigone, 3 May 1947 (Home Service)
The Frogs, 3 February 1947 (Light Programme); repeated 20 February (Third Programme), followed by scenes in the original Greek (Carpenter 1996, 59)
* *The Frogs*, 27 April 1947
* *Electra*, 9 February 1948, repeated 12 February, 24 October
Medea, 26 September 1949 (Home Service)
Choephoroe, 6 October 1949 (Third Programme)
* *The Frogs*, 3 December 1950
* *The Frogs*, 9 December 1951
* *Electra*, 13 April, 1 November 1953
The Arbitration of Menander, 3 August 1952 (Third Programme)
* *The Arbitration of Menander*, 11 July 1956
* *The Rape of the Locks*, 13 July 1956

Appendix 2

Murray's other broadcasts for the BBC

1926

Address Broadcast by Professor Gilbert Murray, 13 May. Broadcast at the end of the General Strike.

1928

Extracts from Alcestis, 3 December. (Schools Broadcast, National Service)

1930

International Co-operation, 5 March. (National Service)
Nansen: Explorer and Internationalist, 12 March. (National Service)

1934

Lecture on Prometheus Bound, 16 May. (Schools Broadcast, Empire Service)

1937

Talk on Euripides, 8 October. (Schools Broadcast, National Service)

As I See It, 14 December. (National Service)

1938

Progress of the Mind, 8 February. (National Service)

Matters of Moment: Greece, 17 March. (National Service)

Why Greek? A series of 6 programmes, 31 May–28 June. (Empire Service)

Matters of Moment, 17 March. (Empire Service)

1940

In My Opinion: Greece, 22 November. (Foreign Language Service)

1941

Calling Australia, 21 January. (Pacific Service)

What Greece Stands For, 23 March. (Foreign Language/Arabic)

Books We Remember: Shelley's Poems. Talks for Sixth Formers, 9 May. (Schools Broadcast, Home Service)

Unity Through Understanding, 29 May. (Hindustani Service)

In My Opinion: Socrates, 5 June. (Home Service)

The Commonwealth of Man—Leisure, 13 September. (Home Service)

Talks for Sixth Formers, 3 October. (Home Service)

Message to Greece, 12 October. (European News)

1942

Books and Authors: F. M. Cornford's Translation of Plato's Republic, 16 March. (Overseas Service)

Brains Trust, 26 April. (Home Service) The first of 18 appearances on this programme.

Books and Authors, 27 April. (Overseas Service)

German Atrocities in Poland, 18 June. (Home Service)

1943

Why We Enjoy Poetry, 6 September. (Home Service)

Classical Humanism, 12 December. (Home Service; later translated into Spanish and Portuguese and broadcast on the Overseas Service.)

1944

Message to Norway, 5 April. (European Service, in Norwegian)

Personal Choice: Tennyson's Ulysses, 19 June. (Home Service)
Calling Australia, 10 October. (Pacific Service)
Christmas Talk, 24 December. (General Overseas Service)

1945

Book Talk. Eternal Championship of the Underdog: Shelley's Prometheus Unbound, 22 January. (Home Service)
Books and People: Old Friends and New, 9 March. (Home Service)
Europe and Ourselves, 12 March. (Home Service)

1946

Australians in Britain, 19 July. (Pacific Service)
Australians and Civilization, 19 July. (Pacific Service)
A Future Home for Civilization, 8 August. (Pacific Service)
The Hard Road to Peace, 29 September. (Home Service)
A Victorian Looks Back on Twenty-Five Years, 13 November. (Home Service)

1947

Great Lives: Socrates, 14 January. (General Overseas Service)
Calling West Africa, 14 January. (General Overseas Service)
Great Books: Homer, 8 October. (African Service)
How it Strikes a Victorian, 11 December (Home Service)

1948

Mind of Man: Reason. Talks to Sixth Formers, 30 January. (Home Service)
The Olympic Games, 18 July. (Home Service)
Should This be the Last Olympics?, 28 August. (General Overseas Service)
The Right Thing to Do, 2 November. (General Overseas Service)

1949

Is Regional Association the Most Practical Step towards World Government?, 6 June. (General Overseas Service)
My Library, 9 August. (General Overseas Service)
Myself when Young, 14 August. (Home Service)

1950

These Fifty Years. Appeal on behalf of the Oxford Committee on Famine Relief, 7 August. (Home Service)
Introduction to Antigone, 8 October. (Third Programme)
Euripides, 11 October. (Third Programme)
1900–1950: Summing Up, 20 December. (European Services)

1951

Courage—The Secret of Freedom, 11 January. (European Service)
Jane Ellen Harrison, 3 March. (Third Programme)
T. P. Marriott Memorial Lecture, 2 June. (Third Programme)
Introduction to The Frogs, 3 December. (Home Service)

1952

This I Believe, 26 February. (North American Service)
Asquith's Achievements as a Statesman, 18 September. (Third Programme)
The Experience of Age. With Laurence Housman, Bertrand Russell, and Walter de la Mare; 19 November. (Home Service)
These Fifty Years, 19 December. (Pacific Service)

1953

Hellenism and the Modern World. Series of six broadcasts. (Home Service: see Appendix 3 for details.)

1954

The Author of The Golden Bough, 7 January. (Third Programme)
Foundations of Strength: Truth, 2 February. (Home Service)
I Remember. A series of six broadcasts, 25 February–15 April. (Home Service: see Appendix 3 for details.)
Are our Pearls Real? Presidential Address at the Classical Association's Jubilee Meeting, 8 April. (Third Programme)
At Home, 18 October. (Home Service)
Memories of Gandhi, 10 December. (Home Service)

1955

Foundations of Western Values: Truth the Sovereign Virtue, 26 May. (Home Service)
Memories of the Peace Movement, 2 October. (Home Service)

1956

Menander: Inventor of Modern Comedy, 12 July. (Third Programme)
British Prime Ministers since 1900, 3 September. (Home Service)
Spirit of the Olympic Games. With Dr Roger Bannister; 8 October. (Home Service)
Thoughts on Refugees, 8 October. (Home Service)
These Twain Shall Meet, 12 November. (General Overseas Service)
Unfinished Battle, 14 December. (Home Service)

Appendix 3

Broadcasts and articles by Gilbert Murray published in the *Radio Times* and *The Listener*

On many occasions Murray's broadcasts were reprinted in part or in whole in *The Listener*. Where no radio station is indicated it would appear that these were commissioned articles. With one exception all those listed below were printed in *The Listener*.

Broadcasting the News, 28 May 1926. (*Radio Times*)
International Co-operation, 12 March 1930. (National Service)
Nansen: Explorer and Internationalist, 12 March 1930. (National Service)
As I See It, 29 December 1937.
Progress: Anything to Save Trouble, 16 February [1938?].
The League from Within, 27 April 1938.
What Greece Stands For, 5 December 1940.
Unity Through Understanding, 29 May 1941. (Hindustani Service)
What Has Socrates to Say to Us?, 26 June 1941.
The Hard Road to Peace, 3 October 1946.
A Victorian Looks Back on Twenty Five Years, 13 November 1947. (Home Service)
Myself when Young, 18 August 1949. (Home Service)
Courage—the Secret of Freedom, 11 January 1951. (European Service)
A Great Scholar: Gilbert Murray on Jane Harrison, 8 March 1951. (Third Programme)
Asquith's Achievements as a Statesman, 18 September 1952. (Third Programme)
Hellenism and the Modern World. 1: The Christian Tradition, 16 April 1953. (Home Service)
Hellenism and the Modern World. 2: Historical Hellenism, 23 April 1953. (Home Service)
Hellenism and the Modern World. 3: The Logos, 30 April 1953. (Home Service)
Hellenism and the Modern World. 4: Civilization Wrecked by War, 7 May 1953. (Home Service)
Hellenism and the Modern World. 5: The Hellenistic Age, 14 May 1953. (Home Service)

Hellenism and the Modern World. 6: Hellene and Barbarian, 21 May 1953. (Home Service)
The Author of The Golden Bough, 7 January 1954. (Third Programme)
I Remember, 25 February 1954. (Home Service)
I Remember: Glasgow University in the 1890s, 4 March 1954. (Home Service)
I Remember: Friendship at Cambridge, 11 March 1954. (Home Service)
I Remember: Famous Americans and a Governor of Papua, 18 March 1954. (Home Service)
I Remember: General Smuts and Dr Nansen, 1 April 1954. (Home Service)
I Remember: An International Committee and Refugees, 15 April 1954. (Home Service)
Foundations of Western Values: Truth the Sovereign Virtue, 26 May 1955. (Home Service)
Memories of the Peace Movement, 6 October 1955. (Home Service)
The Unfinished Battle, 5 January 1956. (Home Service)
Menander: Inventor of Modern Comedy, 12 July 1956. (Third Programme)
Thoughts on Refugees, 18 October 1956. (Home Service)
A Future Home for Civilization, 8 August 1956. (Pacific Service)

Appendix 4

Murray recordings held at the British Library Sound Archive

The dates given beside some recordings here do not correspond to the dates given in Appendices 1 and 2. This is because the British Library and/or the BBC have given, in some cases, the date of the repeat of the original broadcast.

Lecture on Prometheus (1934) AA 631.
As I See It (1937) LP2SS17.
Rape of the Locks (1942) T28077.
Why Do We Enjoy Poetry? (1943) 6363–5.
Brains Trust (1945) LP 25890.
Hippolytus (1945) T28114.

Trojan Women (1946) LP25695-7.
Homer (1947) X11688.
How it Looks to a Victorian (1947) X111301-2.
The Frogs (1947) LP26050-l.
The Mind of Man (1948) 11894-6.
Electra, a Play by Euripides (1948) 0X11258-64.
The Right Thing to Do (1948) X12610.
London Forum (1949) X13926.
Antigone (1950) 15796–7.
The Experience of Age (1952) X18629-30.
The Hellenistic Age (1953) LP24247.
As I Remember (1954) 20365-6.
Gandhi (1954) LP24555.
Glasgow University (1954) 20305–6.
The Peace Movement (1955) LP23291.
Asquith (1956) LP23265.
In Twain Shall Meet—Radio Biography of Sir F. Younghusband (1956) LP23342.
The Unfinished Battle (1955) LP 22809.

15

'Yours Obediently, Gilbert Murray': Letters to *The Times*

William Bruneau and Russell Wodell

Gilbert Murray wrote or co-signed almost three hundred letters to the Editor of *The Times*.[1] His topics ranged from Liberal politics and the League of Nations to reform of the national diet, simplification of English spelling, humane treatment of animals, and the banning of smoking in cinemas. Our excerpts from this formidable corpus can only suggest the range of Murray's epistolary art, force of argument, ready literary technique, and dry wit. To encourage reassessment of Murray as writer-activist, we offer letters illustrating Murray's hard-won eminence as professor, writer, Hellenist, politician, and citizen.

Not known for its sympathy to liberal-humanist causes or to upper-case Liberalism, *The Times* mattered to Murray because its readers numbered among them the great and, sometimes, the good.[2] From the beginning his epistolary strategy was to keep his rhetoric understated and unostentatious. Making no secret of his political outlook and credentials, he argued his views with due respect to

[1] A record we believe exceeded only by the indefatigable George Bernard Shaw.

[2] 'Editors of *The Times* (1788?–2002)', *Oxford Dictionary of National Biography* [*ODNB*], online edition, Oxford University Press, May 2005; online edn., Jan 2006 [http://www.oxforddnb.com/view/themes/93184, accessed 6 April 2006]. For convenient and balanced assessments of the twentieth-century readership of *The Times*, see *ODNB* articles on particular editors during Murray's adult lifetime: G. E. Buckle (editor 1884–1912), Geoffrey Dawson (1912–19 and 1922–41), H. Wickham Steed (1919–22), R. M. Barrington-Ward (1941–8), W. F. Casey (1948–52), and W. J. Haley (1952–67). Peter Dawson's article on Geoffrey Dawson, with its bibliography and source list, is especially relevant here.

evidence, adding sufficient drollery to attract unsympathetic readers. This combination of cultural and political *savoir faire* enabled Murray to make complex points in the space of a few column-inches—any editor's dream. In politics as in literature, it is best to transmit one's message in the shortest possible time.

Certainly Murray's humour and rhetorical force gave his letters and reported speeches a tone and an argumentative force that *Times* readers expected to see. Murray thus joined an elect company of regular correspondents—Bishop Gore, Sir Edward Grey, G. B. Shaw, and Bertrand Russell. Consider Murray's letter of 4 May 1939 (included below) on Neville Chamberlain's unhappy government, and the Prime Minister's errors in public life and in the House:

> The common toad under the harrow is, I believe, silent. Doubtless its feelings are obvious and no verbal comment would make them clearer. But a human toad may be allowed certain privileges, and would, if permitted, say something like this . . .

The self-deprecating humour and the rhetorical strategy were typical. Murray often as not began his letters with an unexpected and distant analogy. His speeches and lectures relied on the same strategy, moving slowly through metaphors and similes—one or two to a page, putting readers at ease, persuading them to suspend judgement. Then came the decisive thrust. It worked every time.

His writing was deliberate, even sly. In a letter we have not included, on the necessity of a National Government to deal with the problems of the Great Depression of the 1930s, Murray pleaded for expert opinion as opposed to political posturing—fighting, as usual, against extremism, whether of the right or the left. Ramsay MacDonald and Stanley Baldwin, at the King's urging, agreed in 1931 to form a temporary National Government to get the country through the great political and economic crisis of the moment. One Labour candidate of that government was George Lansbury, by now Commissioner of Works, and a strong proponent of workers' rights. Here is Murray speaking of the forthcoming election of 27 October 1931:

> But if I am asked at the Election to put the country at the mercy of an unchecked Tory majority or else of Mr. Lansbury, I feel just like Fair Rosamond at Woodstock. (*The Times*, 2 Oct. 1931, 14e)

Murray trusted his readers to recall Queen Eleanor's legendary offer to her husband's mistress Rosamond: the choice between suicide by a chalice of poison or a dagger, an offer decidedly not to be refused. The opening analogy, the closing thrust, the historical-literary reference—all were vintage Murray.

One of the difficulties in excerpting Murray's *Times* correspondence is that he more often than not joined debates-in-progress, announcing his own views as a common-sense alternative to previous arguments. He was unfailingly polite to those whose rhetoric he swiftly demolished; only occasionally did he express impatience with those on the extreme Right ('The only difficulty in answering Sir Alexander Gordon is the difficulty of knowing where to begin. He seems to be living in another world') or the extreme Left ('I am ashamed to ask for more of your valuable space for answering my Communist critics, but it might do harm to leave Mr. Rothstein altogether unanswered').

From the very start of his *Times* letter-writing, Murray left few doubts about his outlook. He opposed British involvement in the Boer War and the worst features of Imperial immigration and economic policy, yet held that a Just War was possible.[3] Even so, Murray's positions were not entirely consistent. He faithfully recommended free trade, even when that policy threatened—in 1903—to split the Liberal Party. On the other hand he felt nothing less than horror at the spectacle of indentured Chinese workers on the South African Rand after 1904—although industrialists thought free trade should include a 'trade' in Chinese workers. In Murray's defence, he thought a proper and adequate understanding of freedom could mean only that Chinese workers would be released, while the world economy grew unfettered and untariffed.

Murray changed his mind on occasion, most importantly on the rightness of British policy in the Great War. Still, he was consistent on principles and purposes. His friends and colleagues knew what Murray was likely to say about Greek literary history, about British foreign policy, about women's rights, about temperance, or about the basis of good physical health. Murray might surprise readers with

[3] On Murray's attitude to the Boer War, see D. Wilson 1987, 70–4; on 'Just War', see Murray 1917a, 20–45.

an unexpected rhetorical flourish, or a factual discovery, but his ethics and politics in 1956 were recognizably what they had been in 1896. Throughout his life and in changing political circumstances, Murray's orientation was unwaveringly utilitarian and liberal.[4]

He steadfastly espoused partisan Liberal views, particularly as they fell into disfavour after 1919.[5] Murray found political friends and accomplices in the 1920s, 1930s, and 1940s despite the decline of the Liberal Party. He was fond of asserting, perhaps with tongue in cheek, that upper-case Liberalism was nearly indistinguishable from its lower-case philosophical cousin.

In fact Murray's name first appeared in *The Times* not at the end of a letter, but in a friendly review of his *History of Ancient Greek Literature* (1897). The anonymous assessor applauded Murray's understanding of who (or what) Homer was, and congratulated him on a book that proved Greek and Latin classics 'had not lost their hold upon the modern world'.[6]

His early *Times* letters on education concerned the teaching of Classics, as one might expect of a Regius Professor of Greek. Yet increasingly, and particularly after the Great War, Murray proposed broad civic and historical education for as many children as possible.

[4] Murray repeatedly declared himself a utilitarian and a humanist, but most explicitly in his correspondence with Bertrand Russell. On these matters, see esp. Russell to Murray, 3 April 1902, Bertrand Russell Archives, McMaster University, Hamilton, Ontario, RA 3 071:

'Our differences seem to spring from the fact that you are a ulititarian, whereas I judge pleasure & pain to be of small importance compared to knowledge, the appreciation & contemplation of beauty, & a certain intrinsic excellence of mind which, apart from its practical effects, appears to me to deserve the name of virtue.'

And Murray's reply to Russell, 5 Apr. 1902, RA 1 710.053451:

'As to Utilitarianism, I think its great strength is that (1) it is nearly the truth, and generally accepted as such; (2) it provides a fairly intelligible basis of discussion. People who differ in their moral intuitions are mostly—though I admit not always—at a deadlock, unless they can agree to argue from the Utilitarian point of view—i.e. considering what the result of the two courses of action is likely to be, and whether they will, on the whole, LIKE one better than the other. (Those capitals are an accident; but I welcome them. The word 'like' is of the essence of the matter.)'

[5] For a brief and telling discussion of the decline of the British Liberal Party, see Russell 1999, esp. 7–11.

[6] 'Murray's Greek Literature', *The Times* (19 Mar. 1897), 13a. The author of the review was Thomas Humphry Ward (1845–1926), a special and leader writer for *The Times* from 1880 until his death.

After the 1918 Education Act, and especially in the difficult years of government cut-backs in education and health funding, Murray changed emphasis. He favoured after 1925 the extension and the 'intellectual enrichment' of *state* schooling, not just the democratization of private schooling.

Murray's letters to *The Times* eventually included nearly thirty on the problem of Greek at Oxford and in the schools—whether undergraduates should have Greek before admission; whether Greek literature should anchor the undergraduate curriculum; whether and how schoolgirls and schoolboys could be drawn to Greek and Latin; on Greek admission requirements at Oxford; on the value of classical literature in translation in a liberal education; and on the study of Greek religion and Greek social history using the methods of archaeology, philology, and even physics. Greek poetry, drama, and philosophy threw light on the motives of human action in all times and all places. Greek studies must, then, be present in schools, universities, and everyday life. Their good effects on reasoning and character meant that Greek studies, and the study of Hellenist thought and literature, deserved a central role in education.

We represent this ongoing concern with the full text of Murray's (uncharacteristically long) 1910 letter on compulsory Greek, arguing a position from which he later deviated only slightly. Another dozen letters not included here offer detailed arguments against those who favoured retention of nineteenth-century admissions policy, and those who opposed any compulsion whatsoever, in any subjects whatsoever, at universities ancient or modern.

Murray's maturing view of ancient Greek literature and religion illustrates his willingness to reconsider points of detail while maintaining basic hypotheses. Taking into account the discoveries of Greek archaeology, and the arguments of colleagues in England and the continent, Murray eventually concluded that Greek religion had passed through five, rather than four, stages of development.[7]

Similarly, his commitment to women's rights took new forms once universal suffrage was established in the United Kingdom. Murray had opposed the suffragette political strategy but always supported

[7] Cf. Robinson 2002, 161–83, 246–7. Harrison and Murray had a long, if fraught, professional friendship in which Harrison's lengthy researches on Greek religion played a great part.

women's rights, particularly in his own sphere of higher education. He welcomed the 1918 Reform Act, and its grant of voting rights to women aged over thirty, but was, of course, satisfied only in 1928 when that right was extended to all adults from the age of majority. Murray's attention moved in the 1920s to family welfare and social policy, and to the creation of institutions to ensure women's equality as a practical rather than a theoretical achievement.

As in his published lectures and books, discussions of a central theme typically led Murray to a type of logical dissection learned from such friends as Bertrand Russell. He offered clarification, examples *per contrarium*, comparisons with neighbouring concepts, exemplary or opponent cases, and, sometimes, extended logical claims. In this sense his letters were as philosophical as they were political or educational. We provide two delightful letters from 1954, an amusing exchange with Mr S. Naish, in which Murray recalls Professor Jebb's famous comment on hypotheses (see p. 347).

Each new letter gave Murray a chance to try his rhythm and balance in prose, to show his fondness for metaphor, and to display vocabulary that recalled his long career as translator of Greek drama. For any reassessment of Murray, the letters stand as evidence of his powers as a practical logician *and* a prose stylist.

Our selection points directly to Murray's moral principles and practice. Although he accepted the doctrine of Just War, Murray's opposition to wars of aggression was consistent. His vegetarianism and teetotalism, his multifarious acts of charity, and his life as parent and grandparent are of a piece: Murray was a kindly and, so far as an outsider can tell, a fair man. His was a practical ethic, as shown by his 1955 letter about Princess Margaret, who, Murray thought, had been unjustly treated in the press over her unhappy romantic attachment to the divorced Captain Peter Townsend.

Murray's very first letter to *The Times* was an anxious comment on the Russian government's treatment of the prisoner Nicholas Tchaikovsky (15 May 1908). Prisoners and refugees appeared and reappeared through Murray's letters of the 1930s and 1940s (particularly those concerned with refugees from Germany, Spain, and Italy, and, after 1945, with the forced relocation of starving Europeans). If Murray's ethics of fairness were those of a life-long liberal, his practices were those of a person with considerable bureaucratic *savoir faire.*[8] In Murray's view, ethics and politics were of a piece. Energetic voluntarism in national and international associations was far more than an avocation: it was a duty. His work in public associations—for improved teaching of the Classics, for women's political rights, or for justice in the world, to name but three—was Murray's way of being fair and equitable. He hoped and expected to change the world thereby. Whether or not he succeeded, however effective he may have been, Murray could always truthfully say that he had *lived* fairly and equitably.

Murray's goals were not, of course, all high-flown. Where he thought he might save a life or remedy poverty and hunger directly, by raising awareness through *The Times*, he did so. Where he found it best to achieve these things through endlessly bureaucratic work, chiefly in the League, again he did so. (Criticism of Murray as a generally ineffectual agent of change was to be expected, and he indeed received his share. During much of his life Murray was seen as a prophet of lost causes, and not a terribly effective one at that. The clear-sightedness of many of his directly political letters may help to rehabilitate his reputation in this regard.)

Murray's many arguments against arbitrary state power show an impressive grasp of modern European history. His inclination was always to ask large (possibly over-large) questions about liberty, power, human rights, and causal relations in history. Murray worries—about war, social unrest, 'world systems' and, above all, the conditions that permit these miseries in the first place. A long sequence of letters to *The Times* dealt with the causes of the Great War, and with ways of persuading League of Nations members to give up their rivalries and mutual suspicions. In a still broader sense, the letters sustained Murray's claim that a practical ethic was essential for world peace. In an intriguing and prescient letter (his 1933 letter on 'Bombing from the Air'), Murray applied

[8] Murray was responsible for much day-to-day work in the League of Nations Association through several decades, and acted as chair and secretary of the League's Committee for Intellectual Cooperation in the 1920s and 1930s. These administrative tasks required Murray to calm the egotistical fantasies of well-known British and continental figures, people whose real intellectual capacities were not always self-evident. On this aspect of Murray's work, see de Madariaga 1960, but especially 183–5.

these high-minded worries to practical ends. On 10 November 1932, Stanley Baldwin as Lord President of the Council told the House of Commons that 'the bomber will always get through'. Murray's letter was intended to keep the debate about armament on an even keel, and to restrain warmongers (Lord Winterton among them, as this letter reveals). On another hand, Murray wrote relatively little about appeasement and rearmament, hoping against hope that the League might yet guarantee the peace of nations.

In all but two cases, we have selected letters by Murray alone, not by Murray with others. It is well to remind those who look for him in *The Times* that Murray co-signed over 100 collective letters (many of which we suspect he wrote). These contain important evidence of liberal opinion and liberal networks in Britain from 1908 through 1956. They begin with a circular against Britain's prosecution of the Boer War,[9] signed by a galaxy of turn-of-the-century liberals (and often Liberals). In a 1907 letter, Murray joined sixty-eight other playwrights in a sharp rebuke to official censorship. Both letters affirmed the crucial value of civil liberty in peace and in war. The collective letters on censorship, the condition of prisoners of war and prisoners of conscience in both world wars, and the exact legal status of the Covenant of the League—all are valuable guides to much twentieth-century history.

Our selection will succeed best if it leads readers to return to the whole body of Murray's writing, and to the causes to which he devoted much of his life. We had no room for important letters on Murray's pleas for civic education in primary and secondary schools, including training in international affairs, explicit education about the aims of the League and of the UN, and the like. Murray's letters on education, the theatre, publishing and literature, all deserve a place in print, and one day, we hope, shall have it.

Despite his 'dated' politics (his own word), Murray by 1956 had earned his reputation as a fluent speaker and writer, and wide recognition and respect for his work in support of the League of Nations

[9] *The Times* (26 Mar. 1900). Signatories included Arthur Sidgwick, brother of the moral philosopher Henry Sidgwick—and among twenty-one others, Alexander Bain, Herbert Spencer, and James Murray, lexicographer and first begetter of the *Oxford English Dictionary*.

and its successor the United Nations. His letters to *The Times* amount to a long, variegated essay on the values of peace, civility, humane utilitarianism, individualism in ethics and politics, and renewed Hellenism in the twentieth century. An annotated edition of his *Times* correspondence would provide a valuable cross-section of reformist and internationalist British political thought in the first half of the twentieth century.

* * *

M. Tchaikovsky's Imprisonment, 15 May 1908

Sir,

In December last many persons in England received with a painful shock the news that M. Nicholas Tchaikovsky,[10] a man known and greatly respected by thousands in this country, had been seized by the Russian secret police and imprisoned in the fortress of St. Peter and St. Paul. The ground of his arrest is still unknown. He had escaped from Russia as a suspect in 1873, but that incident was presumably cancelled by the amnesty of November 2, 1905, especially as the original charge against him had no relation to crime, but only to liberal propaganda.

Two petitions, one drawn up in America and one in England, were addressed to the Russian Government, and signed by a most striking number of distinguished people of all shades of political opinion. The English petition pointed out that 'the fate of such a man as M. Tchaikovsky could not be a matter of indifference in the countries in which he was well known'; and 'ventured at least to hope that his treatment might be regulated with consideration for his age, indifferent health, and liability to recurrent attacks of malaria'. The American petition also specially begged that a charge might be formulated against him. Favourable answers were returned to both petitions, and M. Stolypin[11] definitely promised, in answer to the

[10] Nicholas Tchaikovsky was loosely identified with the Populist Socialist grouping in the Russian parliament before the climactic Bolshevist takeover of November 1917.

[11] Pyotr Arkadyevich Stolypin (1862–1911) was Nicholas II's Chairman of the Council of Ministers (Prime Minister), 1906–11. Stolypin launched heavy-handed

Americans, that he 'would personally interest himself in the case and would expedite the trial, which should be before an open and competent court'.

From the information which I receive, no word of this promise has been carried into effect. There has been no trial. This distinguished man of science, who has lived peaceably in England and America for the best part of 30 years, and whose family are British subjects, is being left to rot, unaccused, in prison.

Of course, Mr. Stolypin is, in a sense, fighting for his life, and is, therefore, bound to be rough in his methods. It would be absurd to demand from him the same liberal and scrupulous administration of justice which is possible in countries not threatened by revolution. But it is not too much to ask, in a case which has aroused such strong interest both in England and in America, that he should remember his promise, and direct that this particular prisoner should be granted a trial, or else a release. There seems to be no case for any action, however friendly or informal, on the part of the Foreign Office, and I consequently venture to ask for the hospitality of your columns.

Compulsory Greek, 7 March 1910

Sir,

The name of this humble contributor has continued for weeks to flame at the head of your columns in connexion with 'compulsory Greek', although he himself has taken but slight part in the controversy. He does not complain. He began it by reviewing Mr. Snow's book;[12] and he only mentions the point now as a sort of apology for plunging once more into the fray. The cause of this particular plunge

attacks on revolutionary groups while in office. He tried also to save the Tsarist regime by legislation to allow peasants to secure plots of land as freehold. The 1911 assassination was controversial then, as it is now. Was Stolypin shot by a Social Revolutionary party member or by a double agent working for the Okhrana, the Tsarist secret police?

[12] Snow 1910; Gilbert Murray's review was in *The Times* (4 Feb. 1910), 8a. T. C. Snow had been Murray's tutor at St John's College, and had recommended Murray for his Glasgow professorship (1889–99). On Snow as Murray's tutor, see D. Wilson 1987, 18–19, 53.

is the Rector of Exeter[13] and his repeated back-slidings. He began by pleading eloquently for exemptions from Greek in the entrance examination, and Professor Turner[14] and I agreed with him. In his next two letters he slipped into advocating the entire abolition of Greek in that examination. He now proceeds to language of alarming vagueness and even of denunciation; the 'so-called friends of Greek' remind him of Mr. Asquith's Cabinet. What language to apply to a set of quiet and God-fearing teachers!

However, I can bear these hard words. But I wish to point out two things. First, the Rector, who apparently speaks for some influential party in Council,[15] is no longer considering hard cases or the relief of special classes. He is proposing to alter the whole character of Oxford and assimilate it educationally to the 16 modern Universities. Secondly, I feel in all his argument a kind of intangible misconception or false implication, which seems to show that he has not understood what his opponents are arguing about. I am not a partisan. I am anxious to listen to every argument and consider every interest before adopting an attitude of definite opposition to the proposals of Council. But I must state frankly that unless the Rector will make more of an effort to understand the attitude of us younger 'friends of Greek', he will find great difficulty in carrying with him even those of us who are closest to his views.

I will begin by stating, without prejudice to future reconsideration, that sort of entrance examination that I should like. It would be generally like Mr. Godley's;[16] I certainly do not want Latin prose in

13 The Rev. William Walrond Jackson (1838–1931), Rector of Exeter College, Oxford.

14 Herbert Hall Turner (1861–1930), astronomer and seismologist. He became Professor of Astronomy at Oxford in 1893. According to the *Oxford Dictionary of National Biography*, he was literally done in by university politics: 'Turner entered fully into the life of New College, but was blind to the necessity of making his case carefully in the university... The combination of overwork, vituperative personal attacks by Lindemann, his budget in the red, and his observatory once more a pawn in university politics overwhelmed him, and may have contributed to the stroke he suffered shortly afterwards.'

15 Oxford University's Hebdomadal Council, which represented college heads, professors, and tutors.

16 Alfred Denis Godley (1856–1925), classical scholar and tutor at Magdalen College; elected public orator of Oxford in 1910. Murray is referring to Godley's letters to *The Times* of 16 Feb. 1910, 6f, and 3 Mar. 1910, 12a.

it, and I certainly do want some Greek and some elementary science, as—almost—'indispensable constituents of the highest and most truly liberal education'. I only differ from Mr. Snow and Mr. Godley in adding the word 'almost'. When once the University, in the interests of what it believes to be the highest education, has laid down its list of subjects to be normally required, I am ready to consider claims for special exemption quite liberally as they occur. These exemptions should apply not to Greek only, but to every single subject. I know scores of clever men who have a sort of congenital inability to do mathematics. Well, let them off mathematics, on condition that they give proof of real ability by taking some other subject on a definitely higher standard. And do the same for Greek, for Latin, and even for English. Many very good students in science and mathematics have extreme difficulty in writing a passable English composition. (This is no scoff at science. It is no whit more discreditable for a scientific man to be unable to write English than it was, say, for Ruskin not to be able to understand what was meant by a logarithm.)

What I complain of is that Greek is singled out alone for attack. The odious word 'compulsory' is attached to Greek alone among all the 'compulsory' subjects. It alone is to be made optional, while the compulsion is kept up in the other cases. This is not an honest demand for freedom—it is a mere onslaught upon Greek. And if we ask for the reasons why Greek should be thus attacked, we find that they are purely commercial or conventional. The other subjects have financial pressure behind them or are connected with strong vested interests. Greek has little to recommend it except its intellectual and educational qualities. That is why we are asked to single it out and throw it as a prey to the Philistine.

There is another point on which I should like to reason with the Rector, or rather with those outside Oxford who are listening to his persuasions. I can understand the wish to destroy the whole system of classical education in England. Classical education has been in many ways narrow, oppressive—even obscurantist. Still, on the whole, for reasons that need not be detailed here, I wish to keep it. But if we are to keep classical education, it seems to me mere folly to attempt to keep it by insisting on Latin (and Latin composition, too) while dropping Greek. First, you cannot understand Latin literature without knowing Greek. Secondly, the things for which most scholars chiefly read the

Classics are in Greek and not in Latin. In trying to be brief I may be unjust to Latin literature, of which I am very fond. But, to put the matter shortly, Greek poetry and philosophy and historiography are still alive; as a great English scholar wrote to me the other day, 'they affect what one is going to say and think to-morrow'. That is not true, or is very much less true, of Latin. If you lighten your classical course by leaving out Greek, you will find that you have left out nearly everything that makes a classical course, with all its labour, worth pursuing.

Here I shall be met by the pedagogic argument, 'Latin prose is a better mental gymnastic than the translation of a Greek play. Its hardness is its value.' First, I doubt the accuracy of that statement in itself. But, more important, I believe that classical education has been greatly damaged by too much pedagogy. Grammar is good, but we have had too much of it. We want less of Dr. Syntax and more of Milton and Shelley and Browning—considering those great men for the moment as Greek scholars, not merely as poets or supporters of Mr. Asquith.

Next comes the cynical argument. A weary schoolmaster will tell you, 'Boys do not care for literature. You will never get your passmen intelligently interested in a Greek play.' If you wait a moment he may add: 'I am not even interested in it myself.' I venture to reply that in this argument everything depends on the last sentence. I certainly know many masters in public schools who would strongly deny that boys were normally incapable of enjoying Greek plays. And I know that their pupils would bear them out enthusiastically. I have myself taught the elementary stages of Greek to some thousands of students in classes both small and large, and I believe it is mere nonsense, either wilful cynicism or else a confession of incompetence, to pretend that young students in the early stages of Greek cannot get literary enjoyment out of Homer or Herodotus, or a Greek tragedy or comedy. I find, on the whole, that, if not overworked, they are eager for the literature—that is, for the real essence of the book they read; and they continue to be so until we choke them with our pedagogy.

As to Mr. Godley's proposal for a compulsory science paper, I am relieved to find that all the Rector has to say against it is that it is 'illusory and impracticable'. If that is all, we may feel fairly hopeful about it. Most good proposals begin in that condition. But the reason why I mention the subject is not that. It is that the Rector seems quite to misunderstand Mr. Godley's intention. For my own part, at any rate, I do not advocate a science paper as a kind of compliment to sooth the science professors. I advocate it because I want it. I think that a complete lack of scientific knowledge is a dreadful flaw in education. A man who knows no science at all is debarred from understanding the movement of the age he lives in and, so far, is not, in the normal sense of the word, an educated man.

Mr. Godley is pleasantly attacked by my redoubtable ally, Professor Turner, because, in making a list of the great Oxford men of the 18th century, he left out the names of Halley and Bradley. Very bad of him. And, unless this comet had opportunely warned me, I should probably have done the same.[17] That is one of the reasons why Mr. Godley and I feel that we ought to have had some little training in science when we were younger and had the time for it.

I have run to great lengths, I fear, and have perhaps spoken somewhat cavalierly of various subjects for which I really have a great respect—such as Latin prose, grammar, pedagogy, and the claims of the honest Philistine. I am sorry for this; and I will gladly state a case for all of them when they do not come into conflict with what I regard as a higher interest.

Viscount Grey's Speech, 26 October 1916

Sir,

May an ordinary British citizen be allowed to express in your columns the profound sense of relief and encouragement with which he has read the speech of Viscount Grey to the representatives of the foreign Press?

One of the hardest things to bear in a long war like the present is the gradual forgetting of the cause in the mere struggle. We grow so absorbed in the business of fighting that we cease to remember what

[17] Halley's Comet appeared in 1910, but did not transit the sun until 19 May. Murray may be thinking of the Great Daylight Comet, much brighter than Comet Halley but often confused with it, which had appeared in the middle of January. Murray's error, ironically, confirms his point.

we are fighting for. Men's nerves, especially if they are not actively at work, grow jaded or irritable, and according to their various natures they relapse into dreamy and self-deluding pacifism or into the self-indulgence of mere prejudice and pugnacity.

I believe that the average Englishman, consciously or unconsciously, has always in his mind some such thought as this: 'You ask me to go on facing death, or facing my children's death; you ask us collectively to endure more and more, to give more and more of all that is dear to us; and we are ready both to endure and to give. Of course we will go on. We have no faintest temptation anywhere to refuse the last sacrifice that is needed for victory. Only, for Heaven's sake, in mercy to the dying and respect for the dead, do not lower or forget the cause for which we are giving it!'

The Prime Minister and others have stated our cause as well as it can be stated. Mr. Lloyd George has made the country ring with his great appeals. But no one except the Foreign Secretary was in the position to give us a speech like that of Monday, going patiently and with absolute truthfulness over the whole ground, showing again exactly why we were compelled in honour to declare war and are now compelled to continue it; how we entered the lists as the champions of all national safety and freedom, and can appeal to the brotherhood of civilized mankind to support us simply because we are fighting for the right and not for conquest. This seems to me to be just what the country at his moment needed to hear again; and I think I know of more than one young soldier who will go back to France with a higher heart and more serene spirit because of it.

I write only of the effect of the speech among ourselves. But there are thousands of well-disposed neutrals in America and Scandinavia who will read with keen appreciation Viscount Grey's words of welcome to the proposed League to Enforce Peace, and, one may hope, be led seriously to search their hearts on the one point of difficulty which he puts to them. Can they make sure that the temper of their own countries can be raised to the point of undertaking the full responsibility which the formation of such a league involves? This is for us the vital point to be faced. That the leaders of the movement have faced it no one who has personally talked with them can have any doubt; but it may need all their leadership to convert the mere generous impulses of a good-natured majority into the practical policy of a nation. We can trust their power for compelling peace so vastly more if once we know that they are prepared, in the last resort, to fight for it.

Lord R. Cecil's Challenge—A Liberal Point of View, 26 April 1922

Sir,

May a firm Liberal, who has had the privilege of working in some intimacy with Lord Robert Cecil, add something to your comment on his remarkable manifesto?

I fully agree with you that the manifesto is not really a Centre Party document, but a Liberal document. It expresses, perhaps with new force and vitality, the doctrines in which I believe, and I am ready, without reservation, to vote or speak for Lord Robert as one of my leaders. Furthermore, I do not see how the writer can in the long run avoid cooperation with the Liberal Party.

Why, then, is he justified—as I think he is—in not forthwith calling himself a Liberal, and inviting his Unionist supporters to become Liberals with him? I think there are two reasons.

In certain conditions of a nation's history a particular form of policy, formerly disputed, becomes inevitable. It has to be followed, reluctantly or not, by the party that formerly opposed it. I think it will be found that in its main lines the Liberal policy, which in 1918 was denounced by the Prime Minister and under his influence overwhelmingly rejected by the electorate, has gradually proved to be right, and is being even now accepted as more or less inevitable. The result is that old Liberal speeches, like Mr. Asquith's Paisley policy,[18] or his denunciations, in the teeth of such obloquy, of the Irish reprisals, seem now to have had almost a prophetic quality. They have almost all 'come true'.

But the Liberals, like every beaten party, have an after-swell of unpopularity to contend with. Many people will agree point by point with all the Liberal programme who would indignantly repudiate it if

[18] Herbert Henry Asquith (1852–1928), formerly a distinguished Liberal Prime Minister and war leader, was elected to the Commons from the Paisley constituency

it came to them as a whole, labelled Liberal. And, from their point of view, they are right. Names have such wide and vague connotations. If they once accepted the name 'Liberal,' they might feel themselves committed to all sorts of unknown possibilities which they fear and dislike. If Lord Robert speaks to them without a label, they will at least listen, and I think that, point by point, they will agree.

My second observation is this: Lord Robert's policy, which I accept, has, after all, its Conservative side. One of the things most needed now in public policy is the restoration of orderly habits. I need not specify details, but the Government's handling of the coal crisis, of reparations, of Irish reprisals, and of Russia, to say nothing of the recent confusion at Genoa, supplies abundant illustration of the disastrous effects of slipshod, incorrect, and violent methods, of not playing according to the rule, or not taking the trouble to use the machine of government without sabotage. In these matters—and they are very important matters—we need Conservatism. We need a return to the old habits of upright and consistent negotiation, as practised by Gladstone and Peel, by Lord Salisbury and Lord Grey.

If I can draw any conclusion from public meetings in many parts of England, Lord Robert Cecil has now a position in politics of a quite exceptional kind. He has escaped the stains of the war; he has escaped the stains of the Coalition. He is known to be disinterested, he is felt to be wise, and people of all parties will listen with respect to what he says. I am told that he has little influence in the present House of Commons, and can well believe it. For that also is an asset in the country.

Bombing from the Air—Arguments for Total Abolition—British Interests, 7 June 1933

Sir,

The letter from Lord Winterton[19] and others in defence of the use of bombing aircraft for police purposes is clearly worthy of the most

in 1920. In 1925 he became Earl of Oxford and Asquith. Asquith tried in the early 1920s to recommend, or even to construct, a broad post-Liberal yet still Liberal political movement: he was unsuccessful.

[19] Edward Turnour, sixth Earl of Winterton, was in 1933 without government post but strongly agreed with Churchill's urging of a strong British defence policy. In 1938

careful consideration, and since the society of which I am chairman has taken throughout the country a strong line on the other side I should be grateful for an opportunity of explaining our position.

If I may speak for the League of Nations Union as a whole, we do not for a moment accuse the Air Force of 'inhumanity'; nor do we deny the extreme convenience, cheapness, and effectiveness, under present conditions, of the use of aircraft for police purposes on certain troubled frontiers. I do not even wish to press the consideration that perhaps, if the use of aircraft continues, it will not for very long be confined to one side. There are important nations who object strongly to the dominant position of Great Britain in Asia and who have plenty of aircraft and pilots to spare.

Our case is that the total abolition of bombing from the air is of such vital importance to the civilized world, and particularly to Great Britain, as to outweigh utterly a sacrifice of 'convenience, cheapness, and effectiveness' in Iraq or on the North-West Frontier. If bombing is abolished, Great Britain recovers her insular security; if bombing continues, our capital, our industrial centres, our shipping, and our food are exposed to sudden and devastating attack against which there is no effective protection. To maintain bombing for the sake of operations against the Pathans is to sacrifice the heart for the finger.

For consider what are the consequences of our present demand for the retention of bombing 'in certain regions'. We keep in existence a force of machines and skilled bombers, a training school, and arrangements for research into methods of making bombing more deadly; we maintain the whole system, as a legitimate method of war, to be developed further as need occurs. Furthermore, if Great Britain has savage frontiers, so have other countries. France, Italy, Holland, and Russia will keep their bombing establishments; and who can feel confident that, in some time of intense international suspicion and excitement, the bombing forces will not be transferred to Europe?

Apart from the special interests and perils of Great Britain, we should also remember that more than any other weapon the bombing aeroplane creates insecurity. No other weapon can cross frontiers and strike

he served briefly as deputy to the Secretary for Air, Lord Swinton. He was Conservative member for the Horsham division of Sussex 1905–1. See the collective letter 'Aircraft for Police Purposes', *The Times* (2 June 1933), 15f.

at the very heart of an enemy nation with such complete suddenness and surprise. If we keep alive the practice of bombing we make it almost impossible for Europe to attain the security which is its greatest need.

May I conclude by expressing my warm appreciation of your own leading article on the subject?

Abyssinia and Italy—The Covenant of the League, 23 May 1935

Sir,

I am one of those many millions who believed, and believe still, that, amid all sorts of confusions and inconsistencies, the World War was on our part essentially a fight for justice in international relations, as against naked Machtpolitik; an attempt, in Mr. Gladstone's words, to 'establish public right as the common law of Europe'. If the League of Nations stands, the War will have been justified, or at least compensated; if it comes to nothing, our whole action will have been a series of vain cruelties and blunders.

One cannot expect perfection from any human institution. I am not disposed to judge harshly the failure of the League to stop the Japanese aggression. It did try; it did make inquiries and pronounce judgment; but it could not impose its will or its sense of justice on a highly armed non-Christian people at the other end of the world.

But the action of Italy towards Abyssinia threatens us with a catastrophe of an utterly different kind. One member of the League is openly planning against another member, under the eyes of all Europe, aggression of the most extreme kind, and is claiming the right actually to prohibit any consideration of the matter by the League. If the League submits there is no law left between nations. The Covenant is gone. By Article XI:—

> Any war or threat of war is a matter of concern to the whole League ... which will take ... whatever action is deemed wise and effectual to safeguard the peace.

And no one denies the existence of a threat of war. By Articles XII to XV all members are bound to seek means of peaceful settlement for any dispute likely to lead to a rupture. Nay more, by Article X all members of the League are explicitly bound to respect and preserve against external aggression the territorial integrity and existing political independence of all members of the League.

I say nothing of the special treaties between Italy and Abyssinia or of the Kellogg Pact. My concern is with the Covenant of the League. I do not see what will be left of the Covenant, or what will remain to show that the Great War was anything but a battle of the kites and crows, if Signor Mussolini is allowed to set his will above the law and make war as if no League existed. Who will dare to speak of 'cooperation to achieve international peace' or 'the prescription of open just and honourable relations between nations'?

For those, if there are such persons in this country, who care nothing for what they call 'ideal arguments', but think only in terms of immediate national convenience, I would suggest two other considerations. The nations of Europe are engaged at this moment in building a system of security based on a series of pacts of mutual assistance. Who will trust those pacts, who will trouble to fulfil them, if the Great Powers show at the very outset that they regard all such obligations as minor matters compared with the wishes of any one Great Power? What degree of trust will nations like Turkey or Persia, or the lesser States of Europe, put in the League? What will be the future value in foreign exchange of the word of Great Britain or France?

And will it look well, so soon after the Council's solemn condemnation of Germany for a breach of treaty for which, as your columns have shown, there were at least some extenuating circumstances, to condone and commit a far more flagrant breach of treaty for which no casuist has yet invented a shade of justification?

What the world wants is to be sure that the members of the League mean to keep their Covenant. Then at last we shall have security—and also self-respect.

'Sanctions', 13 July 1936

Sir,

The essence of sanctions in the Covenant is simply a refusal by loyal members of the League to cooperate in a criminal undertaking. Do those of your correspondents who write so glibly about the abolition of sanctions really wish the Assembly of the League to say to a war-maker in the same breath:—

> You are committing a crime against God and man. We condemn your action; and now, what can we sell you to help in making it a success? Arms, oil, ships, money: they are all at your disposal.

If they do not mean this, what do they mean?

Government and Public Opinion—Mr. Chamberlain's Critics, 4 March 1939

Sir,

The common toad under the harrow is, I believe, silent. Doubtless its feelings are obvious and no verbal comment would make them clearer. But a human toad may be allowed certain privileges, and would, if permitted, say something like this:—

I take it as fairly certain that the Conservatives will remain in office for the rest of my life. Their political machine is still whole; the other two are broken; and even if much more than half the country were against the Government it would still be sure of thumping majorities in the House of Commons. In critical times like these that is a dangerous situation. Unless it is very wise, such a Government will mistake its Parliamentary majorities for an expression of the national will, and forget that it needs the allegiance of a united nation.

Now the Baldwin Government, though open in my opinion to much criticism, did not make this fundamental mistake. They tried to be 'National'; they were at least Conservative in the best sense of that much-abused word. They believed in the generous and kindly traditions of the British people and its concern for moral ideals.

That is what seems to have gone. I can never remember a time when the nation was so bitterly divided, and a large minority at any rate so full of an almost savage mistrust of the real aims of the Prime Minister. No doubt they are unreasonable. But, to take one instance, anyone who is familiar with the Youth Movements will have observed on the one hand their eager readiness for public service and self-sacrifice, and on the other hand their intense reluctance to put their lives at the disposal of a Government whose whole aims and purposes they regard with extreme—and no doubt unjustified—suspicion. It is not enough to say that these young people are unreasonable. It is not enough for a Government in times like these to confute the Opposition by smart party speeches and vote them down triumphantly in the House. It must possess or regain the general confidence of the nation.

Though confessedly an old Liberal I am almost entirely concerned with a cause which is above party, and I am clear that the bitterness of which I speak is not for the most part due to party spirit. There is no bitterness, there is general sympathy, towards the Government's activities in the Home Office, the Colonial Office, the Board of Education, and elsewhere. In foreign affairs, no doubt, there have been specially difficult problems and strong differences of opinion. But that is not the real cause of the trouble. It is that when a large part, and perhaps the most thoughtful part, of the nation is daily and hourly harassed by thoughts of the hideous suffering inflicted on millions of innocent human beings, and the monstrous crimes against humanity which are being daily perpetrated, and perpetrated with success, the Prime Minister somehow leaves the impression—no doubt an unjustified impression—of being entirely indifferent to such issues. His kind words are all for the oppressors; his unkind words for the sufferers. His words of comfort are devoted to showing how this country can, after all, make money out of the agonies of others. He seems to ignore completely that moral idealism which lies near the root of the British character, he pours contempt upon the League of Nations, and when people passionately protest in the streets against this attitude, he imagines—apparently he really does imagine—that they are Communists.

His answer to Mr. Attlee's attack in the House on Monday was both dignified and convincing. He is not a trickster, not a cynic, not a man utterly without heart. But why has he goaded not merely Mr. Attlee but millions of people throughout the country into imagining that he is? There must be some way in which the Government can convince us that it has some generous enthusiasm, that its policy has some moral basis, that it is not always ready to side with the strong against the weak and to radiate satisfaction over the calamities of the innocent. Lord Baldwin once admitted frankly that events in Abyssinia were to him 'a bitter humiliation,' and that one phrase took the sting out of opposition criticism. His sympathies were on the right side, and that made all the difference.

Alien Refugees—Discrimination in Interment—Friends and Enemies, 8 July 1940

Sir,

I had exactly the same experience as Mr. H. G. Wells. I also supported the naturalization of a German friend who had spent his early life combatting German militarism and had to fly, leaving almost all that he possessed, when the Nazis came into power. He has since then been trying in every way, by writing, lecturing, broadcasting, digging, or, best of all, fighting, to be allowed to help the Allied cause. All we have done is to intern him. However, I should not venture to ask for your space except that this case throws light on a wider danger.

Much of the deplorable mismanagement of the refugee questions is due to haste and lack of thought, which, however cruel in its results, may be excused in a nation faced by imminent and deadly peril. But it is partly due to a deeper cause, of which there were many signal instances in the last War: the tendency of wise and reasonable men to yield to public hysteria. There are now two dangerous cries: One is 'Intern all Germans', which is already taking the form 'Intern all foreigners'. This is the reaction of the average ignorant and unthinking man, who can see no difference between one German and another, or, if it comes to that, between one foreigner and another. Oppressor and victim, Fascist and anti-Fascist, are all the same to him. Another dangerous cry comes not from the ignorant man but from the strong party man, who, when things go wrong, wishes to find a scapegoat and fixes instinctively on his old political opponents. I am thinking particularly of the cry against Mr. Chamberlain and Lord Halifax, as 'crypto-fascists,' though there are many similar examples.

Surely our great asset in the eye of the world is not merely that we are fighting for a righteous case, but that we are a decent nation with a high standard of honour. We trust one another and keep our heads. We do not in misfortune cry out that we are betrayed. We do not allow cruelties to be done in our name towards those who are fled to us for protection. We do not become so blinded by the emotions of war as to be unable to distinguish between friends and enemies. I am not pleading for any slackening of precautions, but, if anything, for greater precautions. Let our rulers listen to every word which comes from Scotland Yard or the responsible Intelligence Services. If ever there are real differences in the Cabinet let the Prime Minister, in whom we all have confidence, deal with them as he thinks right. But I tremble for any democracy which yields either to party faction or to mob hysteria.

Too Many Germans in Italy—Mussolini's Method—An Anecdote of 1915

Sir,

Current events in Milan give some point to the following anecdote told to me by a French friend who was engaged in propaganda in Italy in 1915.

Early in that year he was visited by a young stranger, who gave his name as Benito Mussolini. 'Don't you think,' said the young man, 'that there are too many Tedeschi in Milan?' The Frenchman warmly agreed. 'Give me 100,000 francs and I will remove them.' 'How will you do that?' 'You will see.' The money was given.

Next morning every important German in Milan was wakened early by three or four young Italians armed with clubs; he was directed to dress quickly and hurry to his train; his luggage would be sent after him.

One recognizes the master's early manner in the treatment of a fine traditional subject. A pity he is no longer interested in it.

Electoral Reform, 16 February 1944

Sir,

May a member of the inarticulate public be allowed a word on the electoral question? It is a subject on which M.P.s of the two great parties have an interest which is not that of the nation. The position of the Labour Party is quite intelligible; some of their spokesmen have explained it. The mass of the nation is not Socialist but there is much resentment against the Conservatives who, with a minority in the country, have had an overwhelming majority in the

House for a long and unhappy period. The Labour Party may well win the election, form a Socialist Government, and be able to carry out a socialist revolution against the real wishes of the country. With Proportional Representation this could not be done.

It seems odd that the Conservatives should not wish to avert this danger. Apparently they calculate on raising such a scare against it that they will be able to raise another House of Commons majority from an unwilling country. It is, of course, to the interest of every candidate that his opponent should be as unattractive as possible. The Socialist naturally likes his rival to be a 'Blimp'; the Conservative likes his to be the sort to frighten the bourgeoisie. The helpless public, I venture to think, has largely lost enthusiasm for both the great parties. It would like, first, to have candidates who were prepared to work in a national Government much like the present but based on a more progressive House; secondly, to have many more members of the type generally returned by universities under P.R.... few of whom would ever be selected by a Labour or Conservative caucus.

The Liberal Party is no doubt just as capable of sin as the others, but in present circumstances it supports P.R. for very sound reasons; that it sees the grave dangers involved in the victory of either a revolutionary or a reactionary minority, and that it believes Liberal principles to be much needed in the post-war world.

Nuremberg—The Verdict of History—Victor and Vanquished, 2 May 1946

Sir,

Dr. C. K. Allen's[20] letter emboldens, nay, almost compels, me to utter one perfectly obvious thought which has caused me profound disquiet from the beginning.

[20] Carlton Kemp Allen (1887–1966), by 1946 secretary to the Rhodes Scholarship Trustees and Warden, Rhodes House, Oxford. Allen was a legal scholar of the first order, and had a good classical education. He wrote to *The Times* on the Nuremberg trials 26 Apr. 1946, 5f.

Granted that the trials are being conducted with the most scrupulous justice; granted further that since the acceptance by the League of Nations of the rule that 'aggressive war is a crime against the international community', certain actions not previously regarded as criminal may have become so; granted lastly that the monstrous and demoniac cruelties introduced into warfare by the Nazis must receive some definite world-wide condemnation; nevertheless how can it be just, or to future generations ever seem just, that after a war the victors, because they are victors, should judge the offences of the vanquished, and, merely because they are victors, escape all judgment themselves? Do we claim that no war crimes were committed by any member of the British, American, or Russian armies?

I doubt if these trials will produce in history that moral effect which is claimed to be their main justification. A soldier judged and hanged by his enemies is to his own people an object of sympathy rather than horror.

Delegates to U.N. Assembly, 12 November 1946

Sir,

Is it not strange that, at a time when social and philanthropic questions are notably important, the British delegation to the U.N. assembly contains no woman member? At the League assembly there were always women delegates, and I never heard any doubt expressed as to the value of their work, especially on the social and humanitarian side. The change cannot be due to any difference between the League and the U.N.; on the contrary, a declaration presented to the assembly in January, and moved by Mrs. Roosevelt, urged that 'women should occupy more important positions in the various delegations'. It cannot be due to any lack of competent women among the Government's supporters, nor surely to some new and unsuspected deduction from Socialist principles.

Why in the world has so reactionary a change been made?

Germany and Europe—Seeking a Middle Way, 22 August 1949

Sir,

The problem how we are to live with some 60m. Germans in a more or less United Europe is an extremely serious one, not to be solved by undue deference to German election cries, which presumably are subject to the same weaknesses as election cries elsewhere; and certainly not by the policy, favoured by Mr. de la Mahotière,[21] of keeping Germany permanently hostile and permanently beggared

In principle we had at the beginning of the occupation two fairly obvious tasks: to destroy our late enemy's war potential and to see that the people for whose government we had made ourselves responsible did not starve or sink into hopeless misery. The first task was plain and straightforward. We went on destroying Germany's industrial resources. We even at one time entertained the famous proposal to annihilate the whole of German industry and leave nothing but agriculture. (Presumably without such highly convertible instruments as ploughshares and reaping hooks.) But this policy made our second task unachievable and incidentally cost us £80m. a year or more.

Clearly some compromise combination is necessary. We cannot have Germany permanently a 'slum of misery'. We cannot have her so strongly armed as to be again a public danger. The obvious solution lies in making Germany a member of United Europe, contributing by her own prosperity to the prosperity of the whole, and at the same time surrounded by such strong and united forces as to make a revival of nationalistic war policies neither tempting nor practicable. I do not presume to make any detailed proposals. I have not enough knowledge. But the reports which I get from Germany indicate that, while a year or two ago

[21] Stuart R. de la Mahotière (1918–), commentator on European political economy, and in 1961 author of a popular guide to *The Common Market* (London: Hodder and Stoughton).

common opinion in Germany regarded war as inevitable, there is now, since the Atlantic Pact, a fairly general expectation of peace.

Impasse in Far East, 12 March 1953

Sir,

The letters of various eminent people on the Chinese problem leave me bewildered. How can any one think it 'right' or 'expedient' or remotely possible for a Government which is at war with the United Nations to have a seat on the Council of the U.N.? War cancels previous treaties.

Further, have we any reason to believe that China cares at all about a seat on the U.N. Council? Her purpose, clearly stated and confirmed by action, is to 'liberate Asia from the rule of the white man' by driving the Americans out of Korea, the British out of Malaya, and the French out of Cochin China.

In this policy she has a leading seat on a very great informal union of nations, consisting not only of Russia and her satellites but of almost all Asia. Even Mr. Nehru has said that 'the foot of a single European soldier in Asia is an insult to the whole continent.' Theoretic Communism is perhaps a secondary consideration, though I see from a letter from a Chinese woman student in a Hongkong paper that after liberating Korea she hopes to go on and liberate New York.

Hypotheses, 14 May 1954

Sir,

A Cambridge professor of logic, holding forth in an upper lecture room, made a remark which caused his audience to stamp their feet, and precipitated plaster in the room below. A classical lecturer underneath observed the ceiling and remarked, 'I see that Professor Blank's premises are not equal to his hypotheses.'

Your obedient servant,

S. Naish

The Oaks, Bosham, Sussex.

Hypotheses, 17 May 1954

Sir,

The historical and logical incident mentioned by Mr. Naish in his letter of May 14 occurred very close to me and I can report it in a more strictly accurate form. It occurred in Glasgow University, where the Professor of Logic and Rhetoric often gave full scope to the second of these subjects at the end of his lecture. The Greek classroom is underneath, and when I occupied it I was not allowed to forget Professor Jebb's[22] famous comment: 'I fear my premises will not support Professor Veitch's[23] conclusion.'

Princess Margaret, 28 October 1955

Sir,

Your leading article to-day states with scrupulous fairness and consideration one view of our beloved Princess's marriage to the man of her choice. Your arguments are all sound in themselves, but they are based on a principle that is surely open to question. It may be true that a large minority of the British people will not regard her proposed union as a marriage; but are we to accept, as a special rule for the Royal Family, that, when public opinion is divided, the more backward and timid opinion should, for safety's sake, always prevail over that of the ordinary educated man?

Out of Favour—to the Editor of *The Times*, 19 July 1956

Sir,

Many, many moons ago, it seems, a walking-stick was almost an essential part of an Englishman's walking out outfit. I often wonder

[22] Richard Claverhouse Jebb (1841–1905), Professor of Greek at Glasgow (1875–89) and Regius Professor of Greek at Cambridge (1889–1905). For the 'famous comment', see Jebb 1907, 190.

[23] John Veitch (1829–94), professor of logic in the University of St Andrews and of Glasgow. On the occasion in question, Veitch had concluded a session with a quotation

why this highly respectable attitude, which added dignity and bearing to one's stride, has gone out of favour.

I beg to remain, Sir, most sincerely,
GILBERT HAMMOND

43, Girlington Road, Bradford, 8.

This prompted many replies, among which was Murray's last published letter to The Times, *at age 90*:

28 July 1956

Sir,

Have your correspondents forgotten the solemn judgment of a Chinese sage upon the English, that even the best of them like to take a stick with them when they go for a walk? 'For what purpose except to beat the innocent?'

Yours, &c.,
GILBERT MURRAY

Yatscombe, Boar's Hill, Oxford.

from his own book on the Border Ballads. The traditional form of applause among Glasgow students was 'pedal approbation': stamping on the floor with their feet.

16

Gilbert Murray and Psychic Research

N. J. Lowe

> It is hard to see how language can originally have grown, or how an infant can learn it, or how we can ever, by means of language, understand a new idea, without telepathy. [...] The basis of this so-called telepathy is unconscious sense-perception, the sensory disturbance itself being too slight for consciousness, but the state of mind resulting from it being fully perceptible ... but we must be prepared for the possibility that this sense-perception is not confined to the canonical five channels of Sight, Sound, Smell, Taste, Touch. (Murray 1916, 61–2)

> The points on which I speak with some conviction are, first, that telepathic communication does take place, and secondly that as far as my own experience goes it seems to me to be a communication of feeling rather than of cognition, though the cognition may follow as the feeling is interpreted. (Murray 1952, 169)

Accounts of Gilbert Murray's life and work traditionally sideline his psychic activities, as indeed Murray himself largely tried to do. But the story is an important one; Murray was the most significant telepath of his age, amateur or professional, and his fifty years of so-called 'experiments'[1] were still being cited into the 1970s as the most important and compelling existing evidence for extra-sensory

[1] In chronological order, the principal discussions of Murray's 'experiments', with asterisks indicating primary publications of results, are: *Murray 1916; *Verrall 1916; *Sidgwick 1924; Thouless 1925; More 1925; Salter 1936; *Salter 1941; Murray 1952; Heywood 1971, 145–54; *Dodds 1972; *Dingwall 1973 (including the only published account of J. A. Hadfield's 1919 experiments with Murray); D. Wilson 1987, 273–82.

powers. Yet the material has not been seriously examined for over thirty years, during which time parapsychology has been subjected to new kinds of scrutiny that have affected the very nature of the field. It has had to respond to the renewed challenge to its credibility from the association with New Age movements; to the rise of sceptic organizations such as CSICOP, the Committee for the Scientific Investigation of the Claims of the Paranormal, in which stage magicians such as James Randi have been prominent in the exposure, and sometimes the deliberate perpetration, of scientific irregularities; and perhaps above all to the perception in the 1980s that the sceptics had effectively won the debate, with some prominent researchers publicly crossing the floor. The same period has also seen some groundbreaking work on the importance of psychic research as a chapter in long-Victorian intellectual history—although comparatively little has so far been said about the central role of classical scholars in the establishment of the field.[2] But the standard histories of psychic research—Gauld, Oppenheim, Luckhurst—leave off before the Murray phenomenon broke in 1915; and the last sustained critical discussion of Murray's psychic activity was the psychologist and disillusioned psychic veteran Eric Dingwall's dyspeptic 1973 summary of the sceptics' case, in response to Dodds's publication of the posthumous records of Murray's later experiments.[3]

These are not the only reasons why the Murray experiments are overdue for reconsideration. At the very least, Murray's ambivalent feelings about his apparent psychic abilities are an important window into unresolved complexities in his personality and beliefs, and there is more to be said about his management of those complexities in the light of the way in which those abilities were reported and debated, particularly in the responses to Eleanor Sidgwick's paper of December 1924. It is also now possible to see more clearly, in the light of recent research on the cultural history of the paranormal, how deeply the historical prominence of Murray's performances is connected with the institutional structures of psychic research in the early

[2] See especially Cerullo 1982, Brandon 1983, J. P. Williams 1984, Oppenheim 1985, Winter 1998, Luckhurst 2002, and for the post-war generation Hazelgrove 2000.

[3] For an attempt at a compromise defence see Inglis 1984, 202–8 (cf. 1985, 60–2, 307–8).

part of the last century, and how their subsequent reception history is something of a weathercock for the changes that the field underwent thereafter. Not least of all, there is the enduring fascination of the colourful and perplexing material itself—including some fundamental features of the evidence that both the psychics and the sceptics have largely missed.

Readers unfamiliar with the history of paranormal studies may find a brief background sketch useful.[4] The story of psychic research is shaped by three year zeroes: three moments at which not only the methods but the very terminology of the field sought to mark themselves off as qualitatively different from what had gone before. The first is 1848, the year when the Fox sisters of Hydesville, New York, drew worldwide attention by their claims to be able to communicate with the spirits of the dead, marking the beginning of the movement that came to be known as spiritualism. Though the Foxes were swiftly exposed as fakes, their taps from beyond actually the product of virtuoso knuckle-cracking, imitators flourished despite repeated debunking by stage magicians. In 1880 the American mentalist Washington Irving Bishop, who took the 1881 London season by storm and introduced Victorian Britain to the new wave of mind-reading acts from across the Atlantic, published a fat pamphlet explaining how self-styled clairvoyants performed their mind-reading tricks. Bishop himself, in contrast, made a point of allowing himself to be examined by scientists of the day, as did his more durable British disciple 'Stuart Cumberland' (Charles Garner).[5]

[4] Useful general histories include Heywood 1971, Bauskopf and McVaugh 1980, Inglis 1985, Beloff 1993.

[5] Bishop's career in Britain was cut short when he made the mistake of libelling his rival, the great stage magician J. N. Maskelyne, and at the end of 1884 he fled the country rather than stand trial; a staggering fine of £10,000 was imposed, and he never returned. After a bigamous marriage and allegations of cocaine, alcohol, and spousal abuse, Bishop (who suffered from a peculiar form of catalepsy) met a bizarre end when he collapsed on-stage and a pair of overenthusiastic doctors in the audience removed his brain in a premature autopsy. For a full account of this remarkable figure and his legacy see Jay 1986, 155–99 (not known to Luckhurst 2002, 63–9), who reproduces a contemporary satirical song: 'Oh! Mr. Cumberland, and Irving Bishop too, | With the pins you try to find, I'd like to run you through, | For you have marr'd my happiness and it is very plain | That all the family now have got thought-reading on the brain.'

But the year after Bishop's London debut a second year zero dawned. 1882 saw the foundation of the Society for Psychical Research,[6] and the debut issue of the SPR's *Proceedings* that year was dominated by investigations of what was initially termed 'thought-transference' (to replace the earlier 'thought-reading', with its undesirable associations with stage mentalism), but for which the Society's co-founder F. W. H. Myers now coined the classicizing term 'telepathy'. The SPR itself was a slightly uneasy marriage of spiritualist money with hard-nosed Cambridge scientism, founded and dominated for its first generation by a circle of Trinity and Newnham classicists centred on Henry and Eleanor Sidgwick and run by the Trinity–Newnham cabal that included Walter Leaf, Eleanor's brothers Arthur and Gerald Balfour, and the wife, daughter, and sister of A.W. Verrall; and it was this circle that adopted Murray as one of their flagship projects.[7]

It was the SPR's activities and publications that dominated psychic research until 1934, when J. B. Rhine published his monograph *Extra-Sensory Perception*: the first classic in the library of what from this point on would be called parapsychology, and a work whose laboratory-centred approach swept away the amateur researches of the SPR over the preceding half-century. In the longer term, it also swept away most of the credibility of psychic research; the story of parapsychology since Rhine has generally been one of disappointment, with promising-looking result after result proving irreplicable, fraudulent, or statistically insignificant, and by the 1980s the scientific literature pointed fairly inexorably to what was tactfully called the null hypothesis. Yet even in this climate, older researchers continued well into the seventies to cite the so-called Murray 'experiments' as the single weightiest body of evidence for telepathy yet produced.[8]

[6] On the foundation and early history of the SPR see especially T. Hall 1964, Gauld 1968, Nicol 1972, J. P. Williams 1984, Luckhurst 2002.

[7] The Verralls are the key dynasty in the history of psychic research in England in the first half of the 20th cent.: first Mrs Verrall, whose last published work was the documentation of Murray's telepathic activities in the same issue of the *Proceedings* that carried his presidential address (1916) and her obituary, and then her daughter Helen and Helen's husband W. H. Salter, a Verrall pupil from Trinity who later became President of the SPR in his own right. See further Lowe 2005.

[8] Heywood 1971; Burt in Gregory 1975, 65–6 ('of the various qualitative experiments on record by far the most convincing').

To understand this, we need to appreciate the cachet that the SPR enjoyed in its pre-war heyday. Roger Luckhurst has well noted how 'the core figures of the SPR constituted nodal points in late Victorian society. They linked into professional scientific and traditional academic communities, crossed between aristocracy, society elites, and middle classes, whilst marginalizing the Spiritualist constituency in a process of exclusionary institutionalization that paralleled that of other scientific societies' (Luckhurst 2002, 52). Freud, Jung, and William James all contributed to its journals, and James served a term as president, as did Henri Bergson and both the brothers Balfour, Arthur and Gerald. Among those who passed through the portals were Gladstone, Ruskin, Tennyson, Lord Leighton, H. M. Stanley, Lewis Carroll, Henry James, W. B. Yeats, and Radclyffe Hall. Among the classical activists may be found not only some of the familiar suspects like Murray, E. R. Dodds, and W. F. Jackson Knight, but such enduring teams as Butcher and Lang, Leaf and Bayfield (and indeed Lang, Leaf, and Myers), as well as Jane Harrison, Cyril Bailey, A. S. Owen, and many others. Murray differed from these in being only ever an experimental subject, never an active investigator; but he was one of only four figures to serve two terms as SPR president.[9]

Prior to the Murray phenomenon, however, SPR investigations into telepathy had been disappointing at best, and at worst a public embarrassment. The first issue of the *Proceedings* reported on studies of Bishop and Cumberland, whose routines included finding a pin hidden in a room by simply holding the hand of the person thinking of it, as well as more spectacular demonstrations such as Bishop's showpiece of driving a team of horses pell-mell through the city streets blindfolded.[10] It was quickly established that the mind-reading techniques which used physical contact relied on

[9] The others were Henry and Eleanor Sidgwick and the physicist Sir Oliver Lodge, who wrote a poignant memoir *Raymond* about the son he lost on the front in 1915 and the spirit's attempts to alert his father through a series of esoteric allusions to Horace's *Odes*.

[10] 'Twelve months ago, the performances of Mr. Irving Bishop having attracted considerable attention, a small committee of distinguished men investigated the matter, and after a few and rather hastily conducted experiments, a report, approved of by the other members of the committee, was drawn up by Mr. G. J. Romanes, and published in *Nature* for June 23rd, 1881 ... Mr. Stuart Cumberland has obtained

the perception of involuntary movements and tensions on the part of the subject, and the Reverend E. H. Sugden duly trained himself in what became known as 'muscle-reading' and reported back to the SPR on his successes. For something more authentically paranormal, the SPR (especially its co-founder W. F. Barrett) invested heavily in the amazing performances of the daughters of the Rev. Creery of Buxton ('a clergyman of unblemished character', apparently notwithstanding a curious history of denominational tergiversation)—only to discover five years into the study that the girls had been communicating by gestural and auditory codes, which had been masked by their constant fidgeting. Gurney's similar deception by the stage act of Blackwood and Smith is a suspected motive in his mysterious apparent suicide.[11]

It is against this background that we have to set the impact of Murray's 'experiments'—the sceptics contending that they were nothing of the kind—and the weight given to them by the recognized integrity and status of the experimental subject. The performances themselves date from Murray's time in Glasgow in the late nineties, where he developed a famous thought-guessing routine with his eldest daughter Rosalind. But notwithstanding the 11-year-old Murray's formative encounter with the psychic lady on the voyage to England,[12] there was no outward sign of a serious interest in the

considerable notoriety by experiments somewhat similar to those of Mr. Bishop, but his performances have no sort of relationship to our experiments, as he expressly disclaims thought-reading and denies the possibility of obtaining any results without contact. Mr. Bishop, on the other hand, professes to obtain results without contact, but the experiments for which he makes this claim are never obtained without the very closest proximity, nor without accompaniments of needless flurry and excited pantomime which are eminently calculated to distract and mislead the attention.' (Barrett et al. 1882, 14) Cf. Barrett 1882, 63–4:

'It is, however, very difficult to arrive at any satisfactory conclusions from these experiments, owing to the extraordinary pantomime of wriggling excited action which Mr. Bishop invariably employs, so utterly different from the silent, passive condition to which we have been accustomed in the experiments recorded in our report.'

The muscle-reading act was revived in 2005–6 by the television illusionists Criss Angel in the US and Derren Brown in the UK, both clients of magic consultant Luke Jermay.

[11] As argued by T. Hall 1964. Hall, like Dingwall, was a conjuror and sceptic in the SPR ranks who eventually turned against the Society and the subject.

[12] D. Wilson 1987, 10–11; Paludan in this volume, p. 22.

paranormal before 1898, when Murray was staying with the Verralls in Cambridge while working on his Euripides. This was at a time when May Verrall was discovering in herself the capacity for automatic writing that was to obsess her and the psychic elite for the next couple of decades; and it was she who introduced Murray to the work of the SPR, which he himself joined soon after.

Murray's telepathic act remained essentially invariate over the course of half a century.[13] Murray would leave the room while one of the company nominated a subject, which was then written down, and the door opened to signal that they were ready to proceed. Murray would then come from the next room or the far end of the corridor, and take the hand of the transmitting 'agent'[14] (or sometimes Rosalind's, if someone else were the agent) and try to describe what she was thinking of, while his remarks were scribbled down on scraps of paper and afterwards typed up. The subjects were sometimes literary, sometimes episodes in the experience of one or more members of the company, sometimes entirely imaginary. Murray would start by trying to get a feel for the kind of topic, and then to zoom in on specifics—though on occasion he would get it in one before he even entered the room.

The really astonishing thing about the Murray experiments, which has been surprisingly little remarked, is the statistics. Looking back on them from a Rhinean perspective of decades of slightly-above-chance results being pounced on as of massive significance, Murray's success rate of *over seventy per cent*, with half or more of these direct hits, is so anomalous that it is easy to understand the impact they had on witnesses, such as the sceptical psychologist J. A. Hadfield in 1919 who concluded there was no paranormal mechanism but nevertheless admitted it was the most extraordinary performance he had attended (Hadfield, letter in *The Times*, 22 Dec. 1924). No non-fraudulent subject had ever achieved such a success rate, and the backlash was not long in coming. The first of four sets of published results, assembled by May Verrall to accompany Murray's coming-out speech in the Society's proceedings for 1916, had its wider impact

[13] The last documented performances were in 1946, and he had abandoned them by the time of the 1952 presidential address.

[14] Mrs Verrall's term, adopted by subsequent reports.

blunted by the delay in publication until after the war; but the second, by Eleanor Sidgwick in 1924, prompted a public debate in the letter pages of *The Times* and *The Guardian* which drew in J. S. Haldane, Gerald Balfour, and the veteran sceptics Sir Horatio Bryan Donkin and E. Ray Lankester, both of whom had been involved in the original tests on Washington Irving Bishop. The impact was international. Freud wrote to Ernest Jones that Sidgwick's paper had finally convinced him of the reality of telepathy, and conducted similar experiments of his own with Anna Freud and Sandor Ferenczi, apparently with some success.[15] Others, however, were less readily won over. In January 1925 Houdini pronounced Murray a fraud, and replicated his routine for an invited audience of New York celebrities including Ralph Pulitzer—though Houdini's brother revealed after the master's death that the trick had been achieved by using the new technology of the microphone to bug the room, an option hardly available to Murray.

But the most trenchant critique came in a 1925 article by C. K. Ogden under his punning pseudonym Adelyne More, who laid ruthlessly into the way Murray's perceived integrity and close relationship with his investigators had allowed them to forego their normal standards of experimental rigour:

> In this subject sound evidence cannot rest upon social distinction and personal position; rather it must rest upon the solid foundation of controlled and rigid conditions under which the experiments are conducted. It is only when all normal processes have been effectually eliminated that supernormal agencies can be assumed. Such a demand on the part of the investigator in no way presupposes fraud on the part of the medium; it merely implies the use of a method which is essential if the experiments are to be scientifically valuable. In the following remarks upon Professor Murray's work, it must not be assumed that his good faith is in any way doubted. Questions are asked and observations are made which would be necessary with other mediums, and are therefore pertinent in this case. (More 1925, 290)

[15] Jones 1957, 420; the letters quoted by Jones appear unfortunately to have been unavailable to Paskauskas 1993. Particular thanks to Barbara McManus for this reference.

This disclaimer is then enthusiastically subverted, using a careful frame of conditionals and hypotheticals to engage in what amounts to a frontal assault on Murray's good faith. Murray himself is referred to throughout as 'the medium', a banausic and pejorative term scrupulously avoided by Murray's own supporters, tainted as it was with associations of charlatanry and vulgar showmanship. Even apparent manifestations of spontaneous integrity are stigmatized as a charade:

> On two occasions the experiments were stopped because the medium said that he had heard part of what was said, which he attributed to the loud speaking of one of the sitters due to excitement. If the success of the experiments can be accounted for normally, these last mentioned cases would be an ordinary piece of mis-direction on the part of the medium. (292–3; note the artful syntax of the last sentence.)

Nor is the wider family immune from stain: the greater success rate when a family member was the transmitting agent

> may be due to the causes that Mrs. Sidgwick indicates, but, on the other hand, it is possible that it may be due to collusion between the medium and his family. Under the given conditions the use of a code is naturally easy, and until a control is enforced which makes its use impossible, the supernormal qualities of the experiments can in no way be accepted. Mrs. Sidgwick records two cases when outsiders chose the subject, and a member of the family acted as agent; both were failures. This rather points away from the use of a code and suggests pre-arrangement beween the medium and the agent. (291–2)

Ogden concludes, stingingly: 'Until this medium consents to sit under controlled conditions his powers, however real they may be, can be given no credence' (295).

Such barely-veiled imputations of chicanery were daring stuff to level at a figure of Murray's reputation and standing. Most discussions of the Murray results made a point of vigorously deprecating the very thought of any dishonesty; even in 1934 the British Rhinean S. G. Soal was induced by SPR pressure first to tone down and then to abandon a critical paper on the experimental evidence for telepathy which allowed itself to question the integrity of Murray's performances (Bauskopf and McVaugh 1980, 213, and see H. Price 1939, 171). The attitude persisted long after his death: 'Gilbert Murray, a sceptical rationalist and one of the most honest and conscientious persons I have known, could not possibly be accused of cheating either during the experiment or in reporting the results' (Burt 1975, 66—a comment soon to seem peculiarly ironic from this particular arbiter of experimental integrity[16]); 'There was no attempt to exclude collusion or other forms of trickery and though we may be sure that Professor Murray's experiments were perfectly straightforward, the mere possibility is enough to damn his experiments from a scientific point of view' (Ellis 1974, 61). And indeed, the principal effect of the 1924–5 criticism seems to have been to push Murray's already ambivalent feelings about offering his powers to investigation into a deep disinclination to further public scrutiny. The only further publication of results in his lifetime was the record of the Salters' 1931 experiments, which attempted to address some of Ogden's requirements, but only saw publication ten years after the event and in the SPR's lower-profile *Journal*; even Dodds misses them in his retrospective round-up of publications. Murray himself made no further public statement on the subject until the 1952 presidential address, by which time the performances had been safely abandoned, and the fifteen years of further records remained unpublished until 1973.

Murray himself was pointedly reticent on the matter, and publicly cautious about relaxing a rationalist stance of sceptical materialism. His original suggestion in his 1916 SPR presidential address was that the mechanism at work was a non-paranormal form of hyperaesthesia—that he was subliminally catching some of the oral discussion of the topic while out of conscious earshot. This was also the explanation favoured by Hadfield and Dingwall, who both noted that the effect fell away to nothing when the subject was written down without being spoken or Murray was made to wait on a different floor. But the Verrall–Sidgwick–Dodds axis argued vigorously for something spookier being at work, pointing to what (they argued) were hits that did not form part of the spoken subject at all, and in the 1941 paper reporting their own experiments on the acoustics of the rooms

[16] The allegations that Burt had falsified key data in his work on the genetic basis for intelligence broke in the *Sunday Times* in October 1976, though in recent years the charge has been interestingly challenged.

and corridor at Yatscombe, complete with floor plan.[17] By the time of his 1952 presidential address Murray himself had come round to their view; but even his earlier rationalization has to be taken with caution. As Wilson points out from correspondence and Ann Paludan from personal memory, Murray was acutely aware that a too-active involvement in psychic research did nothing for his credibility in public affairs; and Dingwall suggests, though perhaps over-glibly, that Murray secretly wanted to believe but preferred others to take the public responsibility for it. Certainly a familiar narrative in accounts of early psychic research is that it was all about rationalists giving themselves permission to believe in the irrational—a kind of Sidgwickian rationalism that got rid of the embarrassments of God while letting the immortal soul back in by the servants' entrance.[18]

At any rate, Dingwall was right to point out that Murray's professed scepticism is hard to reconcile with a number of facts about his life: particularly his fifteen years' membership of the SPR before coming out as a telepath, and his extreme reluctance to engage in experiments under scientific conditions, or indeed any kind of experiment at all apart from his family parlour-game—no tests on his hearing, for example. Part of the explanation lies in the institutional history of the subject: the Verrall–Sidgwick group belonged to the first generation of psychic researchers, and their agenda and methods had something of a stranglehold on the SPR's work. Gauld characterizes the Eleanor Sidgwick regime that ran the society after 1910 as 'dominated by a group of elderly and closely linked persons whose immediate interests were in communications from their own deceased intimate friends',[19] and Ogden archly questioned the relaxation of normal standards of

[17] Like other elements in the 1941 paper, this was a clear if unacknowledged response to Ogden criticism of the earlier publications (More 1925, 291 n. 1).

[18] This is the theme of e.g. Cerullo 1982, J. P. Williams 1984 (esp. 118–38), and see now Schultz 2004.

[19] Gauld 1968, 337–8. The conversion of the Society's nucleus from scepticism to obsession on the matter of 'survival' did not go unnoticed. In 1911 Ernest Jones wrote to Freud:

'You ask me of the Society of [sic] Psychical Research. I am sorry to say that in spite of the good names in it, the society is not of good repute in scientific circles. You will remember that they did some valuable work in the eighties on hypnotism, automatic writing etc., but for the past 15 years they have confined their attention

experimental rigour when one of their own was the object of study. Fifty years on, Dingwall felt able to write more frankly, noting a scientific health inspector's nightmare kitchen of experimental flaws in the Murray data: the uncontrolled environment, non-random subjects, and involvement of close family members (never fewer than two). A sample is sufficient to indicate the tone:

> Before examining certain of these results I must point out what has always seemed to me an extraordinary feature of all the Murray tests, namely the inability or unwillingness on the part of the observers to record the precise conditions under which the tests were carried out (24) [...] These so-called experiments were obviously conducted in a slipshod fashion with no systematic form of control whatever... The tests are not carefully controlled experiments: they are a kind of parlour game after luncheon (26) [...] Did it really not strike Mrs Verrall that *experiments* were useful in science and that in this case a few simple *experiments* were desirable? Indeed, one such experiment had been tried. Hadfield stated that when Murray was living at Woodstock Road in Oxford some of the tests were on the first floor, but when Murray was asked to wait on the ground floor farther away from the room where the agents were gathered telepathy mysteriously ceased to operate (28) [...] Is it possible that Murray had a deep-seated, perhaps to some extent unconscious, wish to convince himself that telepathy and all that it implied was true and that therefore he shunned any test or experiment which might tend to show the contrary in his own case? If this were so, he would have found additional support for his own position when he realised the passionate desire of his distinguished friends to find evidence through him to support their own views (37) [...] The whole case and the conditions under which the tests are made are extremely puzzling and contain elements which to me still remain frankly inexplicable (39).

The question persists, however: what was really going on? It remains an unfortunate by-product of Murray's own reluctance to become an object of study and debate that he left the parsimonious hypothesis of simple fraud—overhearing or collusion—beyond the reach of refutation and only likely to increase with distance from personal

to 'spook-hunting', mediumship, and telepathy, the chief aim being to communicate with departed souls.' (Paskauskas 1993, 97)

Even the lifelong sceptic A. W. Verrall, who died in 1912, dictated a posthumous palinode through 'Mrs Willett', the SPR's favourite automatist: 'This kind of thing is harder to do than it looked' (Balfour 1917, 199).

acquaintance and memory, for all that it remains extremely difficult to square with Murray's character and conduct and that of the family members who would have to be supposed to play along, as well as a bizarrely high-stakes game to play over decades with the risk of exposure. And indeed, everyone who actually witnessed the experiments yet rejected a psychic explanation fell in instead with the hyperaesthetic theory, despite the fact that the entire basis for this kind of subliminal acoustic influence was a few flimsy anecdotes with no stronger evidential basis than the telepathic explanation. Ogden, for one, was not having this; if there was an auditory mechanism at work, it could only be conscious—and therefore, by an implication that did not need spelling out, an engine of deliberate deception.

But one feature of the Murray case records has not been adequately foregrounded since it was originally queried by Ogden in 1925, and has to do less with the control conditions than with the actual conduct and recording of the experiments. As Ogden noted, many of the published results show quite clearly that the form in which they were recorded, which seems to be the Murray family's own and was later followed in the published casebooks by May Verrall, Eleanor Sidgwick, Helen Salter, and Eric Dodds, gives a quite misleading impression of what was going on. They look like verbatim transcripts, but even in their published form they show vestiges of interaction between Murray and the others present that have been edited out of the format. There are a couple of famous occasions when Murray is supposed to have come straight out with a spot-on guess as soon as he enters the room, but these are very much the exception. For the most part, the guesses do not come at once, but are progressive, and responsive to encouragement and egging on from the others in the group. It cannot have hindered that Murray would always be holding the hand of one of the guessee's party, usually his daughter or wife, throughout the guessing process, which was recognized by the circle as naturally proceeding from general to particular.

The range of such incidental interaction can be seen from a selection of representative cases. In what follows, the notes are as originally published by Verrall 1916, Sidgwick 1924, Salter 1941, or Dodds 1972, with the following names abbreviated to initials: Lady

Mary Murray, Rosalind [Murray] Toynbee, Basil Murray, Agnes Murray, Stephen Murray, Helen Salter, W. H. Salter. Only the 1941 publication identifies the note-takers (as one or other of the Salters, not specified case-by-case).[20]

(i)

AM 'Alice in Wonderland, falling down the rabbit hole and landing where Bill the Lizard is watching, and White Rabbit is going by at the same time.'

GM (as he enters the room) 'I want to say 'Oh my ears and whiskers.' (Sidgwick 1924, 243)

This is one of a handful of occasions when Murray comes straight out with a literary quotation immediately on entry. It looks impressive, though of course we know nothing of how likely or otherwise Agnes had been to choose this (slightly misremembered) episode from *Alice*.

(ii)

Mr. Tatham 'Xenophon's soldiers coming in sight of the sea and saying *Θάλαττα*, etc.'

GM 'Not Xenophon's people coming to the sea and saying *Θάλαττα*—?' (ibid., 256)

Again this *looks* like an impressive direct hit, if recorded fully.

(iii)

BM 'I'll think of the singing in *The Wasps*, when the Athenian citizens, dikasts, come and sing outside Bdelycleon's house, and Philocleon tries to climb out to them.'

GM 'I think it's Greek—I think it's Aristophanes—it's a chorus of Gerontes—the people in *The Wasps*.' (ibid., 270–1)

This illustrates Murray's tendency to zoom in from general to particular; the final leap is an easy one, as there is only one other chorus of old men in extant Aristophanes and that (*Acharnians*) would be more naturally characterized as farmers. The dashes are a standard punctuational feature; it remains unclear what kinds of unrecorded interaction occurred in the pauses (if such they be), but some of the examples that follow suggest it could have been considerable.

[20] Alexander Murray suggests to me that José 'Bombie' Blomfield is likely to have been the uncredited note-taker for many of the performances.

(iv)

BM I'm thinking of Adam and Eve in the Garden of Eden, and Eve knitting a muffler for Adam.

GM A *[word illegible]*. Nothing at all. I can hear all the maids singing in the next room. (Dodds 1972, 383)

This example is often cited in connection with Murray's sensitivity to noise as a potential distraction, in mundane as well as psychic matters. But it is the only reference anywhere in the published record to where the servants were during the experiments; they remain as invisible as slave attendants in Greek tragedy.

(v)

W. Mellor I'm thinking of the operating theatre in the nursing home in which I was operated.

GM I get an impression of a theatre. No. I can't get it. I'm now guessing—Covent Garden and Oedipus. (Sidgwick 1924, 232)

A much-discussed failure, in which the Verrall analysis is that Murray gets the idea of 'theatre' but misinterprets it as the more conventional performance kind. Dingwall pointed out, however, that the Covent Garden reference could easily come out of the word 'operating', suggesting again an essentially auditory mechanism at root.

(vi)

HS (subject suggested by MM). Jane Harrison angry with Belloc in the study at Barford.

GM [to HS] I think this isn't you. Well, the thing I'm getting is something I don't think you know. Is it you? If it's you, Mary, it's Miss Harrison and Belloc, when she bit her lip. (Salter 1941, 32)

Notice here how Murray uses the identity of the transmitting agent to assist in narrowing the subject, which in this and many other cases is something so familiar to the Murrays as to be referred to by a kind of shorthand.

(vii)

RT 'This he hasn't read—a book (of) Strindberg, called *Marriage* about a horrid old schoolmaster, I think, who goes into a restaurant and asks for female crabs to eat.'

GM 'This is a book—I haven't read it, and it's all nasty—it's a cross, tired sort of man—oh it must be Strindberg—a cross tired sort of man going into a restaurant—he seems to be eating crabs and tearing them up—I mean tearing them malignantly—I feel inclined to say that they are female crabs but—'

[At this point we laughed at the hesitation which accompanied the final success with 'female' crabs. I have not read the book, but I understood from Mrs. Toynbee that no motive is assigned for the eating of female crabs, nor is the tearing 'malignant.'] (Verrall 1916, 109)

Another interesting progressive sequence, notable for the way the company intervenes to confirm the guess so forcefully as to terminate the experiment. Murray's own account (1916, 61) records a crucial prompt.

(viii)

MM I think of the cathedral at Lund in 1916 when they were apologising because the little Privatdozent only spoke German.

GM I think it's something to do with Sweden. Is it?

MM Yes.

GM That little man shifting about in the cathedral at Lund, because he could only speak German.

(He added here, 'I think that's because there is a roll, diploma or something from Sweden in the hall.')
Contemporary note from WHS. There was lying in the hall a roll of cartridge paper wrapped round the middle with brown paper, length about 30 inches. It had not come through post but by hand, and was in fact a drawing by Emery Walker of Hertford College: nothing to do with Sweden or to suggest a connection with Sweden. A real Swedish Diploma had come by post a few days before.
[*Later note by HS.* This is a good example of G.M. inventing something to use as a peg on which to hang a veridical impression. Compare the incident of the horses' hooves quoted in *Proc.* xxix, pp. 60, 92, 93.] (Salter 1941, 33)

HS's rationalization misses the point: if there had been a Swedish diploma in the hall in the last few days, it would recall to both Murrays their favourite Swedish anecdote from the stock of family stories taken out and polished at such times. For the hoofs, see next item.

(ix)

MM 'Mr. Z— riding on the sea-shore on a horse.'

GM 'Is this a thing of your own? Let me try it with Rosalind. Well, absurd, same impression from both. I have Z—'s manuscripts there—and I have a noise of hoofs. I expect it's the noise of hoofs in the street that makes me think of it.' *(No noise of hoofs in the street.)*

Note by Professor Murray. The record here is not quite complete. It should end thus: 'It is Z— riding on a horse. *('Where?')* I suppose in Greece.' (Verrall 1916, 92–3)

Notice the gaps in this interesting example. Murray's opening question may or may not have been answered, with or without spoken words; but clearly there is an unstated physical reconfiguration of the experiment with Rosalind instead of Lady Mary as the 'agent'. More remarkably still, someone in the party (we are not told who) is recorded as prompting Murray on with a leading question, to which his reply is inferential rather than impressionate. How much more of this kind of prompting has been edited out of the records? Other examples, as we shall see, tell a similar story.

(x)

Professor Murray then suggested that I should choose an incident and tell Mrs. Toynbee. But after he had left the room, at an unspoken suggestion, by sign, of Lady Mary Murray's, we decided to pursue the usual plan.

RT 'I'll think (of the) Master of Trinity—[to HS] your Master walking along the Backs and a gardener with a wheelbarrow sweeping up dead leaves and getting out of his way.'

GM 'I don't think this is Mrs. Verrall's—it's the Master of Trinity walking in a garden—and a gardener sweeping leaves.'

RT 'Any special place?'

GM 'The Backs.' (Verrall 1916, 110)

Here it is Rosalind who is recorded as asking a specific leading question, to which the answer is an easy guess.

(xi)

RT 'I think of Helena Cornford and Tony grown up, walking beside the river at Cambridge.'

GM 'This is not a book. It's got a sort of Cambridge feel in it. It's the Cornfords somehow.—No—it's a girl walking beside the river, but it isn't Frances [Mrs. Cornford]. Oh! is it baby Cornford grown up? Ought I to know what she is doing?' ('Who she is with'). 'No, I don't get who she is with—No—I should only be guessing.' *(EVERY ONE: 'go on').* No. I should only think of another baby grown up—Tony [a small grandchild].' (Sidgwick 1924, 215)

This time Murray himself appeals to the company for a prompt, receives one, declines it, and only upon general encouragement goes on to supply the missing information, which he admits is a guess. For the information carried by 'Who she is with', see on 'cold reading' below.

(xii)

BM 'I'm thinking of the Etruscan seer who during the siege of Veii was captured by a young Roman warrior. He told them to drain the Alban lake in order to take Veii.'

GM 'I don't think it's Balaam, but it's something like—It's a prophet who's serving the wrong side—not Hebrew. I think it's early Roman—I've got the impression that he's telling them to drain a marsh.—Does he come in Livy? I get an impression that he's caught and made to reveal a secret.' (ibid., 239)

Here a completely false start is recovered from. It would take a strong poker player to betray nothing at all in response to the prompt 'Does he come in Livy?'

(xiii)

BM 'I'm thinking of the sinking of the Titanic and one of the bandsmen who was playing Nearer my God to Thee to nearly the end, and then he dived off and sat on his 'cello until he was picked up by a boat.'

GM 'This is something awful—a big shipwreck. I suppose it is the Lusitania. No it's not the Lusitania. It's the thing that ran into the iceberg—the Titanic. Singing of hymns. Is there some special incident? *('Yes.')* I feel as if somebody was crashing a fiddle or a 'cello or breaking up a musical instrument—people being picked up out of the water—saved. Don't much think I shall get it clearer than that.'

(*[Professor Murray said afterwards]* 'I knew it was Nearer my God to Thee. I ought to have said it.') (ibid., 271–2)

But he did not.[21] And he could not have got the instrumental tune, being tone deaf; rather, he knows it because it was and remains the single most famous detail of the *Titanic* sinking. Again a prompt is

[21] 'Another extraordinary feature of [Mrs Sidgwick's] report is that in a so-called scientific publication it is thought to be worth while to record what the agents or medium *said* they had thought after the event has proved that such thoughts would have been applicable' (More 1925, 205).

needed, and if a 'special incident' is required for the *Titanic*, most would think of this one.[22]

(**xiv**)

MM 'A Russian man giving out the quinine to the population in the steppes, near Samara, and being rude to them, so they had to complain to the Friends.'

GM 'Oh, I think it's that man who had to distribute coffee or whatever it was to the people at Samara. *(Not coffee: try to get it—its taste.)* Quinine. *(GM got the taste of the quinine in the end.)*' (Dodds 1972, 387)

Whether or not GM 'got the taste', the fact that he was familiar with the story shows that the necessary information was already in his head, and merely needed a leading question to draw it out.

(**xv**)

SM 'George Rickey and me riding the motor-bike past the inhabitants of Moulsford Lunatic Asylum, and one cheery-looking man with gold spectacles on his forehead barking furiously at us like a dog.'

GM 'A curiously confused and ridiculous scene. You and someone on a motor-bicycle, and a scene of great confusion—perhaps the bicycle is broken down. But there's a confused rabble and—I know it sounds ridiculous—but someone on all fours barking like a dog. *(Then, after a little encouragement.)* Are they lunatics by any chance?' (ibid.)

Here again one would like to know what form the 'encouragement' took.

(**xvi**)

BM 'He stood, and heard the steeple
Sprinkle the quarters on the morning town.
One, two, three, four, to market-place and people
It tossed them down.'

GM 'A poem, Housman, can't quite remember:
"de dum de dum the steeple
Sprinkle the quarters on the morning town.
One, two, three, four..."'

[22] On the *Lusitania*, Sladek 1973, 182 notes that this experiment dated from the year after the sinking. 'It is about as remote an item to guess as someone's thought "the battle of Waterloo" in 1816.'

[Housman, *Last Poems*, XV. Basil had set the same subject twice before, B28 and C47. Murray's response was strikingly similar on all three occasions, though only on this third attempt did he identify the poem as Housman's.] (Dodds 1972, 389)

Dodds's note here is almost as remarkable as the fact that it took three goes at the same text before Murray was able to name the author. Clearly there was a rather higher-than-chance likelihood that any subject beamed by Basil would be this fragment. Of how many other subjects chosen seemingly at random was this also true?

(xvii)

BM 'I am thinking of a scene which has been in my head all the afternoon, from that book 'No Mean City', in which the hero leads his gang in an attack on a rival gang in Glasgow, and he is waving his razors in front of his face like a drum-major as he goes to the attack.'

GM 'I get a horrid impression of squalor and general disagreeableness. I should think it was Glasgow slums, and I should think it was that book. (Right: we had been talking about the book before dinner.) A general impression of squalor. Faint impression of a man going away from somewhere.' (ibid., 392)

If the whole company had just been talking about the book, GM's guess was hardly a shot in the dark. Even so, he does not in fact get the episode, though some details can with some effort be seen as appearing to fit it. Here again we see that the subjects chosen were far from random, and that the identity of the sitter and composition of the party could constrain the choice quite tightly.

In these examples we see a number of ways in which the guessing process itself, and the interactions between Murray and others present involved, could draw out significant information by a combination of familiarity or freshness of subject, leading questions in both directions, and unrecorded responses (spoken or otherwise) to Murray's progressive guesses.[23] This is exactly the kind of thing that stage mentalists are able to massage into the illusion of mindreading

[23] The lone testimony against such activity comes from the Salters in 1941: 'Sometimes the answer came at once, e.g. "Switzerland and glaciers". In the case where I [WHS] was agent he held my hand for (I judge) 30 seconds before speaking. There was never any fishing or beating about the bush. None of the incidents had been discussed between the Murrays and ourselves.' (Salter 1941, 31)

through techniques of 'cold reading', which is clearly what was practised on the impressionable 11-year-old by the lady who took his father's ring or watch.[24] The difference, of course, is that if we accept there was no conscious fraud or collusion involved, Murray himself was apparently taken in by his own virtuoso performance. Again the studies made of muscle-readers in the 1880s may be indicative here. Luckhurst aptly adduces the conclusion of Dr Charles Gatchell, who in summing up this work in 1891 noted that 'the testimony of all muscle-readers . . . has been that they do not know what their methods are. Early success is a self-surprise. It creates the impression that one is possessed of a weird power.'[25] May Verrall in 1916 already saw the superficial similarities in Murray's 'experiments' to Bishop and Cumberland's muscle-reading technique, and had to argue quite carefully and not entirely convincingly for the differentness of what Murray was doing.

There seems sufficient prima facie reason to continue to credit that Murray was doing something pretty extraordinary, and that at the bottom of it was an extremely close rapport with Rosalind and Lady Mary in particular. But the more one looks, as Hadfield, Ogden, and even Dingwall (in his time an honorary Vice-President of the Magic Circle) did not, at the techniques of mind-reading used by professional mentalists in Murray's time and beyond, the less paranormal the findings seem and the more even Murray's own hyperaesthetic mechanism seems a smokescreen for more subtle kinds of people-reading skills.[26] Perhaps Murray resisted more scientific kinds of testing, even with the increased exposure this brought to imputations

[24] A good walk-through of the technique can be found in Brown 2003, 117–26.

[25] C. Gatchell, 'The Methods of Mind-Readers', *Forum* 11, 1891, 197ff, quoted by Luckhurst 2002, 67. A pinch of salt is necessary, however; both Bishop and Cumberland learned their technique by assisting established stage practitioners.

[26] The verdict of Ellis 1974, 59–61 is worth quoting here:
'Many alternative explanations are possible. Intuition must have played some part at least. Many of the senders were colleagues, close friends or members of his family, and he must often have known what subjects were currently in their minds. Some were experiences which he himself had shared. An unintentional signal at the beginning of a reading could easily tell him whether he was on the right track, even though he may not have been consciously aware of it.'

of fraud, precisely because he suspected at some level that any such testing could only disappoint the family and friends who had invested so heavily in the mystery—which seems exactly the kind of consideration that would have weighed more heavily with him than the concern for scientific rigour which so irritated Ogden and Dingwall by its absence.

Bibliography

Ackerman, R. A. (1973). 'Verrall on Euripides' Suppliants 939ff.', *Greek, Roman and Byzantine Studies*, 14, 103–8.

—— (1986). '"Euripides and Professor Murray"', *Classical Journal*, 81, 329–36.

—— (1991a). 'The Cambridge Group: Origins and Composition', in Calder 1991, 1–19.

—— (1991b). *The Myth and Ritual School: J. G. Frazer and the Cambridge Ritualists*. New York: Garland.

A[llen], T. W. (1914). 'Review of *Studies in the Odyssey*', *Journal of Hellenic Studies*, 34, 335.

—— (1924). *Homer: The Origins and the Transmission*. Oxford: Clarendon Press.

—— (1931). *Homeri Ilias*. 3 vols. Oxford: Clarendon Press.

Allen & Unwin papers. Dept of Special Collections, Reading University Library.

Angell, N. (1910). *The Great Illusion*. London: Heinemann.

Archer, C. (1936). 'G.M. – W.A. 1895–1924', in Thomson and Toynbee 1936, 31–48.

Arlen, S. (1990). *The Cambridge Ritualists*. Metuchen, NJ: Scarecrow Press.

Arnold, M. (1887). 'Up to Easter', *Nineteenth Century*, 21, 629–43.

Aron, R. (1966). *Peace and War: A Theory of International Relations*. London: Weidenfeld and Nicolson.

Ashworth, L. (1999). *Creating International Studies: Angell, Mitrany and the Liberal Tradition*. Aldershot: Ashgate.

—— (2002). 'Did the Realist–Idealist Great Debate Ever Happen? A Revisionist History of International Relations', *International Relations*, 16, 33–51.

Aster, S. (2004). *Appeasement and All Souls: A Portrait with Documents, 1937–1939*. Cambridge: Cambridge University Press.

Backemeyer, S. (1998). *Eric Fraser, Designer and Illustrator*. London: Lund Humphries.

Bailey, C. et al., (eds.) (1936). *Greek Poetry and Life: Essays Presented to Gilbert Murray on His Seventieth Birthday, January 2, 1936*. Oxford: Clarendon Press.

Baldwin, T. (2003). 'From Knowledge by Acquaintance to Knowledge by Causation', in N. Griffin (ed.), *The Cambridge Companion to Bertrand Russell*. Cambridge: Cambridge University Press, 420–48.

Balfour, G. W. (1917). 'The Ear of Dionysius: Further Scripts Affording Evidence of Personal Survival', *Proceedings of the Society for Psychical Research*, 29, 197–243.

Barker, E. (1953). *Age and Youth*: Memories of Three Universities *and* Father of the Man. *London: Oxford University Press.*

Barrett, W. F. (1882). 'Appendix to the Report on Thought-reading', *Proceedings of the Society for Psychical Research*, 1, 47–64.

——, Gurney, E., and Myers, F. W. H. (1882). 'First Report of the Committee on Thought-reading', *Proceedings of the Society for Psychical Research*, 1, 13–34.

Bauskopf, S. H. and McVaugh, M. R. (1980). *The Elusive Science: Origins of Experimental Psychical Research*. Baltimore and London: The Johns Hopkins University Press.

Beard, M. (2000). *The Invention of Jane Harrison*. Cambridge, MA: Harvard University Press.

Bebbington, D. W. (2004). *The Mind of Gladstone: Religion, Homer, and Politics*. Oxford: Oxford University Press.

Beloff, J. (1993). *Parapsychology: A Concise History*. London: Athlone Press.

Bentley, M. (1977). *The Liberal Mind, 1914–29*. Cambridge: Cambridge University Press.

—— (2005). *Modernizing England's Past: English Historiography in the Age of Modernism, 1870–1970*. Cambridge: Cambridge University Press.

Bhagwati, J. (2004). *In Defence of Globalization*. Oxford: Oxford University Press.

Birn, D. S. (1981). *The League of Nations Union 1918–1945*. Oxford: Clarendon Press.

Bishop, W. I. (1880). *Second Sight Explained: A Complete Exposition of Clairvoyance or Second Sight, as Exhibited by the Late Robert Houdin and Robert Heller, Showing How the Phenomena May be Produced*. Edinburgh: John Menzies.

Blackwell, K. (1985). *The Spinozistic Ethics of Bertrand Russell*. London: Allen & Unwin.

Blake, R. (1998). 'Gladstone and Disraeli', in P. J. Jagger (ed.), *Gladstone*. London: Hambledon, 51–70.

Blakemore, M. (2004). *Arguments with England*. London: Faber and Faber.

Blunt, W. S. (1919). *My Diaries: Being a Personal Narrative of Events 1888–1914*. 2 vols. London: Martin Secker.

Bone, A. G. (ed.) (2003). *Bertrand Russell: Man's Peril, 1954–55*. London: Routledge.

Booth, K. (1991). 'Security in Anarchy: Utopian Realism in Theory and Practice', *International Affairs*, 67, 527–45.

Bowra, C. M. (ed.) (1930). *The Oxford Book of Greek Verse.* Oxford: Oxford University Press.

—— (1966) *Memories 1898–1939.* London: Weidenfeld and Nicolson.

Brandon, R. (1983). *The Spiritualists: The Passion for the Occult in the Nineteenth and Twentieth Centuries.* London: Weidenfeld and Nicolson.

Briggs, A. (1961–79). *The History of Broadcasting in the United Kingdom.* 4 vols. Oxford: Oxford University Press. Vol. 1, *The Birth of Broadcasting* (1961); Vol. 2, *The Golden Age of Wireless* (1965); Vol. 3, *The War of Words* (1970); Vol. 4, *Sound and Vision* (1979).

—— (1985). *The BBC: The First Fifty Years.* Oxford: Oxford University Press.

Briggs, W. W. and Calder, W. M. (eds.) (1990). *Classical Scholarship: A Bibliographical Encyclopedia.* New York: Garland.

Brooke, S. (1996). 'Evan Durbin: Reassessing a Labour "Revisionist"', *Twentieth-Century British History*, 7.1, 27–52.

Brown, D. (2003). *Absolute Magic: A Model for Close-Up Performance*, 2nd edn. Humble, TX: H & R Magic Books.

Bull, H. (1966). 'The Grotian Conception of International Society', in H. Butterfield and M. Wight (eds.), *Diplomatic Investigations: Essays in the Theory of International Politics.* London: George Allen & Unwin, 51–73.

—— (1972). 'The Theory of International Politics, 1919–1969', in B. Porter 1972, 30–55.

—— (1977). *The Anarchical Society: A Study of Order in World Politics.* London: Macmillan.

Burian, P. (2000). 'Gilbert Murray 1866–1957: British Classicist and Translator', in O. Classe (ed.), *Encyclopedia of Literary Translation into English*, ii. London: Fitzroy Dearborn, 981–3.

Burkert, W. (1966). 'Greek Tragedy and Sacrificial Ritual', *Greek, Roman and Byzantine Studies*, 7, 87–121.

—— (1972). *Homo Necans: Interpretationen von Griechischen Opferriten und Mythen.* Berlin; New York: W. de Gruyter

—— (1983). *Homo Necans. The Anthropology of Ancient Greek Sacrifical Ritual and Myth.* Berkeley: University of California Press.

—— (1987). *Ancient Mystery Cults.* Cambridge, MA: Harvard University Press.

Burrow, J. W. (1988). *Whigs and Liberals: Continuity and Change in English Political Thought.* Oxford: Clarendon Press.

Burt, C. (1966). 'Parapsychology and its Implications', *Journal of Neuropsychiatry*, 2, 363–77, reprinted in Gregory 1975, 63–82.

Buzan, B. (2004). *From International to World Society: English School Theory and the Social Structure of Globalization.* Cambridge: Cambridge University Press.

Calder, W. M. (1989). 'Ulrich von Wilamowitz-Moellendorff to Sir Alfred Zimmern on the Reality of Classical Athens', *Philologus*, 133.2, 303–9.

—— (ed.) (1991). *The Cambridge Ritualists Reconsidered* (*Illinois Classical Studies*, supplement 2). Atlanta GA: Scholars Press.

—— (2004). 'Allen, Thomas William (1862–1950)', in Todd 2004, i, 10–12.

—— and Kopff, E. C. (1977). 'The Student-Teacher Topos in Biographical Fiction: Gilbert Murray and Ulrich von Wilamowitz-Moellendorff', *Classical Philology*, 72, 53–4.

Campbell, J. L. and Hall, T. H. (1968). *Strange Things: The Story of Fr Allan McDonald, Ada Goodrich Freer, and the Society for Psychical Research's Enquiry into Highland Second Sight.* London: Routledge & Kegan Paul.

Campbell, L. (1898). *Religion in Greek Literature: A Sketch in Outline.* London: Longmans.

Carpenter, H. (1996). *The Envy of the World: Fifty Years of the BBC Third Programme and Radio 3.* London: Weidenfeld and Nicolson.

Carr, E. H. (1939). *The Twenty Years' Crisis 1919–1939: An Introduction to the Study of International Relations.* London: Macmillan.

Carter, J. (ed.) (1961). *A. E. Housman: Selected Prose.* Cambridge: Cambridge University Press.

Ceadel, E. B. (1940). 'The "Askew Collations" of Aeschylus', *Classical Quarterly*, 34, 55–60.

—— (1941a). 'Resolved Feet in the Trimeters of Euripides and the Chronology of the Plays', *Classical Quarterly*, 35, 66–89.

—— (1941b). 'The Division of Parts among the Actors in Sophocles' *Oedipus Coloneus*', *Classical Quarterly*, 35, 138–47.

Ceadel, M. (1980). 'The First British Referendum: The Peace Ballot, 1934–1935', *English Historical Review*, 95, 810–39.

—— (2000). *Semi-detached Idealists: The British Peace Movement and International Relations, 1854–1945.* Oxford: Oxford University Press.

Cerullo, J. (1982). *The Secularisation of the Soul: Psychical Research in Modern Britain.* Philadelphia: Institute for the Study of Human Issues.

Clarke, P. (1978). *Liberals and Social Democrats.* Cambridge: Cambridge University Press.

Claude, I. L. (1962). *Power and International Relations.* New York: Random House.

Coleridge, M. E. (1910). *Gathered Leaves from the Prose of Mary E. Coleridge*, with a Memoir by Edith Sichel. London: Constable.

Collard, C. (1981). *Euripides*, New Surveys in the Classics, 14. Oxford: Clarendon Press.

—— (1993). 'Gilbert Murray on Rudyard Kipling: An Unpublished Letter', *Notes and Queries*, 238 (n.s. 40), 63–4.

—— (2007). 'Schoolmaster, Don, Educator: Arthur Sidgwick Moves to Corpus in 1879', in Stray 2007b.

Collini, S. (1991). *Public Moralists: Political Thought and Intellectual Life in Britain, 1850–1930.* Oxford: Clarendon Press.

—— (2006). *Absent Minds: Intellectuals in Britain.* Oxford: Oxford University Press.

Davies, C. S. L. (1979). 'The Great Wadham Row', *Wadham College Gazette,* n.s. 1.6 (Michaelmas Term), 29–32.

Davies, M. (1999a). 'Leaving Out the Erinyes: The History of a Misconception', *Prometheus,* 25, 117–28.

—— (1999b). 'The Three Electras: Strauss, Hofmannsthal, Sophocles, and the Tragic Vision', *Antike und Abendland,* 45, 36–66.

—— (2006). *Housman and Murray: A Syncrisis.* Oxford: Information Press.

Dawe, R. D. (1964). *The Collation and Investigation of Manuscripts of Aeschylus.* Cambridge: Cambridge University Press.

—— (1965). *A Repertory of Conjectures on Aeschylus.* Leiden: Brill.

—— (1973). *Studies on the Text of Sophocles,* i. Leiden: Brill.

—— (1985). *Sophoclis Tragoediae,* ii, 2. verbess. Aufl. Leipzig: Teubner.

—— (1990). 'Richard Porson', in Briggs and Calder 1990, 376–88.

—— (1996). *Sophocles, Oedipus Rex,* 3rd edn. Stuttgart: Teubner.

Dawkins, R. M. (1906). 'The Modern Carnival in Thrace and the Cult of Dionysus', *Journal of Hellenic Studies,* 26, 191–206.

De Madariaga, S. (1960). 'Gilbert Murray and the League', in Smith and Toynbee 1960, 173–97.

Denniston, J. D. (1934). *The Greek Particles.* Oxford: Clarendon Press.

Diggle, J. (ed.) (1981). *Euripidis Fabulae,* ii. Oxford: Clarendon Press.

—— (ed.) (1984). *Euripidis Fabulae,* i. Oxford: Clarendon Press.

—— (1994a). *Euripidea.* Oxford: Clarendon Press.

—— (ed.) (1994b). *Euripidis Fabulae,* iii. Oxford: Clarendon Press.

—— (2007). 'Housman's Greek' [forthcoming in a Festschrift].

Diggle, J. and Goodyear, F. R. D. (1972). *The Classical Papers of A. E. Housman.* 3 vols. Cambridge: Cambridge University Press.

Dingwall, E. J. (1973). 'Gilbert Murray's Experiments: Telepathy or Hyperaesthesia?', *Proceedings of the Society for Psychical Research,* 56, 21–39.

Dixon, J. (2001). *Divine Feminine: Theosophy and Feminism in England.* Baltimore: Johns Hopkins University Press.

Dodds, E. R. (1944). *Euripides, Bacchae.* Oxford: Clarendon Press. (2nd edn, 1960)

—— (1957). 'Gilbert Murray', *Gnomon,* 29, 476–9.

—— (1960). Introduction, in Smith and Toynbee 1960, 13–19.

Dodds, E. R. (1972). 'Gilbert Murray's Last Experiments', *Proceedings of the Society for Psychical Research*, 55, 371–402.

—— (1977). *Missing Persons: An Autobiography.* Oxford: Oxford University Press.

Donnelly, J. (2000). *Realism and International Relations.* Cambridge: Cambridge University Press.

Driver, D. (1981). *The Art of the* Radio Times. London: BBC Books.

Dunn, D. H. (2006). 'A Doctrine Worthy of the Name? George W. Bush and the Limits of Pre-emption, Pre-eminence and Unilateralism', *Diplomacy and Statecraft*, 17, 1–29.

Dunne, T. (1998). *Inventing International Society: A History of the English School.* London: Macmillan.

Easterling, P. E. (1997). 'Gilbert Murray's Reading of Euripides', *Colby Quarterly*, 33, 113–27.

Eliot, T. S. (1920). 'Euripides and Professor Murray. A Performance at the Holborn Empire', *Art and Letters*, 3.2, 36–43 = Eliot 1951, 59–64.

—— (1951). *Selected Essays*, 3rd enl. edn. London: Faber.

Ellis, K. (1974). *Science and the Supernatural.* London: Wayland.

Esslin, M. (1971). 'The Mind as Stage', *Theatre Quarterly*, 1.3, 5–11.

Evans-Pritchard, E. E. (1956). *Nuer Religion.* Oxford: Oxford University Press.

Farnell, L. R. (1896–1908). *The Cults of the Greek States*, 5 vols. Oxford: Oxford University Press. Vols. 1 and 2 (1896); vols. 3 and 4 (1907); vol. 5 (1908).

—— (1912). *The Higher Aspects of Greek Religion.* London: Williams and Norgate.

—— (1913a). 'The Dionysiac and the Hero Theory of the Origin of Tragedy', *Hermathena*, 17, 1–28.

—— (1913b). 'Greek Religion and Mythology', in C. Bailey (ed.) *The Year's Work in Classical Studies.* London: John Murray, 129–37.

—— (1920). *Outline-History of Greek Religion.* London: Duckworth.

Field, G. C. (1949). *The Philosophy of Plato.* London: Oxford University Press.

Fischer-Lichte, E. (2004). 'Thinking about the Origins of Theatre in the 1970s', in Hall, Macintosh, and Wrigley 2004, 329–60.

Fitzsimons, R. (1980). *Death and the Magician: The Mystery of Houdini.* London: Hamish Hamilton.

Fowler, R. L. (1990). 'Gilbert Murray', in Briggs and Calder (eds.) 321–34.

—— (1991). 'Gilbert Murray: *Four (five) Stages of Greek Religion*', in Calder 1991, 79–96.

Fraenkel, E.(ed.) (1950). *Aeschylus, Agamemnon.* 3 vols. Oxford: Clarendon Press.

Freeden, M. (1978). *The New Liberalism*. Oxford: Clarendon Press.

—— (1986). *Liberalism Divided: A Study in British Political Thought, 1914–1939*. Oxford: Clarendon Press.

Friedman, T. (1999). *The Lexus and the Olive Tree*. New York: HarperCollins.

Gauld, A. (1968). *The Founders of Psychical Research*. London: Routledge and Kegan Paul.

Gerson, G. (2004). *Margins of Disorder: New Liberalism and the Crisis of European Consciousness*. Albany: State University of New York Press.

Gielgud, V. (1957). *British Radio Drama 1922–1956*. London: Harrap.

—— (1965). *Years in a Mirror*. London: Bodley Head.

Girard, R. (1977). *Violence and the Sacred*, tr. P. Gregory. Baltimore: Johns Hopkins University Press.

Goff, B. (2005). 'Dionysiac Triangles. The Politics of Culture in Wole Soyinka's *The Bacchae of Euripides*', in V. Pedrick and S. M. Oberhelman (eds.), *The Soul of Tragedy: Essays on Athenian Drama*. Chicago: University of Chicago Press, 73–88.

Goold, G. P. (2000). 'Housman's Manilius', in A. W. Holden and J. R. Birch (eds.), *A. E. Housman: A Reassessment*. Basingstoke: Macmillan, 134–53.

Grainger, J. H. (1986). *Patriotisms: Britain, 1900–1939*. London: Routledge.

Gregory, A. (ed.) (1975). *ESP and Psychology*. London: Weidenfeld and Nicolson.

Gribble, F. H. (1910). *The Romance of the Oxford Colleges*. London: Mills and Boon.

Griffith, M. (2003). 'Robinson Jeffers and Greek Tragedy', *Jeffers Studies*, 7.1, 19–50.

Grove, G. (1980). *The New Grove Dictionary of Music and Musicians*, ed. by S. Sadie, 6th edn., 20 vols. London: Macmillan.

Gurney, E., Myers, F. W. H., Podmore, F., and Barrett, W. F. (1882). 'Third Report of the Committee on Thought-reading', *Proceedings of the Society for Psychical Research*, 1, 161–215.

Haggard, H. R. (1926). *The Days of My Life: An Autobiography*, ed. C. J. Longman. 2 vols. London: Longmans, Green.

Hall, E. M. and Macintosh, F. (2005). *Greek Tragedy and the British Theatre, 1660–1914*. Oxford: Oxford University Press.

—— and Wrigley, A. (eds.) (2004). *Dionysus Since 69: Greek Tragedy at the Dawn of the Millennium*. Oxford: Oxford University Press.

Hall, T. (1964). *The Strange Case of Edmund Gurney*. London: Duckworth.

Halliday, W. R. (1925). 'Stages of Greek Religion' [review of Murray 1925a], *Classical Review*, 39, 185–6.

Harris, W. V. (1989). *Ancient Literacy*. Cambridge: Harvard University Press.

Harrison, J. E. (1899). 'Delphica', *Journal of Hellenic Studies*, 19, 205–51.
—— (1903). *Prolegomena to the Study of Greek Religion*. Cambridge: Cambridge University Press.
—— (1905). *The Religion of Ancient Greece*. London: Constable.
—— (1908a). 'The Greek Epic' [review of Murray 1907b], *Albany Review*, 2.10 (January), 453–8.
—— (1908b). *Prolegomena to the Study of Greek Religion*. 2nd edn. Cambridge: Cambridge University Press.
—— (1912). *Themis. A Study of the Social Origins of Greek Religion*. Cambridge: Cambridge University Press.
—— (1925). *Reminiscences of a Student's Life*. London: Hogarth.
—— (1927). *Themis: A Study of the Social Origins of Greek Religion*, 2nd edn. Cambridge: Cambridge University Press.
Harrison, T. (2000). *Divinity and History: Religion in Herodotus*. Oxford: Oxford University Press.
Haslam, J. (2002). *No Virtue Like Necessity: Realist Thought in International Relations since Machiavelli*. New Haven and London: Yale University Press.
Hazelgrove, J. (2000). *Spiritualism and British Society Between the Wars*. Manchester: Manchester University Press.
Hazlehurst, C. (1971) *Politicians at War, July 1914 to May 1915*. London: Jonathan Cape.
Henderson, J. G. (2007). 'The Euripides Series: Well-laid Plans at OUP', in Stray 2007a.
Henderson, M. I. (1960). 'The Teacher of Greek', in Smith and Toynbee (1960), 125–48.
—— (1971). 'Murray, George Gilbert Aimé (1866–1957), Classical Scholar and Internationalist', in E. T. Williams and H. M. Palmer (eds.), *The Dictionary of National Biography, Supplement 1951–60*. Oxford: Oxford University Press, 757–61.
Henig, R. (ed.) (1973). *The League of Nations*. Edinburgh: Oliver and Boyd.
Henrichs, A. (1984). 'Loss of Self, Suffering, Violence: The Modern View of Dionysus from Nietzsche to Girard', *Harvard Studies in Classical Philology*, 88, 205–40.
Heywood, R. (1971). *The Sixth Sense. An Inquiry into Extra-sensory Perception*, rev. edn. London: Chatto & Windus.
Hinchcliffe, L. G. (1983). *Trust and Be Trusted: The Royal Army Pay Corps and Its Origins*. Winchester: Royal Army Pay Corps.
Hirst, F. W., Murray, G., and Hammond, J. L. (1900). *Liberalism and the Empire: Three Essays*. London: R. B. Johnson.
Hobhouse, M. H. (1917), *'I Appeal Unto Caesar': The Case of the Conscientious Objector*. London: Allen & Unwin.

Hobson, J. A. (1902). *Imperialism: A Study.* London: Nisbet.

Hofmannsthal, H. von (1911). *König Ödipus.* Berlin: Fischer.

—— (1968). *Briefwechsel 1898–1929*, ed. H. Burger. Frankfurt: Insel.

—— (1997). *Sämtliche Werke: Kritische Ausgabe* 7.5, ed. by K. E. Bohnenkamp and M. Mayer. Frankfurt: Fischer.

Holroyd, M. (1988). *Bernard Shaw*, i: *The Search for Love.* London: Chatto & Windus.

—— (1989). *Bernard Shaw*, ii: *The Pursuit of Power, 1898–1918.* London: Chatto & Windus.

—— (1991). *Bernard Shaw*, iii: *The Lure of Fantasy, 1918–1950.* London: Chatto & Windus.

Hooper, S. (ed.) (1940). *The Deeper Causes of the War.* London: George Allen & Unwin.

Housman, A. E. (1892). Introductory lecture, in Carter 1961, 1–22.

—— (ed.) (1903a). *M. Manilii, Astronomicon liber I.* London: Grant Richards.

—— (1903b). 'Owen's *Persius* and *Juvenal*', *Classical Review*, 17, 389–94 (= Diggle and Goodyear 1972, ii, 602–10).

—— (ed.) (1905). *D. Iunii Iuvenalis Saturae.* London: Grant Richards.

—— (1917). 'A Georgian History of Victorian Literature' [review of *The Cambridge History of English Literature*, vols. 13 and 14], *Cambridge Review*, 38 (23 May 1917), 358–60 = Carter 1961, 114–20.

—— (1920). 'Bywater's *Four Centuries of Greek Learning in England*', *Classical Review*, 34, 110–11 (= Carter 1961, 120–3, = Diggle and Goodyear 1972, iii, 1004–6).

—— (1922). 'The Application of Thought to Textual Criticism', *Proceedings of the Classical Association*, 18, 67–84 (= Carter 1961, 131–50, = Diggle and Goodyear 1972, iii, 1058–69).

—— (1930). *M. Manilii Astronomicon liber 5.* London: Grant Richards.

—— (2007). *The Letters of A. E. Housman*, ed. A. Burnett. Oxford: Oxford University Press.

Hurrell, A. (1992). 'Collective Security and International Order Revisited', *International Relations*, 11, 37–55.

—— (2005). 'Legitimacy and the Use of Force: Can the Circle be Squared?' *Review of International Studies*, 31, 15–32.

Ignatieff, M. (1998). *Isaiah Berlin: A Life.* London: Chatto & Windus.

Inglis, B. (1984). *Science and Parascience: A History of the Paranormal.* London: Hodder & Stoughton.

—— (1985). *The Paranormal.* London: Granada.

Ironside, P. (1996). *The Social and Political Thought of Bertrand Russell: The Development of an Aristocratic Liberalism.* Cambridge: Cambridge University Press.

Jackson, R. (2000). *The Global Covenant: Human Conduct in a World of States.* Oxford: Oxford University Press.

—— and James, A. (eds.) (1993). *States in a Changing World: A Contemporary Analysis.* Oxford: Oxford University Press.

James, A. (ed.) (1973). *The Bases of International Order: Essays in Honour of C. A. W. Manning.* London: Oxford University Press.

—— (1986). *Sovereign Statehood: The Basis of International Society.* London: Allen & Unwin.

Jay, R. (1986). *Learned Pigs and Fireproof Women.* New York: Villard.

Jebb, R. C. (1870). *The Characters of Theophrastus.* London: Macmillan.

—— (1886). *Sophocles, Oedipus Coloneus.* Cambridge: Cambridge University Press.

Jebb, C. (ed.) (1907). *Life and Letters of Sir Richard Claverhouse Jebb.* Cambridge: Cambridge University Press.

Jefferson, D. W. (ed.) (1969). *The Morality of Art. Essays Presented to G. Wilson Knight by his Colleagues and Friends.* London: Routledge.

Jeyifo, B. (ed.) (2001). *Conversations with Wole Soyinka.* Jackson, MS: University Press of Mississippi.

Jones, E. (1957). *Sigmund Freud: Life and Work*, iii: *The Last Phase 1919–1939.* London: Hogarth Press.

Kennedy, D. (1985). *Granville Barker and the Dream of Theatre.* Cambridge: Cambridge University Press.

Kenney, E. J. (2006). 'D. R. Shackleton Bailey', *Independent* (4 January), 32.

Kenny, M. (2004). 'The Case for Disciplinary History: Political Studies in the 1950s and 1960s', *British Journal of Politics and International Relations*, 6.4, 565–83.

Leavis, Q. D. (1943). 'The Discipline of Letters: A Sociological Note', *Scrutiny*, 12.1, 12–26.

Lenz, J. R. (1987–8). 'Bertrand Russell and the Greeks', *Russell*, 7.2, 104–18.

Lewis, J. (2005). *Penguin Special: The Life and Times of Allen Lane.* London: Viking.

Linklater, A. (2000). 'E. H. Carr, Nationalism and the Future of the Sovereign State', in M. Cox (ed.), *E. H. Carr: A Critical Appraisal.* London: Palgrave, 234–57.

—— and Suganami, H. (2006). *The English School of International Relations: Contemporary Reassessment.* Cambridge: Cambridge University Press.

Lloyd-Jones, P. H. J. (1956). 'Zeus in Aeschylus', *Journal of Hellenic Studies*, 76, 55–67.

—— (1965). Discussion Review of W. S. Barrett (ed.), *Euripides, Hippolytos. Journal of Hellenic Studies*, 85, 164–71.

—— (1973). 'A Review of *The Classical Papers of A. E. Housman*', *Times Literary Supplement* (8 February), 345 = Lloyd-Jones 1982, 182–7.

—— (1982). *Blood for the Ghosts*. London: Duckworth.

—— (1990). *Greek Epic, Lyric and Tragedy*. Oxford: Oxford University Press.

—— (1991). *Greek in a Cold Climate*. London: Duckworth.

Lloyd-Jones, H. and Wilson, N. G. (1990). *Sophoclea*. Oxford: Clarendon Press.

Long, D. and Wilson, P. (eds.) (1995). *Thinkers of the Twenty Years' Crisis: Inter-war Idealism Reassessed*. Oxford: Clarendon Press.

Loveday, P. J. and Martin, A. W. (1969). *Parliament, Factions and Parties: The First Thirty Years of Responsible Government in New South Wales, 1856–1889*. Carleton, Vic.: Melbourne University Press.

Lowe, N. J. (2005). 'Problematic Verrall: The Sceptic-at-Law', in Stray 2005, 142–60.

Luckhurst, R. (2002). *The Invention of Telepathy 1870–1901*. Oxford: Oxford University Press.

McManus, B. F. (2007). 'Grace Harriet Macurdy: The Role of British Classics in the Self-fashioning of an American Woman Scholar', in J. P. Hallett and C. A. Stray (eds.), *British Classics Beyond England*. Waco, TX: Baylor University Press.

MacNeill, W. H. (1989). *Arnold J. Toynbee: A Life*. New York: Oxford University Press.

Maine, H. S. (1905). *Ancient Law: Its Connection with the Early History of Society and its Relation to Modern Ideas*. London: John Murray. (First published in 1861.)

Malinowski, B. (1929). *The Sexual Life of Savages in North-Western Melanesia*. London: Routledge.

Manning, C. A. W. (ed.) (1937). *Peaceful Change: An International Problem*. London: Macmillan.

—— (1962). *The Nature of International Society*. London: The London School of Economics and Political Science and G. Bell and Sons.

Markland, J. (ed.) (1728). *P. Papinii Statii Silvarum libri quinque*. London: G. Bowyer.

—— (ed.) (1763). *Euripidis Drama Supplices Mulieres*. London: G. Bowyer.

Martin, A. W. (1980). *Henry Parkes: A Biography*. Carleton, Vic.: Melbourne University Press.

Michelini, A. N. (1987). *Euripides and the Tragic Tradition*. Madison: University of Wisconsin Press.

Millett, P. C. (2007). 'Zimmern's *Greek Commonwealth* Revisited', in Stray 2007b, forthcoming.

Monk, R. (1996). *Bertrand Russell: The Spirit of Solitude.* London: Jonathan Cape.

Moorehead, C. (1992). *Bertrand Russell: A Life.* London: Sinclair-Stevenson.

More, A. [C. K. Ogden] (1925). 'Recent Experiments in Thought-Transference', *Psyche*, 5, 290–5.

Morefield, J. (2005). *Covenants without Swords: Idealist Liberalism and the Spirit of Empire.* Princeton: Princeton University Press.

Morgenthau, H. J. (1978). *Politics Among Nations: The Struggle for Power and Peace*, 5th edn., rev. New York: Alfred A. Knopf.

Morwood, J. (2005). Introduction, in Murray 2005, vii–xxxv.

Msiska, M.-H. (1998). *Wole Soyinka.* Plymouth: Northcote House.

Murray, G. (1889). *The Place of Greek in Education.* Glasgow: James MacLehose.

—— (1897). *A History of Ancient Greek Literature.* London: Heinemann.

—— (1900a). 'The Exploitation of Inferior Races in Ancient and Modern Times' in F. W. Hirst, G. Murray, and J. L. Hammond, *Liberalism and the Empire: Three Essays.* London: R. Brimley Johnson, 118–57.

—— (1900b). 'National Ideals: Conscious and Unconscious', in Murray 1921a, 160–82.

—— (ed.) (1902a). *Euripidis Fabulae*, i. Oxford: Clarendon Press.

—— (1902b). 'Introductory Essay: *The Bacchae* in Relation to Certain Currents of Thought in the Fifth Century' in *Euripides translated into Rhyming Verse*, in G. C. Warr (ed.), *The Athenian Drama: A Series of Verse Translations from the Greek Dramatic Poets*, iii. London: G. Allen, pp. xix–lxviii.

—— (ed.) (1904). *Euripidis Fabulae*, ii. Oxford: Clarendon Press.

—— (1907a). 'Olympic Houses' [review of L. R. Farnell, *The Cults of the Greek States*, vols. 3 and 4], *Albany Review*, 2, 199–208.

—— (1907b). *The Rise of the Greek Epic.* Oxford: Clarendon Press.

—— (1908–9). 'The Hymn of the Kouretes', *Annual of the British School at Athens*, 15, 357–65.

—— (ed). (1909a). *Euripidis Fabulae*, iii. Oxford: Clarendon Press.

—— (1909b). 'Wherewith Shall it be Salted', *The Sociological Review*, 2, 260–73.

—— (1910). *The Iphigenia in Tauris, Translated into English Rhyming Verse with Explanatory Notes.* London: Allen & Unwin.

—— (1912a). 'Excursus on the Ritual Forms Preserved in Greek Tragedy', in Harrison 1912, 341–63.

—— (1912b). *Four Stages of Greek Religion.* New York: Columbia University Press.

—— (1912c). 'Greek and English Tragedy: a Contrast', in G. S. Gordon (ed.), *English Literature and the Classics*. Oxford: Clarendon Press, 7–24.

—— (1912d). 'The Ritual of Dionysus', *Proceedings of the Classical Association*, 9, 35–45.

—— (1912e). 'What English Poetry May Still Learn from Greek', *Atlantic Monthly*, 110, 660–73 (originally in *Essays and Studies*, 3, 7–31).

—— (1913). *Euripides and his Age*. London: Williams and Norgate.

—— (1914a). 'Hamlet and Orestes: A Study in Traditional Types', *Proceedings of the British Academy*, 6, 389–412; also published separately by Oxford University Press in 1914 and reprinted in Murray 1927a, 205–40.

—— (1914b). *How Can War Ever Be Right?* Oxford: Oxford University Press, reprinted in Murray 1917a = Murray 1918a.

—— (1914c). *Thoughts on the War*. London: Oxford University Press.

—— (1915a). 'The Conception of Another Life', *Edinburgh Review*, 221, 122–39.

—— (1915b). *Ethical Problems of the War: An Address*. Edinburgh: Nelson.

—— (1915c). *The Foreign Policy of Sir Edward Grey 1906–1915*. Oxford: Clarendon Press.

—— (1915d). 'German scholarship', *Quarterly Review*, 223, 330–9.

—— (1915e). 'Introduction', in J. A. K. Thomson, *The Greek Tradition: Essays in the Reconstruction of Ancient Thought*. London: Allen & Unwin, pp. ix–xiii.

—— (1915f). *The Stoic Philosophy*. London: Watts (reprinted in Murray 1950, 19–85).

—— (1916). 'Presidential Address', delivered on 9 July 1915, *Proceedings of the Society for Psychical Research*, 29, 46–63.

—— (1917a). *Faith, War, and Policy: Addresses and Essays on the European War*. Boston: Houghton Mifflin.

—— (1917b). *The Way Forward: Three Articles on Liberal Policy*. London: George Allen & Unwin.

—— (1918a). *Faith, War and Policy: Lectures and Essays*. London: Oxford University Press.

—— (1918b). *The League of Nations and the Democratic Idea*. London: Oxford University Press.

—— (1918c). 'Religio grammatici' (presidential address), *Proceedings of the Classical Association*, 15, 74–97. Reprinted in Murray 1921a, 11–30.

—— (1919). 'Is an Estimate of Our Own Age Possible?', *Contemporary Review*, CXVI.2, 131–43.

—— (1920). *The League and its Guarantees*. London: British Periodicals.

—— (1921a). *Essays and Addresses*. London: Allen & Unwin.

Murray, G. (1921b). *The Problem of Foreign Policy: A Consideration of Present Dangers and the Best Methods of Meeting Them.* London: Allen & Unwin.

—— (1921c). 'The Value of Greece to the Future of the World', in R. W. Livingstone (ed.), *The Legacy of Greece.* Oxford: Clarendon Press, 1–23.

—— (1924). *The Rise of the Greek Epic.* 3rd edn. Oxford: Clarendon Press.

—— (1925a). *Five Stages of Greek Religion.* Oxford: Clarendon Press.

—— (1925b). 'Homer', *Classical Review,* 39, 71–3.

—— (1925c). 'What Liberalism Stands For', *Contemporary Review,* 128, 681–97.

—— (1927a). *The Classical Tradition in Poetry.* London: Oxford University Press; Cambridge, MA.: Harvard University Press.

—— (1927b). 'Dithyramb, Tragedy and Comedy', *Classical Review,* 41, 221–3.

—— (1927c). 'Excursus on the Ritual Forms Preserved in Greek Tragedy', in Harrison 1927, 341–63.

—— (1928). *Jane Ellen Harrison. An Address.* Cambridge: Heffer.

—— (1929a). 'Religion and Philosophy', in *The History of Christianity in the Light of Modern Knowledge.* London and Glasgow: Blakrie.

—— (1929b). *The Ordeal of This Generation: The War, the League and the Future.* London: Allen & Unwin.

—— (1931). *Prometheus Vinctus, Translated into English Rhyming Verse.* London: Allen & Unwin.

—— (1932). 'Allen's *Iliad*', *Classical Review,* 46, 12–14.

—— (1933). *Aristophanes. A Study.* Oxford: Clarendon Press.

—— (1934). *The Cult of Violence.* London: Lovat Dickson.

—— (1935). *Then and Now: The Changes of the Last Fifty Years.* Oxford: Clarendon Press.

—— (1936). 'Pagan Religion at the Coming of Christianity', in A. J. Peake, *A Commentary on the Bible* (1919: cited from the edn. with supplement by A. J. Grieve). London: Jack, 627–35.

—— (1937). *Aeschyli septem quae supersunt tragoediae.* Oxford: Clarendon Press.

—— (1938). *Liberality and Civilization.* London: Allen & Unwin.

—— (1939). *The Persians.* London: Allen & Unwin. Translated from Aeschylus' *Persians.*

—— (1940a). *Aeschylus, Creator of Tragedy.* Oxford: Clarendon Press.

—— (1940b). *Stoic, Christian and Humanist.* London: Watts.

—— (1943a). *The Anchor of Civilization.* The Philip Maurice Deneke Lecture (24 November 1942). London: Oxford University Press.

—— (1943b). 'Francis Macdonald Cornford, 1874–1943', *Proceedings of the British Academy,* 29, 421–32.

—— (1943c). 'Ritual Elements in the New Comedy', *Classical Quarterly*, 37, 46–54.

—— (1944a). *A Conversation with Bryce.* The James Bryce Memorial Lecture. London: Oxford University Press.

—— (1944b). 'Religion in State Schools', *The Rationalist Annual.* London: Watts, 3–6.

—— (1945). *The Arbitration: The Epitrepontes of Menander.* London: Allen & Unwin.

—— (1946). *Greek Studies.* Oxford: Clarendon Press.

—— (1947). *The Wife of Heracles.* London: Allen & Unwin. Translated from Sophocles' *Trachiniae.*

—— (1948). *From the League to U.N.* London: Oxford University Press.

—— (1949). 'Myself when young'. *The Listener,* 42 (18 August), 272–3.

—— (1950a). *Stoic, Christian and Humanist,* 2nd edn. London: Watts.

—— (1950b). 'What is Liberalism?', *World Review,* n.s. 12, 7–16.

—— (1951). 'Dis geniti', *Journal of Hellenic Studies,* 71, 120–8.

—— (1952). 'Presidential Address', *Proceedings of the Society for Psychical Research,* 49, 155–69.

—— (ed.) (1953). *Aeschyli Fabulae,* repr. with corrections. Oxford: Clarendon Press.

—— (1954). *Hellenism and the Modern World.* Boston: Beacon Press.

—— (ed.) (1955). *Aeschyli Fabulae.* 2nd edn. Oxford: Clarendon Press.

—— (1960). 'Autobiographical Fragment', in Smith and Toynbee 1960, 23–103.

—— (1965). *Euripides and his Age.* 2nd edn. Oxford: Oxford University Press.

—— (2005). *Gilbert Murray's Euripides.* Exeter: Bristol Phoenix Press.

Murray, H. (1970). *Selected Letters of Hubert Murray,* ed. F. J. West. Melbourne: Oxford University Press.

Nardin, T. (1983). *Law, Morality and the Relations of States.* Princeton: Princeton University Press.

Nicol, F. (1972). 'The Founders of the S.P.R.', *Proceedings of the Society for Psychical Research,* 55, 341–67.

Nietzsche, F. (1872). *Die Geburt der Tragödie aus dem Geiste der Musik.* Leipzig: E. W. Fritzsch.

Northedge, F. S. (1986). *The League of Nations: Its Life and Times, 1920–1946.* Leicester: Leicester University Press.

Norwood, G. (1908). *The Riddle of the Bacchae: The Last Stage of Euripides' Religious Views.* Manchester: Manchester University Press.

Nuttall, A. D. (1988). 'Hamlet: Conversations with the Dead', *Proceedings of the British Academy,* 74, 53–70.

Nuttall, J. (2003). 'The Labour Party and the Improvement of Minds: The Case of Tony Crosland', *Historical Journal*, 46.1, 133–54.

Ogden, C. K. (1925). *see* More, A.

Olson, S. D. (2002). *Aristophanes, Acharnians*. Oxford: Oxford University Press.

Oppenheim, J. (1985). *The Other World: Spiritualism and Psychical Research in England, 1850–1914*. Cambridge: Cambridge University Press.

Page, D. L. (1934). *Actors' Interpolations in Greek Tragedy*. Oxford: Oxford University Press.

—— (1962). *Poetae Melici Graeci*. Oxford: Clarendon Press.

—— (ed.) (1972). *Aeschyli septem quae supersunt tragoediae*. Oxford: Clarendon Press.

Page, N. (1983). *A. E. Housman: A Critical Biography*. London: Macmillan.

Paskauskas, P. A. (ed.) (1993). *The Complete Correspondence of Sigmund Freud and Ernest Jones 1908–1939*. Cambridge, MA: Belknap Press.

Peacock, S. (1988). *Jane Ellen Harrison: The Mask and the Self*. New Haven: Yale University Press.

Pearson, A. C. (1912). 'Murray's *Euripides*: Vol. III', *Classical Review*, 26, 155–8.

Pickard-Cambridge, A. W. (1927). *Dithyramb, Tragedy and Comedy*. Oxford: Oxford University Press.

Pike, A. F. (1966). 'Gibbes, J.G.N.', *Australian Dictionary of Biography*, i. Melbourne: Melbourne University Press, 439.

Pollard, A. W. (1890). *Odes from the Greek Dramatists*. London: D. Stott.

Pomeroy, S. B. (1994). *Xenophon, Oeconomicus: A Social and Historical Commentary, with a New English Translation*. Oxford: Oxford University Press.

Porter, B. (ed.) (1972). *The Aberystwyth Papers: International Politics, 1919–1969*. London: Oxford University Press.

—— (2002). 'Lord Davies, E. H. Carr and the Spirit Ironic: A Comedy of Errors', *International Relations*, 16, 76–96.

Porter, J. I. (2000). *The Invention of Dionysus: An Essay on the 'Birth of Tragedy'*. Stanford: Stanford University Press.

Potter, M. 2005. 'Russell's Integrated Emotivism', unpublished paper, Annual Meeting of the Bertrand Russell Society, Hamilton, Canada, 15 May 2005.

—— (2006). *Bertrand Russell's Ethics*. Bristol: Thoemmes Continuum.

Powell, J. U. (1925). *Collectanea Alexandrina: Reliquiae minores poetarum Graecorum aetatis Ptolemaicae, 323–146 A.C.* Oxford: Oxford University Press.

—— (1933). *New Chapters in the History of Greek Literature*, Third Series. Oxford: Oxford University Press.

—— and Barber, E. A. (1921). *New Chapters in the History of Greek Literature.* Oxford: Oxford University Press.

Preisendanz, K. (1928). *Papyri Graecae Magicae*, i. Leipzig: Teubner.

Price, H. (1939). *Fifty Years of Psychical Research: A Critical Survey.* London: Longmans, Green.

Price, S. R. F. (1999). *Religions of the Ancient Greeks.* Cambridge: Cambridge University Press.

Rae, J. (1970). *Conscience and Politics: The British Government and the Conscientious Objector to Military Service 1916–1919.* London: Oxford University Press.

Reith, J. (1975). *The Reith Diaries*, ed. by C. Stuart. London: Collins.

Rich, P. (1995). 'Alfred Zimmern's Cautious Idealism: The League of Nations, International Education, and the Commonwealth', in Long and Wilson 1995, 84–5.

Richards, G. (1941). *Housman 1897–1936.* Oxford: Oxford University Press.

Richards, H. (1895). 'Catulliana', *Classical Review*, 9, 304–6.

—— (1907). *Notes on Xenophon and Others.* London: Grant Richards.

—— (1909). *Aristophanes and Others.* London: Grant Richards.

—— (1911). *Platonica.* London: Grant Richards.

Ricks, C. (ed.) (1968). *A. E. Housman: A Collection of Critical Essays.* Englewood Cliffs NJ: Prentice-Hall.

—— (ed.) (1988). *A. E. Housman: Collected Poems and Selected Prose.* London: Allen Lane.

Roberts, S. H. (1964). *The Squatting Age in Australia 1835–1847*, rev. edn. Melbourne: Melbourne University Press.

Robinson, A. (2002). *The Life and Work of Jane Ellen Harrison.* Oxford: Oxford University Press.

Roe, M. (1965). *The Quest for Authority in Eastern Australia 1835–51.* Melbourne: Melbourne University Press.

Rose, J. E. (2001). *The Intellectual Life of the British Working Classes.* New Haven: Yale University Press.

Russell, B. (1912). *The Problems of Philosophy.* London: Thornton Butterworth.

—— (1915). *The Policy of the Entente, 1904–1914: A Reply to Professor Gilbert Murray.* Manchester and London: National Labour Press.

—— (1916). *Principles of Social Reconstruction.* London: Allen & Unwin.

—— (1930). *The Conquest of Happiness.* London: Allen & Unwin.

—— (1932). *Education and the Social Order.* London: Allen & Unwin.

—— (1946). *History of Western Philosophy.* London: Allen & Unwin.

—— (1947a). 'The Faith of a Rationalist', *The Listener*, 37 (29 May), 826.

—— (1947b). *Philosophy and Politics.* Cambridge: National Book League.

Russell, B. (1954). 'The Hydrogen Bomb and World Government', *The Listener* 52 (22 July), 133–4.

—— (1960). 'A Fifty-six Year Friendship', in Smith and Toynbee 1960, 205–11.

—— (1961). 'The Reconciliation of Individuality and Citizenship', in *The Basic Writings of Bertrand Russell, 1903–1959*, ed. R. E. Egner and L. E. Denonn. New York: Simon and Schuster, 445–53.

—— (1988). *Prophecy and Dissent, 1914–16. Collected Papers of Bertrand Russell*, xiii. London: Unwin Hyman.

Russell, C. (1999). *An Intelligent Person's Guide to Liberalism*. London: Duckworth.

Ryan, A. (1988). *Bertrand Russell: A Political Life*. New York: Hill and Wang.

Ryan, J. A. (1976). 'Wise, G. F.', *Australian Dictionary of Biography*, vi. Melbourne: Melbourne University Press, 429.

Salter, H. de G. (Verrall). (1936). 'The Evidence for Telepathy', in Thomson and Toynbee 1936, 261–277.

—— (1941). 'Experiments in Telepathy with Dr. Gilbert Murray', *Proceedings of the Society for Psychical Research*, 32, 29–38.

Sandys, J. E. (ed.) (1893). *Aristotle, Constitution of Athens. A Revised Text, with an Introduction, Critical and Explanatory Notes, Testimonia and Indices*. London: Macmillan.

Schechner, R. (1977). *Essays on Performance Theory, 1970–1976*. New York: Drama Book Specialists.

—— (1993). *The Future of Ritual: Writings on Culture and Performance*. New York: Routledge.

Schmidt, B. (1998). 'Lessons from the Past: Reassessing the Interwar Disciplinary History of International Relations', *International Studies Quarterly*, 42, 433–59.

Schultz, B. (2004). *Henry Sidgwick: Eye of the Universe*. Cambridge: Cambridge University Press.

Seaford, R. (1994). *Reciprocity and Ritual. Homer and Tragedy in the Developing City-State*. Oxford: Clarendon Press.

—— (ed.) (1996). *Euripides Bacchae*. Warminster: Aris and Phillips.

—— (2001). *Euripides' Bacchae*. Repr. with corrections. Warminster: Aris and Phillips.

Shannon, R. (1974). *The Crisis of Imperialism, 1865–1915*. London: Paladin/Granada.

Shaw, G. B. (1960). *Major Barbara*, ed. D. H. Laurence. Harmondsworth: Penguin.

Sheppard, J. T. (1925). 'The Rise of the Greek Epic', *Classical Review*, 39, 73–4.

Shils, E. (1955). 'The Intellectuals: (1) Great Britain', *Encounter*, 4, 5–16.

Sidgwick, E. (1924). 'Report on Further Experiments in Thought-transference Carried Out by Professor Gilbert Murray, LL.D, Litt.D', *Proceedings of the Society for Psychical Research*, 34, 212–74, with Appendix 336–41.

Silk, M. and Stern, J. P. (1981). *Nietzsche on Tragedy*. Cambridge: Cambridge University Press.

Simon, L. (1920). *Studies in Jewish Nationalism*. London: Longmans.

Sladek, J. (1973). *The New Apocrypha: A Guide to Strange Science and Occult Beliefs*. London: Hart-Davis, MacGibbon.

Slater, J. G. (1994). *Bertrand Russell*. Bristol: Thoemmes Press.

Smith, J. (1960). '1889–1957: Some Personal and Chronological Notes from the Correspondence', in Smith and Toynbee (1960), 104–16.

Smith, J. and Toynbee, A. J. (eds.) (1960). *Gilbert Murray: An Unfinished Autobiography, with Contributions by his Friends*. London: Allen & Unwin.

Snow, T. C. (1910). *How to Save Greek, and Other Paradoxes of Oxford Reform*. Oxford: Basil Blackwell.

Soyinka, W. (1969). 'The Fourth Stage (through the Mysteries of Ogun to the Origins of Yoruba Tragedy)', in Jefferson 1969, 119–134.

—— (1973). *The Bacchae of Euripides: A Communion Rite*. London: Eyre Methuen.

—— (1976). *Myth, Literature and the African World*. Cambridge: Cambridge University Press.

Stapleton, J. (2001). *Political Intellectuals and Public Identities in Britain since 1850*. Manchester: Manchester University Press.

—— (2005). *Sir Arthur Bryant and National History in Twentieth-Century Britain*. Lanham, MD: Lexington Books.

Stevenson, C. L. (1970). 'The Emotive Conception of Ethics and Its Cognitive Implications', in W. Sellars and J. Hospers (eds.), *Readings in Ethical Theory*, 2nd edn. New York: Meredith, 267–75.

Stewart, J. G. (1959). *Jane Ellen Harrison: A Portrait from Letters*. London: Merlin Press.

Stone, J. (1958). *Aggression and World Order: A Critique of United Nations Theories of Aggression*. London: Stevens.

Stray, C. A. (1991). [Review of Peacock 1988.] *Liverpool Classical Monthly*, 16, 103–11.

—— (1998). *Classics Transformed: Schools, Universities, and Society in England, 1830–1960*. Oxford: Clarendon Press.

—— (2004a). 'Gilbert Murray, 1866–1957', in H. C. G. Matthew and B. Harrison (eds.), *The Oxford Dictionary of National Biography*. Oxford: Oxford University Press, xxxix, 912–18.

Stray, C. A. (2004b). 'Livingstone, Richard Winn (1880–1960)', in Todd 2004, iii, 585–7.

—— (ed.) (2005). *The Owl of Minerva: The Cambridge Praelections of 1906* (*Proceedings of the Cambridge Philological Society*, Supplementary Volume 28).

—— (ed.) (2007a). *Classical Books: Scholarship and Publishing in Britain since 1800.* London: Institute of Classical Studies.

—— (ed.) (2007b). *Oxford Classics: Teaching and Learning 1800–2000.* London: Duckworth.

Suganami, H. (1989). *The Domestic Analogy and World Order Proposals.* Cambridge: Cambridge University Press.

Sugden, E. H. (1882). 'Note on Muscle-reading', *Proceedings of the Society for Psychical Research*, 1, 291–3.

Sulloway, F. J. (1996). *Born to Rebel: Birth Order, Family Dynamics and Creative Lives.* New York: Pantheon Books.

Symonds, R. (1986). *Oxford and Empire: The Last Lost Cause?* London: Macmillan.

Thomson, J. A. K. (1914). *Studies in the Odyssey.* Oxford: Clarendon Press.

—— (1957). 'Gilbert Murray 1866–1957', *Proceedings of the British Academy*, 43, 245–70.

—— and Toynbee, A. (eds.) (1936). *Essays in Honour of Gilbert Murray.* London: Allen & Unwin.

Thorndike, S. and Casson, L. (1960) 'The Theatre and Gilbert Murray', in Smith and Toynbee 1960, 149–75.

Thouless, Robert H. (1925). 'Professor Murray's Experiments in Telepathy', *Journal of the Society for Psychical Research*, 22, 51–4.

Todd, R. B. (ed.) (2004). *The Dictionary of British Classicists.* 3 vols. Bristol: Thoemmes Continuum.

—— (2006). 'Ernest Barker and the Classical Tradition: Two Studies', *Polis*, 23.2 = Special Issue, *Ernest Barker, The Political Thought of Plato and Aristotle (1906): A Centenary Tribute*, ed. J. Stapleton, 368–85.

Toye, J. and Toye, R. (2007). 'Alfred Zimmern, Julian Huxley and the Initial Leadership of UNESCO', *Journal of World History* (forthcoming).

Toynbee, A. J. (1959). *Hellenism: The History of a Civilisation.* London: Oxford University Press.

—— (1960). 'The Unity of Gilbert Murray's Life and Work', in Smith and Toynbee 1960, 212–20.

Trilling, L. (1955). *Freud and the Crisis of Our Culture.* Boston: Beacon Press.

Turner, F. M. (1981). *The Greek Heritage in Victorian Britain.* New Haven: Yale University Press.

Turner, V. W. (1969). *The Ritual Process.* Chicago: University Press.

—— (1982). *From Ritual to Theatre: The Human Seriousness of Play.* New York: Performing Arts Journal Publications.

Turyn, A. (1957). *The Byzantine Manuscript Tradition of the Tragedies of Euripides.* Urbana: University of Illinois Press.

Uhlig, K. (2003). *Hofmannsthals Anverwandlung antiker Stoffe.* Freiburg im Breisgau: Rombach.

Vasunia, P. (2005). 'Greek, Latin and the Indian Civil Service', *Proceedings of the Cambridge Philological Society*, 51, 35–69.

Verrall, A. W. (1895). *Euripides the Rationalist: A Study in the History of Art and Religion.* Cambridge: Cambridge University Press.

—— (1907). 'The Scholar and Critic', in C. Jebb 1907, 429–87.

—— (1910). *The Bacchants of Euripides and Other Essays.* Cambridge: Cambridge University Press.

Verrall, M. De G. (1916). 'Report on a Series of Experiments in "Guessing"', *Proceedings of the Society for Psychical Research*, 29, 64–110.

Wallace, S. (1988). *War and the Image of Germany: British Academics, 1914–1918.* Edinburgh: John Donald.

Walsh, W. H. (2000). 'The Zenith of Greats', in M. G. Brock and M. C. Curthoys (eds.), *The History of the University of Oxford*, vii: *Nineteenth-Century Oxford*, Part 2. Oxford: Oxford University Press, 311–26.

Walters, F. P. (1952). *A History of the League of Nations*, ii. Oxford: Oxford University Press.

Waltz, K. N. (1959). *Man, the State, and War: A Theoretical Analysis.* New York: Columbia University Press.

Wecklein, N. (1902). [Review of Murray 1902a], *Berliner philologische Wochenschrift*, 22, cols. 929–35.

—— (1911). [Review of Murray 1909a], *Berliner philologische Wochenschrift*, 31, cols. 257–60.

West, F. J. (1968). *Hubert Murray: The Australian Pro-Consul.* Melbourne: Oxford University Press.

—— (1973). *Biography as History.* Sydney: Sydney University Press.

—— (1980). 'The Australian Expatriates: Gilbert and Hubert Murray', in A. F. Madden and W. H. Morris-Jones (eds.), *Australia and Britain: Studies in a Changing Relationship.* London: Frank Cass, 57–70.

—— (1982). '"Ghosts Can Not Speak Until They Have Drunk Blood": A. E. Housman and Gilbert Murray as Donors', unpublished paper, read to Staff Seminar, Schools of Social Science and Humanities, Deakin University, Geelong, Vic., Australia, Aug. 1982, in Francis West Papers, National Library of Australia.

West, F. J. (1983). 'Psychobiography', unpublished paper, in Francis West papers, National Library of Australia.

—— (1984). *Gilbert Murray: A Life*. London: Croom Helm.

—— (2006). 'Two Pacific Biographies', in *Texts and Contexts: Reflections in Pacific Islands Historiography*, ed. D. Munro and B. V. Lal. Honolulu: University of Hawai'i Press, iii. 120–1.

West, M. L. (1974). *Studies in Greek Elegy and Iambus*. Berlin: De Gruyter.

—— (1984). *Carmina Anacreontea*. Leipzig: Teubner.

—— (1990). *Studies in Aeschylus*. Stuttgart: Teubner.

Wheeler, N. J. (2000). *Saving Strangers: Humanitarian Intervention in International Society*. Oxford: Oxford University Press.

Whitaker, G. H. (2007). '... brevique adnotatione critica ...: A Preliminary History of the Oxford Classical Texts', in Stray 2007b.

Whitehead, K. (1989). *The Third Programme: A Literary History*. Oxford: Clarendon Press.

Wight, M. (1991). *International Theory: The Three Traditions, ed. G. Wight and B. Porter. London: Leicester University Press.*

Wilamowitz-Moellendorff, U. von (ed.) (1889). *Euripides, Herakles*. Berlin: Weidmann.

—— (ed.) (1914). *Aeschyli Tragoediae*. Berlin: Weidmann.

—— (1991). *The Prussian and the Poet: The Letters of Ulrich von Wilamowitz-Moellendorff to Gilbert Murray (1894–1930)*, ed. by A. Bierl, W. M. Calder, and R. L. Fowler. Hildesheim: Weidmann.

Wilkinson, L. P. (1974). 'A. E. Housman, Scholar and Poet', *Housman Society Journal*, 1, 32–46.

Williams, J. P. (1984). 'The Making of Victorian Psychical Research: An Intellectual Elite's Approach to the Spiritual World'. Dissertation, University of Cambridge.

Williams, M. (2005). *The Realist Tradition and the Limits of International Relations*. Cambridge: Cambridge University Press.

Wilson, D. (1987). *Gilbert Murray OM, 1866–1957*. Oxford: Clarendon Press.

Wilson, G. (1968). *Murray of Yarralumla*. Melbourne: Oxford University Press.

Wilson, N. G. (1990). 'Thomas William Allen, 1862–1950', *Proceedings of the British Academy*, 76, 311–19.

Wilson, P. (1998). 'The Myth of the First Great Debate', *Review of International Studies*, 24, 1–15.

—— (2000). 'Responses to *The Twenty Years' Crisis*, 1939–1946', in M. Cox (ed.), *E. H. Carr: A Critical Appraisal*. London: Palgrave, 165–97.

—— (2003). *The International Theory of Leonard Woolf: A Study in Twentieth-Century Idealism.* New York: Palgrave.

—— (2004). 'Manning's Quasi-Masterpiece: *The Nature of International Society* Revisited', *The Round Table*, 93, 755–69.

Winter, A. (1998) *Mesmerized: Powers of the Mind in Victorian Britain.* Chicago: University of Chicago Press.

Woolf, V. (1977). *The Diary of Virginia Woolf,* i: *1915–1919*, ed. A. O. Bell. London: Hogarth Press.

Wrigley, A. (2005). 'Aeschylus' *Agamemnon* on BBC Radio, 1946–1976', *International Journal of the Classical Tradition*, 11, 216–44.

Young, G. M. (1937). 'The New Cortegiano', in *Daylight and Champaign: Essays.* London: Jonathan Cape, 140–59.

Zeitlin, F. (2004). 'Dionysus in 69', in Hall, Macintosh, and Wrigley 2004, 47–75.

Zimmermann, B. (1991). *Greek Tragedy: An Introduction.* Baltimore and London: Johns Hopkins University Press. (German original 1985)

—— (1992). *Dithyrambos: Geschichte einer Gattung*, Hypomnemata 98. Göttingen: Vandenhoeck and Ruprecht.

Zimmern, A. E. (1911). *The Greek Commonwealth: Politics and Economics in Fifth-Century Athens.* Oxford: Oxford University Press.

—— (1918). *Nationality and Government: With other Wartime Essays.* London: Chatto & Windus.

—— (1923). 'The Evolution of the Citizen', in O. Stanley (ed.), *The Way Out.* London: Oxford University Press.

—— (1924). *The Greek Commonwealth: Politics and Economics in Fifth-Century Athens*, 4th edn. Oxford: Clarendon Press.

—— (1931). *The Study of International Relations.* Oxford: Clarendon Press.

—— (1935). *The State as a 'Mortal God'.* London: Industrial Christian Fellowship.

—— (1939). *Spiritual Values and World Affairs.* Oxford: Clarendon Press.

Zuntz, G. (1965). *An Inquiry into the Transmission of the Plays of Euripides.* Cambridge: Cambridge University Press.

Index